THE HEDGE FUND EDGE

Wiley Trading Advantage

THE HEDGE FUND EDGE

MAXIMUM PROFIT/MINIMUM RISK
GLOBAL TREND TRADING STRATEGIES

Mark Boucher

JOHN WILEY & SONS, INC.

New York • Chichester • Weinheim • Brisbane • Singapore • Toronto

This book is printed on acid-free paper. ∞

Copyright © 1999 by Mark Boucher. All rights reserved.

Published by John Wiley & Sons, Inc.

Published simultaneously in Canada.

No part of this publication may be reproduced, stored in a retrieval system or transmitted in any form or by any means, electronic, mechanical, photocopying, recording, scanning or otherwise, except as permitted under Section 107 or 108 of the 1976 United States Copyright Act, without either the prior written permission of the Publisher, or authorization through payment of the appropriate per-copy fee to the Copyright Clearance Center, 222 Rosewood Drive, Danvers, MA 01923, (978) 750-8400, fax (978) 750-4744. Requests to the Publisher for permission should be addressed to the Permissions Department, John Wiley & Sons, Inc., 605 Third Avenue, New York, NY 10158-0012, (212) 850-6011, fax (212) 850-6008, E-Mail: PERMREQ @WILEY.COM.

This publication is designed to provide accurate and authoritative information in regard to the subject matter covered. It is sold with the understanding that the publisher is not engaged in rendering professional services. If professional advice or other expert assistance is required, the services of a competent professional person should be sought.

Library of Congress Cataloging-in-Publication Data:

Boucher, Mark, 1962–
     The hedge fund edge : maximum profit/minimum risk global trend
trading strategies / Mark Boucher.
          p.   cm. — (Wiley trading advantage)
     Includes index.
     ISBN 0-471-18538-8 (alk. paper)
     1. Hedge funds.   I. Title. II. Series.
HG4530.B68   1998
     332.64'5—dc21   98-18230

10   9   8   7   6

Acknowledgments

Two broad groups of people deserve recognition and thanks for the making of this book and for the events in my life that have led up to it. The first people are what I term "the wind beneath my wings." These are the people who directly helped me in ways that made this book possible. The second group is what I term "the shoulders of greatness on which I stand." These are people whose work indirectly has been of enormous benefit and help to me not only in putting this work together, but also in developing the concepts described in many of the chapters.

Among those who have been the wind beneath my wings, I want to thank my parents, particularly my mother, who throughout my life has been willing to sacrifice anything to help me to achieve my dreams. I want to thank my significant other, Anita Ellis, without whose consistent help and support none of this would have been possible. I am grateful to my coworkers for all their hard work and effort. Thank you Larry Connors and others for proofreading and offering moral support. I also thank my first partners in the hedge fund business, Tony Pilaro and Paul Sutin, whose faith and support led me into this industry. And I want especially to thank Tom Johnson, my partner and friend, whose research, faith, fascination, and support made this possible.

This book is greatly enhanced by the previous efforts of others who act as the shoulders of greatness on which this effort stands. First and foremost, I must acknowledge with gratitude the contribution of Mr. "X," a great European money manager. He asked to remain anonymous, but near the end of his life, he shared with me his knowledge and system for financial success. Mr. X, your work will indeed live on and not just with me.

Next I thank Marty Zweig and Dan Sullivan for their work on avoiding negative periods in U.S. markets, which provided a model of what to strive for, both internationally and across other asset classes. Also, thanks Marty, for all those wonderful correlation studies you filled your newsletter with each month for decades—I saved them all and sought to apply my own reworking of them to our master models.

William O'Neil has done tremendous work on stock selection criteria, emphasizing ways to find the top-performing stocks in each market, and Frank Cappiello has done pioneering work on the importance of institutional discovery in the odyssey of a stock's rise from obscurity to prominence. Meanwhile, Nelson Freeburg has applied a never-ending, incredible stream of timing systems to a whole host of asset classes providing me with many insights. Also, I am tremendously indebted to all the people at Bank Credit Analyst for their rigorous work and insight into the liquidity cycle across most tradable markets on the globe.

My heartfelt thanks go to Ludwig von Mises, Ayn Rand, and Murry Rothbard for their selfless preservation of Austrian economics, the ideals of capitalism, and truth. I am grateful for the work of Paul Pilser for putting economic myth in its place and bringing forth the theory of alchemy. I want to acknowledge Stanley Kroll for his work on money management and Jay Schabacker for his brilliant melding of the liquidity cycle and mutual fund selection.

Finally, I thank Tony Robbins for reteaching me how to change and grow and for exposing me to some of the ideas on which this work is based. If there is anyone out there who has not yet drunk of the knowledge of any of the great innovators I have acknowledged here, let me encourage you to partake immediately for your own enrichment.

M.B.

Contents

Introduction

This book is written for every investor or trader—large or small—who wants a methodology to consistently profit from the markets without incurring huge risks.

In this era of exploding U.S. and global stock markets, many investors are focusing most of their attention on returns, not on risk. I can safely say that the methodologies advocated in this book offer highly pleasing potential returns. Our newsletter to clients has shown average annual returns of over 32 percent per year since 1992, without a losing year and, more significantly, without a drawdown of over 10 percent (this has more than doubled the total return of the Standard & Poor's 500 [S&P] over this period). During this same period, the funds I have consulted for have done even better in terms of both risk and return, with real money, investing millions of dollars globally. And in researching the concepts on which these methodologies are based, my colleagues and I have gone back to the early 1900s to verify their rigor. Thus while I am confident that the methodologies described here can enable you to pull consistently large profits from the markets, I also hope that the book sharpens your focus on two equally important factors of investment—risk and market understanding.

1

THE IMPORTANCE OF RISK

Recounting a personal experience may be the most effective way to explain why risk should be of paramount importance to investors. In the early 1970s, when I was just nine years old, my father died of cancer. He had struggled to try and leave me a trust fund with enough money to finance my future college education. Since I had at least a decade to go until reaching college age when my father set up the trust, he put it into stock funds managed by a bank. From the end of World War II to the late 1960s, stocks had been in a wonderfully profitable bull market. The public was participating in stocks to the highest degree since 1929, and the prevailing wisdom was that if one just hung onto stocks over the long run, they showed a better return than nearly any other type of asset. (This type of environment should sound quite familiar to investors of the late 1990s.)

Things did not go according to plan beginning in 1972. From 1972 to 1975, the value of that trust fund declined by over 70 percent along with the decline in U.S. and global stock prices of a commensurate amount (the S&P and Dow dropped by around 50% during this period, but the broader market dropped by much more than that). By the time I started college in the early 1980s, even the blue chip indexes had lost more than 70 percent of their value from 1972 in after-inflation terms. While my trust had recovered somewhat from 1975 to the early 1980s, it was nowhere near the level it had been before my father died. In the early 1970s, he believed he had provided enough funds for me to go to an Ivy League school—but a decade later the diminished trust led me to opt for U.C.-Berkeley instead. In no way could the trust have covered the cost of an elite private school.

The historical fact is that it would have been difficult to pick a worse investment class than stocks from 1972 to 1982. Even experts like John Templeton and Warren Buffett did poorly. This experience left me with a keen desire to understand what led to such a huge disparity in the returns of equities over such a long period. It also provided an extremely valuable lesson regarding risk, which I sadly had to learn again with my own money before it really sank in.

I began investing my savings from summer jobs and such when I was a sophomore in high school. My first real killing came during the 1979 runup in gold prices. I had read several books convincing me that gold could do nothing but explode in price, and I plunged my entire savings into options on gold stocks. The options took off, and my account surged by nearly 500 percent from March 1979 to January 1980. Pure luck helped, as I was forced to exit my December 1979 options just before the gold market peaked and crashed beginning in January 1980.

I had caught the speculative bug. By early 1980, I was regularly speculating in a host of highly leveraged commodity positions. Not knowing what I was doing, I lost small amounts of money consistently until 1981, when I got caught short March '81 Orange Juice during a freeze in early 1981. I was short Orange Juice, which shot up from around 80 to 130 in a series of limit-up moves that lasted for more than a week and prevented anyone short from being able to get out of positions. By the time I could cover my shorts, I had lost nearly half of my account and more than half of the profits I had gained from gold's runup. My real education had begun, and I realized that I needed to study the subject much more thoroughly to profit consistently from the markets. The easy money I had first thought was for the taking had really been luck. Having seen two accounts lose more than half their value, I now realized the importance of limiting risk.

The mathematics of losses and risk is sometimes lost on investors until they actually experience it up close and personally. When your account drops 70 percent in value, that means you won't get back to breakeven until you have made over 230 percent on your remaining money. It hardly seems fair! One would think that if you dropped 70 percent, you ought to be able to get back to even when you made 70 percent—but that is not the way it works. As I started to voraciously study the works of investors who had made significant long-run gains, I noticed that most great investors and traders sought to keep drawdowns (their largest loss from an equity high) around 20 to 30 percent or less—and most measured their gains in terms of the drawdowns they had to sustain to generate those gains. An investor who loses more than 20 percent must show gains of 30 percent or higher just to get back to even—and that could take more than a year to produce, even for an excellent investor.

As the concept of weighing risk against reward hit home, investment performance suddenly meant more to me than making big gains: it meant measuring those gains against the risk I was taking to achieve them.

If I can prevent just one person out there from going through the same painful experience I had from 1972 to 1982, then writing this book has been a worthwhile effort. I hope I will convince more than one of you. Similarly, if I can get one or more investors and traders to think of performance not just in terms of total returns over the short run, but in terms of reward compared with drawdown and consistency over the long run, I will be pleased. Far too many fund-rating services only list performance in terms of return, while totally ignoring risk. Investors wanting to consistently perform well in the markets have to be much smarter than that.

The goal of this book is to present a methodology for achieving market-beating long-run returns with substantially lower risk than the long-run risk of U.S. and global equities. However, just as important as giving the reader such a methodology is to do it with honesty and integrity, based on the philosophy I have identified as essential for achieving low-risk consistent market gains. To do this, I must explode some myths and misconceptions. And perhaps the most important lesson I have for market participants is that the answer to their quest for superior performance doesn't lie in a Holy Grail system, but in their own development of the skills necessary to understand major market movements.

While I provide dozens of specific systems and rules along with their historical records of market-beating risk/reward performance, I also stress that it is far more important to understand what lies behind their success and to keep abreast of anything that could change those underlying principles than it is to follow those exact rules and systems. This distinction is, in fact, the difference between market novices and market masters over the long term. The market novice constantly searches for "magic" systems that will deliver a fortune. The master tries to develop the necessary skills and insight into markets and economics to consistently see what methodologies will work in the forthcoming environment.

As I discuss in Chapter 6, the novice tries to find fish holes where the fish are biting today, while the master learns how to find the fish holes where the fish are biting every day. The book is designed to provide the skills that can convert novice investor/traders into potential market masters.

HOW IT ALL STARTED

After graduating from the University of California–Berkeley in the mid-1980s, I first traded on my own for a bit. While at a conference on trading where I was a speaker, I met two key individuals: Tom Johnson, a Stanford Ph.D., and Paul Sutin, his student at the time. They liked some ideas I had expressed on seasonal commodity straddles, and we decided to begin doing historical research together, initially on ways to dispel the myth of the efficient market hypothesis, which had broad academic acceptance and basically held that achieving higher than average profit with lower than average risk was impossible.

Dr. Johnson and I began a research effort that lasted more than three years and involved testing and developing nearly every theory we could get our hands on that had to do with achieving market-beating performance. We tested every concept we could find going back to the early 1900s (or earlier, where data exist; we found records for bonds and some stock indexes from as long ago as the 1870s). We were striving to find something historically rigorous.

Our research concentrated on two areas of study: (1) the testing of market-beating concepts and methods, and (2) the detailed study of all those who had achieved market-beating performance on a risk/reward basis historically and in the present. Tom put significant resources into developing software that could test and show intricate statistics for any simple or complex trading system or data-set/concept for trading stocks, bonds, commodities, and currencies. As a result of building this huge database and accompanying software, Tom and I also started a small business selling the use of this software for testing other people's ideas. Many large and small investors, traders, and institutions hired us to test their ideas or systems on our long-term database. This research effort is the basis for the ideas presented in this book, and I am grateful to Tom Johnson, Paul Sutin, and the many others who helped put that research effort together. I also owe a huge debt of gratitude to the great market masters whose ideas we retested and found to be rigorous. I have no false pride about acknowledging ideas from others—my primary concern is with what actually works. Appendix B provides a list of the great investors and researchers whose work I have found to be exceptional; I urge you to read as many of their works as you can.

HOW TO RECOGNIZE A MARKET MASTER

A real-life example will illustrate the difference between a market master who strives for understanding and a market novice who searches for magical systems. By some strange coincidence, Tom and I handled two projects within the span of a year or so that depended on the same basic concept. Both of these investors had attended a seminar by Larry Williams, in which Larry proposed a system based on the discount/premium disparity between the S&P cash and nearby futures. Simplifying a bit, the concept was that one should buy the S&P futures any time that the futures were closing at a discount to the cash S&P, and hold to the following profitable close. Larry didn't use any stop-loss in the version of the system we were given by our first customer.

The first customer—a market novice—had attended Larry's seminar and began to trade this particular system (Larry usually packs more systems into a seminar than just about anyone, so I'm sure this was just one of many such systems at the seminar). The customer, who was showing consistent profits through this trading, was shocked at the success of the system and wanted a third party to evaluate it before committing more capital to it. The year was late 1986.

I backtested the system and found almost identical performance to that illustrated by Larry Williams in his seminar. The problem was that S&P futures only began to trade in 1982, so there wasn't a timeframe long enough to evaluate the system properly. I met with the client and explained two serious reservations that I had about the system. The first was the lack of stop-loss protection—any system that does not limit losses is an accident waiting to happen according to my research. The second problem had to do with understanding futures markets in general. Again simplifying greatly, most nearby contract futures markets trade at a premium to underlying cash during a bull market, but trade at a discount to the underlying cash market during a bear market. Theoretically, the futures should trade at a premium to cash equal to the T-bill

rate for the period between entry and futures delivery, but in reality the premium/discount of nearby futures reflects whether
there is a short-term shortage or overly large inventory of product
(or a reason for investors to panic-buy or panic-sell the underlying instrument immediately). Since other financial instruments
such as currencies had shown a tendency to trade at a premium
most of the time, but at a discount during severe bear markets, I
reasoned that the S&P would be similar. This meant that the system would likely fail in a severe bear period. I tried to convince
the client to add stop-losses and some sort of filter to protect him
against a bear market period if he wanted to continue to trade the
system on its own.

I described two types of stop-loss and trend filters the client
might use; these filters, however, would have cut total profits from
1982 to 1986. I was surprised by the client's response. He said
something like, "You mean, it really does work!?" He took off from
our meeting very excited about the original system, and I had the
strange feeling that he hadn't heard a thing I said about stop-losses
and trend filters.

This client called back every few months to gloat that he was
still making money with the original system and had been able to
add to his exposure to it. And in fact, for so simple a system, it had
worked remarkably well, generating thousands of dollars a year
per contract since 1982. It was very rare that one needed an extra
$5,000 beyond normal initial margin to maintain each per contract
position, since it was usually only held until the first profitable
close, and so the client had increased his trading size every time he
had extra margin plus $5,000. He had made around $10,000 per
contract, by his reckoning, up until October 1987. On October 27,
1987, the day of the great market crash, the S&P December futures
closed at a discount to the cash S&P, and this novice trader had du-
tifully bought as many contracts as he could on the close at
around the 874.00 level. The next morning, the December S&P
opened at 859.00 and proceeded to plummet to the 844.00 level
very quickly thereafter (the S&P contract was $500 per 1.00 point
at that time). This meant that on the open, the novice trader faced
a potential margin call, because he had a $7,500 per contract loss
and had only allowed $5,000 room. The trader exited as quickly as
he could to avoid potential ruin. He sold out very near the lows at
around 846.00 average fill for a one-day loss of just over $14,000

per contract, which basically wiped him out completely. Had he used the trend filter and stop-loss I had recommended, he would have made far less profit until October 27, 1987, but he would have still made money through the crash. It is also worth noting that if he had had hugely deep pockets and courage of steel, he could have survived the day—the system actually did work, it just required a ton of margin, but this trader was going for maximum profits.

A few months later, we were reviewing the trading of an excellent investor for input on how he could improve his already stellar performance. Among the concepts he listed as exploiting was the same Larry Williams concept of looking for buy signals near the close of a day or on the day following one in which the nearby S&P futures closed at a discount to cash. I inquired about the concept and found that he had gone to the same seminar. However, I noted in this trader's actual trades that he had done no buying on October 27, nor during future signals during the October–November 1987 period.

I asked this second trader why he had avoided these trades. "Are you nuts?" he replied. "Sure I try to look for those opportunities, but only when I can do so with limited risk and use a stop-loss. Besides, the risk of the market falling further was just too large—no one understanding what was going on at the time would have even considered going long on the close. And in fact, I ignored all of those signals until I was pretty sure we weren't in a consistent downtrend, because in a consistent downtrend, closing at a discount to cash might be normal."

Now while the novice trader made several mistakes besides ignoring the basic rules of limiting risk and understanding what underlies a system being used, what really differentiated him from the master trader was what he was looking for. The novice trader was looking for a magical system that, when applied, would print cash for him. He didn't want to be bothered with potential shortcomings because he wanted so badly to find his pot of gold in a system. Conversely, the master trader was simply looking for ideas or systems that he could understand and utilize to help find low-risk, high-reward potential trading/investing opportunities. He wouldn't have dreamed of trading a system he didn't understand, or investing without proper stop-loss protection. He wasn't looking for magic; he was searching for ideas, concepts, systems, and methods that would help him add another arrow to his quiver of potential situations where he would find low-risk opportunities for profit. One wanted to be camped out by a fishing hole someone else had found where the fish were biting and bait his hook as fast as possible. The other was simply looking for another way to find a fishing hole where fish might be biting for a while.

UNDERSTANDING IS KEY TO SUCCESS

There are many books, courses, and software that purport to sell Holy Grail systems. They are mostly hype that is based on a perception of the world that does not jibe with reality. One of the reasons there are so many such books and services is that there are so many traders and investors hunting for such systems. The pot of gold they are hunting for, however, isn't at the end of the rainbow. That pot is built, coin by coin, based on your skills as a trader/investor, and on your ability to consistently find reliable ways to limit your risk while participating in opportunities that have much more reward than the risk you are taking. The pot of gold doesn't lie in some system outside yourself; it lies in the set of skills and degree of understanding and insight that you build within. That is why I want to give investors more than a methodology; I want to help them understand what builds profitable methodologies and what underlies investing and trading success.

So this book has chapters that are purely methods and systems based on a concept, but it also has chapters that give the reader insight and understanding into basic principles of success required to profit from the markets long term as well as to understand the economics behind market profits. Although Chapter 6, in particular, may seem long and complex to the reader who just wants techniques, investors who do not understand the concepts in that chapter will ultimately shoot themselves in the foot as investors, and may even contribute to destroying the mechanism that makes investing profit opportunities possible in a free economy.

OVERVIEW OF THE APPROACH IN THIS BOOK

First of all, it is impossible to include all the complex tools and models that I use in my investment approach in a book of this size. I have, however, presented the basic concepts that make up my approach as fairly simple tools, indicators, and models that any investor, trader, or money manager can use. Whenever possible, I include decades of historical track record of each tool, so you can see for yourself that it works. And by building each new concept on the foundation of the prior one, I try to underscore that the sum of the parts makes a much greater whole.

The system presented here is based on our research from the mid-1980s. We tried to test every concept we could find for investing profitably to learn how we could use it, whether it was valid, and what made it tick. When we found a promising theory, we tried to integrate it into a composite or model that included other things that worked, independently. We also analyzed the practices of great investors and then condensed their methodology into the concepts and principles on which it was based. In this way, we could develop insight into not only what worked, but what consistently was required, and what modifications created different performance profiles. We also tried to rigorously test the methods of successful investors on very different historical periods to search out weaknesses: Did they just happen to fit the period under which they were utilized, but fail during other periods?

The strategies employed by an investor who is trying to beat a specific market over the long run differ greatly from those of one who is trying to profit consistently from the markets. Most mutual fund managers are trying to beat a specific benchmark index. They may have excellent stock selection criteria that will allow the elite among them to outperform their benchmark in both good and bad market environments. However, their performance is also highly correlated with their benchmark. This means that their strategies work wonderfully when their chosen benchmark is doing well. But when their benchmark is plummeting, these investors' strategies are also faltering.

Great investors like Peter Lynch, John Templeton, and Warren Buffett have phenomenal stock selection criteria that other traders try to emulate when investing in stocks. But investors also need to understand that there are periods when being in the market at all is a losing proposition. As mentioned in Chapter 1, any person who just happened to buy an investment property in California in 1972 and hold it for the next 10 years did substantially better than the previously named illustrious investors during that decade. Similarly, the average Joe who bought a mutual fund in 1982 and has held on to it probably has done better than Donald Trump or most other real estate experts (in the United States) during this period. I am going to explain why this is so, and strive to get investors to participate in the asset class that is moving in a reliable and profitable trend. If you could have bought real estate between 1972 and 1982, and then switched to stock funds in 1982, you would have done much better than the experts in either field. A key principle to be discussed is the importance of correctly determining the tide of investment flows. I will explore several ways to do this.

Certain environments allow stocks to move up in reliable and strong trends. These are the times that investors seeking consistent returns invest heavily in stocks. There are also periods (1929–1932, 1937, 1939–1942, 1946–1949, 1957, 1960, 1962, 1965–1975, 1981–1982, 1984, late 1987, 1990, 1994), when investors were far better served avoiding heavy allocations to stocks. Investors who are more concerned with avoiding drawdown and achieving consistent profits will therefore seek to avoid severe bear market periods that can ruin annual profitability, and can shave from 25 to 90 percent of their capital during a down phase. Such investors will want to determine when trends in different markets are reliable and invest only among reliable trends across many asset classes such as global equities, global bonds, currency trends, commodities, real estate, precious metals, and any other asset class that is not highly correlated with the others in its profit performance profile. These traders will shoot for average annual returns that are higher than those of U.S. or global equities (10%–12%) over the long run, but will show a performance profile that is only correlated to equities when they are investing heavily in stocks as opposed to other investments.

How does one determine when to invest in one country's equity market versus another? How does one determine when to avoid equities altogether? These are some of the questions answered with models and tools in the following chapters.

In general, I use five investing concepts to answer the asset allocation question: Austrian Liquidity Cycle, Valuation Gauges, Technical Tools, Money Management, and Understanding of long-run profit-building characteristics. Before explaining and building on these concepts, I issue a warning in Chapter 7: I explain that buy-and-hold investing 100 percent in the U.S. or any other single equity market is far too volatile a strategy for any reasonable investor in terms of risk and return. If you don't want to go through what I did after 1972; if you want to avoid a 70 percent plus drawdown including inflation after a decade of holding; or if you would rather not wait up to 30 years before breaking even after inflation, read this chapter closely and heed its warning. Even if you had nerves of steel and could avoid the fear that develops in a multiyear negative market environment, there are few investors who will want to be down after two or more decades of investing.

In Chapter 2, I discuss the first component of my five-pronged strategy for isolating reliable trends in global equity markets: the Austrian Liquidity Cycle. Here you'll learn how to isolate the most reliable equity markets on the globe using a strategy that a successful European money manager used for decades to substantially beat global and U.S. market averages with a fraction of the drawdown and risk. The idea here is that if you simply switch to investing only among those markets where liquidity trends are clearly favorable along with technical trends of the markets themselves, you can slash risk and enhance return. This model itself is worth hundreds of times the price of this book.

In Chapter 3, valuation is considered on a country-index basis. It is critical not only to monitor trends, but to be sure you are not paying too much for the stocks you buy. When a whole country index starts to get overvalued, potential rewards drop, and potential risks rise rapidly. You can incorporate this valuation concept into a tool that will help you improve on the liquidity model covered in Chapter 2.

In Chapter 4, I cover technical tools. You want to make sure the tide of the market you are preparing to invest in is moving clearly and reliably in your favor. Even if you find a stock whose earnings are soaring, if the overall market is moving lower, chances are your stock is falling, too. So before moving to individual stock selection criteria, you want to be sure you are investing in only those markets where technical strength is excellent. At the end of Chapter 4, I show you how to add a simple technical element to the liquidity-valuation model based on Chapters 2 and 3, which will substantially increase profitability, cut risk, and reduce drawdown. By the end of this chapter, you'll know how to cut the long-run risk of global equity market investing by almost 60 percent, while increasing annual profits by almost 50 percent.

Chapter 5 is devoted to one of the most important components of any successful investing methodology—money management strategies along with the principles of character needed for investment success. If you have a great system and poor money management, you're much less likely to succeed than the person with just a mediocre system and sound money management strategies. Simply applying these money management techniques to the strategy described in earlier chapters will put you substantially ahead of most professional investors and money managers over the long run.

Chapter 6 focuses on the final segment of our five-pronged strategy—an understanding of the elements that create investment profits. This long and challenging chapter includes some of the most important information in the book. When you have assimilated this material, you will be on your way toward becoming a top global investor because you will have insight into what underlies the major trends that create investment profits in any asset class:

- This chapter explores Austrian Alchemy, an approach toward economics that will allow you to understand what drives prices and supply and demand forces.
- In this chapter, I cover the long-run growth paradigm, which explains what lies behind stock market profits and human economic progress.
- Another major topic in Chapter 6 is the effect of government policies on GDP growth and stock market gains, as well as a look at how investors must try to weed through media stories to separate fact from hype.

Although this may be new and difficult material, by the end of this chapter—and especially by the end of the book—you will gain new insight into how to locate profitable investments and how to understand what is going on in the financial world. You will also be able to resist government power grabs and learn how to vote with your capital to support policies that favor investors around the world. This chapter has little appeal for novices (who have the greatest need to read it), but investment masters (and those who hope to be masters) will find it to be the most rewarding section of the book.

In Chapter 7, we concentrate on stock selection criteria. Once you have gone through the valuation, liquidity, and technical models and have identified good profit opportunities in a particular market, this chapter will show you how to zero in on the top individual stocks within that market, for maximum profits. The criteria in this chapter for both long positions and short sales have been tested thoroughly on decades of data, as well as used in real time to build substantial profits since the late 1980s. You will learn how to find top growth stocks in runaway technical trends that are set to outperform their markets, yet sell at reasonable prices that will slash your risk and improve your potential profits. You will also learn how to find stocks to sell short, and when to use such strategies as a hedge against a systemic market decline, or in a two-way market environment. Here, too, many lengthy books incorporate less valuable information than can be found in this chapter alone. Our criteria have been real-time tested and have outperformed their respective markets in each year since 1989.

In Chapter 8, we move from equities to other asset classes. Here you will learn models for timing your investments among global bonds, commodities, gold and silver, real estate, and other asset classes, such as arbitrage funds and hedge funds, which should be included in nearly any portfolio. For each asset class, I include a simplified version of my own methodology for timing and choosing investments, just as provided for global equities in earlier chapters. You will learn when it is appropriate to invest in bonds, or commodity funds—and which ones to choose and why. You will know when to switch to gold stocks and emerging market debt. Not only will you understand how and when to switch among different asset classes, but simple models will signal you when to make such changes. I provide the full track record for these models along with information on how to find out even more about them should you want to expand your knowledge.

In Chapter 9, I explain how to put all the components covered so far together in a custom-tailored portfolio using a portfolio strategy that best fits your own risk/reward characteristics and desires. By putting together timing models from a host of different asset classes and combining disparate investments into a diversified portfolio, you can substantially increase returns while cutting risks to a fraction of traditional asset-allocation portfolios. You will also learn about flexible asset allocation and how to use global relative strength tables to help you screen out top investments and asset classes at any one time. This is where we bring the power of all the previous chapters together.

Appendix A covers short-term trading strategies. You will learn why understanding is even more critical for short-term traders than for any other type of investor. And I will give you one of my favorite short-term trading patterns and strategies.

Finally in Appendix B, you will learn many of the shoulders of greatness on which this work stands. There are many excellent services, letters, data vendors, and software vendors that are critical sources of information for top investors. In this section, I list my favorites so that those who want to explore what I consider to be the best in the business, know exactly what to read and where to go.

The bottom line is that reading this book should help you become a totally different investor. You will know strategies for substantially increasing the profitability of investing, while slashing risk to the bone. You will see how others have accomplished this feat, and will understand exactly how and why it works. I have tried to put more valuable information in this book than in any I have ever read. Sometimes the information is compressed, and the concepts are complex. But if you read and understand each chapter of this book, you will gain decades of investing insights and techniques in an unbelievably short time.

The Risk of Traditional Investment Approaches

From 1982 through most of 1997, the global financial markets have been very generous to investors. Both bonds and stocks in the United States and abroad have returned investment gains far above their long-term average levels. The American and global financial markets have been in one of the most dramatic secular (or long-term) bull markets seen in the past 150 years of financial market history.

THE EFFECTS OF A LONG-TERM BULL MARKET

This spectacular long-lasting bull market in global financial assets has made traditional investing approaches, such as buy-and-hold and dollar cost averaging into both bonds and stocks a wildly lucrative venture—investors have grown accustomed to average annual gains in the upper teens or higher on long-term investments. Seldom in history has it been so easy for investors to make such high average annual returns over such a long time span.

Many factors have contributed to this global secular bull market. The computer revolution has been a primary accelerant radically improving worker productivity and allowing companies' profit growth and margins to move up at a much higher rate than GDP growth levels. The demographic shift of the baby boom generation through its spending life cycles has led to a portfolio shift in favor of financial assets. Government tax policies and free-trade policies have become less intrusive (though they still have a long way to go in this regard). Freer market approaches have been gaining ground globally as 70 percent of the world's population once held back by statist governments have joined the ranks of the global marketplace.

These secular trends have helped propel the global financial markets into historically high valuation levels at average annual returns that dwarf almost any other 15-year period. And many of these trends appear likely to continue building into the next decade. Restructuring based on computer technology—a long trend in the United States—is just now gaining steam in many of the other developed nations. Government cuts in spending and taxes appear to be marching forward, albeit at a grindingly slow but steady general pace. And the baby boomers are feeling the pinch to awaken before their retirement needs (directly ahead) hit them in the face.

However, traders, investors, and speculators of all stripes also need to be aware that no trees grow to the sky—and no secular trend lasts forever. Baby boomers' massive savings and portfolio shifts are likely to reverse beginning around 2005. As the Figure 1.1 shows, the average peak savings age (for baby boomers will occur in 2005, and this group of savers will begin to fall into the retirement category of dis-savers soon after that point in time.

As described throughout this book, the marginal gains from computer technology take off in the initial years, but even with the present breathtaking pace of innovation, those gains also slow down after the first wave of restructuring and retechnology tooling.

The same overwhelming needs of retiring baby boomers that will lead to their dis-savings will also create unprecedented government spending problems (especially in developed nations) as massive transfer payments become due (Medicare, Medicaid, Social Security in the United States, and their equivalents abroad). The lower taxes and lower spending that has characterized recent government fiscal policy is therefore likely to be temporary as

Figure 1.1 **THE SPENDING WAVE**

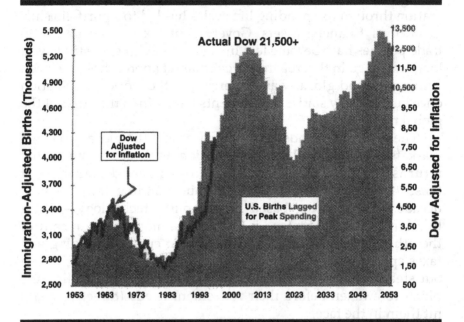

Source: Reprinted with the permission of Simon & Schuster from *The Roaring 2000s* by Harry S. Dent, Jr. Copyright © 1998 by Harry S. Dent, Jr.

virtually no developed nations are attacking these imminent major problems.

Investors who intend to participate in investment markets in the decade ahead and beyond may not be able to depend on the wild global financial bull market alone to achieve the same high returns they have grown accustomed to over the past 15 years. In fact, an adjustment, or reversion to the mean return, may develop; and a bear market larger in both duration and extent than we have seen in many decades may bring our current high returns closer to long-term average annual returns for financial markets.

Reviewing and understanding the long-term averages and implications of how secular bull and bear markets intertwine may therefore be valuable for long-term investors. It can also serve to warn investors that continued achievement of high average annual returns means adopting a more flexible and adaptive global approach with many asset classes, not just equities and bonds. Investors may also need to relearn the concept of timing their moves among different asset classes to avoid negative environments that could be devastating to capital.

LONG-TERM RETURNS IN EQUITIES

Figure 1.2 shows a long-term average annual return perspective on the Standard & Poor's (S&P) 500 Index since 1900. The chart tells you if you had held the S&P for the prior decade what your average annual return would have been at any year-end since 1900. Four secular bull markets during the past century managed to push the 10-year average annual return of the S&P up past 10 percent. During these periods—if you had held the S&P for the

Figure 1.2 **S&P 500 AVERAGE ANNUAL 10-YEAR RETURN**

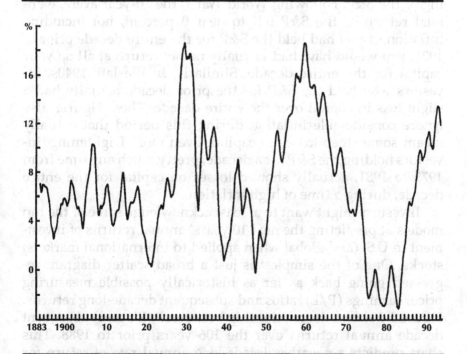

Source: Reprinted by permission of the *Bank Credit Analyst.*

preceding decade—you would have had average annual returns in each of those 10 years of 10 percent or more. The first secular bull market ended just before World War I; the second ended in 1929; the third ended in the mid 1960s. Both the 1929 peak and the 1965 peak ended with 10-year average annual gains in the 18 percent to 20 percent range. Although the chart is not fully up to date, 10-year average annual rate of return for the S&P in 1997 was around 18 percent.

Does this mean the S&P is destined to decrease its rate of annual returns immediately? No, certainly not; the past does not equal the future. However, the wise investor also does not ignore historical norms and should constantly be on the lookout for historical resistence levels in the amount of return the S&P has generated and on the valuation levels investors are willing to pay for blue-chip stocks.

Investors should notice that, historically, following every secular bull market of high annual returns for a decade, there has been a sharply falling rate of return on the next decade holding of the S&P. Following World War I, the 10-year average annual return of the S&P fell to near 0 percent, not including inflation. If you had held the S&P for the entire decade prior to 1921, you would have had virtually no net return at all on your capital for the entire decade. Similarly, in the late 1940s, investors who held the S&P for the prior decade actually had a slight loss in capital over the entire decade. These figures also ignore considerable inflation during this period that actually meant some steep losses to capital. Even more frightening, investors holding the S&P for a decade, pretty much any time from 1975 to 1981, actually showed losses on capital for the entire decade, during a time of high inflation.

Investors might want to at least acknowledge some of the top models at predicting the next 10 years' annual returns of investment in U.S. (and global when applied to international markets) stocks. One of the simplest is just a broad scatter diagram regressed going back as far as historically possible measuring price/earnings (P/E) ratios and subsequent decade-long returns. Figure 1.3 shows the relationship between P/E's and subsequent decade annual returns over the 106 years prior to 1988. This chart predicts a negative decade-long annual rate of return for

Figure 1.3 **HISTORY LESSON**

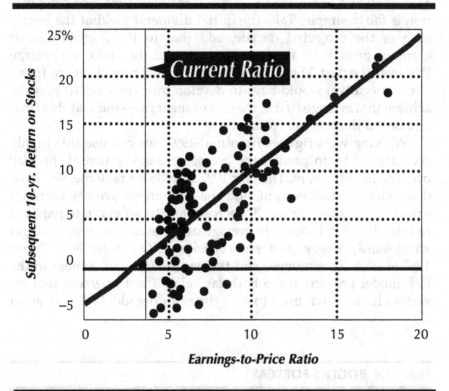

Note: When the ratio of earnings to stock prices is low, as it is today, the returns to stocks over the following 10 years are often low. Each dot shows the earnings-to-price ratio for one year between 1881 and 1987 and the annual return to stocks over the subsequent decade. Earnings are averaged over the previous 10 years. All data are adjusted for inflation.

Source: Robert Shiller, Yale University. Reprinted by permission of *Investor's Business Daily*.

the S&P over the decade 1997–2006 based on 1997's 23 P/E (price earnings) ratio.

Bogle's Model

A far more accurate model was created by John Bogle, founder and chairman of the $200 billion (and growing) Vanguard Mutual Fund Group. Since 1957, this model has an extremely accurate

0.78 correlation to the actual decade-long annual return of the S&P, as shown in Figure 1.4, graphed through 1993. The computation is fairly simple. Take the initial dividend yield at the beginning of the projected decade, add that to the average annual earnings growth for the past 30 years, and then take the average P/E over the past 30 years and compute what rate of return (positive or negative) would have to develop over the next 10 years to achieve that average P/E at the end of the term—and add this final number to the previous total.

Working with figures from mid-1997, we can use this highly accurate model to predict the average annual return of the S&P over the next 10 years. Thus for 1997 to 2006 we take the S&P dividend yield of 1.65 percent, add the 6.5 percent average earnings growth, and then subtract 3.5 percent for the annual rate required to take the 23 P/E down to average over the next 10 years—to get an *estimated average annual return of 4.6 percent a year for the S&P from 1997 to 2006.* This number and the negative return number in the P/E model prediction are both far below the 18 percent that investors have grown used to over the prior decade. Will you, as an

---

Figure 1.4 **BOGLE'S FORECAST**

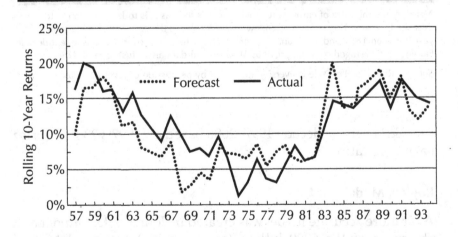

Source: Bogle on Mutual Funds by John Bogle of Vanguard (McGraw-Hill, 1993). Reprinted by permission of The McGraw-Hill Companies.

investor, be satisfied with an average annual return of between –2 percent a year and +4.6 percent a year over the next decade?

Corrections in the Market

If history is any guide to the future, possible poor decade-long annual returns are not the only pitfall for long-term equity investors. As mentioned, historically every secular bull market peak has been followed by a large and lengthy correction that took many decades to recover from when inflation is considered. Big secular bear markets (e.g., 1929–1932; 1966–1981) took 90 percent and 72 percent respectively off the value of blue-chip stock investments, after inflation. Each secular bull market peak was accompanied by a sense of euphoria that led investors to believe all they needed to do was buy stocks and hold them to make money over the long term—and by a series of innovations that encouraged financial reporters of the period to think they were in a "new era." In this novel financial environment, the violation of past valuation and historical return extremes supposedly would be meaningless.

Figure 1.5 provides a closer look at the real-life effects of long-term investing during a secular bear market period that directly followed a high-return secular bull market.

The charts shown in Figure 1.5, courtesy of the Chartist, show the results of investment in the Wies Growth Fund Index, an index of growth mutual funds. From 1960 to 1969, investors in growth funds had a very high rate of annual return (over 15%), as their capital grew from $10,000 initially to $35,728. However, $10,000 invested in 1969 actually fell in value at an average annual rate of 8.21 percent through 1975, leading to a 57.3 percent loss in that 6-year period, not including inflation. The entire 16-year period showed an average annual gain of under 2 percent, with investors needing to sit through a drop in capital of over 60 percent in a 6-year period to achieve that less than 2 percent annual gain. Even this steep decline in capital underestimates the real devastation felt by investors.

As Figure 1.6 shows, the after-inflation effects of holding blue chips like the S&P or Dow Jones Industrial Average (DJIA) from the mid-1960s to 1981 were practically incomprehensible. The DJIA in constant dollars shows just how brutal the last secular bear market was to investors in after-inflation terms. In constant

Figure 1.5 **PERFORMANCE OF GROWTH FUNDS 1960–1975**

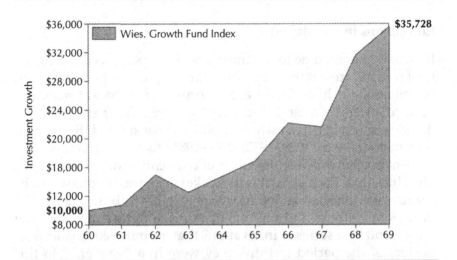

Note: Compounded growth, +15.2%; initial capital through January 1, 1960, $10,000; ending capital through December 31, 1968, $35,728.

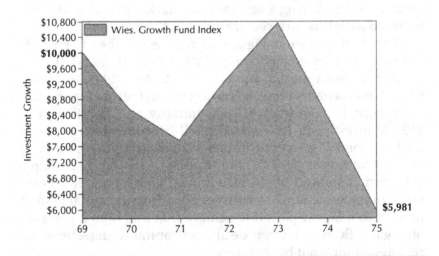

Note: Compounded loss, –8.21%; initial investment through January 1969, $10,000; ending investment through December 1974, $5,981.

Source: Reprinted by permission of *The Chartist.*

Figure 1.6 **STILL IN THE CHANNEL: INFLATION-ADJUSTED DOW**

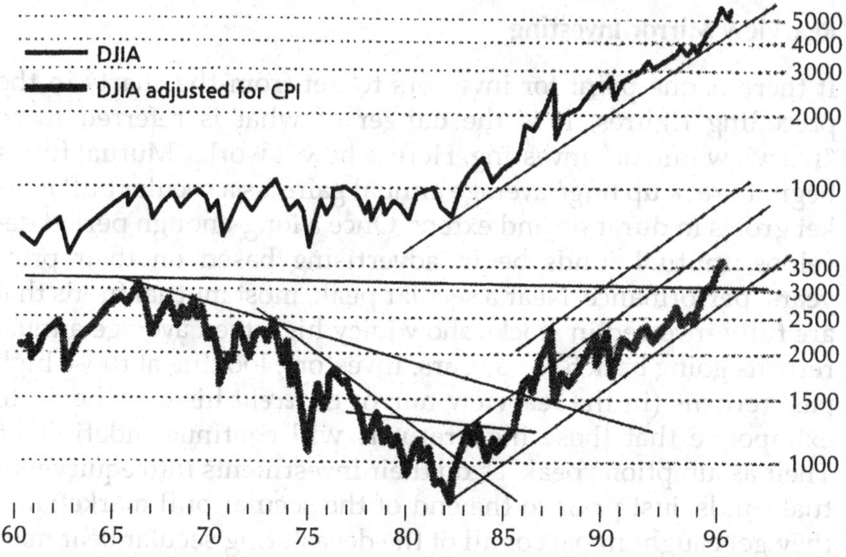

Source: Used by permission of Salomon Smith Barney.

dollar (inflation-adjusted) terms, the Dow peaked near 3100 in the mid-1960s and then plummeted to around 850 by 1981—a decline in real terms of over 72 percent for holding stocks during this 15-year period. Imagine for a few seconds being down more than 72 percent in real terms after holding stocks for 15 years.

How long did it take investors to recover from this debacle? Figure 1.6 says it all. In the most resilient segment, the Dow blue chips, *investors had to hold on for 30 years* from 1965 to 1995 before they broke even in after-inflation terms. Investors buying at the last secular peak, in 1929, had to wait even longer to get their principal back after inflation. That is why at a minimum, long-term investors need to realize that secular bull markets have repeated periodically in the past and that it is wise to develop a strategy for avoiding at least part of any such bear market. Few people have a retirement plan that would allow them to retire comfortably if they simply break even on their investments after a 30-year period. Yet with a 100 percent U.S. equity approach, this is the kind of devastation a secular bear market can wreak on investments.

Rearview Mirror Investing

If there is one point for investors to get from the charts in the preceding figures, it is the danger of what is referred to as "rearview mirror" investing. Here is how it works. Mutual funds begin to rack up huge average annual gains as a secular bull market grows in duration and extent. Once a long-enough period develops, mutual funds begin advertising based on their prior years' performance. Near a secular peak, most mutual funds that are fully invested in stocks show juicy high-teen average annual returns going back 5 to 15 years. Investors, looking at those high past returns (in the rearview mirror of *recent* history), begin to extrapolate that those high returns will continue indefinitely. Their assumptions peak, as do their investments into equity mutual funds, just prior to the end of the secular bull market; and they get caught in part or all of the devastating secular bear market that inevitably follows. In the early to late 1960s, most university economics classes taught students that all they had to do to retire wealthy was invest consistently in the stock market blue chips or Nifty Fifty. The studies that "proved" this thesis were looking in the most recent rearview mirror—not at the current investment merits of equities in terms of valuations and future growth rates (as the Bogle Model does). Investors following such advice not only failed to achieve double-digit annual returns, but actually had to wait three decades just to get their principal back in full after the ravages of inflation.

PROTECTION AGAINST BEAR MARKETS

Are there ways that investors can at least partially sidestep secular bear markets and the ravages to capital they contain for equity-only investors? Are there other asset classes that investors can profit from during periods when equities are not representing a good risk/return investment? The answer to both questions is "Yes!" and these are the questions that much of this book will be concerned with answering. Dealing with these issues involves stepping back a bit and looking at some of the critical measures of the performance of any investment or set portfolio to better understand the merits of different investments and be able to make comparisons.

Most nonprofessional investors as well as most fund rating services, are primarily concerned with one set of numbers—total return. The typical investor and rating service is constantly poring over numbers to find the top 1-year return fund, the top 5-year return fund, the top 10-year return fund. While these numbers certainly tell an investor one aspect of a fund's performance, they often receive concentrated attention at the expense of more important performance measures.

When talking in Europe to multimillionaire professional investors and asset-allocation specialists of European banks, I discovered that the total return of a fund was one of their last questions of inquiry. Much more important to these investors were things like the risk, the volatility, the drawdown, the duration and frequency of drawdowns, the sharp ratio (a ratio comparing volatility and return), and the correlation of the fund to global equities or other benchmarks. Only after they had found a potential fund that offered low risk, small and quick drawdowns, market-independent performance, and less than market volatility did they then check to see what the total return was. What these astute professionals were trying to find was not a fund with great 1-, 5-, or 10-year performance over the past—but a fund that offered *a superior rate of return per unit of risk* when compared with those of other funds and asset classes.

The viewpoint that total return is a valid measure of performance only when the downside risk is taken into consideration can be illustrated by analyzing which of the following two prospects is a better investment: (1) Over the past 30 years, investment Fund A has returned 12 percent annually on average, has a strategy that is not dependant on any particular market doing well, and has had a 5 percent worst-case historical drawdown; (2) over the past 30 years, investment Fund B has returned 17 percent per year on average, has had performance highly correlated with U.S. stock indexes, and has had a 15 percent worst-case historical drawdown (both investments are vastly superior to the S&P). Many investors, and rating services, would highlight investment B, which showed greater total returns for the period. And many investors would say, "Hey, I'm willing to take a worst-case 15 percent hit without a problem, so the extra protection of the lower drawdown in investment A does me no good."

However, most professional investors would prefer investment A. Even if the higher drawdowns are acceptable to you, leveraging investment A is a better choice than risking investment B. If you simply buy A on margin (put 50 percent down), you are going to achieve something close to a 19 percent annual return after margin costs (24% – 5%) for only 10 percent expected risk, compared with a 17 percent return on investment B for a 15 percent expected risk. For any risk posture, investment A is superior because its return in relation to its risk is better. A's return/risk ratio is 12 percent/5 percent = 2.4 to 1, while B's is 17 percent/15 percent = 1.13 to 1. Therefore A returns 2.4 units of profit per unit of maximum drawdown risk, whereas B returns only 1.13 units of profit per unit of maximum drawdown risk. Instead of hunting for top total return numbers, in general, astute investors should be hunting for top returns in relation to risk. Although there are other aspects to consider in evaluating potential investments, superior return per unit of risk is one of the most important concepts for investors to understand to be better than average over the long term. It is essential to consider traditional investments in terms of not just total return, but return, drawdown, volatility, duration of drawdown, and reliability.

BLUE CHIP STOCKS

A brief look at blue chip U.S. stocks will provide a benchmark to compare against, and a base to build on. A critical criterion in judging an investment is the maximum drawdown. If you had invested in this vehicle in the past at the worst possible time, how much of a drop in principal would you have had to withstand, and how long would it have taken you to recover? Looking at the historically worst-case scenario helps an investor answer the questions: "What is the downside?" and "What is the risk?"

As Figure 1.7 illustrates, the drawdowns in U.S. stocks are sometime breathtakingly steep. In fact, an investor in even the least volatile blue chips should expect a drawdown of around 30 percent every seven years or so. Drawdowns, before inflation,

Figure 1.7 **SIZE OF BEAR MARKETS**

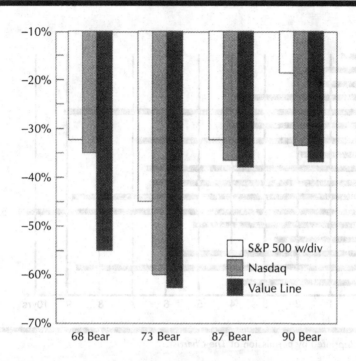

reached as high as 90 percent in the 1930s and 54 percent in the 1970s. NASDAQ (National Association of Securities Dealers Automated Quotations System) and Value-Line indexes had much steeper drops than blue chips in virtually every major bear market this century—dropping over 40 percent three times since World War II, and over 50 percent twice since World War II. During 1973 and 1974, even market legends like Warren Buffett and John Templeton had drawdowns of over 40 percent: *Even the best manager cannot profit when using a strategy that is wrong for the overall environment.*

How long would it take you to recover from these drawdowns? Our next chart, Table 1.1, shows just how long it took to recover not including the effects of inflation. On average, it took an investor 7 years to recover from a bear market, many times it took 1 to 4 years, but on some occasions it took 13 to 25 years. And as noted,

Table 1.1 **TIME FROM BEAR MARKET PEAK TO FULL RECOVERY**

Bear Markets										
1990										
1987										
1981										
1976										
1973										
1968										
1966										
1961										
1946										
1938										
1937										
1929										25.3yrs
1919										
1916										
1909										
1906										
1901										
	1	2	3	4	5	6	7	8	9	10yrs

Source: Reprinted by permission of *The Chartist.*

after adjusting for inflation it took over 30 years to recover from the mid-1960s and over 40 years to recover from 1929. These are very long and very deep drawdowns, to be sure. The only silver lining is that such deep and long drawdowns are not very common occurrences—happening once every 40 years or so (or about once in every long-term investor's investing lifetime).

INVESTMENT CRITERIA

Figure 1.8 shows a chart that we use often as an overall summary of an investment or asset class. It shows five key perspectives on investment performance: (1) compound annual return, (2) average annual volatility (or fluctuation from high to low), (3) worst drawdown over the period evaluated, (4) average downside volatility (the largest drop from a high during the course of a

Figure 1.8 **U.S. STOCKS SINCE WORLD WAR II (1943)**

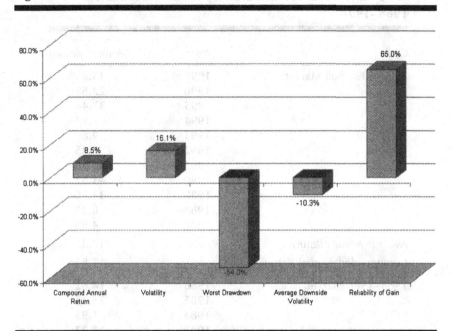

year on average), and (5) the reliability of gains (what percentage of years are profitable). Shown on the chart are the figures for blue chip stocks since World War II, and three ways to improve on this performance: (1) by increasing compound annual returns, (2) by slashing drawdown and volatility (i.e., risk), and (3) by increasing the reliability of annual gains. Here then are our initial benchmarks on which to improve performance as they are the long-term performance numbers for the S&P: an 8.5 percent or so compound annual return; 16 percent volatility with an occasional drawdown as high as 50 percent, 10 percent average annual drops from a high; and profits in 65 percent of years.

Before discussing these criteria, it is necessary to understand the difference between compound annual return and a statistic most investors are probably more familiar with—average annual return. Table 1.2 shows the S&P's annual returns since 1968. For this period, the S&P's average annual return has been 10.35 percent, while its compound annual return has been 9.23 percent.

Table 1.2 **STANDARD & POOR'S ANNUAL RETURNS, 1968–1997**

Cycle	Year	Annual Return
1987–1997 Bull Market	1997	33.20%
	1996	22.85
	1995	37.44
	1994	1.17
	1993	9.89
	1992	7.45
	1991	30.18
	1990	−3.32
	1989	31.36
	1988	16.22
	1987	4.66
Average Annual Return		17.37
Compounded Annual Return		13.83
1968–1986 Market	1986	14.62
	1985	26.33
	1984	1.95
	1983	17.27
	1982	14.76
	1981	−9.73
	1980	25.77
	1979	11.58
	1978	2.44
	1977	−11.50
	1976	19.14
	1975	31.54
	1974	−29.72
	1973	−18.10
	1972	15.63
	1971	10.78
	1970	0.10
	1969	−11.36
	1968	8.06
Average Annual Return		10.35
Compounded Annual Return		9.23

Since the 1987 crash lows, when the S&P has been on one of the swiftest and longest bull markets in its history, the S&P has achieved an incredible 17.37 percent average annual return, which equates to a 13.83 percent compound annual return. For the entire period going back to 1943, the S&P's average annual returns have been just under 10 percent, while the compound annual returns have been 8.5 percent. What investors need to see here is that a 13 percent compound annual return equates to a 15 percent to 20 percent average annual return, based on the S&P's normal historical reliability and volatility. The reason we use compound annual return instead of average annual return is that average returns fail to show as vividly the effects of large negative years on long-term returns when compared with compound annual returns—particularly in the early years of an investment plan. This concept is illustrated later in this chapter.

When evaluating market performance in terms of past performance, investors need a sound rationale for believing such returns will continue. It is also critical to look at such criteria as compound annual return, average downside volatility, worst-case historical drawdown, frequency of drawdown and recovery time, the percentage of years the investment has been profitable, and how dependent and correlated the investment is to returns in specific asset classes.

If these criteria become the camera lens through which we see and evaluate investment strategies, then it is easy to envision an ideal investment. It would have a market rate or better compound annual return with a below-market average drawdown and maximum drawdown. It would have fewer and shorter drawdowns than the market, and it would be profitable a higher percentage of years. In addition, the ideal investment strategy would not be dependent on the stock or bond market for its returns—it would be able to profit in nearly any market environment that has existed in the past, not just during bull markets in stocks or bonds.

Many investors do not give enough credit to this last criterion—the reliability of gains. Nor do they give enough weight to the harm to capital growth caused by negative years. Table 1.3 illustrates just how important it is to long-term investment gains. The table shows two theoretical examples of returns over a 10-year period. The first strategy looks superior because if you average the annual returns you get a 20.7 percent average annual

Table 1.3 **THE IMPORTANCE OF RELIABLE GAINS ON LONG-TERM WEALTH-BUILDING**

Year	Volatile Returns Annual Return (%)	Principal	Dependable Gains Annual Return (%)	Principal
1	21	1,210,000	18	1,180,000
2	35	1,633,500	18	1,392,400
3	20	1,960,200	18	1,643,030
4	-26	1,450,550	18	1,938,780
5	32	1,914,720	18	2,287,760
6	12	1,347,450	18	2,699,560
7	42	3,045,170	18	3,185,480
8	-16	2,557,950	18	3,750,887
9	31	3,350,910	18	4,435,460
10	56	5,233,000	18	5,233,850
	Average Annual Return = 20.7%		Average Annual Return = 18%	
	Compound Annual Return = 17.98%		Compound Annual Rate = 18%	

return. However, this average return comes at the cost of an occasional double-digit losing year—16 percent in year 8 and 26 percent in year 4. The second strategy calls for investing in a high-yield instrument that returns a simple 18 percent per year and is renewed each year at that same rate so that the average of its annual returns is lower—18 percent. Which strategy builds more long-term capital?

What most investors fail to realize is that you make more money investing in a consistent 18 percent per year than in a volatile 20.7 percent per year as Table 1.3 shows. This illustrates the false bias of average annual return that compound annual return shows clearly: while the average annual return of volatile returns is higher, these investments earn less money than a consistent investment with a lower average annual return, but a higher compound annual return. The cost of an occasional double-digit losing year on long-term appreciation is high—especially if those costs arise in year one or two of an investment program. A strategy that delivers consistent positive returns and rarely shows a negative annual period can build more capital and be easier to stick to than a strategy that delivers several percentage points higher annual returns but has a double-digit loss about as often as U.S. and global equities do. Compound annual rates show this discrepancy, while average annual returns often do not. So do not discount the importance of reliable returns in building an investment strategy.

HIGH RETURNS AND HIGH CONSISTENCY—THE TRADEOFF

The U.S. stock market shows a positive return about 65 percent of years. Since I have described secular bull and bear markets, I will briefly run through the more intermediate-term movements of the U.S. market since World War II to provide insight into stock investment strategy.

Figure 1.9 **BULL AND BEAR MARKETS (CHANGE IN S&P 500)**

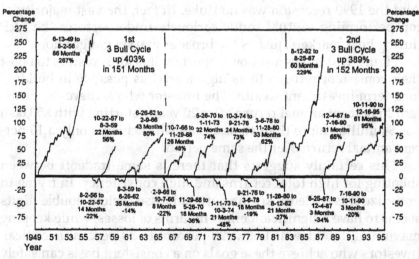

Note: All data are monthly averages except for the initial and terminal months of the cycle, which are the S&P 500 close for that date.

Sources: S&P's Corporation; Crandall, Pierce & Company. Reprinted by permission of Crandall, Pierce & Company, copyright © 1998.

As is apparent from Figure 1.9, the U.S. stock market has experienced 9 bear markets from World War II to 1996 that dropped an average of 26.9 percent in an average 15.7 months, and has experienced 10 bull markets rising an average of 104.9 percent in 41.8 months. These shifts underscore the large degree of variability in returns of stock investment. It also is a reminder that no market goes up forever; if you have yet to experience a bear market—and if history is any guide—you are likely to witness one in the years ahead. There are many years when the market rises rapidly and consistently, but there are also many years when it drops like a rock.

Some investors feel that holding a fund with a superior long-term performance can help insulate them from the effects of bear markets. Table 1.4 shows the fallacy of that expectation. Notice how severe the hits were in the top Relative Strength mutual funds of the 1987–1990 bull market during the brief 1990 bear market. This was one of the shallowest and shortest bear markets of the twentieth century, and yet top managers like Peter Lynch, Templeton, Auriana/Utsch, Baron, and others showed losses of 25 percent or more compared with the S&P's loss of 20 percent. And the 1990 recession was no fluke. In fact, the vast majority of top performing mutual funds seriously underperform the S&P during bear markets, just as the broader market gauges do.

Figure 1.10 shows just how important it is for investors to boost their consistent returns to as high a level as possible in building long-term investment wealth. The investor who achieves a consistent 25 percent annual return after 20 years (starting with $50,000) has $4 million more than an associate who achieves only a 10 percent annual return over the same period.

This certainly suggests that there is some tradeoff between shooting for high total returns and high consistency. In trying to optimize this tradeoff, keeping annual losses below double digits seems to have a significant effect in terms of losses, while keeping maximum drawdowns below 20 percent to 30 percent is critical. Investors who achieve these goals on a consistent basis can safely build significant long-term investment wealth if they are able to achieve compound annual returns of 11 percent or more. Strategies in this range over the long term should be sought; we will be exploring many such strategies and building many that do substantially better, throughout this book.

Table 1.4 **MUTUAL FUNDS DURING THE 1990 BEAR MARKET**

Templeton Global Growth	−25.50%
Fidelity Magellan	−27.36
Investco Dynamics	−27.51
Twentieth Century Growth	−27.54
Gardison McDonald Oppor.	−27.85
GIT Equity Special Growth	−28.07
Federated Growth Trust	−28.18
Twentieth Century Ultra	−28.29
MIM Stock Appreciation	−29.26
Investco Strategic Leisure	−30.05
Scudder Development	−30.14
Longleaf Partners Fund	−30.22
T. Rowe Price New America	−30.28
Clipper Fund	−30.79
Olympic Equity Income	−31.29
Kaufmann	−31.35
T. Rowe Price New Horizons	−31.36
Baron Asset	−32.25
Fund Trust Aggressive	−33.64
Safeco Growth	−35.32
Columbia Special	−35.32
Twentieth Century Vista	−36.91
PBHG Growth	−36.99
Stein Roe Capital Oppor.	−37.66
Oberweis Emerging Growth	−39.01
Bull & Bear Special Equity	−48.83

Using these criteria to judge a strategy (such as buy and hold U.S. stocks), we will look at a simple example of an improvement in that strategy in the attempt to improve at least two of the following three main criteria: (1) increasing compound annual returns, (2) cutting drawdown and downside volatility, and (3) increasing the consistency of gains.

Figure 1.11 shows that with a portfolio 50 percent invested in non-U.S. stocks and 50 percent invested in U.S. stocks, we can achieve a higher compound annual return with the same risk/ short-term volatility.

Figure 1.10 **DRAMATICALLY INCREASING YOUR WEALTH**

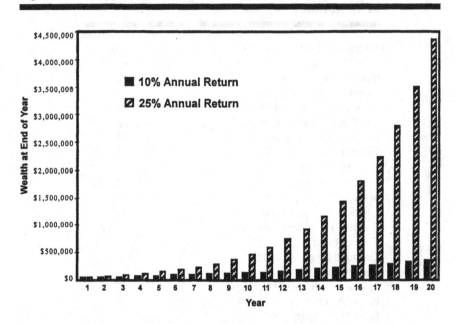

Investing simply in the world index, a capitalization weighted index of all global equities over the long run will return higher compound annual returns with a slightly lower (but still unacceptable) maximum drawdown, and less downside volatility, with the same 65 percent reliability. By increasing two of our top three criteria, global investing certainly qualifies as an improvement compared with long-run investing in U.S. stocks with 100 percent of a portfolio.

While Figure 1.12 shows clear improvement versus buy-and-hold investing in U.S. stocks, it is also far short of our goals. Global equity diversification may be one component in the search for profitable returns with low risk, but it alone does not achieve that goal. The main difficulty with global equity investing is similar to the problem of U.S. equity investing—the drawdowns can be huge and long-lasting during bear markets. One reason we didn't get

Figure 1.11 **DIVERSIFICATION RISK AND RETURN (EUROPE, AUSTRALIA, AND FAR EAST INDEX)**

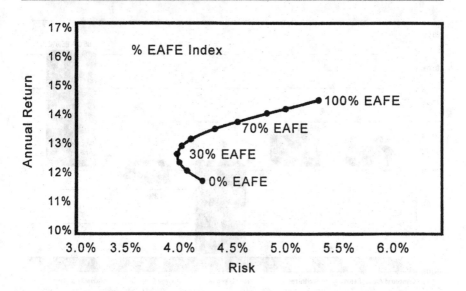

Note: Starting from the bottom and moving along the curve, first to the left and then up and to the right, we move from a 100% U.S. portfolio to a 90% U.S./10% foreign portfolio, to an 80% U.S./20% foreign portfolio, and so forth. At the top right end, we eventually get to a 100% foreign portfolio. This chart reveals interesting facts: (a) A portfolio of 100% U.S. stocks has a lower rate of return than portfolios with a mix of foreign stocks; (b) as the percentage of foreign stocks increases, the volatility initially goes down as returns rise; (c) the least volatile portfolio (for this time period) was the one with 70% U.S. stocks and 30% foreign stocks; and (d) a 50%–50% portfolio mix gives a higher return with less volatility than a 100% U.S. portfolio. Even though the exact performance of these different mixes of U.S. and foreign stocks changes, the shape of the curve has remained consistent over periods of time. Therefore, investing in foreign stocks offers the opportunity to improve your portfolio's return and reduce its volatility.

Source: Reprinted by permission of the *Global Investing Newsletter.*

more benefit from diversifying into global equities is illustrated in Table 1.5.

Most global equity markets around the globe are highly correlated with the U.S. market during market declines. Although they rise at different rates at different times, during U.S. bear markets, most global markets tend to decline in sync with U.S. stocks. In

Figure 1.12 **S&P 500 AND WORLD INDEX PERFORMANCE SINCE WORLD WAR II (1943)**

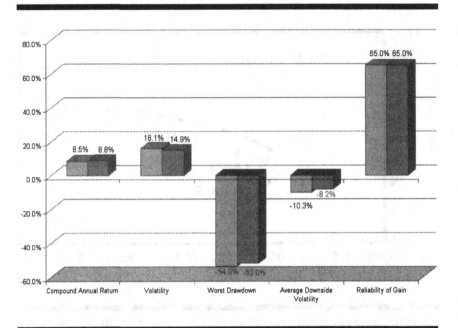

Table 1.5 **GLOBAL STOCK MARKET DECLINE DURING U.S. MARKET RETREATS**

Country	1987	1990	1994	Average
United States	21.8%	15.1%	10.0%	15.6%
Australia	42.5	11.6	22.8	25.6
Japan	21.2	20.8	29.3	23.8
United Kingdom	26.7	16.2	19.6	20.8
Germany	22.4	23.1	17.1	20.9
France	24.2	19.5	27.5	23.7
Italy	15.2	25.6	31.5	24.1
Switzerland	25.4	21.9	23.6	23.6
Emerging markets	44.0	48.0	25.6	39.2

this book, therefore, we look beyond global equities to other asset classes that are more independent of U.S. and global stocks for their gains. We also examine ways of nullifying the effects of equity bear markets.

SUMMARY

Before taking further steps to develop a strategy that can produce market-size or larger gains with less than market-size risk and drawdowns, at market-or-higher reliability, it is helpful to review what has been covered so far.

First, there are some long-term problems with many traditional buy-and-hold approaches. If history is any guide, investors cannot reasonably expect that using a buy-and-hold strategy in the U.S. stock market during the decades ahead will achieve anything close to the 18 percent annual return (and 13% compound annual return) of the past decade. U.S. (and global) stocks make long-term secular trends up and down—and also have intermediate-term bull and bear markets within those secular trends. Many past secular peaks have come with valuations near 1997 levels and with average 10-year annual returns at 1997 levels, and some of the top long-term return predicting models point to much lower expected returns over the next decade than have been achieved in the past decade. Therefore it is imprudent for investors and traders to deploy an investment strategy (such as buy-and-hold) with goals that depend on the continuation of strong gains in the U.S. stock market over the decades ahead. Nor is this plan advisable for investors wishing to maximize long-term gains. Shorter-term traders should be even more dubious of such approaches, because bear markets can completely wipe them out if their strategy is not prepared for them.

Investors in all stocks need to understand the risks as well as the rewards. U.S. and global stocks have experienced huge drawdowns of 50 percent or more several times during the twentieth century, some of which required 30 years or longer for recovery after adjusting for inflation.

To compare investments, we have devised a key set of criteria. While most investors look only at total returns, those returns must be measured in terms of the risk required to achieve them.

Key criteria in analyzing the potential success of investment strategies are factors such as compound annual return, average downside volatility, worst-case historical drawdown, frequency of drawdown and recovery time, in what percentage of years the investment is profitable, and how dependent and correlated the investment is to returns in specific asset classes. These factors, which can achieve better than market returns at less than market risk, underlie the strategies we will develop and explore in the chapters that lie ahead.

Liquidity—The Pump That Artificially Primes Investment Flows

In Chapter 1 we explored some of the major problems facing long-term investors in U.S. and global equities: large drawdowns, high volatility, large variability of returns, and inconsistent returns on an annual basis. In this chapter and in the chapters ahead, we are going to examine factors that contribute to a favorable market climate for a particular asset class thus enabling us to favor one asset class over another in our portfolios.

Next, we will develop methodologies for determining which assets in which countries are experiencing reliable factors that will push their prices up or down. Finally, we will learn strategies for exploiting this information to shift our investment capital among asset classes and countries to the areas that show the best risk/reward potential at any one time. In this way, we can profit from virtually any investment environment. These strategies for achieving above market returns more consistently and with lower than market risk can then be combined into a coherent approach that produces substantially higher average annual returns than equities, with risk and volatility substantially lower than stocks.

The factors that we seek to explore, understand, and exploit as strategies can be referred to as "fuel" because they are energizing sources that lead to appreciation in stocks, bonds, commodities, currencies, futures instruments, real estate, and other asset classes.

A critical test for determining robust fuel factors is whether we can achieve better than market returns just by using the one factor independently (or perhaps just with a technical filter to confirm that the market is behaving as anticipated). If we can find many such independently reliable factors and put them together with other unrelated but also independently reliable factors, we can often get a synergy that allows us to leverage our efforts, boost our returns, and slash the risk of investing at a particular time in any one asset or asset class.

If you had started investing in the mid-1960s and put much of your money into real estate (California in particular), you would have enjoyed a phenomenal secular bull market that led to percentage gains in the thousands by the early 1980s. If sometime in the early 1980s you had been able to see that the next secular bull market was not going to continue to be in real estate but would shift to stocks and bonds, you would have had another 1000 percent opportunity (especially in Hong Kong and Chile). All investors would like to understand the factors that lead toward such major shifts in investment flows and performance in different investment vehicles.

Here's another important point to think about. Who achieved better investment performance from 1965 to 1981—a stock market legend like Warren Buffett or John Templeton, or the average Joe who just happened to buy an investment property in California with most of his spare capital? The average Joe kicked the experts' backsides! Or consider this—who did better from 1982 to 1997, the expert property investor in New York or the average Jane who bought a mutual fund? This is the point alluded to in Chapter 1: even the best manager cannot profit with a strategy that is wrong for the overall environment. Furthermore, if you can align your strategy with the overall environment and can shift your strategy to fit that environment when it changes, you can profit from nearly any set of circumstances.

So, how do we discover the factors that can help us analyze the current investment environment and identify potential investment gains. We want to monitor all sorts of investment vehicles while watching for signals of success. When you find investment success by anyone—dissect it, determine what makes it tick, and then *mimic its essential components.* Add those components to your arsenal after you have fully analyzed their strengths and weaknesses, paying particular attention to determining the environments they are vulnerable in. And finally, *seek constantly for understanding.* The more you understand about markets, about how people succeed in markets, and about human nature, the more successful you will become in the markets yourself. Achieving consistent investment gains is a constantly changing quest, an exploration of self, human behavior, and the world itself. As stressed in Chapter 1, not only must investors have reliable tools, they must also acquire insight and understanding. Investors who understand the markets and the logic behind strategies will be able to adapt when a critical aspect underlying their success suddenly changes. They will be able to consistently profit in any environment.

After decades of research and real-time trading and investing, we have found that the study of the Austrian interpretation of the Liquidity Cycle (ALC) can help give investors both rules of thumb and insight into future investment gains. Once you understand it, you will find it hard to believe that anyone could invest without knowledge of the Austrian Liquidity Cycle, because it is based on cause and effect. In addition, it is one of the easiest and simplest methodologies for improving long-term profitability and cutting risk in investing in equities, bonds, and other asset classes.

UNDERSTANDING THE AUSTRIAN INTERPRETATION OF THE LIQUIDITY CYCLE

The Austrian Liquidity Cycle (ALC) is a composite of the classic Liquidity Cycle model mixed with the "Austrian Economic" model, or free market model. We will be discussing Austrian economics in more detail later on in this book. There is, however, a critical aspect of the Austrian Model that investors must grasp to better understand, interpret, and utilize the Liquidity Cycle. The Austrian Model simply views an economy as though it were totally free from interference (except for prevention of the violation of the rights of individuals to life, liberty, and property), and views any exception to that freedom (whether it be a law, an institution, or some government or corporate construct), as an artificial obstruction to free market forces. An artificial obstruction to such forces leads to a dichotomy between real unencumbered supply-and-demand forces and artificially manipulated supply and demand forces. This dichotomy results in a misallocation of true underlying incentives and resource utilization. The larger this dichotomy grows, the more severe the ultimate correction of resource allocation must eventually be, when free market forces ultimately prevail by forcing realignment in the long run.

Rent control provides an example of how the Austrian Model interprets an artificial manipulation. Under an unencumbered free market, if demand grows strongly for housing in a particular area, prices for rents (and property) rise sharply. That rise in price sets in force a signal to producers that the market is demanding more production of housing. If real estate is scarce, skyscrapers are built because they are profitable. Higher prices create an incentive structure for more supply to come on line. There may be a lag between building completions and demand, which will cause prices to move up sharply, but the higher the prices rise, the greater the incentive becomes for builders and owners of buildings to provide housing, and the more the supply expands. On a macroeconomic basis, the higher the profit margin to property development compared with other industries, the more the percentage of total resources that will be allocated to property development by the economy as a whole. Thus excess demand sets in motion a process that naturally pulls resources to the area, and eventually leads to a more equitable alignment of supply and demand again. High demand leads to higher prices, which leads to higher profit margins for supplying, which leads to higher supply.

What if we throw rent control (or price controls of any kind) into the mix? Rent control advocates see prices rising and lament that poorer people may not be able to afford living in an area. They attack the symptom of excess demand, higher prices, by locking prices at a particular level. But this action has a negative effect on the supply-and-demand forces that underlie the higher price symptom. Prices begin to rise, reflecting excess demand. At some point, however, the government arbitrarily writes a law that says to property owners, "You can charge no more than 'x' price for rent, or we will put you in jail or take your property." Abruptly prices are prevented from rising to reflect excess demand. Incentives to housing producers can only go up to the level arbitrarily chosen by government instead of the level chosen by the verdict of the free market; therefore, new supply incentives remain artificially low. And the threat of rent-control makes housing supply a dangerous business because the participants' profits could be limited even more in the future. So supply dries up and there is no incentive to increase it. Meanwhile because prices have been locked below free-market levels, demand increases not only by the free-market amount, but by a higher level because those individuals who would not ordinarily seek high-priced housing are able to demand it at artificially low prices. So excess demand increases while supply slows down. Rationing of some sort must take place to deal with the demand (after all, rationing is what higher prices were doing in the first place). In addition, property owners have little or no incentive to maintain their property; since demand is in excess, there is not enough competing supply to weaken the demand for run-down property, and maintaining property does not increase profits. In fact, maintenance cuts profits since rents can be raised an arbitrary amount whether the property is upgraded or not. The result of rent control is that there is more demand and less supply creating an even greater imbalance than existed before the price manipulation. Usually, properties become neglected by owners, and values fall slowly until it becomes cost-competitive to own property instead of renting it. Eventually, after the supply/demand gap has existed for years (often decades), a majority of tenants become owners and they vote to repeal rent control laws. Whereupon property prices soar and demand and supply can eventually realign. The law actually exacerbated the supply/demand differential problem that was the source of rising prices. Legislators simply substituted some sort of government rationing scheme for price rationing, while destroying the mechanism that encouraged supply to meet excess demand. The misalignment of resources away from housing production leads to a huge catch-up phenomenon once the artificial barriers are removed. In the meantime, those without the political connections to receive rationed housing are forced out of the market—and they are much larger in number than the population originally seeking rental units.

An investor understanding the implications of rent-control laws on real estate would know to stay out of real-estate where rent control is possible, and also to buy in rent-controlled areas where repeal is likely.

This rent-control (artificial manipulation of free market forces) example is critical to understanding the implications of government policies on investments. Here are some key rules of thumb concerning the impact of artificial interference:

1. Interference that attacks a symptom without addressing the forces behind the symptom usually leads to worse underlying problems and eventually worse underlying symptoms when the interference must be abandoned or corrected in the opposite direction.

2. In the long run, the cost of artificial interference often grows to a breaking point; whereupon free market forces usually prevail even though interference can be maintained for decades.

3. The indirect effect of an artificial interference on incentives is usually much more important, in terms of ultimate effect, than the direct results of that interference because the forces of dynamic change in an economy are more powerful than existing resources over the long run.

THE LIQUIDITY CYCLE ILLUSTRATED WITH AN ISLAND ECONOMY

These rules of thumb, along with the rent control example, provide a foundation for studying the Liquidity Cycle in terms of the Austrian Model.

For stock prices to rise, there must be excess demand for them, meaning money is flowing into the equity market. There are three main places for this money to come from: (1) increased savings and investment, (2) portfolio shifts out of other asset classes and into equities, and (3) new liquidity generated by the central bank. In a fractional reserve central bank banking system, such as that in the United States and most other countries of the world, the liquidity from the central bank far outpaces the liquidity from shifts in savings and portfolios. For this reason, investors can learn much from studying the status of central bank policy and liquidity flows.

It is also important for investors to realize that from an Austrian perspective, a central bank is an artificial manipulation and an economic distortion (similar to rent control). A free-market economy might have a currency similar to that authorized in the original U.S. Constitution, where the government or a bank is permitted only to coin money in order to verify the weight and measure of a free market chosen store of value such as gold and silver. In such a system, individuals are allowed to freely choose such coinage as one (of many possible) forms of currency. However, using government force to create a monopolistic body that prints the only allowable legal tender without any backing whatsoever is both a distortion and manipulation of an economy and of the value of the currency used by all participants in that economy. Investors need to understand not only the status of current policy, but also the implications of current policy distortions on future flows of funds and on the value of the underlying currency.

One of the main determining factors in valuing a currency is its inflation rate. An analogy will be helpful here. From the Austrian perspective, "real inflation" is simply an increase in the sum of the prices of absolutely everything in an economy. Suppose you were taking a cruise aboard an ocean liner that sank and left you stranded on a deserted island with nine of your fellow survivors and a few items you were able to bring aboard your life raft. When you inventoried your goods, you found that your combined cash equaled exactly $1,000 (or $100 for each person).

As you and your companions attempted to deal with your plight, you started to develop a small economy: some of you tried fishing, one person built huts, some picked coconuts, and others purified water—and you each used your $100 to trade among the 10 survivors. At times, coconuts were in shortage, and their price would rise—but that only meant that the price of fish or water had to fall commensurately, because there was only the same $1,000 total in circulation; and that was as much as the sum of the price of absolutely everything could be worth. There was no "real inflation" because the sum price of absolutely everything in the economy remained the same.

But then one member of the group happened to find some debris from the ship that included $500 in cash. He decided not to tell the other islanders about it, and slowly but steadily he began to spend an extra dollar here and there until he had spent over $120 of the new loot. Because more dollars were competing for goods and services, prices of most goods began to rise until the other islanders noticed the increases and realized that someone must have extra undisclosed money. The "real" (or Austrian) inflation rate had risen 12 percent because the sum of the price of absolutely everything had gone up 120/1000 or 12 percent.

After a long meeting in which the islanders all tried to get the guilty party to come clean to no avail, they decided to appoint one of the group to be an economic analyst. This person would study prices to determine when inflation was occurring. Several islanders offered to take on this task, but the job went to a man who proposed monitoring the price of coconuts as the means for watching inflation. He reasoned that it was too difficult to monitor the price of everything in the growing island economy, but that coconuts were an absolute staple being a source of liquid, a fruit, a plate for fish, a critical component of clothing, and an ingredient in virtually every meal. Monitoring inflation with a Coconut Price Index (CPI for short) seemed to be a sensible way of gauging when any islander spent money beyond the initial pool of cash that had been agreed on and declared.

About this time, the cash finder decided he had better cut back on spending any new money for a while. However, he also decided to scan the island for any further debris. So, when the other islanders were laboring and not looking, he went on a scouting trip to see what he could find. Low and behold, he discovered a box with a safe in it, and after battering it open, he found it contained over $100,000 in cash. The person who found this extra cash had an odd name—Central Bank—CB for short. CB was a smart fellow, and began to realize that he could spend money pretty much however he saw fit, at least until the Coconut Price Index began to head higher.

Although he was now wealthy, CB never spent his new money directly on coconuts. First he spent money to get a bigger hut. The hut-builder was willing to work harder and put in longer hours because CB could pay the going hut-rate for the extra time. After a couple weeks of this, the hut-builder got hungrier and began buying more coconuts with some of the "new money" he earned from CB. The CPI would rise a little bit, triggering suspicion and outcry from the island economist. The hut-builder, however, also put money into buying more fish, savings, and other goods, so that only a fraction of his new spending ever hit the coconut market. Thus after CB had spent another $40 on his hut improvements, only $2 had gone into more coconuts, and the economist was only declaring a small price increase and minimal inflation number with his CPI. With coconuts representing only about 10 percent of the original $1,000 economy, the $2 increase in demand had only raised prices about 2 percent, which is what the economist declared as the official inflation rate. There was a significant difference between real inflation ($40/1120 = 3.57\%$) and CPI inflation (2%)—yet it was only when CPI inflation began to spiral that CB had to rein in his new money spending.

THE LIQUIDITY CYCLE IN MODERN ECONOMIES

How the Central Bank Stimulates the Economy

Like this island economy, most fractional reserve central bank economies have indexes of inflation that reflect price increases on a small representative basket of goods. Just as on the island, however, price inflation of this small sampling of goods dictates much of the reactions of the marketplace. And like CB himself, if you can begin to see when and how a central bank is spending money, you can often anticipate when the CPI will increase and be one step ahead of other investors.

Moreover in most economies around the world, the central bank doesn't find an old hoard of money—it just prints it. Examining how this process works and observing how this money flows through the economy are preliminary steps in learning how to profit from the system.

One of the main implications of the distortion of a central bank is the creation of a boom-bust cycle, known as the Liquidity Cycle, but often referred to as the business cycle (although it has nothing to do with business or an economy in the absence of the distortion of a central bank). Figure 2.1 illustrates the main cyclical phenomenon created by central bank activity (although long-term devaluation of the value of the currency is usually another prominent feature of central bank unbacked currencies).

Most central banks are either created or increase their power during wartime to allow the government to spend beyond its means, or during a recession or depression to kick-start an already distorted economy. Thus, it is easiest to follow the Liquidity Cycle chart by starting at its bottom during a state of recession or depression.

Figure 2.1 **THE LIQUIDITY CYCLE**

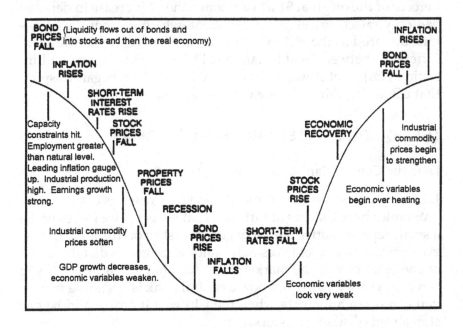

Note: This cycle depicts the rise and fall of liquidity. An expansion in liquidity during disinflation influences the most liquid assets first then into the general economy.

In a recession trough (near the trough of the Liquidity Cycle shown in Figure 2.1) GDP growth is slowing and then is negative, bond prices, property prices, equity prices, and inflation are falling, and financial intermediaries (like banks) are cautious and cutting back on the pace of loaning activities. Banks cut lending because company earnings are falling, balance sheets are deteriorating, property values are declining, and they're worried about getting back their principal on loans. Negative general sentiment is pervasive. As the recession deepens, the central bank begins to notice that capacity utilization and pricing pressures are so low that the central bank (Federal Reserve Board, or Fed) will be able to pump up money supply without affecting inflation negatively (more money is unlikely to flow into coconuts until the rest of the economy is producing near capacity). So the Fed cuts the discount rate (which is a short-term interest rate it charges member banks to borrow from it), and very short-term interest rates in the markets move lower in response.

As the Fed essentially cuts short-term rates by reducing its discount rate, the effect is felt to a diminishing degree all along the yield curve, meaning that long-term rates also fall, but to a much lesser extent than the very short-term interest rates that the Fed is manipulating directly. The yield curve is the difference between short-term rates and long-term interest rates, plotted by duration, as shown in Figure 2.2.

This yield curve is relatively normal: long-term rates are slightly higher than short-term rates. People lending over a longer period of time generally demand a higher rate of interest to compensate them for the increased opportunity cost of tying up their capital for a longer period. In addition, there is a great deal more risk of rates rising the longer the duration of a loan.

Figure 2.2 **YIELD CURVE EXAMPLE**

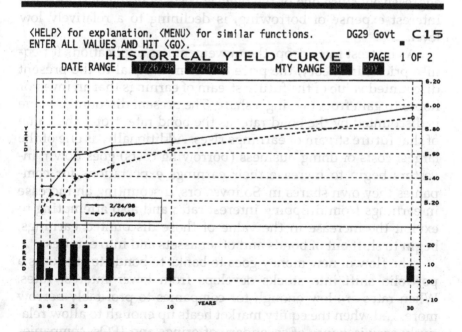

Source: Bloomberg Financial Markets. Copyright © 1998 Bloomberg LP. All rights reserved.

As the Fed continues to cut the discount rate, the yield curve begins to steepen and short-term rates fall significantly far below long-term rates. The steeper the yield curve, or the more short-term rates fall below long-term rates, the greater the incentive banks have to borrow from the Fed at the discount rate (up to their full fractional reserve requirement limit) and loan to the long-bond market at a higher rate, profiting from the difference. Banks with excess reserves begin to borrow up to the full extent of their reserve capacity to maximize profits by borrowing at the lower short-term rate and loaning to the government at a higher long-term rate. So the first recipients of Fed money printing are the banks, who in turn loan the money to the bond market forcing interest rates down all along the yield curve. As banks loan to the longer-term bond markets, the yield curve behaves like a rubber band, eventually forcing long-term rates lower as well.

The lower short- and long-term interest rates become, the more enticing it becomes for companies to borrow in order to expand. Less profitable ventures become more viable when interest costs are low. Eventually, companies begin to try borrowing more aggressively since one of the biggest costs of doing business, the interest expense of borrowing, is declining to a relatively low level.

As interest rates drop, the movement has implications for equity prices. In theory, the price of a firm is equal to the present discounted value of the future stream of earnings that an investor hopes to gain from owning a share. The present discounted value is discounted by the bond rate: as the bond rate drops, the value of that future stream of earnings rises. Additionally, as one of the largest costs of doing business (borrowing costs) goes down, investors begin to increase their earnings expectations for companies they own shares in. So investors, discounting an increase in earnings from dropping interest rates and also attempting to exploit the increase in the value of those discounted earnings, begin to shift out of bonds and other assets and into equities.

The flow of new money goes to banks to bonds to stocks as a portfolio shift into stocks develops from lower interest rates. When rates are low enough for companies to profitably borrow more, and when the equity market heats up enough to allow relatively easy issuance of secondary offerings and IPOs, companies are also able to get money readily from the equity markets. The result is that the new money liquidity eventually flows from equities and bonds to companies that in turn finally invest money in new businesses and business expansion feeding into the real economy. The new liquidity has flowed from banks to bonds to stocks to corporations to the real economy, and economic activity begins to pick up. This entire process has a long time lag; anywhere from 6 to 18 months may pass after initial Fed action before results begin to be felt in the real economy. This means that the Fed has a very difficult job. As an analogy, imagine you are controlling the rudder for a huge ship, but your steering does not affect the ship's movement until 6 to 18 minutes after you have made the adjustment.

Figure 2.3 shows clearly the relationship between bond prices and stock prices (S&P 500) since 1954 in the United States. Virtually every major stock market advance since 1954 was preceded in time by a bond market rally meaning a decline in bond rates, as the dotted lines indicate. Astute investors will also see that most major tops in the S&P were also preceded by a sharp drop in bond prices, or higher bond rates. This is not just an arcane academic theory, it is cause and effect and is an extremely valuable tool in determining the right time to aggressively buy or move out of equities in any one country.

Investors should also note that Figure 2.4 shows the incredible relationship between the yield curve and economic growth rates. The middle section is the yield curve as represented by the 10-year T-note divided by the 3-month T-bill. The top panel is the annual real GDP growth rate. As highlighted by the arrows, virtually every major advance in GDP growth rates has been preceded by a steepening of the yield curve (a move by the ratio above 1.5), and virtually every major drop in GDP growth rates has been preceded by flattening or inversion of the yield curve (a move by the ratio to 1 or less). Once again, this is not coincidence; it is cause and effect as the liquidity created by the Fed finds its way into the economy or as banks pull back lending and cease borrowing from the Fed under an inverted yield curve. An inverted yield curve occurs when short-term rates rise above long-term rates creating a loss for any bank borrowing from the Fed and therefore drying up new borrowing incentives. Many observers call the yield curve the gas pedal and brake pedal of the Fed—a steep yield curve indicates full throttle, while an inverted yield curve indicates full braking.

Figure 2.3 **BONDS LEAD STOCKS IN U.S. FRACTIONAL RESERVE SYSTEM**

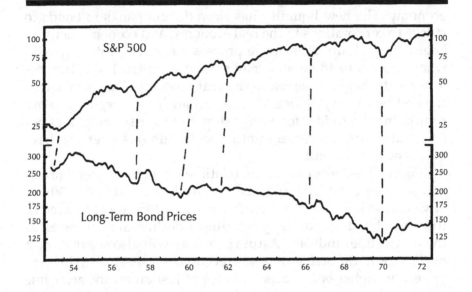

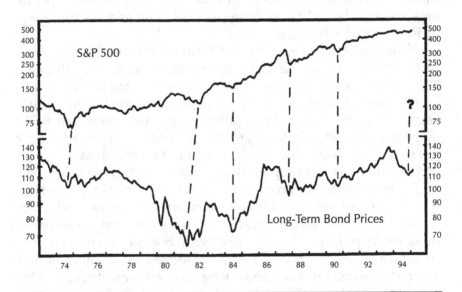

Source: Reprinted by permission of the *Bank Credit Analyst.*

Figure 2.4 **YIELD CURVE AND ITS IMPACT ON GDP GROWTH**

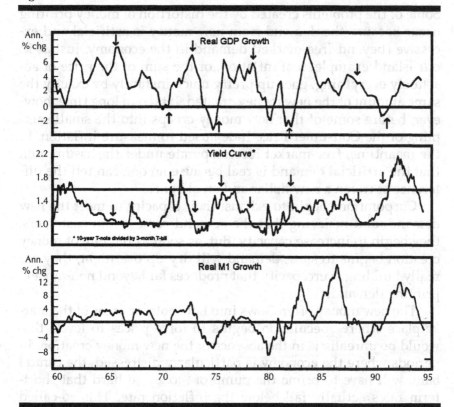

Note: Notice the amazing correlation between the yield curve and real GDP growth. Down arrows show that whenever the yield curve becomes inverted (<1), real GDP quickly turns down. Conversely, whenever the yield curve moves from inversion to steepness (≥ 1.5), the top arrows on the GDP chart show that GDP growth picks up.

Source: Reprinted by permission of the *Bank Credit Analyst.*

To return to our original Liquidity Curve, as the economy begins to pick up, we move up the Curve. Bond prices rally first, then stocks, then the economy picks up. Up to this point, printing money looks like an almost magical elixir for whatever ails the economy. Print enough funny money and things will pick up, it would seem. The problem is that what likely ailed the economy in the first place was some sort of distortion to free-market forces, and the new money printing distortion causes problems of its own. You can rarely get something for nothing in the world of economics.

How the Central Bank Distorts the Economy

Some of the problems created by the distortion of money printing occur because the demand from new money is artificial and excessive (beyond free-market) demand in the economy. Just as in our island example, real inflation, or the sum of the price of absolutely everything, goes up pretty much instantly by exactly the same amount of the new money created. It takes a long time, however, before some of that new money creeps into the small sampling of the Consumer Price Index used to measure inflation. In the meantime, free market forces operate under the assumption that the artificial demand is real because no one can tell the difference between a new dollar and an old one.

Corporations begin to exhaust their capacity to meet the new demand, and believing that the demand comes from customers, they begin to increase capacity. But, as soon as the rate of money creation begins to slow, demand will dry up overnight; they are really building overcapacity that produces far beyond non-money-printing demand.

The new money often flows into hot spots, or areas of the marketplace where speculation begins to force prices to levels that would be unrealistic in the absence of the new money creation. In periods where the economy is particularly distressed, the central bank will have to prime the pump of money so hard that short-term rates actually fall below the inflation rate. This so-called negative real interest rate (the real interest rate is the interest rate minus inflation) usually leads to excessive real estate speculation because investors are paid to borrow money and put it into real assets that will appreciate at the rate of inflation while they can leverage the gain by paying off debt at the lower interest rate. It also leads to another chronic problem associated with fractional reserve central banking systems—the explosion and proliferation of debt assumption.

An increasing inflation period can actually be secular, meaning it can last over several Liquidity Cycle booms and busts until finally the bond market stops the inflation spiral (or, in the absence of a large freely traded bond market, hyperinflation can develop). Once speculation in real estate and real assets has boomed and busted, and inflation has become excessive and begun to recede, a new hot spot emerges. During high inflation, the bond market crashes until bond investors are so concerned about future inflation potential that real interest rates stay very high during both booms and busts. Naturally, equity prices also will have crashed from higher interest rates. Eventually, the bond market becomes smart enough to quickly choke off speculation in real estate or any expansion that threatens CPI inflation. When the bond market becomes inflation-wise in this manner, a new hot spot begins to emerge: financial markets.

An inflation-wary bond market that slowly chokes down inflation rates causes a period of disinflation and forces hot money away from real assets like real estate and toward financial assets like stocks and bonds, which are hurt by inflation but benefit from lower interest rates under relatively lower inflation. Financial markets continue to be the hot area where most new money ends up as long as the disinflation period continues, which again, could be several Liquidity Cycles long. But, once financial markets become wildly overvalued under mania conditions, if a persistently slow economy, government spending program, or other inflation excuse arises, a secular move back into inflation-benefiting real estate or real assets is likely to begin again. These are the secular forces of inflation increase and disinflation that led to the huge gains in real estate from the late 1960s to the early 1980s and then to the huge gains in stocks from 1982 through today in the United States. As inflation rose, long-term real estate and real assets (e.g., gold, silver, commodities) became the hot spots and were pushed to wildly overvalued levels at the same time that bonds and equities were pushed to wildly undervalued levels. Conversely as disinflation trends took hold, financial asset markets became the hot spots and while bonds and stocks are being pushed to overvalued levels, real assets are becoming quite undervalued.

Manipulating the Island Economy

Going back to our island example, suppose that after several months on the island, a monsoon season develops. The islanders are relatively unprepared for the rains, and they all need hut renovations immediately to avoid getting drenched. Demand for the hut-builder skyrockets and the islanders compete heavily with each other for his limited time by raising the price they pay for his services. In the absence of CB's new money, as the price of hut-building rises the prices of some other goods must decline commensurately. Soon the price of farmed vegetables and gathered island food declines as this is not the best season for such activity anyway, so the farmer/gatherer decides it is more lucrative to stop planting/gathering and start helping the hut-builder. The island economy has just allocated more resources to hut-production. When the monsoon season eases up and most islanders are satisfied with their new roofs, demand slows back down, prices for hut-building time drop back down, and the farmer begins to calculate that farming/gathering island food is again as lucrative as hut-building and so he shifts back.

Now imagine what happens if CB is using lots of new money at the time of the monsoon. Since demand for huts is paramount, almost all the new money ends up in this hot area. Naturally, CB is spending new money on improving his hut roof, but in addition nearly every dollar he spends elsewhere is taken by other islanders and put immediately into demand for hut-building services. With CB's new money, prices of hut production don't just skyrocket, they literally explode to much higher levels because more money is chasing the same good (service). This high price translates into an acute signal to the other islanders—several decide to drop their tasks and move toward hut production even though this is essentially a false signal. It is not that islanders want huts so much compared with other goods, but merely that new money is being funneled into a hot area masking as real demand. CB, the richest man on the island (for some reason), is approached by several islanders who ask for a loan to help build up hut-production tools and facilities. It is obvious that demand is acute, and that the fisherman, coconut picker, clothier, and other islanders cannot drop their absolutely necessary daily chores to build roofs, so CB makes the loan.

In this situation, the new entrants spend most of their time gearing up new hut-production facilities instead of helping the existing hut-builder. After they have created new tools and roof-factories, they compete to solve the excess demand problem. But, a new problem begins to develop as the roof problem is cured and the monsoon season begins to dry up. Prices for hut-building with the new money drop severely because there is now more competition for providing hut-building services. Since the original hut-maker has tools without any debt attached, he can lower prices below that required by the other builders, who try to stick out the price war as long as their savings allow. The fisherman, clothier, and coconut producers don't want their fellow islanders to starve or freeze, so they extend them credit, but eventually their debts become too large to facilitate. Now what will they do? Perhaps the island will have to develop some bankruptcy infrastructure. In any case, the false signal of artificial demand has led to a misallocation of resources in favor of a hot area—and the fallout from this misallocation has serious repercussions. It requires significantly more loss of total island production in terms of time and utilization of the new hut-producers for as long as they remain in the wrong business; in terms of the loss of investment in the new factors of production that will not be utilized; and in terms of the lost credit extended by everyone to the entrepreneurs. The overall production or gross domestic product (GDP) of the island falls from the misallocation below what it would be if the farmer/gatherer simply went back to his old vocation in the proper allocation of resources. In addition, the adjustment from the misallocation takes longer, and is much more painful and widely felt by everyone on the island, than it was without the new money.

Other Problems Related to Manipulating an Economy

Misallocation of resources and false signals of demand are not the only problems with printing money. Returning to the Liquidity Cycle (see Figure 2.1), as excessive demand signals cause money to flow from hot areas to the rest of the economy, the whole economy-wide demand eventually begins to pick up at an unsustainable rate. The new money causes demand to rise to a level beyond the new production being generated in the economy, which is the real level of GDP growth. This excessive demand causes the economy to overheat. Unemployment drops below the natural level of job shifting. Capacity utilization rises to above 85 percent of capacity throughout all industries. As the capacity to produce begins to be exhausted and demand for goods is still rising, the only way to ration the limited production relative to this artificially high demand rate is to raise prices. A similar phenomenon happens concurrently in the labor market as demand for labor outpaces the supply of labor with the necessary skills. Successful strikes, wage raises, and pay-hike settlements begin to proliferate, first in the high-skilled labor group, and then among lower skilled labor.

Industrial commodity prices begin to rise, and the goods in that tiny basket of the economy known as the Consumer Price Index gradually begin to rise, signaling to economists and all market watchers that inflation is somehow mysteriously creeping into the economic background. The Fed, realizing that it can no longer print money without the populace noticing the ensuing inflation increase, begins to contemplate taking action to cool things off. While the Fed is contemplating, the bond market sells off substantially, and long-term interest rates rise in response to perceived increased risks of inflation, which will eat away at the principal involved in the long-term loan that a bond represents. When the Fed sees both long-term and short-term rates are rising, it throws in the towel and follows the market action by raising the discount rate.

The yield curve begins to flatten as the Fed plays catch-up. If the economy is not very overheated and other parts of the globe are not near capacity constraints, the flattening of the yield curve may slow down economic growth quickly enough to avoid a recession, or an actual negative rate of GDP growth. This is what is known as a "soft landing." Eventually, however, excess demand and misallocation of resources must be corrected, and the overheating gets excessive enough that the Fed must create an inverted yield curve to slow things down. As the central bank raises short-term rates above long-term rates, bank borrowing at the discount-rate window becomes an unprofitable venture, so it dries up almost completely. When short-term and long-term rates rise sufficiently, bond prices, equity prices, and eventually even real-estate prices fall as the Fed is no longer pumping artificial new money demand into the system, creating a sharp dropoff in demand. A recession develops and the cycle repeats from where we started once again.

TIMING THE LIQUIDITY CYCLE

If you understand the Liquidity Cycle, you can comprehend how an economy works in a fractional reserve banking system. Liquidity is a critical determinant of which asset class you want to emphasize in your portfolio—both in the intermediate term and long term.

On average, around 97 percent of all equities decline during a pronounced tightening phase when an inverted yield curve is required. Conversely during a steep yield curve, more than 90 percent of all equities rise. The charts shown in Figure 2.5 (courtesy of Bank Credit Analyst, a top macroeconomic analysis group whose services I highly recommend), show the yield curve, real interest rate, and S&P since the 1920s. These charts indicate that almost every major decline in the S&P was led by a flattening or inversion in the yield curve, and most major rallies were led by a steepening in the yield curve.

The following set of monetary "timing systems" (and later macro-economic timing systems) are our own revisions of original studies done by such notable investors/innovators as Marty Zweig, Ned Davis, Dan Sullivan, Edson Gould, Gerald Appel, Nelson Freeburg, John Hussman, Stephen Leeb, Martin Pring, Edward Renshaw, Richard Eakle, Joe Kalish, William Omaha, Norman Fosback, and many other great pioneers. These timing systems will help illustrate how using monetary (and economic)

Figure 2.5 **MONETARY CYCLES AND THE STOCK MARKET**

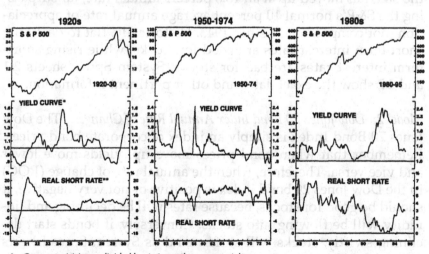

* Corporate AAA rate divided by 4–6 months commercial paper rate.
** 4–6 month commercial paper rate minus inflation rate.

Source: Reprinted by permission of the *Bank Credit Analyst.*

variables can help investors time the liquidity cycle to know when it is safe to invest in equities and when it is risky from the viewpoint of Liquidity Cycle Theory. Investors wanting to create their own models can also use these to help build successful timing tools or to give them a sense of the environment from a liquidity perspective.

Monetary Conditions

Model 1: 3-Month T-Bill Yields, 12-Month Rate of Change. This is simply the percentage change up or down of the yield in the 3-month Treasury bill (T-bill) today versus one year ago. As shown in Spreadsheets 2.1 and 2.2, whenever T-bill yields are moving up at a 6 percent or higher rate, year over year, the S&P does very poorly, underperforming cash, with a 2.2 percent annual rate of appreciation. Thus if today's 3-month T-bill rate were 4.26 percent and one year ago 3-month T-bills yielded 4 percent, then the yield would have risen 6.5 percent year over year—a bearish situation because 6.5 percent is greater than a 6 percent increase. Conversely, when 3-month T-bill yields are relatively flat or declining, with a year-over-year yield change of 6 percent or less, the S&P has moved up at an 18.8 percent annual rate, far surpassing the S&P's normal 10 percent average annual rate of appreciation (not compounded!) since 1943. Historically, flat to declining short-term interest rates are good for stocks, while rising short-term interest rates are bad for stocks. System Spreadsheets 2.1 and 2.2 show the exact dates and other pertinent information.

Model 2: Dow Jones 20 Bond Index Annual Rate of Change. The Dow Jones 20 Bond Index is simply an index of corporate bond prices. Remember that when bond prices move up, yields move lower and vice versa. Therefore, when the annual rate of change (ROC) in the Dow Jones 20 bond index is positive or not very negative, it should be good for stocks, because rates will be declining and liquidity will be flowing into stocks. Conversely, if bonds start declining swiftly, stocks will suffer. And as System Spreadsheets 2.3 and 2.4 show clearly, whenever the annual rate of change in the Dow Jones 20 Bond Index was greater than −1.5 percent, the S&P moved up at a brisk 17.4 percent annual rate. We can also see that when the annual rate of change in the Dow Jones 20 Bond Index fell at a 12-month ROC rate of −1.5 percent or below, the

System Spreadsheet 2.1 3-MONTH T-BILL YIELD ROC ≤ 6%

System Description: Buy S&P when the 12-month rate of change of 3-Month T-Bill Yield ≤ 6.0%. Exit when > 6.0%.

Significance: When T-Bill rates aren't rising rapidly, stocks rise nicely.

Data: Monthly close of 3-Month T-Bills and monthly close of S&P 500.

From: 1/29/43   To: 12/31/97

Annual Rate of Return: 18.8%

Entry Date	Entry Price	Exit Date	Exit Price	Profit/ Loss	Days in Trade	Percent Change
3/31/47	$ 15.17	7/31/47	$ 15.76	$ 0.59	89	3.89%
7/29/49	15.04	7/31/50	17.84	2.80	262	18.62
3/31/52	24.37	4/30/52	23.32	(1.05)	23	−4.31
9/30/52	24.54	10/31/52	24.52	(0.02)	24	−0.08
8/31/53	23.32	1/31/55	36.63	13.31	371	57.08
11/29/57	41.72	1/30/59	55.42	13.70	306	32.84
6/30/60	56.92	10/31/61	68.62	11.70	349	20.56
11/30/61	71.32	12/29/61	71.55	0.23	22	0.32
2/28/63	64.29	3/29/63	66.57	2.28	22	3.55
4/30/63	69.80	5/31/63	70.80	1.00	24	1.43
8/31/64	81.83	11/30/64	84.42	2.59	66	3.17
1/31/67	86.61	8/31/67	93.64	7.03	153	8.12
9/29/67	96.71	1/31/68	92.24	(4.47)	89	−4.62
8/30/68	98.86	9/30/68	102.67	3.81	22	3.85
3/31/70	89.63	5/29/70	76.55	(13.08)	44	−14.59
6/30/70	72.72	3/31/72	107.20	34.48	459	47.41
4/28/72	107.67	10/31/72	111.58	3.91	133	3.63
7/31/74	79.31	8/30/74	72.15	(7.16)	23	−9.03
9/30/74	63.54	10/31/74	73.90	10.36	24	16.30
11/29/74	69.97	8/31/77	96.77	26.80	719	38.30
5/30/80	111.24	11/28/80	140.52	29.28	131	26.32
2/27/81	131.27	4/30/81	132.81	1.54	45	1.17
11/30/81	126.35	8/31/83	164.40	38.05	458	30.11
11/30/84	163.58	7/31/87	318.66	155.08	696	94.80
10/30/87	251.79	11/30/87	230.30	(21.49)	22	−8.53
12/31/87	247.08	1/29/88	257.07	9.99	22	4.04
2/29/88	267.82	5/31/88	262.16	(5.66)	67	−2.11
10/31/89	340.36	2/28/94	467.14	126.78	1,130	37.25
10/31/95	581.50	12/31/97	970.43	388.93	567	66.88
Total				$831.31	6,362	476.37%
			Percent of Days Invested			44%
			Annual Rate of Return			18.8%

System Spreadsheet 2.2 **3-MONTH T-BILL YIELD ROC > 6%**

System Description: Buy S&P when the 12-month rate of change of 3-Month T-Bill Yield > 6.0%. Exit when ≤ 6.0%.

Significance: When T-Bill rates are rising, stocks move up less than cash.

Data: Monthly close of 3-Month T-Bills and monthly close of S&P 500.

From: 1/29/43   To: 12/31/97

Annual Rate of Return: 2.2%

Entry Date	Entry Price	Exit Date	Exit Price	Profit/ Loss	Days Long	Percent Change
7/31/47	$ 15.76	7/29/49	$ 15.04	($ 0.72)	522	−4.57%
7/31/50	17.84	3/31/52	24.37	6.53	436	36.60
4/30/52	23.32	9/30/52	24.54	1.22	110	5.23
10/31/52	24.52	8/31/53	23.32	(1.20)	217	−4.89
1/31/55	36.63	11/29/57	41.72	5.09	740	13.90
1/30/59	55.42	6/30/60	56.92	1.50	370	2.71
10/31/61	68.62	11/30/61	71.32	2.70	23	3.93
12/29/61	71.55	2/28/63	64.29	(7.26)	305	−10.15
3/29/63	66.57	4/30/63	69.80	3.23	23	4.85
5/31/63	70.80	8/31/64	81.83	11.03	327	15.58
11/30/64	84.42	1/31/67	86.61	2.19	567	2.59
8/31/67	93.64	9/29/67	96.71	3.07	22	3.28
1/31/68	92.24	8/30/68	98.86	6.62	153	7.18
9/30/68	102.67	3/31/70	89.63	(13.04)	392	−12.70
5/29/70	76.55	6/30/70	72.72	(3.83)	23	−5.00
3/31/72	107.20	4/28/72	107.67	0.47	21	0.44
10/31/72	111.58	7/31/74	79.31	(32.27)	457	−28.92
8/30/74	72.15	9/30/74	63.54	(8.61)	22	−11.93
10/31/74	73.90	11/29/74	69.97	(3.93)	22	−5.32
8/31/77	96.77	5/30/80	111.24	14.47	718	14.95
11/28/80	140.52	2/27/81	131.27	(9.25)	66	−6.58
4/30/81	132.81	11/30/81	126.35	(6.46)	153	−4.86
8/31/83	164.40	11/30/84	163.58	(0.82)	328	−0.50
7/31/87	318.66	10/30/87	251.79	(66.87)	66	−20.98
11/30/87	230.30	12/31/87	247.08	16.78	24	7.29
1/29/88	257.07	2/29/88	267.82	10.75	22	4.18
5/31/88	262.16	10/31/89	340.36	78.20	371	29.83
2/28/94	467.14	10/31/95	581.50	114.36	437	24.48
Total				$123.95	6,937	60.61%

Percent of Days Invested	48%
Annual Rate of Return	2.2%

System Spreadsheet 2.3 DOW JONES 20 BOND INDEX CLOSE ROC > −1.5%

System Description: Buy S&P when the 12-month rate of change of the Dow Jones 20 Bond Index close is > −1.5%. Exit when ≤ −1.5%.

Significance: When corporate bonds are moving up or flat, stocks perform very well.

Data Used: Monthly close of Dow Jones 20 Bond Index and monthly close of S&P 500.

From: 1/29/43   To: 12/31/97

Annual Rate of Return: 17.4%

Entry Date	Entry Price	Exit Date	Exit Price	Profit/ Loss	Days in Trade	Percent Change
11/30/48	$ 14.75	4/29/49	$ 14.74	($ 0.01)	109	−0.07%
7/29/49	15.04	4/30/51	22.43	7.39	457	49.14
4/30/52	23.32	3/31/53	25.29	1.97	240	8.45
10/30/53	24.54	11/30/53	24.76	0.22	22	0.90
1/29/54	26.08	8/31/55	43.18	17.10	414	65.57
1/31/56	43.82	4/30/56	48.38	4.56	65	10.41
4/30/58	43.44	12/31/58	55.21	11.77	176	27.09
6/30/60	56.92	8/31/61	68.07	11.15	306	19.59
9/29/61	66.73	10/29/65	92.42	25.69	1066	38.50
3/31/67	90.20	4/28/67	94.01	3.81	21	4.22
8/31/67	93.64	9/29/67	96.71	3.07	22	3.28
10/31/68	103.41	1/31/69	103.01	(0.40)	67	−0.39
12/31/70	92.15	7/31/73	108.22	16.07	674	17.44
9/28/73	108.43	10/31/73	108.29	(0.14)	24	−0.13
5/30/75	91.15	12/30/77	95.10	3.95	676	4.33
2/28/78	87.04	4/28/78	96.83	9.79	44	11.25
4/30/82	116.44	6/30/82	109.61	(6.83)	44	−5.87
7/30/82	107.09	12/30/83	164.93	57.84	371	54.01
1/31/84	163.41	2/29/84	157.06	(6.35)	22	−3.89
10/31/84	166.09	4/30/87	288.36	122.27	652	73.62
4/29/88	261.33	2/28/89	288.86	27.53	218	10.53
4/28/89	309.64	6/29/90	358.02	48.38	306	15.62
12/31/90	330.22	3/31/94	445.77	115.55	849	34.99
4/28/95	514.71	1/31/97	786.16	271.45	461	52.74
3/31/97	757.12	12/31/97	970.43	213.31	198	28.17
Total				$959.14	7,504	519.51%
			Percent of Days Invested			52%
			Annual Rate of Return			17.4%

System Spreadsheet 2.4 DOW JONES 20 BOND INDEX CLOSE ROC ≤ –1.5%

System Description: Buy S&P when the 12-month rate of change of the Dow Jones 20 Bond Index close is ≤ –1.5%. Exit when > –1.5%.

Significance: When corporate bonds are declining sharply, stocks move down.

Data Used: Monthly close of the Dow Jones 20 Bond Index and monthly close of S&P 500.

From: 1/29/43   To: 12/31/97

Annual Rate of Return: –0.3%

Entry Date	Entry Price	Exit Date	Exit Price	Profit/ Loss	Days in Trade	Percent Change
3/31/47	$ 15.17	11/30/48	$ 14.75	($ 0.42)	437	–2.77%
4/29/49	14.74	7/29/49	15.04	0.30	66	2.04
4/30/51	22.43	4/30/52	23.32	0.89	263	3.97
3/31/53	25.29	10/30/53	24.54	(0.75)	154	–2.97
11/30/53	24.76	1/29/54	26.08	1.32	45	5.33
8/31/55	43.18	1/31/56	43.82	0.64	110	1.48
4/30/56	48.38	4/30/58	43.44	(4.94)	523	–10.21
12/31/58	55.21	6/30/60	56.92	1.71	392	3.10
8/31/61	68.07	9/29/61	66.73	(1.34)	22	–1.97
10/29/65	92.42	3/31/67	90.20	(2.22)	371	–2.40
4/28/67	94.01	8/31/67	93.64	(0.37)	90	–0.39
9/29/67	96.71	10/31/68	103.41	6.70	285	6.93
1/31/69	103.01	12/31/70	92.15	(10.86)	500	–10.54
7/31/73	108.22	9/28/73	108.43	0.21	44	0.19
10/31/73	108.29	5/30/75	91.15	(17.14)	413	–15.83
12/30/77	95.10	2/28/78	87.04	(8.06)	43	–8.48
4/28/78	96.83	4/30/82	116.44	19.61	1046	20.25
6/30/82	109.61	7/30/82	107.09	(2.52)	23	–2.30
12/30/83	164.93	1/31/84	163.41	(1.52)	23	–0.92
2/29/84	157.06	10/31/84	166.09	9.03	176	5.75
4/30/87	288.36	4/29/88	261.33	(27.03)	262	–9.37
2/28/89	288.86	4/28/89	309.64	20.78	44	7.19
6/29/90	358.02	12/31/90	330.22	(27.80)	132	–7.76
3/31/94	445.77	4/28/95	514.71	68.94	282	15.47
1/31/97	786.16	3/31/97	757.12	(29.04)	42	–3.69
Total				($ 3.88)	5,788	–7.91%

Percent of Days Invested	40%
Annual Rate of Return	–0.3%

S&P actually moved lower at a –0.3 percent annual rate, far underperforming cash (T-bill or money market returns averaged around 5 percent during this entire period as a reference).

Model 3: Annual Change in 30-Year Government Bond Yield.   This involves looking at the 30-year bond yield today versus one year ago as a percentage change number, positive or negative. As apparent in System Spreadsheets 2.5 and 2.6 when bond yields year over year are rising at 9 percent or less, stocks do quite well, with the S&P rising at 14.8 percent annual rate. Conversely when today's 30-year bond yield is above last year's 30-year bond yield by more than 9 percent, stocks have historically declined at a – 0.9 percent annual rate. So if last year's month-end 30-year bond yield was 5 percent, and the last month-end 30-year bond yield today was 5.47 percent, that would be negative because 5.47 is greater than 9 percent above 5.

Model 4: 30-Year Bond Yield versus 3-Month T-Bill Yield Curve Ratio. Here we simply take the 30-year bond yield and divide it by the 3-month T-bill yield. When the long bond yield is much higher than the short-term yield, then the yield curve is steep, and banks have every incentive to loan out as much as possible and borrow to the limit of their reserves. Conversely when the long bond yield is close to or even below the T-bill yield, banks are not being paid to borrow short and loan long, and loans slow down sharply. Thus when the long bond yield/T-bill yield ratio is greater than 1.15, the yield curve is steep, and stocks move up at a very swift 19.1 percent annual rate. When the long bond yield/T-bill yield ratio falls to 1 or below, however, the yield curve is flat or inverted, and stocks take a major beating, falling at –7.5 percent annual rate. System Spreadsheets 2.7 and 2.8 illustrate this pattern.

Model 5: Composite of Positive Conditions in T-Bill Yields, Dow Jones 20 Bond Index Prices, and 30-Year Bond Yields.   When short-term rates Model 1 is positive for stocks, Dow Jones 20 Bond Index corporate bond prices are in a positive mode for stocks via Model 2, and 30-year bond yields are in a positive mode for stocks via Model 3, then all levels of interest rates are in sync, and the S&P moves up at a swift 20.1 percent annual rate with 91 percent reliability, as shown in System Spreadsheet 2.9.

System Spreadsheet 2.5 30-YEAR TREASURY BOND YIELD ROC ≤ 9%

System Description: Buy S&P when the 12-month rate of change of 30-Year Treasury Bond Yield ≤ 9%. Exit when > 9%.

Significance: When 30-Year Treasury Bond yield is fairly flat or dropping, stocks perform better than average.

Data Used: Monthly close of 30-Year Treasury Bond Yield and monthly close of S&P 500.

From: 1/29/43   To: 12/31/97

Annual Rate of Return: 14.8%

Entry Date	Entry Price	Exit Date	Exit Price	Profit/ Loss	Days in Trade	Percent Change
3/31/47	$ 15.17	1/30/48	$ 14.69	($ 0.48)	220	−3.16%
6/30/48	16.74	8/31/48	15.97	(0.77)	45	−4.60
10/29/48	16.54	12/29/50	20.41	3.87	566	23.40
1/31/51	21.66	3/30/51	21.40	(0.26)	43	−1.20
8/31/51	23.28	10/31/51	22.94	(0.34)	44	−1.46
3/31/52	24.37	4/30/53	24.62	0.25	284	1.03
10/30/53	24.54	4/29/55	37.96	13.42	391	54.69
5/31/55	37.91	7/29/55	43.52	5.61	44	14.80
1/31/56	43.82	4/30/56	48.38	4.56	65	10.41
5/31/56	45.20	8/31/56	47.51	2.31	67	5.11
9/28/56	45.35	10/31/56	45.58	0.23	24	0.51
4/30/57	45.74	5/31/57	47.43	1.69	24	3.69
11/29/57	41.72	12/31/58	55.21	13.49	284	32.33
10/30/59	57.52	11/30/59	58.28	0.76	22	1.32
2/29/60	56.12	2/28/66	91.22	35.10	1566	62.54
12/30/66	80.33	10/31/67	93.90	13.57	218	16.89
6/28/68	99.58	1/31/69	103.01	3.43	156	3.44
5/30/69	103.46	6/30/69	97.71	(5.75)	22	−5.56
2/27/70	89.50	4/30/70	81.52	(7.98)	45	−8.92
7/31/70	78.05	8/31/70	81.52	3.47	22	4.45
9/30/70	84.21	10/30/70	83.25	(0.96)	23	−1.14
11/30/70	87.20	3/30/73	111.52	24.32	610	27.89
4/30/73	106.97	5/31/73	104.95	(2.02)	24	−1.89
2/28/74	96.22	3/29/74	93.98	(2.24)	22	−2.33
8/30/74	72.15	9/30/74	63.54	(8.61)	22	−11.93
12/31/74	68.56	12/30/77	95.10	26.54	784	38.71
2/28/78	87.04	5/31/78	97.29	10.25	67	11.78
6/29/79	102.91	9/28/79	109.32	6.41	66	6.23
2/27/81	131.27	4/30/81	132.81	1.54	45	1.17
11/30/81	126.35	1/29/82	120.40	(5.95)	45	−4.71
4/30/82	116.44	6/30/82	109.61	(6.83)	44	−5.87
7/30/82	107.09	11/30/83	166.40	59.31	349	55.38
1/31/84	163.41	3/30/84	159.18	(4.23)	44	−2.59
8/31/84	166.68	4/30/87	288.36	121.68	695	73.00
5/31/88	262.16	8/31/90	322.56	60.40	589	23.04
11/30/90	322.22	7/29/94	458.26	136.04	956	42.22
3/31/95	500.71	1/31/97	786.16	285.45	481	57.01
3/31/97	757.12	12/31/97	970.43	213.31	198	28.17
Total				$1,000.59	9,216	513.86%

Percent of Days Invested	64%
Annual Rate of Return	14.8%

System Spreadsheet 2.6 30-YEAR TREASURY BOND YIELD ROC > 9%

System Description: Buy S&P when the 12-month rate of change of 30-Year Treasury Bond Yield > 9%. Exit when ≤ 9%.
Significance: When 30-Year Treasury Bond Yields are rising sharply, stocks move down.
Data Used: Monthly Close of 30-Year Treasury Bond Yield and monthly close of S&P 500.
From: 1/29/43   To: 12/31/97
Annual Rate of Return: −0.9%

Entry Date	Entry Price	Exit Date	Exit Price	Profit/ Loss	Days in Trade	Percent Change
1/30/48	$ 14.69	6/30/48	$ 16.74	$ 2.05	109	13.96%
8/31/48	15.97	10/29/48	16.54	0.57	44	3.57
12/29/50	20.41	1/31/51	21.66	1.25	24	6.12
3/30/51	21.40	8/31/51	23.28	1.88	111	8.79
10/31/51	22.94	3/31/52	24.37	1.43	109	6.23
4/30/53	24.62	10/30/53	24.54	(0.08)	132	−0.32
4/29/55	37.96	5/31/55	37.91	(0.05)	23	−0.13
7/29/55	43.52	1/31/56	43.82	0.30	133	0.69
4/30/56	48.38	5/31/56	45.20	(3.18)	24	−6.57
8/31/56	47.51	9/28/56	45.35	(2.16)	21	−4.55
10/31/56	45.58	4/30/57	45.74	0.16	130	0.35
5/31/57	47.43	11/29/57	41.72	(5.71)	131	−12.04
12/31/58	55.21	10/30/59	57.52	2.31	218	4.18
11/30/59	58.28	2/29/60	56.12	(2.16)	66	−3.71
2/28/66	91.22	12/30/66	80.33	(10.89)	220	−11.94
10/31/67	93.90	6/28/68	99.58	5.68	174	6.05
1/31/69	103.01	5/30/69	103.46	0.45	86	0.44
6/30/69	97.71	2/27/70	89.50	(8.21)	175	−8.40
4/30/70	81.52	7/31/70	78.05	(3.47)	67	−4.26
8/31/70	81.52	9/30/70	84.21	2.69	23	3.30
10/30/70	83.25	11/30/70	87.20	3.95	22	4.74
3/30/73	111.52	4/30/73	106.97	(4.55)	22	−4.08
5/31/73	104.95	2/28/74	96.22	(8.73)	196	−8.32
3/29/74	93.98	8/30/74	72.15	(21.83)	111	−23.23
9/30/74	63.54	12/31/74	68.56	5.02	67	7.90
12/30/77	95.10	2/28/78	87.04	(8.06)	43	−8.48
5/31/78	97.29	6/29/79	102.91	5.62	283	5.78
9/28/79	109.32	2/27/81	131.27	21.95	371	20.08
4/30/81	132.81	11/30/81	126.35	(6.46)	153	−4.86
1/29/82	120.40	4/30/82	116.44	(3.96)	66	−3.29
6/30/82	109.61	7/30/82	107.09	(2.52)	23	−2.30
11/30/83	166.40	1/31/84	163.41	(2.99)	45	−1.80
3/30/84	159.18	8/31/84	166.68	7.50	111	4.71
4/30/87	288.36	5/31/88	262.16	(26.20)	284	−9.09
8/31/90	322.56	11/30/90	322.22	(0.34)	66	−0.11
7/29/94	458.26	3/31/95	500.71	42.45	176	9.26
1/31/97	786.16	3/31/97	757.12	(29.04)	42	−3.69
Total				($45.33)	4,101	−15.00%

Percent of Days Invested	29%
Annual Rate of Return	−0.9%

System Spreadsheet 2.7 **YIELD CURVE < 1.0**

System Description: Buy S&P when the ratio of 30-Year Treasury Bonds Yields to 3-Month Treasury Bills is ≤ 1. Exit when the ratio > 1.

Significance: When the yield curve is flat, stocks perform well below average.

Data Used: Monthly 30-Year Treasury Bonds, monthly 3-Month Treasury Bills, and monthly close of S&P 500.

From: 1/29/43   To: 12/31/97

Annual Rate of Return: −7.5%

Entry Date	Entry Price	Exit Date	Exit Price	Profit/ Loss	Days in Trade	Percent Change
11/30/59	$ 58.28	1/29/60	$ 55.61	($ 2.67)	45	−4.58%
2/29/60	56.12	3/31/60	55.34	(0.78)	24	−1.39
12/31/65	92.43	3/31/66	89.23	(3.20)	65	−3.46
4/29/66	91.06	6/30/66	84.74	(6.32)	45	−6.94
7/29/66	83.60	3/31/67	90.20	6.60	176	7.89
8/31/67	93.64	9/29/67	96.71	3.07	22	3.28
4/30/68	97.59	3/31/69	101.51	3.92	240	4.02
4/30/69	103.69	3/31/70	89.63	(14.06)	240	−13.56
4/30/70	81.52	6/30/70	72.72	(8.80)	44	−10.79
3/30/73	111.52	9/30/74	63.54	(47.98)	392	−43.02
10/31/74	73.90	1/31/75	76.98	3.08	67	4.17
9/29/78	102.54	10/31/78	93.15	(9.39)	23	−9.16
11/30/78	94.70	5/30/80	111.24	16.54	392	17.47
10/31/80	127.47	10/30/81	121.89	(5.58)	261	−4.38
Total				($65.57)	2,036	−60.46%
			Percent of Days Invested			14%
			Annual Rate of Return			−7.5%

Another nice feature of the Liquidity Cycle is that it is useful in almost all countries where bonds and stocks are freely traded. Thus we can use liquidity analysis not only as a timing tool, but as an aid in picking those markets that are likely to be among the strongest or the weakest. The three charts shown in Figure 2.6, courtesy of Morgan Stanley Capital International, show that in the 1993 recovery for example, the countries that showed the sharpest drops in short-term interest rates (the most central bank pump priming) also developed the highest valued equity markets and then showed the strongest recovery in industrial production.

System Spreadsheet 2.8 YIELD CURVE > 1.15

System Description: Buy S&P when the ratio of 30-Year Treasury Bonds Yields to 3-Month Treasury Bills is > 1.15. Exit when the ratio ≤ 1.15.

Significance: When the yield curve steepens, stocks move up rapidly.

Data Used: Monthly 30-Year Treasury Bonds, monthly 3-Month Treasury Bills, and monthly close of S&P 500.

From: 1/29/43   To: 12/31/97

Annual Rate of Return: 19.1%

Entry Date	Entry Price	Exit Date	Exit Price	Profit/ Loss	Days in Trade	Percent Change
3/31/47	$ 15.17	12/30/55	$ 45.48	$ 30.31	2,285	199.80%
1/31/56	43.82	4/30/56	48.38	4.56	65	10.41
7/31/56	49.39	8/31/56	47.51	(1.88)	24	−3.81
1/31/58	41.70	8/31/59	59.60	17.90	412	42.93
3/31/60	55.34	11/30/64	84.42	29.08	1,218	52.55
4/28/67	94.01	7/31/67	94.75	0.74	67	0.79
11/30/70	87.20	7/30/71	95.58	8.38	175	9.61
8/31/71	99.03	11/30/72	116.67	17.64	328	17.81
1/31/75	76.98	7/31/75	88.75	11.77	130	15.29
9/30/75	83.87	10/31/77	92.34	8.47	545	10.10
11/30/77	94.83	6/30/78	95.53	0.70	153	0.74
7/31/78	100.68	8/31/78	103.29	2.61	24	2.59
5/30/80	111.24	8/29/80	122.38	11.14	66	10.01
11/30/81	126.35	12/31/81	122.55	(3.80)	24	−3.01
7/30/82	107.09	8/31/84	166.68	59.59	546	55.64
10/31/84	166.09	11/30/88	273.70	107.61	1,066	64.79
8/31/90	322.56	12/31/97	970.43	647.87	1,914	200.85
Total				$952.69	9,042	687.10%
			Percent of Days Invested			63%
			Annual Rate of Return			19.1%

The Liquidity Cycle tends to work from Hong Kong to Germany to India to the United States. Figure 2.7 courtesy of the China Analyst, shows the incredibly strong relationship between the prime lending rate and earnings in the wildly explosive Hong Kong market since 1980. Note that each major expansion in earnings was preceded by a drop in the prime rate and that each major drop in earnings was preceded by a runup in the prime rate.

System Spreadsheet 2.9 MONETARY COMPOSITE

System Description: Buy S&P when 3-Month T-Bill Yield 12-Month ROC ≤ 6.0%, Dow Jones 20 Bond Index 12-Month ROC > −1.5%, and 30-Year Treasury Bond Rate 12-Month ROC ≤ 9%. Exit when any of these is no longer true.

Significance: When many monetary variables align, the market moves up both rapidly and reliably.

Data Used: Monthly close of 3-Month Treasury bills, monthly close Dow Jones 20 Bond Index, monthly close of 30-Year Treasury Bonds, and monthly close of S&P 500.

From: 1/29/43   To: 12/31/97

Annual Rate of Return: 20.1%

Entry Date	Entry Price	Exit Date	Exit Price	Profit/ Loss	Days in Trade	Percent Change
7/29/49	$ 15.04	7/31/50	$ 17.84	$ 2.80	262	18.62%
9/30/52	24.54	10/31/52	24.52	(0.02)	24	−0.08
10/30/53	24.54	11/30/53	24.76	0.22	22	0.90
1/29/54	26.08	1/31/55	36.63	10.55	262	40.45
4/30/58	43.44	12/31/58	55.21	11.77	176	27.09
6/30/60	56.92	8/31/61	68.07	11.15	306	19.59
9/29/61	66.73	10/31/61	68.62	1.89	23	2.83
11/30/61	71.32	12/29/61	71.55	0.23	22	0.32
2/28/63	64.29	3/29/63	66.57	2.28	22	3.55
4/30/63	69.80	5/31/63	70.80	1.00	24	1.43
8/31/64	81.83	11/30/64	84.42	2.59	66	3.17
3/31/67	90.20	4/28/67	94.01	3.81	21	4.22
12/31/70	92.15	3/31/72	107.20	15.05	327	16.33
4/28/72	107.67	10/31/72	111.58	3.91	133	3.63
5/30/75	91.15	8/31/77	96.77	5.62	589	6.17
4/30/82	116.44	6/30/82	109.61	(6.83)	44	−5.87
7/30/82	107.09	8/31/83	164.40	57.31	284	53.52
11/30/84	163.58	4/30/87	288.36	124.78	630	76.28
10/31/89	340.36	6/29/90	358.02	17.66	174	5.19
12/31/90	330.22	2/28/94	467.14	136.92	826	41.46
10/31/95	581.50	1/31/97	786.16	204.66	329	35.20
3/31/97	757.12	12/31/97	970.43	213.31	198	28.17
Total				$820.66	4,764	382.17%

Percent of Days Invested	33%
Annual Rate of Return	20.1%

Figure 2.6 **FALLING RATES LEAD TO RISING STOCKS AND ECONOMIC GROWTH**

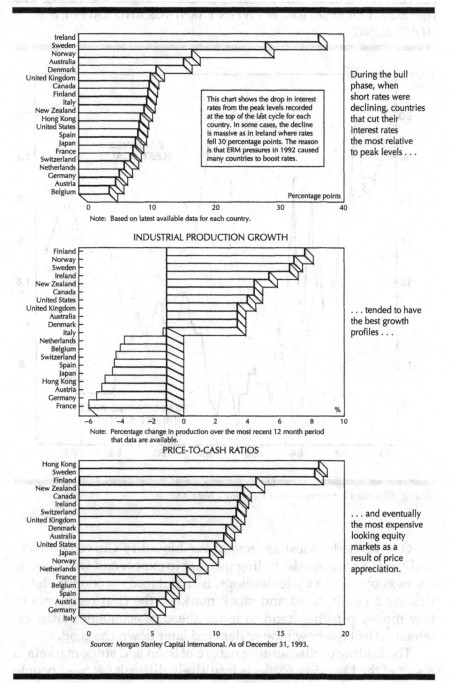

This chart shows the drop in interest rates from the peak levels recorded at the top of the last cycle for each country. In some cases, the decline is massive as in Ireland where rates fell 30 percentage points. The reason is that ERM pressures in 1992 caused many countries to boost rates.

During the bull phase, when short rates were declining, countries that cut their interest rates the most relative to peak levels . . .

Note: Based on latest available data for each country.

INDUSTRIAL PRODUCTION GROWTH

. . . tended to have the best growth profiles . . .

Note: Percentage change in production over the most recent 12 month period that data are available.

PRICE-TO-CASH RATIOS

. . . and eventually the most expensive looking equity markets as a result of price appreciation.

Source: Morgan Stanley Capital International. As of December 31, 1993.

Source: Reprinted by permission of the *Bank Credit Analyst.*

Figure 2.7 **CORRELATION BETWEEN EARNINGS AND RATES IN HONG KONG**

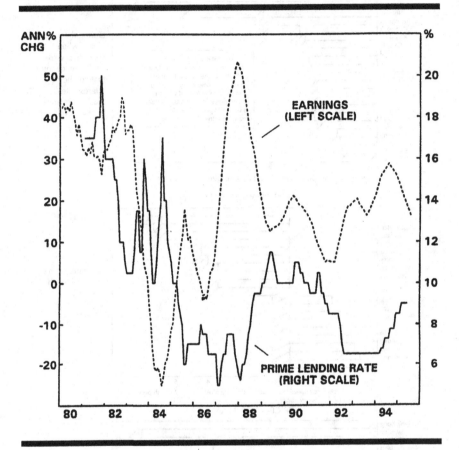

Source: Reprinted by permission of the *Bank Credit Analyst.*

One of the trickiest aspects of the Liquidity Curve, which is really just a basic model telling us what to expect and watch for as the next phase of a cycle develops, is that it leads economic statistics. As a result, bond and stock markets, the first recipients of new money printing, tend to move ahead of economic statistics, which reflect the new money demand later down the road.

The leading or discounting nature of bond and stock markets, a result of the Liquidity Cycle, is intuitively difficult for most people to comprehend. Intuitively, it would seem that the best time to buy stocks is when the economy is booming—earnings, after all, rise most rapidly during such a phase. Conversely, one would think that the worst time to buy stocks would be in the midst of a recession, when earnings are dropping, many firms are actually losing money, and investors are scared to invest. However, the effect of the Liquidity Cycle is to make these intuitive investment timing observations not only inaccurate, but actually dangerous to an investor's financial health.

When economic variables are weak and the Fed begins lowering rates, it is, in fact, the best time to invest in equities because liquidity is flowing into bonds and beginning to flow into equities during weak economic periods. Conversely, the riskiest and poorest time to invest in equities is when the economy looks strong and the bond market is beginning to head lower. The following market timing systems were developed and improved from the original work of the panel of experts we mentioned earlier; these systems will help you see that avoiding stocks during economic strength and buying stocks during economic weakness is a market-beating strategy. It is important that investors not only realize and utilize models based on this idea, but also understand why it is so. Stocks do not magically "discount" recoveries and recessions as much market lore of old relates. The leading nature of stocks and bonds does not reflect their premonition ability, but rather occurs because they are the first recipients of new liquidity in a fractional reserve banking system, and the economy receives the liquidity from the stock and bond markets after they have already been liquified. Thus the economy does not pick up in response to liquidity demand until the stock and bond markets have already done so.

Two subsets of economic gauges are worth watching to determine whether the economy is overheating or underperforming potential. The first subset of economic gauges looks at the production cycle versus production ability: capacity utilization, industrial production, and employment. This subset of tools usually shows trouble first. As an economy overheats, producers begin to compete for resources, which are becoming scarce because everyone is producing very near their total production capacity (remember they are actually overproducing because they are reading liquidity-induced demand as though it were real demand). This competition for resources results in price indexes turning up sharply. So the next economic gauges to watch are input/commodity price measures. Examples of each of these types of gauges are listed in the following section. They help prove the thesis in real profit numbers that a super strong economy is bad for stocks while a weak economy is good for stocks.

Economic Gauges—Productivity

Model 1: Capacity Utilization. Capacity utilization tells us what percentage of productive capacity that exists in a country is

---

System Spreadsheet 2.10 CAPACITY UTILIZATION ≤ 81.5%

System Description: Buy S&P when the Capacity Utilization Rate ≤ 81.5%. Exit when > 81.5%.

Significance: When the economy slows down, stocks preform well.

Data Used: Monthly Capacity Utilization Rate and monthly close of S&P 500.

From: 1/29/43   To: 12/31/97

Annual Rate of Return: 20.4%

Entry Date	Entry Price	Exit Date	Exit Price	Profit/ Loss	Days in Trade	Percent Change
7/31/52	$ 25.40	8/29/52	$ 25.03	($ 0.37)	22	−1.46%
1/29/54	26.08	12/31/54	35.98	9.90	241	37.96
10/31/57	41.06	3/31/59	55.44	14.38	369	35.02
8/31/59	59.60	12/31/59	59.89	0.29	89	0.49
5/31/60	55.83	12/29/61	71.55	15.72	414	28.16
1/31/62	68.84	3/30/62	69.55	0.71	43	1.03
5/31/62	59.63	9/28/62	56.27	(3.36)	87	−5.63
10/31/62	56.52	11/30/62	62.26	5.74	23	10.16
3/31/70	89.63	2/29/72	106.57	16.94	501	18.90
11/29/74	69.97	4/29/77	98.44	28.47	631	40.69
4/30/80	106.29	7/31/87	318.66	212.37	1,893	199.80
9/28/90	306.05	3/31/94	445.77	139.72	915	45.65
12/29/95	615.93	5/31/96	669.12	53.19	111	8.64
8/30/96	651.99	12/31/96	740.74	88.75	88	13.61
1/31/97	786.16	2/28/97	790.82	4.66	21	0.59
5/30/97	848.28	7/31/97	954.29	106.01	45	12.50
Total				$693.12	5,493	446.10%
			Percent of Days Invested			38%
			Annual Rate of Return			20.4%

---

currently being used. In the absence of a fractional reserve federal reserve banking system, it would be logical to assume that as companies use more of their productive ability, they make more money—but not so in a country where liquidity is produced out of thin air. High capacity use in a fractional reserve central banking country tells us that excessive liquidity is being interpreted as real demand by companies and that they will soon begin competing for resources as they will perceive demand to be higher than it really is. Companies compete for scarce resources via paying higher prices and cutting their own margins. This in turn will lead to monetary breaks and downturns in the Liquidity Cycle. Thus when capacity utilization rises above 88.5 percent, the S&P historically falls at a −6.3 percent annual rate. Strong economy—bad for stocks. Conversely when capacity utilization falls to 81.5 percent or less the S&P has historically risen at a steep +20.4 percent annual rate. Weak economy—good for stocks. System Spreadsheets 2.10 and 2.11 illustrate this pattern.

System Spreadsheet 2.11 **CAPACITY UTILIZATION > 88.5%**

System Description: Buy S&P when the Capacity Utilization Rate > 88.5%.
Exit when ≤ 88.5%.

Significance: When capacity use overheats, stocks perform very poorly.

Data Used: Monthly Capacity Utilization Rate and monthly close of S&P 500.

From: 1/29/43   To: 12/31/97

Annual Rate of Return: −6.3%

Entry Date	Entry Price	Exit Date	Exit Price	Profit/ Loss	Days in Trade	Percent Change
10/31/52	$ 24.52	9/30/53	$ 23.35	($ 1.17)	239	−4.77%
12/30/55	45.48	1/31/56	43.82	(1.66)	23	−3.65
1/29/65	87.56	2/28/67	86.78	(0.78)	543	−0.89
10/31/73	108.29	11/30/73	95.96	(12.33)	23	−11.39
Total				($15.94)	828	−20.70%
		Percent of Days Invested				6%
		Annual Rate of Return				−6.3%

Model 2: Industrial Production, 12-Month Rate of Change. Another pretty pure indication of the strength of an economy is its industrial production and the rate of change in industrial production. Intuitively, one would think that strong production would equal strong profits and strong stock performance. But our understanding of the Liquidity Cycle leads us to suspect just the opposite. And indeed our analysis of industrial production, year-over-year percentage changes bears out our suspicion. System Spreadsheets 2.12 and 2.13 show that when industrial production's 12-month rate of change is at 5.6 percent or less, the S&P has historically

---

System Spreadsheet 2.12 **INDUSTRIAL PRODUCTION ≤ 5.6%**

System Description: Buy S&P when the 12-month rate of change of the Industrial Production Index close ≤ 5.6%. Exit when > 5.6%.

Significance: When industrial production growth is not high, stocks move up above average.

Data Used: Monthly close of Industrial Production Index and monthly close of S&P 500.

From: 1/31/45   To: 12/31/97

Annual Rate of Return: 13.2%

Entry Date	Entry Price	Exit Date	Exit Price	Profit/ Loss	Days in Trade	Percent Change
2/28/67	$ 86.78	5/31/68	$ 98.68	$ 11.90	329	13.71%
10/31/68	103.41	2/28/69	98.13	(5.28)	87	−5.11
4/30/69	103.69	11/30/71	93.99	(9.70)	675	−9.35
12/31/71	102.09	1/31/72	103.94	1.85	22	1.81
12/31/73	97.55	2/27/76	99.71	2.16	565	2.21
12/30/77	95.10	4/28/78	96.83	1.73	86	1.82
5/31/78	97.29	6/30/78	95.53	(1.76)	23	−1.81
4/30/79	101.76	6/30/81	131.21	29.45	567	28.94
9/30/81	116.18	8/31/83	164.40	48.22	501	41.50
10/31/84	166.09	7/31/87	318.66	152.57	718	91.86
2/29/88	267.82	6/30/94	444.27	176.45	1,654	65.88
4/28/95	514.71	10/31/97	914.62	399.91	656	77.70
Total				$807.50	5,883	309.17%
			Percent of Days Invested			43%
			Annual Rate of Return			13.2%

System Spreadsheet 2.13 INDUSTRIAL PRODUCTION > 7.0%

System Description: Buy S&P when the 12-month rate of change of the Industrial Production Index close > 7.0%. Exit when ≤ 7.0%.

Significance: When industrial production growth gets too hot, stocks underperform cash.

Data Used: Monthly close of Industrial Production Index and monthly close of S&P 500.

From: 1/31/45   To: 12/31/97

Annual Rate of Return: 1.1%

Entry Date	Entry Price	Exit Date	Exit Price	Profit/ Loss	Days in Trade	Percent Change
4/28/50	$ 18.07	7/31/51	$ 22.40	$ 4.33	328	23.96%
9/30/52	24.54	9/30/53	23.35	(1.19)	262	−4.85
2/28/55	36.76	3/30/56	48.48	11.72	285	31.88
7/31/57	47.91	8/30/57	45.22	(2.69)	23	−5.61
1/30/59	55.42	10/30/59	57.52	2.10	196	3.79
12/31/59	59.89	2/29/60	56.12	(3.77)	43	−6.29
11/30/61	71.32	8/31/62	59.12	(12.20)	197	−17.11
9/28/62	56.27	10/31/62	56.52	0.25	24	0.44
6/28/63	69.37	7/31/63	69.13	(0.24)	24	−0.35
10/31/63	74.01	12/31/63	75.02	1.01	44	1.36
1/31/64	77.04	2/28/64	77.80	0.76	21	0.99
7/31/64	83.18	9/30/64	84.18	1.00	44	1.20
11/30/64	84.42	12/30/66	80.33	(4.09)	545	−4.84
6/28/68	99.58	8/30/68	98.86	(0.72)	46	−0.72
2/29/72	106.57	11/30/73	95.96	(10.61)	459	−9.96
2/27/76	99.71	2/28/77	99.82	0.11	262	0.11
3/31/77	98.42	11/30/77	94.83	(3.59)	175	−3.65
11/30/78	94.70	4/30/79	101.76	7.06	108	7.46
7/31/81	130.92	8/31/81	122.79	(8.13)	22	−6.21
9/30/83	166.07	9/28/84	166.10	0.03	261	0.02
1/31/95	470.42	2/28/95	487.39	16.97	21	3.61
Total				($ 1.89)	3,390	15.23%
			Percent of Days Invested			25%
			Annual Rate of Return			1.1%

risen at a better than average +13.2 percent annual rate. When the 12-month rate of change in industrial production has risen above 7 percent, however, the S&P has historically risen at a subpar +1.1 percent—underperforming cash (5%) significantly.

Model 3: Unemployment, 29-Month Rate of Change. Our least favorite of the three gauges of pure economic strength is the unemployment rate and changes in it. Here we use the 29-month rate of change (ROC) of unemployment. Intuitively, one might think that low unemployment would mean more people working and more money in the economy creating better profits and better stock performance. But our understanding of the Liquidity Cycle leads us to suspect that, once again, the opposite is the case. Our

---

System Spreadsheet 2.14 **UNEMPLOYMENT INCREASING**

System Description: Buy when current unemployment > that 29 months ago.
Exit when current unemployment ≤ unemployment rate 29 months ago.

Significance: When unemployment is increasing, stocks do better.

Data Used: Monthly Civilian Unemployment Rate and monthly close of S&P 500.

From: 1/31/47   To: 12/31/97

Annual Rate of Return: 16.1%

Entry Date	Entry Price	Exit Date	Exit Price	Profit/ Loss	Days in Trade	Percent Change
10/30/53	$ 24.54	5/31/56	$ 45.20	$ 20.66	675	84.19%
10/31/57	41.06	5/31/60	55.83	14.77	674	35.97
3/31/61	65.06	2/28/62	69.96	4.90	239	7.53
5/31/62	59.63	12/31/62	63.10	3.47	153	5.82
1/31/63	66.20	3/29/63	66.57	0.37	42	0.56
1/30/70	85.02	1/31/73	116.03	31.01	784	36.47
9/30/74	63.54	5/31/77	96.12	32.58	697	51.27
4/30/80	106.29	3/30/84	159.18	52.89	1,023	49.76
9/28/90	306.05	8/31/93	463.56	157.51	763	51.47
Total				$318.16	5,050	323.04%
			Percent of Days Invested			38%
			Annual Rate of Return			16.1%

analysis shows that when today's unemployment rate is higher than that of 29 months ago, the S&P moves up nicely at a +16.1 percent annual rate (System Spreadsheet 2.14). However, in a booming economy with an unemployment rate that is actually less than that of 29 months ago (System Spreadsheet 2.15), the S&P has historically moved up at only a +4.4 percent annual rate—underperforming cash (5% average). Not only are the statistics slightly less compelling for unemployment than for other economic gauges, but we see no reason why past norms will continue indefinitely into the future if economic dynamics change. Nonetheless for now and the immediate future, this tool should continue to work reasonably well—although we still prefer the two preceding tools to this one.

System Spreadsheet 2.15 UNEMPLOYMENT DECREASING

System Description: Buy when current unemployment ≤ that 29 months ago. Exit when current unemployment > unemployment rate 29 months ago.

Significance: When unemployment moves down sharply, the economy is getting heated and stocks fare worse than cash.

Data Used: Monthly Civilian Unemployment Rate and monthly close of S&P 500.

From: 1/31/47   To: 12/31/92

Annual Rate of Return: 4.4%

Entry Date	Entry Price	Exit Date	Exit Price	Profit/ Loss	Days in Trade	Percent Change
3/30/51	$ 21.40	10/30/53	$ 24.54	$ 3.14	676	14.67%
5/31/56	45.20	10/31/57	41.06	(4.14)	371	−9.16
5/31/60	55.83	3/31/61	65.06	9.23	219	16.53
3/30/62	69.55	5/31/62	59.63	(9.92)	45	−14.26
3/29/63	66.57	1/30/70	85.02	18.45	1,786	27.72
1/31/73	116.03	9/30/74	63.54	(52.49)	434	−45.24
5/31/77	96.12	4/30/80	106.29	10.17	762	10.58
3/30/84	159.18	8/31/90	322.56	163.38	1,676	102.64
Total				$137.82	5,969	103.48%
		Percent of Days Invested				50%
		Annual Rate of Return				4.4%

Economic Gauges—Inflation and Prices

Model 4: Consumer Price Index Inflation and Gross Domestic Product Quarterly Growth. Here we're looking at both the Consumer Price Index (CPI—and no, in this case it has nothing to do with coconuts) and the quarterly gross domestic product (GDP) growth numbers released by the government. When CPI inflation is less than or equal to 3.2 percent and GDP quarterly growth is less than or equal to 4 percent, if you buy the S&P and hold as long as either of these two criteria are still in place, the S&P has historically risen at a +19.2 percent annual rate. Prices rising at a reasonable rate or dropping prices are good for stocks. However,

---

System Spreadsheet 2.16 **CONSUMER PRICE INDEX (CPI) INFLATION ≤ 3.2% AND QUARTERLY GDP GROWTH ≤ 4%**

System Description: Buy S&P when CPI Inflation ≤ 3.2% and Quarterly GDP Growth ≤ 4%. Exit when *both* move above their respective thresholds.

Significance: When CPI Inflation and GDP growth are not too hot, stocks perform very well.

Data Used: Monthly CPI Inflation, quarterly GDP growth, and monthly close of S&P 500.

From: 4/30/59   To: 12/31/97

Annual Rate of Return: 19.2%

Entry Date	Entry Price	Exit Date	Exit Price	Profit/ Loss	Days in Trade	Percent Change
9/30/71	$ 98.34	6/30/72	$107.14	$ 8.80	197	8.95%
9/30/82	120.45	4/29/83	164.42	43.97	152	36.50
10/31/84	166.09	1/31/85	179.63	13.54	67	8.15
5/31/85	189.55	8/30/85	188.63	(0.92)	66	−0.49
12/31/85	211.28	4/30/87	288.36	77.08	348	36.48
1/31/91	343.93	11/30/92	431.35	87.42	478	25.42
1/29/93	438.78	5/31/94	456.50	17.72	348	4.04
7/29/94	458.26	4/30/96	654.17	195.91	458	42.75
7/31/96	639.95					
Total				$443.52	2,114	161.81%
			Percent of Days Invested			21%
			Annual Rate of Return			19.2%

rising prices are bad for stocks. Thus when CPI inflation is > 3.2 percent and GDP quarterly growth is > 4 percent, for investors who hold the S&P until both criteria are false, the S&P historically has only risen at a +2.9 percent annual rate, making risk-free cash/money market funds/T-bills (5%) a better investment. System Spreadsheets 2.16 and 2.17 illustrate these criteria.

Model 5: Consumer Price Index, Fast and Slow Rate of Change. Just using CPI inflation rates of change themselves, we can show that inflation is bad for stocks. The 11-month rate of change is our "fast" number. For our "slow" number, we take the average CPI for the past 13 months and compare it with the CPI for the 13 months prior to that (months 14 to 26 back in time). The ROC from that

---

System Spreadsheet 2.17 **CONSUMER PRICE INDEX (CPI) INFLATION > 3.2% AND QUARTERLY GDP GROWTH > 4%**

System Description: Buy S&P when CPI Inflation > 3.2% and Quarterly GDP Growth > 4%. Exit when *both* fall below their respective thresholds.

Significance: When CPI Inflation and GDP overheat, stocks underperform cash.

Data Used: Monthly CPI Inflation, quarterly GDP growth, and monthly close of S&P 500.

From: 4/30/59   To: 12/31/97

Annual Rate of Return: 2.9%

Entry Date	Entry Price	Exit Date	Exit Price	Profit/ Loss	Days in Trade	Percent Change
6/30/72	$107.14	9/30/82	$120.45	$13.31	2,675	12.42%
4/29/83	164.42	10/31/84	166.09	1.67	394	1.02
1/31/85	179.63	5/31/85	189.55	9.92	87	5.52
8/30/85	188.63	12/31/85	211.28	22.65	88	12.01
4/30/87	288.36	1/31/91	343.93	55.57	981	19.27
11/30/92	431.35	1/29/93	438.78	7.43	45	1.72
5/31/94	456.50	7/29/94	458.26	1.76	44	0.39
4/30/96	654.17	7/31/96	639.95	(14.22)	67	−2.17
Total				$98.09	4,381	50.17%
			Percent of Days Invested			43%
			Annual Rate of Return			2.9%

13-month average compared with the prior 13-month average is our "slow" rate of change. Now compare the fast ROC and the slow ROC percentage changes. When the fast rate of change of the Consumer Price Index is less than the slow rate of change of the Consumer Price Index, the CPI is either rising less or falling more than it was last quarter, and the S&P has historically risen at a better than average +13.2 percent annual rate. But when the fast ROC of the CPI is above or equal to the slow ROC of the CPI, inflation is picking up, and the S&P has historically risen at only a +1 percent annual rate, substantially underperforming cash (see System Spreadsheets 2.18 and 2.19).

Model 6: Commodity Research Bureau Index, 12-Month Rate of Change. Our liquidity cycle theory implies that when industrial commodity prices start moving up rapidly, the economy is beginning to overheat, and a liquidity crunch will soon develop. It also implies that when commodity prices are falling swiftly that is a good signal for the Fed to begin reliquifying. And when commodity prices are flat, there should be little reason to fear a liquidity crunch. The reality matches the theory. When the 12-month ROC of the Commodity Research Bureau's Index of commodity prices is declining at a −1 percent or less pace, the S&P has historically risen at a very swift +21.5 percent annual rate. When the 12-month ROC of the CRB is between −1 percent and 5 percent, the S&P has risen at a + 21.2 percent annual rate. But when the 12-month ROC of the CRB is +5 percent or more, the S&P has fallen at a −4.8 percent annual rate. System Spreadsheets 2.20, 2.21, and 2.22 demonstrate this pattern. Commodity prices are one of the best inverse indicators to stock price movement in an inflationary banking system; this is why resource funds and commodity funds make some of the best forms of diversification in a portfolio that includes stocks.

Model 7: Sensitive Materials Prices, 18-Month Rate of Change. This is a government-released figure that shows the price movement of materials that are economically sensitive. Again, our ALC would lead us to suspect that when price changes get too hot, stocks should do poorly, while when price changes fall swiftly, stocks should do well. When the 18-month ROC of sensitive materials prices is less than or equal to 18 percent, the S&P has historically risen at a +18.4 percent annual rate (see System Spreadsheet 2.23).

System Spreadsheet 2.18 **CPI FAST AND SLOW ROC BULLISH**

System Description: Buy when the fast CPI ROC < slow CPI ROC where fast CPI ROC is the CPI rate of change from 11 months ago and slow CPI ROC is the ROC of the average of the past 13 months to the average of the prior 13 months. Exit when fast CPI ROC ≥ slow CPI ROC.

Significance: When the rate of change of consumer prices slows down, stocks move up swiftly.

Data Used: Monthly Consumer Price Index and monthly close of S&P 500.

From: 1/29/43   To: 12/31/97

Annual Rate of Return: 13.2%

Entry Date	Entry Price	Exit Date	Exit Price	Profit/ Loss	Days in Trade	Percent Change
4/30/48	$ 15.48	4/28/50	$ 18.07	$ 2.59	521	16.73%
8/31/51	23.28	12/31/53	24.81	1.53	610	6.57
3/31/54	26.94	7/29/55	43.52	16.58	348	61.54
6/28/57	47.37	7/31/57	47.91	0.54	24	1.14
9/30/57	42.42	10/30/59	57.52	15.10	545	35.60
6/30/60	56.92	12/30/60	58.11	1.19	132	2.09
1/31/61	61.78	4/30/62	65.24	3.46	325	5.60
6/29/62	54.75	7/31/62	58.23	3.48	23	6.36
8/31/62	59.12	9/28/62	56.27	(2.85)	21	−4.82
1/31/63	66.20	7/31/63	69.13	2.93	130	4.43
8/30/63	72.50	11/29/63	73.23	0.73	66	1.01
2/28/64	77.80	3/31/64	78.98	1.18	23	1.52
5/29/64	80.37	4/30/65	89.11	8.74	241	10.87
10/29/65	92.42	11/30/65	91.61	(0.81)	23	−0.88
1/31/67	86.61	1/31/68	92.24	5.63	262	6.50
12/31/68	103.86	3/31/69	101.51	(2.35)	65	−2.26
5/30/69	103.46	12/31/69	92.06	(11.40)	154	−11.02
1/30/70	85.02	2/28/73	111.68	26.66	804	31.36
7/31/74	79.31	8/30/74	72.15	(7.16)	23	−9.03
12/31/74	68.56	8/31/78	103.29	34.73	958	50.66
4/30/80	106.29	1/31/84	163.41	57.12	980	53.74
5/31/84	150.55	2/27/87	284.20	133.65	717	88.77
1/29/88	257.07	5/31/89	320.52	63.45	349	24.68
6/30/89	317.98	8/31/90	322.56	4.58	306	1.44
12/31/90	330.22	8/31/94	475.49	145.27	958	43.99
9/30/94	462.69	4/28/95	514.71	52.02	151	11.24
5/31/95	533.40	11/29/96	757.02	223.62	393	41.92
12/31/96	740.74					
Total				$780.21	9,152	479.76%
			Percent of Days Invested			64%
			Annual Rate of Return			13.2%

System Spreadsheet 2.19 CPI FAST AND SLOW ROC CAUTIOUS

System Description: Buy when the fast CPI ROC ≥ slow CPI ROC where fast CPI ROC is the CPI rate of change from 11 months ago and slow CPI ROC is the ROC of the average of the past 13 months to the average of the prior 13 months. Exit when fast CPI ROC < slow CPI ROC.

Significance: When consumer prices heat up, stocks do not do as well as cash.

Data Used: Monthly Consumer Index and monthly close of S&P 500.

From: 1/29/43   To: 12/31/97

Annual Rate of Return: 1%

Entry Date	Entry Price	Exit Date	Exit Price	Profit/ Loss	Days in Trade	Percent Change
3/31/47	$ 15.17	4/30/48	$ 15.48	$ 0.31	285	2.04%
4/28/50	18.07	8/31/51	23.28	5.21	351	28.83
12/31/53	24.81	3/31/54	26.94	2.13	65	8.59
7/29/55	43.52	6/28/57	47.37	3.85	501	8.85
7/31/57	47.91	9/30/57	42.42	(5.49)	44	−11.46
10/30/59	57.52	6/30/60	56.92	(0.60)	175	−1.04
12/30/60	58.11	1/31/61	61.78	3.67	23	6.32
4/30/62	65.24	6/29/62	54.75	(10.49)	45	−16.08
7/31/62	58.23	8/31/62	59.12	0.89	24	1.53
9/28/62	56.27	1/31/63	66.20	9.93	90	17.65
7/31/63	69.13	8/30/63	72.50	3.37	23	4.87
11/29/63	73.23	2/28/64	77.80	4.57	66	6.24
3/31/64	78.98	5/29/64	80.37	1.39	44	1.76
4/30/65	89.11	10/29/65	92.42	3.31	131	3.71
11/30/65	91.61	1/31/67	86.61	(5.00)	306	−5.46
1/31/68	92.24	12/31/68	103.86	11.62	240	12.60
3/31/69	101.51	5/30/69	103.46	1.95	45	1.92
12/31/69	92.06	1/30/70	85.02	(7.04)	23	−7.65
2/28/73	111.68	7/31/74	79.31	(32.37)	371	−28.98
8/30/74	72.15	12/31/74	68.56	(3.59)	88	−4.98
8/31/78	103.29	4/30/80	106.29	3.00	435	2.90
1/31/84	163.41	5/31/84	150.55	(12.86)	88	−7.87
2/27/87	284.20	1/29/88	257.07	(27.13)	241	−9.55
5/31/89	320.52	6/30/89	317.98	(2.54)	23	−0.79
8/31/90	322.56	12/31/90	330.22	7.66	87	2.37
8/31/94	475.49	9/30/94	462.69	(12.80)	23	−2.69
4/28/95	514.71	5/31/95	533.40	18.69	24	3.63
11/29/96	757.02	12/31/96	740.74	(16.28)	23	−2.15
Total				($54.64)	3,884	15.12%

Percent of Days Invested   27%

Annual Rate of Return   1.0%

System Spreadsheet 2.20 CRB INDEX ROC ≤ −1%

System Description: Buy S&P when the 12-month rate of change of the CRB Index ≤ −1%. Exit when > −1%.

Significance: When commodity prices fall, stocks move up rapidly.

Data Used: Monthly CRB Index and monthly close of S&P 500.

From: 1/31/77   To: 12/31/97

Annual Rate of Return: 21.5%

Entry Date	Entry Price	Exit Date	Exit Price	Profit/ Loss	Days in Trade	Percent Change
1/31/78	$ 89.25	5/31/78	$ 97.29	$ 8.04	87	9.01%
6/30/81	131.21	5/31/83	162.39	31.18	501	23.76
7/31/84	150.66	3/31/87	291.70	141.04	696	93.61
5/31/89	320.52	4/30/90	330.80	10.28	239	3.21
11/30/90	322.22	2/28/92	412.70	90.48	326	28.08
3/31/92	403.69	6/30/92	408.14	4.45	66	1.10
7/31/92	424.21	3/31/93	451.67	27.46	174	6.47
6/30/93	450.53	7/30/93	448.13	(2.40)	23	−0.53
12/31/96	740.74	7/31/97	954.29	213.55	153	28.83
8/29/97	899.47	12/31/97	970.43	70.96	89	7.89
Total				$595.04	2,354	201.44%
			Percent of Days Invested			43%
			Annual Rate of Return			21.5%

However, when the 18-month ROC of sensitive materials prices has risen at greater than 18 percent, the S&P has historically fallen at a sharp −10.4 percent annual rate (see System Spreadsheet 2.24).

UNDERSTANDING ECONOMIC GAUGES

The preceding rules of thumb are certainly helpful. But our goal is not just to give you rules and models but to help you understand the how and why behind them, thus enabling you to use the gauges in the most profitable fashion. In fact, probably the best use for economic gauges is to help confirm where you are in

System Spreadsheet 2.21   **5% ≥ CRB INDEX ROC > –1%**

System Description: Buy S&P when 5% ≥ 12-month rate of change of the CRB Index ≤ –1. Exit when CRB Index is outside this range.

Significance: When commodity prices are dropping or rising slowly, stocks do well.

Data Used: Monthly CRB Index and monthly close of S&P 500.

From: 1/31/77   To: 12/31/97

Annual Rate of Return: 21.2%

Entry Date	Entry Price	Exit Date	Exit Price	Profit/ Loss	Days in Trade	Percent Change
5/31/78	$ 97.29	7/31/78	$100.68	$ 3.39	44	3.48%
1/30/81	129.55	3/31/81	136.00	6.45	43	4.98
5/31/83	162.39	7/29/83	162.56	0.17	44	0.10
3/31/87	291.70	4/30/87	288.36	(3.34)	23	–1.15
11/30/88	273.70	12/30/88	277.72	4.02	23	1.47
1/31/89	297.47	2/28/89	288.86	(8.61)	21	–2.89
3/31/89	294.87	5/31/89	320.52	25.65	44	8.70
4/30/90	330.80	5/31/90	361.23	30.43	24	9.20
6/29/90	358.02	7/31/90	356.15	(1.87)	23	–0.52
8/31/90	322.56	9/28/90	306.05	(16.51)	21	–5.12
10/31/90	304.00	11/30/90	322.22	18.22	23	5.99
2/28/92	412.70	3/31/92	403.69	(9.01)	23	–2.18
6/30/92	408.14	7/31/92	424.21	16.07	24	3.94
3/31/93	451.67	6/30/93	450.53	1.14	66	–0.25
11/30/94	453.69	9/29/95	584.41	130.72	218	28.81
10/31/95	581.50	2/29/96	640.43	58.93	88	10.13
7/31/96	639.95	12/31/96	740.74	100.79	110	15.75
7/31/97	954.29	8/29/97	899.47	(54.82)	22	–5.74
Total				$299.54	884	74.70%
		Percent of Days Invested				16%
		Annual Rate of Return				21.2%

the Liquidity Cycle and to know what must occur before you enter the next stage.

Suppose that it is late in an expansionary Liquidity Cycle and economic statistics are starting to get to the overheated level: capacity utilization is above 88.5 percent, industrial production is close to 7 percent above year-earlier levels, and the bond market is

System Spreadsheet 2.22 **CRB INDEX ROC > 5%**

System Description: Buy S&P when the 12-month rate of change of the CRB Index > 5%. Exit when ≤ 5%.

Significance: When commodity prices rise sharply, stocks perform poorly.

Data Used: Monthly CRB Index and monthly close of S&P 500.

From: 1/31/77   To: 12/31/97

Annual Rate of Return: −4.8%

Entry Date	Entry Price	Exit Date	Exit Price	Profit/ Loss	Days in Trade	Percent Change
7/31/78	$100.68	1/30/81	$129.55	$28.87	655	28.68%
3/31/81	136.00	6/30/81	131.21	24.08	66	17.71
7/29/83	162.56	7/31/84	150.66	12.18	263	7.49
4/30/87	288.36	11/30/88	273.70	(2.48)	415	−0.86
12/30/88	277.72	1/31/89	297.47	17.27	23	6.22
2/28/89	288.86	3/31/89	294.87	23.28	24	8.06
5/31/90	361.23	6/29/90	358.02	20.07	22	5.56
7/31/90	356.15	8/31/90	322.56	(13.52)	24	−3.80
9/28/90	306.05	10/31/90	304.00	(15.57)	24	−5.09
7/30/93	448.13	11/30/94	453.69	(10.01)	349	−2.23
9/29/95	584.41	10/31/95	581.50	(12.92)	23	−2.21
2/29/96	640.43	7/31/96	639.95	(13.40)	110	−2.09
Total				$57.85	1,998	57.43%
			Percent of Days Invested			37%
			Annual Rate of Return			−4.8%

starting to soften (as in early 1972, mid-1980, late 1983, early 1987, and late 1993). What should happen next according to the Liquidity Cycle and what do you need to watch to confirm that it is developing?

Once economic variables begin to get heated, the next thing to watch for is evidence that price indexes are starting to move higher. Leading inflation indexes, the CRB and CPI, should begin to turn higher and the bond and T-bill markets should begin a trend lower. In the preceding scenario, investors should probably have one foot poised over the brake in terms of equity invest-ments—but they should also wait until price indexes and interest

---

System Spreadsheet 2.23 **SENSITIVE MATERIALS 18-MONTH
ROC ≤ 18%**

System Description: Buy S&P when the 18-month rate of change of the Sensitive Materials Index close is ≤ 18%. Exit when > 18%.

Significance: When Sensitive Materials prices are not rising too rapidly, stocks perform well.

Data Used: Monthly close of Sensitive Materials Index and monthly close of S&P 500.

From: 4/30/52   To: 12/31/97

Annual Rate of Return: 18.4%

Entry Date	Entry Price	Exit Date	Exit Price	Profit/ Loss	Days in Trade	Percent Change
4/30/52	$ 23.32	11/30/72	$116.67	$ 93.35	5,372	400.3%
11/29/74	69.97	12/31/76	107.46	37.49	546	53.6
3/31/77	98.42	3/30/79	101.59	3.17	522	3.2
5/30/80	111.24	4/30/84	160.05	48.81	1022	43.9
7/31/84	150.66	9/30/87	321.83	171.17	827	113.6
11/30/87	230.30	2/29/88	267.82	37.52	66	16.3
3/31/88	258.89	10/31/94	472.35	213.46	1,718	82.5
10/31/95	581.50	12/31/97	970.43	388.93	567	66.9
Total				$993.90	10,640	780.2%
			Percent of Days Invested			89%
			Annual Rate of Return			18.4%

---

rate vehicles confirm the economic statistics before stepping on the brake and easing out of financial markets.

On the other hand what would one be watching for, and what action would one be looking to take in a situation where inflation indicators are all low, capacity utilization and industrial production rates are the lowest in years, unemployment is creeping to multiyear highs, price indexes like the CRB are plummeting, and the bond market is beginning to move higher, as developed in 1975, early 1982, 1984, near the end of 1990, and late in 1994? In this situation, the only thing lacking is clear evidence that the T-bill and T-bond markets are turning around and moving higher. Investors

System Spreadsheet 2.24 **SENSITIVE MATERIALS 18-MONTH ROC > 18%**

System Description: Buy S&P when the 18-month rate of change of the Sensitive Materials Index close is > 18%. Exit when ≤ 18%.

Significance: When Sensitive Materials prices rise too rapidly, stocks fall swiftly.

Data Used: Monthly close of Sensitive Materials Index and monthly close of S&P 500.

From: 4/30/52   To: 12/31/97

Annual Rate of Return: −10.4%

Entry Date	Entry Price	Exit Date	Exit Price	Profit/ Loss	Days in Trade	Percent Change
11/30/72	$116.67	11/29/74	$ 69.97	($46.70)	522	−40.0%
12/31/76	107.46	3/31/77	98.42	(9.04)	65	−8.4
3/30/79	101.59	5/30/80	111.24	9.65	306	9.5
4/30/84	160.05	7/31/84	150.66	(9.39)	67	−5.9
9/30/87	321.83	11/30/87	230.30	(91.53)	44	−28.4
2/29/88	267.82	3/31/88	258.89	(8.93)	24	−3.3
10/31/94	472.35	10/31/95	581.50	109.15	262	23.1
Total				($46.79)	1,290	−53.5%

Percent of Days Invested	11%
Annual Rate of Return	−10.4%

should probably have their finger on the trigger by searching for equities to watch for breakouts and buy patterns to position in as soon as further bond and bill strength materializes.

The bottom line is that the more investors understand the Liquidity Cycle and the gauges to watch that confirm its position, the better investors they are likely to become.

There are always new twists in every cycle. The current Liquidity Cycle is much longer than and is different from any other in history; in the early 1990s our markets not only were the recipients of one of the steepest yield curves in history from our own Fed, but also received the impetus of massive liquidity from the Japanese central bank.

The Economic Influence of Japan

A quick look at the Japanese situation can provide insight into how foreign influences can affect the Liquidity Cycle. Reviewing Japan also illustrates how much easier it is to understand what is going on in a country when we view it from an Austrian, free-market perspective.

Since World War II, Japan has lived under huge distortions to the free market that have caused problems for the economy. The most pronounced were persistent barriers to spending and artificial incentives to save. Regulations created ridiculously high domestic costs of goods and services, which discouraged spending and consumption. At the same time, huge tax incentives (to save) and overvalued real estate markets making home ownership unlikely for much of the population created an artificially large incentive to save. Savings averaged 35 percent of GDP since the 1950s. Adding to excess personal savings was a trade-as-war mentality that led to chronic underinvestment in infrastructure and large subsidization of big business. The result is that despite a relatively high per-capita income, the real living standard of the average Japanese citizen is below that of most citizens of developed nations. For example, Japan has developed sewage systems for only 45 percent of its citizens.

Underinvestment in infrastructure, personal savings incentives, disincentives to spend, government largesse subsidization of big business, and the trade-as-war mentality to sacrifice for the company that will conquer foreign lands have produced the most marked free-market distortion of chronic excess savings that the world has witnessed in modern history. Much of Japanese economic history is the story of how they have dealt with this distortion.

In the 1950s and 1960s the excess savings was absorbed into rebuilding the Japanese economy after its World War II devastation. Since then the excess Japanese savings have created chronic current account surpluses. In the 1970s, Japan received less flack for chronic current account surpluses because they went into deficit twice during oil shocks (Japan is heavily dependant upon importation of foreign oil). In the early 1980s, the United States needed Japanese excess savings to absorb its huge deficits, but even so, in 1983 and 1984, the United States began to target a lower dollar/yen in response to chronic trade and current account imbalances with Japan.

As the lower dollar policy became clear, Japanese officials worried about possible recession. They responded to this threat by artificially lowering interest rates to avoid recession—throwing more liquidity on an economy that already had chronically excessive savings. Rates fell below the inflation rate creating a negative real interest rate. The cost of capital became so low that capital spending soared at a 10 percent to 15 percent annual rate for the next five years. Artificially low rates diverted savings internally and led to poor and indiscriminate use of low cost capital. Business plans that were marginal suddenly became profitable with a low-cost capital assumption. Ill-advised investments were made and capacity expanded to levels far beyond possible demand. Artificially low interest rates also diverted capital into asset markets and property speculation. At times during 1988 and 1989, the average large Japanese company was making half of its per share earnings in real-estate and stock market speculation. The biggest asset bubble since 1929 was the result.

The asset and property bubbles were popped in 1989 by a tightening of monetary policy as it became evident that loose money had created a huge speculative mania. The Japanese economy plunged into recession one year later, leading to declining capital spending and plummeting spending on imports. But the main distortions that created excess savings continued and once again the current account surplus rose to over 3.5 percent of GDP. Again U.S. and European trading partners responded with a strong yen policy to try to cut the current account surplus of Japan, leading to an almost 60 percent appreciation in the yen from 1990 to 1994.

The strong yen did indeed begin to cut into both the trade and current account surpluses of Japan—but in a deflationary environment following the popping of the excessively large speculative asset and property bubbles, the Japanese economy faced the threat of depression for the first time since World War II. Property markets had dropped by up to 50 percent and equity markets had dropped over 60 percent since 1989, and banks were technically underwater and gasping for balance sheet air. The threat of a global burgeoning effect and global deflation/depression loomed over the world if major Japanese banks, the largest banks in the world, were allowed to fail.

In the early 1990s, the Fed had enormous success reliquifying its own balance-sheet-troubled banking system by engineering the steepest yield curve in decades. Banks were able to borrow short-term and pocket up to 5 percent in profit from loaning to the bond market at the higher long-term rate. This went on for some time, allowing U.S. banks to repair their balance sheets. The Japanese attempted to emulate the Fed's success. However, the deflationary cycle had already forced Japanese bond rates below 3 percent—so even a ¼ percent short-term rate would not have the stimulative effect of a 5 percent spread between short- and long-term rates. It soon became clear that the stimulus from the Japanese yield curve would not be enough to stave off disaster.

The Japanese met with the G-7 (group of seven industrialized nations: the United States, Canada, Japan, Germany, France, the United Kingdom, and Italy) and finally jointly came up with an idea of how to stimulate the Japanese economy despite the deflationary fallout of its speculative bubble. The Japanese central bank and the G-7 made unusually clear statements regarding their intention to devalue the yen and ensure that it would trade at lower rates over the foreseeable future. This allowed Japanese banks an implicit guarantee that if they borrowed at the very low (½%) short-term rates in Japan and loaned to the U.S. bond market (then having rates of over 7%) that they could pocket the difference without fear of currency losses.

The Japanese have since purchased record amounts of U.S. government paper. In 1996, for example, foreign capital financed 100 percent of corporate bond offerings and 200 percent of government borrowing, leaving the excess to feed into equities. Thus since 1994, the U.S. bull market has benefited not only from our own Fed stimulus, but also from much of Japan's record stimulus. The result has been a wildly profitable bull market in U.S. stocks and bonds. The Japanese banks have indeed been able to reliquify to a large extent. However, not surprisingly, the Japanese economy has not done terribly well at recovering from the negative effects of its deflation. The reason, from a Liquidity Cycle perspective is simple. Only a small part of Japanese liquidity has been able to flow into the Japanese economy because only a small part of it has gone into Japanese bonds and stocks; most of the money has gone into the U.S. bond and stock markets, with that market and economy being the main beneficiary.

How long will the Japanese keep spilling money into our markets? Probably until Japanese domestic inflation heats up or until their economy picks up sufficiently to cut back the need for liquification.

Understanding the Southeast Asian Markets

The markets of Southeast Asia, however, are finally suffering the results of years of their own brand of distortions. These export-oriented producers attempted to sterilize their dollar trade surpluses for years by buying the excess dollars from trade surpluses and converting them to reserve holdings to keep their own currencies artificially competitive and linked to the dollar. This meant that they exported lower priced goods and imported domestic inflation. The resultant real estate speculation spiraled for a decade.

Foreign investors, not wanting to miss out on the boom helped fuel even more money than the distorted amount into building export-oriented manufacturing capacity. Then when world growth slowed substantially, their own domestic inflation spiral slowed and the bubble finally burst. In 1994, China devalued its currency, adding competitive pressure to Asian emerging markets, and in mid-1995, the dollar began to soar versus the yen, making Japan much more competitive for similar export markets.

All these factors made debt loads and excess capacity problems too great. Banks were temporarily artificially propped up although the assets behind loans were collapsing in value. The market needed falling prices, which would allow excess capacity to be liquidated at a a price that would allow production to become profitable, but for the central bankers to let prices drop this quickly would destroy the assets underlying the banking system. The central bankers propped up their systems to try to keep the banking system from deflating. As the dollar continued to rally, however, price decline pressures in Southeast Asia grew, and by 1997 global currency traders realized that market forces were in clear opposition to central bank policy. Either central banks would have to let prices fall internally or the currency markets would do the work for them, by deflating the currency prices upon which those assets were based.

Global currency traders, the free market police of the world, finally sensed enough of an imbalance to begin attacking Asian currencies in force. The central banks were faced with the dilemma of either choking their economies with interest rate hikes to defend the currency or devaluing the currencies. Since Asian respect for free-market forces is minimal, these troubled economies tried every strong-arm tactic in the book to ward off the inevitable. Malaysia even tried to make currency trading illegal and is purported to have put out a death contract on large currency traders, for example. Finally global currency speculators forced reality on the central banks of Southeast Asia; and the currencies of Malaysia, Indonesia, Thailand, the Philippines, and others collapsed, followed by their stock markets. Lower currency prices now make Southeast Asian goods unusually cheap globally. The result is that Japan will face some very low-priced competition and is returning to a recession as a result of heightened competitive pressures on its export markets. So Japan will likely continue to need to stimulate via the U.S. yield curve and/or via currency devaluation until their economy strengthens.

In addition, the world will very soon be awash in cheap export goods. It remains to be seen just how much excess export capacity was created in a decade of bubble economies all aiming at similar markets. It is also uncertain how much contagion the excess capacity will create. If the excess is minimal, the world economy will eventually absorb it although global growth rates will suffer temporarily. If the excess capacity problem is acute, however, and similar excess capacity problems develop in China, the world could be facing a severe deflationary incident in the largest trading bloc on earth. Japan sends over 40 percent of its exports to Asia, while the United States sends over 30 percent there.

The Deflation Spiral

It is certainly not the most likely outcome, but a global deflation spiral is not unthinkable. If all of Asia, including China and Japan, should suffer from a large excess export-capacity bubble that cannot be quickly resolved, then most of Eastern Europe and Latin America will also come under competitive attack. The problem is that most emerging markets have built somewhat similar export-oriented capacity. If a glut of goods slows U.S. and European growth enough, a series of competitive devaluations could ripple through the globe and protectionist policies could pop up.

Although the simple liquidity model we provide at the end of this chapter is based on the assumption of an inflationary monetary system, investors must realize that the rules change significantly in a deflationary environment. The reason is simple. In an inflationary system, prices are rising, the only question is how much. Therefore, bond investors are concerned with the rate of change in prices (the inflation rate); whenever inflation picks up, bond investors demand increased risk compensation in the form of higher yields and lower bond prices.

However, imagine an environment where prices are just as likely to fall as to rise. Bond investors need no longer discount future inflation, because it is not clear that any inflation will exist at all. In this environment, bond yields correlate more to general price levels than to the rate of price change. When prices are dropping, one is getting a bonus beyond interest payments in the form of return of principal, which is actually worth more than when the investment was made. In addition, falling prices in an expanding money supply system mean that corporate margins are likely to be dropping. So in a deflation when bond prices rise and yields fall along with price levels, stock prices actually face downward pressure, instead of the normal stock-following-bond-price inflationary model. Conversely, when prices begin to rebound, bond yields head up (and bond prices turn down) as the return of principal stops being a bonus. For the same reason that bond yields head up, stock prices also begin to recover, reflecting more pricing power and an end to margin pressure for corporations. The bottom line is known as Gibson's paradox—*in a deflationary environment* stock prices move inversely to bond prices in opposition to the stock-following-bond-price model outlined earlier. *Investors would have to switch from expecting top relative strength in bond prices to accompany top RS stock markets to expecting top RS bond yields to accompany top RS stock markets* (in the model we will define just ahead). Although Gibson's deflationary paradox was a consistent accompaniment to the gold standard, where price stability and deflation were common, it has yet to show its head since the Great Depression. But since Japan is currently in a deflation and facing Gibson's paradox right now, investors need to understand that the rules of bond/stock relationship turn on their head in a deflationary world. Should Asia or the rest of the world follow Japan into deflation, turn your bond charts upside down to look for top opportunities in equities.

IMPLICATIONS FOR U.S. MARKETS

Investors need to understand some of the implications of Japanese policy and of Asian problems on our markets. They also should follow Japanese bonds, the yen, and Japanese economic gauges to determine when the flow of money out of Japan and into U.S. markets might slow down or even reverse. In that event, the effects on U.S. stock and bond markets could be more severe than the typical cutback of liquidity.

A simple approach can help investors use the Austrian Liquidity Cycle information to improve their investing. There are many

Figure 2.8 **U.S. STOCKS SINCE WORLD WAR II (1943)**

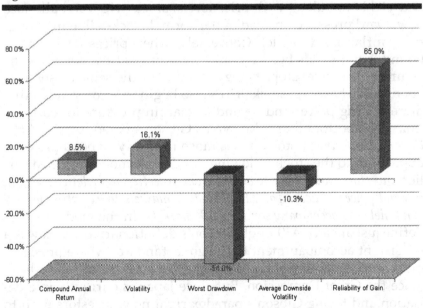

independent ways of using monetary indicators to guide investing in both stocks and bonds. I learned the following simple indicator from a top money manager in Europe; it can be used on
most global equity markets.

We are trying to improve on our base model—buy and hold in
U.S. equities—which produced the long-term performance characteristics shown in Figure 2.8.

We are striving to find factors that can help us improve at
least two of the performance criteria summarized in the chart.
We discussed one small improvement in Chapter 1: simple global
diversification, which improved performance as summarized in
Figure 2.9.

Now we will look at a liquidity indicator that can help us improve the performance of both of the preceding investing methodologies. To compare with the U.S. market, we will only invest in the
S&P if the S&P itself is above its 40-week moving average and
either the bond or T-bill markets are also above their own respective 40-week moving averages. In this way, we can avoid periods

Figure 2.9 **WORLD INDEX SINCE WORLD WAR II**

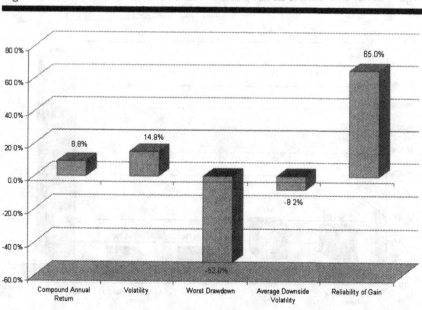

when the liquidity environment, as signaled by the U.S. T-bill and T-bond markets, are negative. And as Figure 2.10 and System Spreadsheet 2.25 show, improvement in investment performance is particularly significant.

Certainly on the U.S. market, our improvement from this simple liquidity tool is substantial: compound annual return rose nearly 2 percent a year while maximum drawdown collapsed to a very acceptable level, and volatility and downside volatility fell slightly.

Now, we will apply the same model concept to foreign markets. We will only invest in markets where either their bond prices are above the 40-week moving average (or bond interest rates are below 40-wk MA) or their short-rate prices are above the 40-week MA (or short rates below 40-wk MA), and their equity index is above its 40-week moving average.

And look at the results! We have been able to boost compound annual returns from 8.5 percent in U.S. equities and 8.8 percent in global stocks to over 12.6 percent while cutting maximum

Figure 2.10 **STOCKS, BONDS, OR T-BILLS OVER 40-WEEK MA**

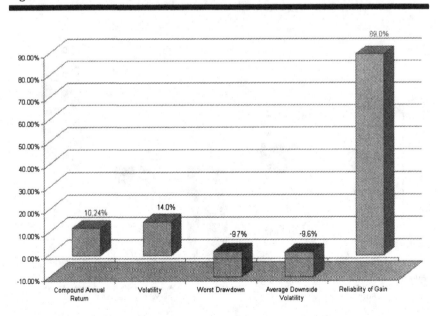

System Spreadsheet 2.25 S&P 500 > 40-WEEK MA AND EITHER T-BILL YIELD < 40-WEEK MA OR T-BOND YIELD < 40-WEEK MA

System Description: Buy S&P 500 when S&P 500 > S&P 500 40-week moving average (MA) and either 3-month T-Bill Yield is < 3-month T-Bill Yield 40-week MA or T-Bond Yield < T-Bond Yield 40-week MA. Exit S&P 500 when the above criteria are not met and hold 3-month T-Bills.

Significance: Using trend and interest rates, one can beat market adverages with substantially less risk.

Data Used: Weekly close of T-Bill Yield, weekly close of Treasury Bond Yield, and weekly close of S&P 500.

From: 1/31/43   To: 12/31/97

Entry Date	Entry Price	Exit Date	Exit Price	Profit/ Loss	Days in Trade	Percent Change	Position	Cumulative Return on $100 Investment S&P and T-Bills	S&P Only
								$ 100.000	$ 100.000
1/7/44	$ 11.87	1/28/44	$ 11.81	($ 0.06)	16	-0.5%	S&P 500	99.495	99.487
1/28/44	0.37	3/10/44	0.37	0.00	31	0.0	T-Bill	99.540	
3/10/44	12.10	3/17/44	12.31	0.21	6	1.7	S&P 500	101.268	103.699
3/17/44	0.38	4/28/44	0.38	0.00	31	0.0	T-Bill	101.315	
4/28/44	11.87	5/12/44	12.00	0.13	11	1.1	S&P 500	102.425	101.088
5/12/44	0.38	7/14/44	0.37	(0.01)	46	0.1	T-Bill	102.496	
7/14/44	13.23	7/21/44	12.78	(0.45)	6	-3.4	S&P 500	99.010	107.659
7/21/44	0.38	8/18/44	0.38	0.00	21	0.0	T-Bill	99.041	
8/18/44	13.04	7/26/46	17.60	4.56	506	35.0	S&P 500	133.675	148.262
7/26/46	0.38	6/13/47	0.38	0.00	231	0.3	T-Bill	134.143	
6/13/47	14.98	6/27/47	15.12	0.14	11	0.9	S&P 500	135.396	127.371
6/27/47	0.38	7/29/49	1.03	0.65	546	0.8	T-Bill	136.516	
7/29/49	15.04	3/10/50	17.09	2.05	161	13.6	S&P 500	155.123	143.966
3/10/50	1.14	2/1/52	1.60	0.46	496	2.3	T-Bill	158.618	
2/1/52	24.30	2/22/52	23.16	(1.14)	16	-4.7	S&P 500	151.176	195.100
2/22/52	1.64	2/29/52	1.51	(0.13)	6	0.0	T-Bill	151.236	
2/29/52	23.26	3/14/52	23.75	0.49	11	2.1	S&P 500	154.422	200.070
3/14/52	1.66	3/28/52	1.60	(0.06)	11	0.1	T-Bill	154.534	
3/28/52	24.18	4/25/52	23.54	(0.64)	21	-2.6	S&P 500	150.444	198.301
4/25/52	1.65	5/2/52	1.62	(0.03)	6	0.0	T-Bill	150.503	
5/2/52	23.56	8/15/52	25.20	1.64	76	7.0	S&P 500	160.979	212.285
8/15/52	1.90	9/26/52	1.63	(0.27)	31	0.2	T-Bill	161.357	
9/26/52	24.73	10/3/52	24.50	(0.23)	6	-0.9	S&P 500	159.857	206.388
10/3/52	1.76	11/6/53	1.31	(0.45)	286	2.0	T-Bill	163.062	
11/6/53	24.61	11/13/53	24.54	(0.07)	6	-0.3	S&P 500	162.599	206.725
11/13/53	1.48	11/27/53	1.49	0.01	11	0.1	T-Bill	162.704	
11/27/53	24.66	10/29/54	31.68	7.02	241	28.5	S&P 500	209.021	266.872
10/29/54	1.01	11/11/55	2.03	1.02	271	1.1	T-Bill	211.301	
11/11/55	45.24	11/18/55	45.54	0.30	6	0.7	S&P 500	212.702	383.629
11/18/55	2.25	1/27/56	2.25	0.00	51	0.5	T-Bill	213.674	
1/27/56	43.35	3/16/56	48.14	4.79	36	11.0	S&P 500	237.284	405.531
3/16/56	2.37	3/30/56	2.17	(0.20)	11	0.1	T-Bill	237.531	
3/30/56	48.48	4/6/56	48.85	0.37	6	0.8	S&P 500	239.344	411.512
4/6/56	2.40	6/15/56	2.58	0.18	51	0.5	T-Bill	240.511	
6/15/56	46.37	8/17/56	48.82	2.45	46	5.3	S&P 500	253.218	411.260
8/17/56	2.60	5/10/57	2.91	0.31	191	2.0	T-Bill	258.228	
5/10/57	46.59	5/24/57	47.21	0.62	11	1.3	S&P 500	261.665	397.697
5/24/57	3.12	7/19/57	3.09	(0.03)	41	0.5	T-Bill	262.998	
7/19/57	48.58	7/26/57	48.45	(0.13)	6	-0.3	S&P 500	262.294	408.143
7/26/57	3.16	4/18/58	1.23	(1.93)	191	2.4	T-Bill	268.602	
4/18/58	42.71	8/22/58	47.73	5.02	91	11.8	S&P 500	300.172	402.078
8/22/58	1.90	10/30/59	4.02	2.12	311	2.4	T-Bill	307.239	
10/30/59	57.52	11/6/59	57.60	0.08	6	0.1	S&P 500	307.666	485.222
11/6/59	4.14	6/10/60	2.72	(1.42)	156	2.6	T-Bill	315.582	

(Continued)

System Spreadsheet 2.25 (Continued)

Entry Date	Entry Price	Exit Date	Exit Price	Profit/ Loss	Days in Trade	Percent Change	Position	Cumulative Return on $100 Investment	
								S&P and T-Bills	S&P Only
6/10/60	57.97	7/15/60	56.05	(1.92)	26	−3.3	S&P 500	305.130	472.165
7/15/60	2.57	8/12/60	2.22	(0.35)	21	0.2	T-Bill	305.786	
8/12/60	56.66	9/9/60	56.11	(0.55)	21	−1.0	S&P 500	302.818	472.671
9/9/60	2.52	11/11/60	2.39	(0.13)	46	0.5	T-Bill	304.217	
11/11/60	55.87	12/2/60	55.39	(0.48)	16	−0.9	S&P 500	301.603	466.605
12/2/60	2.33	12/9/60	2.33	0.00	6	0.1	T-Bill	301.771	
12/9/60	56.65	8/11/61	68.06	11.41	176	20.1	S&P 500	362.551	573.337
8/11/61	2.37	9/1/61	2.32	(0.05)	16	0.2	T-Bill	363.099	
9/1/61	68.19	9/8/61	67.88	(0.31)	6	−0.5	S&P 500	361.448	571.821
9/8/61	2.39	9/15/61	2.33	(0.06)	6	0.1	T-Bill	361.655	
9/15/61	67.65	10/13/61	68.04	0.39	21	0.6	S&P 500	363.740	573.169
10/13/61	2.39	10/27/61	2.33	(0.06)	11	0.1	T-Bill	364.121	
10/27/61	68.34	11/17/61	71.62	3.28	16	4.8	S&P 500	381.597	603.327
11/17/61	2.52	3/30/62	2.72	0.20	96	1.0	T-Bill	385.275	
3/30/62	69.55	4/6/62	68.84	(0.71)	6	−1.0	S&P 500	381.342	579.908
4/6/62	2.76	11/23/62	2.83	0.07	166	1.8	T-Bill	388.302	
11/23/62	61.54	2/15/63	66.41	4.87	61	7.9	S&P 500	419.031	559.438
2/15/63	2.94	2/22/63	2.91	(0.03)	6	0.1	T-Bill	419.325	
2/22/63	65.92	3/1/63	64.10	(1.82)	6	−2.8	S&P 500	407.748	539.978
3/1/63	2.87	4/24/64	3.46	0.59	301	3.4	T-Bill	421.782	
4/24/64	79.75	5/8/64	81.00	1.25	11	1.6	S&P 500	428.393	682.344
5/8/64	3.48	5/22/64	3.48	0.00	11	0.2	T-Bill	429.046	
5/22/64	80.73	9/11/64	83.45	2.72	81	3.4	S&P 500	443.502	702.983
9/11/64	3.51	10/9/64	3.58	0.07	21	0.3	T-Bill	444.804	
10/9/64	85.22	10/16/64	84.83	(0.39)	6	−0.5	S&P 500	442.768	714.608
10/16/64	3.58	11/6/64	3.56	(0.02)	16	0.2	T-Bill	443.779	
11/6/64	85.23	1/8/65	85.37	0.14	46	0.2	S&P 500	444.508	719.157
1/8/65	3.83	1/29/65	3.85	0.02	16	0.2	T-Bill	445.593	
1/29/65	87.56	2/12/65	86.17	(1.39)	11	−1.6	S&P 500	438.519	725.896
2/12/65	3.90	3/26/65	3.92	0.02	31	0.5	T-Bill	440.632	
3/26/65	86.20	4/30/65	89.11	2.91	26	3.4	S&P 500	455.507	750.663
4/30/65	3.92	5/14/65	3.89	(0.03)	11	0.2	T-Bill	456.289	
5/14/65	90.10	6/11/65	85.12	(4.98)	21	−5.5	S&P 500	431.069	717.051
6/11/65	3.78	8/13/65	3.85	0.07	46	0.7	T-Bill	434.056	
8/13/65	86.77	9/3/65	88.06	1.29	16	1.5	S&P 500	440.509	741.817
9/3/65	3.89	1/13/67	4.82	0.93	356	5.5	T-Bill	464.813	
1/13/67	84.53	7/28/67	94.49	9.96	141	11.8	S&P 500	519.581	795.984
7/28/67	4.42	9/8/67	4.32	(0.10)	31	0.5	T-Bill	522.417	
9/8/67	94.36	9/15/67	96.27	1.91	6	2.0	S&P 500	532.992	810.978
9/15/67	4.36	6/21/68	5.58	1.22	201	3.5	T-Bill	551.601	
6/21/68	100.66	10/18/68	104.82	4.16	86	4.1	S&P 500	574.397	883.004
10/18/68	5.35	9/25/70	5.95	0.60	506	10.8	T-Bill	636.347	
9/25/70	83.97	6/25/71	97.99	14.02	196	16.7	S&P 500	742.595	825.468
6/25/71	4.95	7/2/71	5.08	0.13	6	0.1	T-Bill	743.473	
7/2/71	99.78	7/30/71	95.58	(4.20)	21	−4.2	S&P 500	712.179	805.166
7/30/71	5.55	8/27/71	4.75	(0.80)	21	0.5	T-Bill	715.485	
8/27/71	100.48	9/24/71	98.15	(2.33)	21	−2.3	S&P 500	698.894	826.816
9/24/71	4.74	10/1/71	4.68	(0.06)	6	0.1	T-Bill	699.686	
10/1/71	98.93	10/15/71	97.79	(1.14)	11	−1.2	S&P 500	691.623	823.783
10/15/71	4.49	12/17/71	3.94	(0.55)	46	0.8	T-Bill	697.315	
12/17/71	100.26	7/7/72	108.69	8.43	146	8.4	S&P 500	755.946	915.605
7/7/72	4.14	7/21/72	3.95	(0.19)	11	0.2	T-Bill	757.317	
7/21/72	106.66	9/15/72	108.81	2.15	41	2.0	S&P 500	772.583	916.615
9/15/72	4.76	11/10/72	4.67	(0.09)	41	0.8	T-Bill	778.590	

System Spreadsheet 2.25 (Continued)

Entry Date	Entry Price	Exit Date	Exit Price	Profit/ Loss	Days in Trade	Percent Change	Position	Cumulative Return on $100 Investment	
								S&P and T-Bills	S&P Only
11/10/72	113.73	12/29/72	118.05	4.32	36	3.8	S&P 500	808.165	994.453
12/29/72	5.11	10/5/73	7.15	2.04	201	4.1	T-Bill	841.235	
10/5/73	109.85	11/2/73	107.07	(2.78)	21	-2.5	S&P 500	819.946	901.958
11/2/73	7.20	1/31/75	5.61	(1.59)	326	9.4	T-Bill	896.622	
1/31/75	76.98	7/25/75	89.29	12.31	126	16.0	S&P 500	1,040.003	752.179
7/25/75	6.25	10/31/75	5.69	(0.56)	71	1.8	T-Bill	1,058.389	
10/31/75	89.04	12/5/75	86.82	(2.22)	26	-2.5	S&P 500	1,032.001	731.372
12/5/75	5.55	12/19/75	5.49	(0.06)	11	0.2	T-Bill	1,034.511	
12/19/75	88.80	6/4/76	99.15	10.35	121	11.7	S&P 500	1,155.087	835.240
6/4/76	5.58	6/11/76	5.46	(0.12)	6	0.1	T-Bill	1,156.628	
6/11/76	100.92	10/15/76	100.85	(0.07)	91	-0.1	S&P 500	1,155.826	849.560
10/15/76	4.91	10/29/76	4.93	0.02	11	0.2	T-Bill	1,158.313	
10/29/76	102.90	11/5/76	100.82	(2.08)	6	-2.0	S&P 500	1,134.899	849.308
11/5/76	4.86	11/26/76	4.60	(0.26)	16	0.3	T-Bill	1,138.415	
11/26/76	103.15	1/28/77	101.93	(1.22)	46	-1.2	S&P 500	1,124.950	858.658
1/28/77	4.70	9/22/77	7.88	3.18	431	8.1	T-Bill	1,215.740	
9/22/78	101.84	9/29/78	102.54	0.70	6	0.7	S&P 500	1,224.096	863.797
9/29/78	8.11	6/15/79	8.96	0.85	186	6.0	T-Bill	1,297.662	
6/15/79	102.09	7/27/79	103.10	1.01	31	1.0	S&P 500	1,310.500	868.514
7/27/79	9.48	8/3/79	9.15	(0.33)	6	0.2	T-Bill	1,313.470	
8/3/79	104.04	8/10/79	106.40	2.36	6	2.3	S&P 500	1,343.264	896.314
8/10/79	9.32	8/17/79	9.50	0.18	6	0.2	T-Bill	1,346.257	
8/17/79	108.30	8/31/79	109.32	1.02	11	0.9	S&P 500	1,358.936	920.912
8/31/79	9.68	5/16/80	8.60	(1.08)	186	7.2	T-Bill	1,456.415	
5/16/80	107.35	10/3/80	129.33	21.98	101	20.5	S&P 500	1,754.618	1,089.476
10/3/80	11.52	5/7/82	12.68	1.16	416	19.1	T-Bill	2,089.625	
5/7/82	119.47	5/14/82	118.01	(1.46)	6	-1.2	S&P 500	2,064.089	994.116
5/14/82	12.25	8/27/82	7.75	(4.50)	76	3.7	T-Bill	2,140.649	
8/27/82	117.11	6/10/83	162.68	45.57	206	38.9	S&P 500	2,973.621	1,370.416
6/10/83	8.64	11/4/83	8.41	(0.23)	106	3.6	T-Bill	3,082.122	
11/4/83	162.44	11/11/83	166.29	3.85	6	2.4	S&P 500	3,155.171	1,400.827
11/11/83	8.83	1/20/84	8.82	(0.01)	51	1.8	T-Bill	3,211.780	
1/20/84	166.21	1/27/84	163.94	(2.27)	6	-1.4	S&P 500	3,167.915	1,381.031
1/27/84	8.92	9/21/84	10.33	1.41	171	6.1	T-Bill	3,360.428	
9/21/84	165.67	9/20/85	182.05	16.38	261	9.9	S&P 500	3,692.678	1,533.589
9/20/85	7.17	10/11/85	7.14	(0.03)	16	0.5	T-Bill	3,709.556	
10/11/85	184.28	9/12/86	230.67	46.39	241	25.2	S&P 500	4,643.386	1,943.164
9/12/86	5.24	10/10/86	5.20	(0.04)	21	0.4	T-Bill	4,663.743	
10/10/86	235.48	2/13/87	279.70	44.22	91	18.8	S&P 500	5,539.532	2,356.193
2/13/87	5.72	2/27/87	5.40	(0.32)	11	0.3	T-Bill	5,553.418	
2/27/87	284.20	3/20/87	298.17	13.97	16	4.9	S&P 500	5,826.399	2,511.784
3/20/87	5.58	7/17/87	5.55	(0.03)	86	1.9	T-Bill	5,937.793	
7/17/87	314.59	7/31/87	318.66	4.07	11	1.3	S&P 500	6,014.613	2,684.392
7/31/87	6.14	6/24/88	6.51	0.37	236	5.8	T-Bill	6,361.840	
6/24/88	273.78	7/15/88	272.05	(1.73)	16	-0.6	S&P 500	6,321.640	2,291.749
7/15/88	6.72	10/14/88	7.32	0.60	66	1.8	T-Bill	6,433.344	
10/14/88	275.50	11/18/88	266.47	(9.03)	26	-3.3	S&P 500	6,222.480	2,244.743
11/18/88	7.82	12/16/88	7.98	0.16	21	0.7	T-Bill	6,263.191	
12/16/88	276.29	1/13/89	283.87	7.58	21	2.7	S&P 500	6,435.022	2,391.321
1/13/89	8.36	1/20/89	8.30	(0.06)	6	0.2	T-Bill	6,447.882	
1/20/89	286.63	2/24/89	287.13	0.50	26	0.2	S&P 500	6,459.129	2,418.783
2/24/89	8.51	4/14/89	8.71	0.20	36	1.2	T-Bill	6,537.967	
4/14/89	301.36	4/21/89	309.61	8.25	6	2.7	S&P 500	6,716.949	2,608.155
4/21/89	8.57	4/28/89	8.66	0.09	6	0.2	T-Bill	6,730.710	

(Continued)

System Spreadsheet 2.25 *(Continued)*

Entry Date	Entry Price	Exit Date	Exit Price	Profit/ Loss	Days in Trade	Percent Change	Position	Cumulative Return on $100 Investment	
								S&P and T-Bills	S&P Only
4/28/89	309.64	1/26/90	325.80	16.16	196	5.2	S&P 500	7,081.983	2,744.539
1/26/90	7.66	5/18/90	7.67	0.01	81	2.5	T-Bill	7,257.046	
5/18/90	354.64	5/25/90	354.58	(0.06)	6	0.0	S&P 500	7,255.819	2,986.982
5/25/90	7.74	6/8/90	7.69	(0.05)	11	0.3	T-Bill	7,280.431	
6/8/90	358.71	6/15/90	362.91	4.20	6	1.2	S&P 500	7,365.674	3,057.154
6/15/90	7.73	7/20/90	7.62	(0.11)	26	0.8	T-Bill	7,424.653	
7/20/90	361.61	8/3/90	344.86	(16.75)	11	−4.6	S&P 500	7,080.738	2,905.101
8/3/90	7.50	1/25/91	6.14	(1.36)	126	3.8	T-Bill	7,347.324	
1/25/91	336.07	11/22/91	376.14	40.07	216	11.9	S&P 500	8,223.353	3,168.603
11/22/91	4.58	12/13/91	4.21	(0.37)	16	0.3	T-Bill	8,247.361	
12/13/91	384.47	10/2/92	410.47	26.00	211	6.8	S&P 500	8,805.094	3,457.799
10/2/92	2.73	10/23/92	2.94	0.21	16	0.2	T-Bill	8,820.417	
10/23/92	414.10	2/18/94	467.69	53.59	346	12.9	S&P 500	9,961.895	3,939.821
2/18/94	3.28	2/17/95	5.82	2.54	261	3.4	T-Bill	10,301.663	
2/17/95	481.97	6/14/96	665.85	183.88	346	38.2	S&P 500	14,231.928	5,609.120
6/14/96	5.16	6/21/96	5.08	(0.08)	6	0.1	T-Bill	14,249.483	
6/21/96	666.84	6/28/96	670.63	3.79	6	0.6	S&P 500	14,330.470	5,649.387
6/28/96	5.10	8/16/96	5.04	(0.06)	36	0.7	T-Bill	14,435.294	
8/16/96	665.21	8/23/96	667.03	1.82	6	0.3	S&P 500	14,474.788	5,619.061
8/23/96	5.06	10/4/96	5.01	(0.05)	31	0.6	T-Bill	14,565.247	
10/4/96	701.46	3/7/97	804.97	103.51	111	14.8	S&P 500	16,714.548	6,781.067
3/7/97	5.10	5/30/97	5.03	(0.07)	61	1.2	T-Bill	16,921.715	
5/30/97	848.28	12/31/97	970.43	122.15	154	14.4	S&P 500	19,358.396	8,174.902
			Percentage of Years Profitable					89%	69%
			Maximum Drawdown					9.70%	54%
			Compound Annual Return					10.24%	8.50%

drawdown from 52 percent to 13.2 percent, with slight benefits to volatility and downside volatility to boot. Our simple liquidity tool is worth the attention of global investors.

SUMMARY

In this important chapter, we have raised many issues involved in using the Austrian Liquidity Cycle. We discussed the following key points:

- If you can align your investment strategy with the overall economic and liquidity environment, you can maximize

Figure 2.11 GLOBAL STOCKS, BONDS, OR T-BILLS OVER 40-WEEK MA

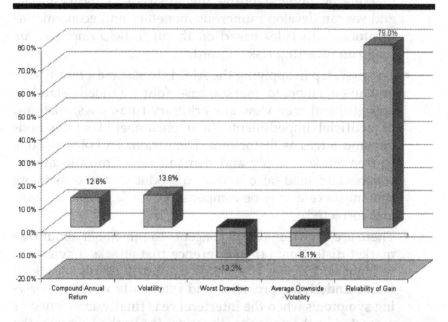

your investments and profit from virtually any investment environment.

- Search for two things—fuel (or the forces that propel prices in one direction or another) and examples of investment success. When you find an example of investment success, dissect it, determine what makes it tick, mimic its essential components, and add those components to your investment strategy arsenal. When you find an example of fuel, test it to make sure it is an independent variable that can improve your investing risk/reward, understand what makes it work, and develop an indicator and rule of thumb that will improve your long-run results. Then be sure to monitor and continue to analyze your fuel concept so that if it changes in some way you will not be fooled by an out-of-date or inappropriate rule. Understanding is much more important to long-run success than the indicator and rule you utilize.

- The Austrian Liquidity Cycle (ALC) is an excellent example of fuel. We can gain enormous insight into what moves markets by understanding the Austrian Liquidity Cycle, and we can develop numerous monetary and economic indicators (with rules based on them) to help improve our long-run investing risk/reward.

- The first step in applying the ALC is to assume a totally free and unencumbered market base (our stranded islanders analogy) and then view any arbitrary rules, laws, customs, or artificial impediments to unencumbered supply-and-demand forces as distortions. Distortions and obstructions to free market supply and demand forces misallocate resources and send false signals to producers and consumers that must eventually be compensated for (e.g., rent-control) and corrected.

- There are three important concepts to remember about free market distortion: (a) Interference that attacks a symptom without addressing the forces behind it usually leads to worse underlying problems and eventually worse underlying symptoms when the interference is finally abandoned or corrected in the opposite direction. (b) In the long run, the cost of artificial interference often grows to a breaking point whereupon free market forces usually prevail even though interference can be maintained for decades. (c) The indirect effect of an artificial interference on incentives is usually much more important than its direct results because in the long run the forces of dynamic change in an economy are more powerful than existing resources.

- Using government force to create a monopolistic body to print legal tender without any backing is both a distortion and a manipulation of an economy and of the value of the currency utilized by all participants in that economy.

- Austrian inflation is an increase in the sum of the price of absolutely everything in an economy—it can only take place when the money supply is expanded so that from an Austrian perspective inflation is purely a monetary phenomenon. Using the price of a small fraction of goods in an economy as an index of inflation (whether coconuts or consumer goods) is therefore an inaccurate measure of inflation and the havoc it wreaks on an economy. There is always a delayed reaction from the actual inflation to the CPI measure. While the actual utility of a CPI is questionable from an inflation measuring standpoint, the perception of its importance wields huge influence on the behavior of individuals in the current economic environment so that being able to anticipate the movement of price of the small basket of goods in the CPI is important for investors.

- For stock prices to rise, money must flow into the market from either increased savings, portfolio shifts, or new money creation. In the fractional reserve central banking system used by much of the world, the liquidity from the central bank far outpaces the liquidity from shifts in savings and portfolios. Therefore monitoring the flow of new money supply from the central bank becomes paramount for successful investing.

- Increasing the supply of money creates artificial demand that gives false signals to market participants. This leads to overconsumption first and overproduction second, creating a boom-bust cycle of expansion and recession. In addition, fractional reserve banking usually generates incentives to borrow; and when enough of the economy is addicted to borrowing, the boom-bust cycle crosses almost the entire economy at the same time with the increase and decrease in the cost of money (interest rates).

- The Liquidity Cycle charts the concurrent movement of markets and economic gauges during each phase of the boom-bust cycle created by central bank fractional reserve banking system money creation. It can tell you what to watch for to confirm the next phase of market movement, and when it is highly likely that markets will move in a particular direction.

- Due to the effect of the Liquidity Cycle, the movement of short-term and long-term interest rates (bonds and bills) often has a leading effect on the movement of equities (except in a deflationary environment). New money generated moves from banks to bonds to stocks to corporations and individuals to the real economy in that order. Stocks and bonds often lead macroeconomic statistics for this reason.

- New money supply creation often fuels speculation in "hot-spot" areas where investors are given an incentive to place their capital. During inflationary waves, real estate and real assets are often the primary hot-spot beneficiaries; whereas during disinflation periods, equities and financial assets are the main beneficiaries. In the case of an outright deflation, bonds are the primary beneficiaries, and stocks tend to follow bond yields instead of bond prices.

- On average, around 97 percent of all equities decline during a pronounced tightening phase when an inverted yield curve is required. Conversely during a steep yield curve, more than 90 percent of all equities rise. The leading nature of interest rates versus equities is fairly consistent throughout the globe so that using an indicator to filter out poor interest rate environments can help investors increase their return while concurrently reducing risk in U.S. and global equity investment.

- The better investors understand the Austrian Liquidity Cycle and the gauges that confirm its position, the more successful they are likely to become.

Index Valuation Gauges— Do Not Ignore the Price You Pay

In Chapter 2, we learned about one of the most important single variables for investing in any asset class—the Austrian Liquidity Cycle—and we learned some simple ways of using the concepts involved in the ALC to improve our equity investing.

The focus in this chapter and several of the chapters ahead will be on learning about other independent variables that can help investors improve their investing performance in equities, bonds, and other asset classes. We will also be developing relatively simple rules of thumb for investors to follow to benefit from each variable. These independent variables can be used in combination for viewing the overall investment environment of stocks, bonds, and other asset classes from which we will build our portfolios. The more accurately we can assess this environment, the more successful our investing is likely to become.

USING INDEX VALUATION GAUGES

In this chapter, we discuss a variable that we refer to as *index valuation*. Valuation has to do with the relationship between what an investment or investment market is realistically worth in relation to the price that it is actually selling for at the current time. Value is a critical variable to understand—many of the most successful investors of our time, including John Templeton and Warren Buffett, use valuation as a primary tool for choosing investments. In Chapter 7, we also describe excellent ways to use individual company valuation gauges to help find good stock investments.

However, another way top investors use valuation gauges is to look at how a whole market is valued, in order to estimate how much potential and how much risk exists in that market. The reason for this is simple. During environments when a market as a whole is being revalued from overvalued to lower-valued somewhere between 75 percent and 99 percent of all individual equities decline. It will do you little good to find a dynamic growth company selling for far less than its intrinsic value if the whole market is being marked down in price. The tidal wave of the whole market environment generally will far overwhelm any individual equity criterion in this situation.

Conversely, when a market as a whole is being revalued from undervalued to overvalued somewhere between 70 percent and 90 percent of all equities rise in value. Short-sellers should beware of this environment. Naturally in this situation, one is paid especially big excess returns for carefully choosing the right kind of stocks.

To see why this is so, we will compare the stock markets of two countries and determine which is a better investment from a risk/reward perspective. Suppose that in these two countries bond rates and short rates are dropping (bond and bill markets are rising) and equity markets are also rising. The average P/E (price/earnings ratio), P/B (price/book value), and P/C (price/cash) (these are three valuation gauges) on one country's index are all very near their highest ever (this could be Hong Kong's Hang Seng Index trading at a 20 P/E in an economy expected to generate 10% average earnings growth, a 3.2 P/B, and a P/C of 16), while the U.S. market is trading below its average P/E, P/B, P/C, and at a P/E (let's say 12) that is less than expected average earnings growth (let's say 18%). If you were going to be investing broadly across one of these two markets, which one would be a better investment, all else being equal?

As discussed in Chapter 1, over the long run there are three main sources of appreciation in any major market index:

(1) dividends (in most developed markets these actually make up 20%–30% of long-term gains); (2) growth in the economic earnings capacity of the underlying equities (earnings growth); and (3) multiple expansion (the change in the P/E).

Therefore if your P/E is already near historic highs, is far above expected earnings growth rates, and is way above long-term average P/Es, you are unlikely to get any gain in price from a further multiple expansion (an increase in the P/E), and you may even face multiple contraction (a decline in the P/E) soon. The historical implications for the S&P Index if the P/E is 22 (which it approached in late summer 1997) are illustrated in Figure 3.1, showing the S&P 400's P/E history since the 1950s.

In theory, the price of a firm is equal to the present discounted value of the future stream of earnings that an investor hopes to gain from owning a share. The P/E of a stock or index defines how much investors are discounting future earnings growth and how much growth they are anticipating.

Figure 3.1 **S&P 400 PRICE/EARNINGS MODEL**

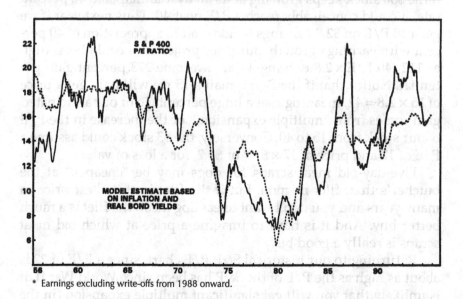

* Earnings excluding write-offs from 1988 onward.

Source: Reprinted by permission of the *Bank Credit Analyst.*

Many investors confuse the concept of price with price/earnings (P/E). Actually P/E is a sort of normalized price, and is a better gauge of what you are really paying than just price. A typical example of confusion is when investors assume that low-priced stocks (under $5 a share) are "cheap." For example, compare a stock priced at $3 a share, where earnings are $.06 a share and analysts' mean estimate for the next year's earnings are $.07 a share, versus a stock priced at $30 a share, where earnings are $2 a share and analysts' mean estimate for next year's earnings are $2.8 per share. On a pure price basis $3 seems cheaper than $30, and many investors make the mistake of assuming that the $3 stock has more upside potential. However, you must look at what you are paying for in relation to its price to understand whether a stock has value or real upside potential from its current price.

Thus when normalized for earnings, the $30 stock is priced at a P/E of 15, while it has an expected earnings growth rate of 40 percent, whereas the $3 stock is priced at a P/E of 50, with an expected earnings growth rate of 17 percent. A good rule of thumb is that a high growth stock or index (with earnings gains of over 25% annually) is near the upper end of its realistic valuation range when its P/E is equal to its expected 3-year earnings growth rate. If the $30 stock keeps growing at its analyst-anticipated 40 percent rate, it could conceivably reach a P/E near 40. Thus next year if we get a 40 P/E on $2.8 earnings in addition to appreciation of 40 percent with earnings growth, our price projections could be as high as 112 (40 P/E × 2.8 earnings)—an awesome 273 percent gain potential. Notice that if the P/E remains 15 we will only get a price of 15 × 2.8 = 42, meaning that a huge percentage of our anticipated gain comes from "multiple expansion," or the increase in the P/E of our stock from 15 to 40. Conversely, the $3 stock could assume a P/E of 17 and price of 17 × $.07 or $1.2, for a loss of value.

Five-day-old meat scraps for dogs may be "cheaper" at the butcher's than filet mignon. But if the filet is at its best price in many years and you don't want to eat dog meat, the filet is a much better buy. And it is hard to imagine a price at which old meat scraps is really a good buy.

Returning to our historical S&P P/E chart, since a P/E of 22 is about as high as the P/E of the S&P has been since World War II, it is unlikely that you will get significant multiple expansion (in the market as a whole) from an investment at these levels. Moreover, virtually every time the P/E reached this extreme, there was a decline in the P/E, which either reduced the value of the S&P, or at least reduced the appreciation of the S&P subsequently (as earnings gains outpaced multiple contraction rate). And, as we explained earlier, the decline in the S&P's P/E from over 20 to under 8 from 1968 to 1982 represented a greater than 50 percent decline in nominal value and a greater than 70 percent decline in the real (after-inflation) value of the S&P. Since most of the other significant declines in the S&P's P/E also represented losses in value of 20 percent or more, a high valuation level as indicated by a historically high P/E level, adds a good deal of risk to any equity investment in addition to detracting from appreciation potential.

From an investment standpoint, this means reward declines and risks rise. Conversely, if an index's P/E is below the long-term average P/E, and is below the expected earnings growth rate, it is much more likely that in addition to getting appreciation due to dividends and earnings growth, you will also get some multiple expansion—the P/E will rise creating further appreciation in the price. Simply for buying at a relatively low price, you are rewarded with much better appreciation potential and less risk. The bottom line is that overvalued markets are riskier and have far less potential upside than markets that are fairly valued or undervalued.

LIMITATIONS OF INDEX VALUATION ANALYSIS

It is important that investors realize the limitations of index valuation analysis and use many valuation tools (e.g., P/Es, P/Bs, P/Cs, price/underlying growth rate, stock/bond yield, earnings/yield comparisons) to gauge overall valuation levels. The reason is that each valuation gauge has periods where it is out-of-phase.

For example, one cannot simply use P/Es to gauge valuation. At the bottom of a recession or depression, when interest rates are dropping sharply, investors begin to take some of the liquidity being pumped into the bond market and invest it in equities, anticipating higher earnings due to lower interest costs. Thus they are valuing equities on future anticipated earnings, not current earnings. For this reason, trailing earnings P/Es explode at market bottoms during recession troughs. The highest P/E of this century in the S&P (this is an anachronism) occurred in 1932 just after the July bottom that marked the best single buying point this century, and the market bottom following the Great Depression.

By using an index made up of several valuation gauges, investors can get a very good idea of what historical relative valuations a particular country's market is selling at as well as whether realistic growth rates are anticipated or not and whether investors are unduly euphoric or depressed.

However, valuation gauges such as P/Es, P/Bs, P/Cs, price/ underlying growth rate, stock/bond yield, and earnings/yield comparisons are not good timing tools and should not be used as such. Valuation gauges can tell an investor whether a market is risky or not, and whether there is high or low upside potential, but they do not tell an investor exactly when to act. Thus an investor needs confirmation from technical tools about when to act on valuation gauges reading over- or undervalued before acting on them.

Valuation gauges are simply ways of measuring what price investors are willing to pay for a stream of earnings or a set underlying intrinsic value. Figure 3.1 shows that there are secular trends in valuations—periods when chronic overvaluation is present for many years, and periods when chronic undervaluation is present for many years. These trends occur because valuation gauges in part measure investor confidence. When stocks have gained ground for a long period and investors feel confident that future gains will match those of the recent past, they are willing to pay high prices for stocks in relation to earnings, and it takes quite a lot to derail this feeling of confidence. Conversely, after years of negative returns, it is difficult for investors to become interested in equity investments at all (as in 1974–1982; and 1931 until the end of World War II).

USING GAUGES FOR MUTUAL FUNDS

Today, mutual funds are considered a primary savings vehicle for most investors. That was true in the 1920s and 1960s as well, and valuations were at similar high extremes. Few investors remember that "mutual funds" in the U.S. used to have the same name they still do in the rest of the English-speaking world, *unit investment trusts* (similar to open-ended mutual funds), and *investment trusts* (similar to today's closed-end funds). From 1929 to 1932 over 90 percent of all investment trusts and unit investment trusts went belly-up, losing investors virtually all of their money. Following World War II, brokerage firms needed to market these vehicles to the public under a new name—mutual funds—to avoid the stigma associated with "investment trust," which no sane investor wanted to touch after the scars of the Depression. Similarly, following the 1972–1974 bear market, it took until the early 1990s before most of the public would touch mutual funds again.

During these periods when investors are chasing greed or feeling scars of fear, valuations stay in ranges of extreme overvaluation or extreme undervaluation. These valuation levels can therefore reveal much about long-term potential risk or reward—but tell little about whether the risk or reward of over- or undervaluation will be realized any time soon.

VALUATION GAUGES FOR INTERNATIONAL MARKETS

Nonetheless, valuation gauges can be used across international markets and are useful to investors in terms of evaluating potential risk and rewards. Figure 3.2 depicts a few valuation gauges in the Hong Kong Hang Seng Index. These charts show that when a broad range of valuation gauges reach near historical extremes concurrently, market risks rise and new investments are probably not warranted. Similarly when a broad range of valuation gauges reach historically relatively low levels, any catalyst or reason to buy is likely to be far more fruitfully rewarded.

Thus an index that utilizes a broad range of valuation gauges for each international market can help investors assess potential gains and risks in the various markets. Figure 3.3 provides an example of our own combination of valuation gauges put into a single index on the Swiss market index. As apparent from the arrows, the overvalued, undervalued levels are helpful assistants, though not the proper lone components of a timing methodology.

We could probably devote an entire book to explaining how to develop a single valuation index for each country's equity market, but much more important than the actual components of an index is simply that investors use one to help them assess risks and

Figure 3.2 **HANG SENG INDEX AND VALUATION TOOLS**

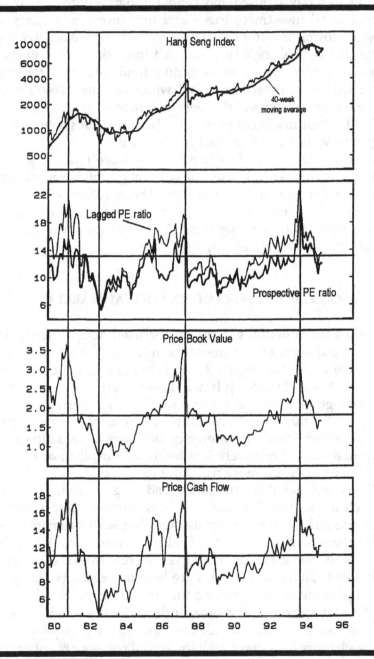

Source: Reprinted by permission of the *Bank Credit Analyst.*

Figure 3.3 **SWISS BANK INDUSTRIALS**

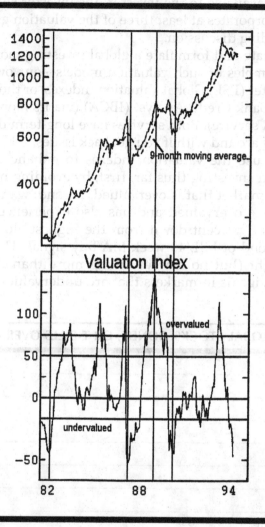

rewards in international markets. Many global valuation index services are available to the investor; the investor should choose one that incorporates at least three of the valuation gauges listed in the preceding discussion.

To illustrate and formulate a global investing model, we will use two examples of such valuation models—our own Portfolio Strategy Letter (PSL) Global Valuation Indexes, or those of the International Bank Credit Analyst (IBCA) (via its monthly service and its EMA service). Both services have long-term data you can test and play around with if you get back issues.

We will use the valuation indexes to enhance the performance of our investing thus far, first, by avoiding new buy signals on any market that is overvalued. Second, we will exit any market that is overvalued and has also experienced a weekly close that is 5 percent down from the highest close since our stock-and-bond-or-bill/40-week MA buy signal. Third, we will double-weight (but no market taking more than 20% of total funds) buy signals in markets that are undervalued when they

---

Figure 3.4 **GLOBAL STOCKS, BONDS, OR T-BILLS OVER 40-WEEK MA**

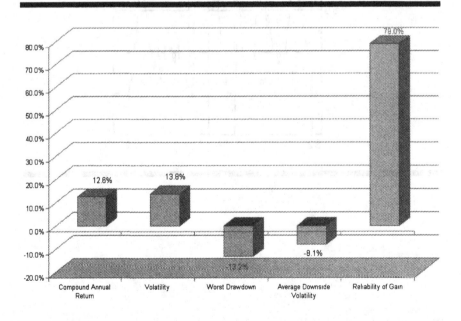

give new stock-and-bond-or-bill/40-week MA buy signals (40 weeks and 200 days are equivalent MAs).

If we add these rules to our Austrian Liquidity Cycle rules for global investing, we get the progression of performance shown in Figures 3.4 through 3.6. As can be seen, which valuation index you use is less important than that investors incorporate valuation tools into their methodology for seeking global investment gains. While compound annual returns are either improved slightly or hardly changed, valuation indexes have a significant impact on drawdowns and volatility (risk reduction). Investors should note that we are achieving gains roughly equivalent to that of the U.S. market since its record run from 1987 to 1997—and we are doing so on average since 1943. In addition, we are accomplishing these outstanding gains with much higher reliability, and much lower drawdowns than the U.S. market exhibited even in that record-breaking bull market period (1987–1997).

Figure 3.5 **GLOBAL STOCKS, BONDS, OR T-BILLS OVER 40-WEEK MA PLUS PORTFOLIO-STRATEGY LETTER VALUATION GAUGES**

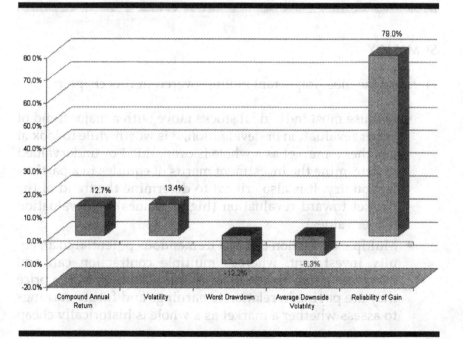

Figure 3.6 **GLOBAL STOCKS, BONDS, OR T-BILLS OVER 40-WEEK MA PLUS BANK CREDIT ANALYST VALUATION GAUGES**

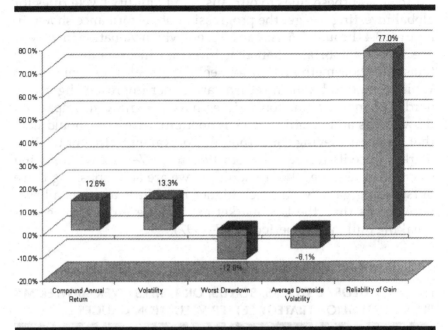

SUMMARY

Here are the most important points covered in this chapter:

- Because most individual stocks move with a major trend of either revaluation or devaluation, it is worthwhile to look at whether a market as a whole is overvalued or undervalued to determine the investment merits of equities in a particular country. It is also critical to determine the trend of the market toward revaluation (higher values) or devaluation (lower values).

- Multiple expansion can add tremendous potential to an equity investment, whereas multiple contraction can add enormous risks. Investors must look carefully at the price they are paying in relation to earnings and future earnings to assess whether a market as a whole is historically cheap or expensive and determine whether that market offers higher than average potential upside or higher than average risk. This analysis of value is intrinsic to a careful analysis of the risk/reward of any stock investment.

- A low-priced stock or index is not necessarily cheap—it is how that market or stock is priced in relation to its earnings and future earnings growth that determines whether it is inexpensive or expensive.

- A combination of valuation tools works better than just one in helping to identify overdone markets on either the upside or downside.

- Markets can stay chronically overvalued or undervalued for many years, so that valuation indexes are not good timing tools in and of themselves. However, these indexes can tell us if potential reward is high or if potential risk is high.

- Most secular bull markets were born in a period of chronic undervaluation reflecting retail investors' fear of past poor returns, while most secular bear markets were born in a period of chronic overvaluation reflecting retail investors' greed in expecting continuation of recent past excellent returns.

- An index that utilizes a broad range of valuation gauges for each international market can help investors to assess potential gains and risks in the markets. The chief benefit to using valuation tools are in risk reduction and market selection.

Macro Technical Tools—
Making Sure the
Tide Is Moving in the
Right Direction

Macro technical models follow the trend, momentum, and relative strength of a particular market. Such models are based on such factors as price action, breadth, momentum, sentiment, pattern recognition, trend-following tools, Elliott wave, volatility, volume and open interest, accumulation and distribution measures, breakout levels, volatility bands, resistence and support levels, price and time turning point analysis, retracement and extension ratios, chaos and Kalman Filtering applications, and many other techniques. There are an incredible number of technical tools and concepts with widely varying usefulness. Unfortunately, many are not even profitable. Perhaps even more frustrating, there are hundreds of books on different technical indicators, but startlingly few of those books are based on completed research that informs investors definitively how to use that indicator to make money in the markets. Even fewer still provide any kind of useful track record of the methodology and indicator usage for comparison purposes.

THE ARGUMENT FOR TECHNICAL ANALYSIS

Nevertheless, I believe that most truly robust trading strategies should have some application of technical analysis incorporated into them. Technical analysis is simply the study of price action, and you cannot have profits without prices moving in your favor. Generally, it is better to have the market tip its hat in some way that proves the scenario you have anticipated before you commit big money to such a scenario. Technical analysis is therefore a last check system that the market is realizing what you have anticipated. It is a final verification tool that the fuel you have found behind an investment is actually beginning to have effect. Other variables such as the Austrian Liquidity Cycle and valuation may help you locate great potential, but technicals can tell you when the market is beginning to perceive and reward that potential. Think of other fuel as the setting of your sights on the target investment; technicals are the final signal telling you when to pull the trigger.

Imagine being a member of a deer hunting team. You have located a large number of deer drinking in a narrow valley with only one exit. You are positioned and rest your sights on the area of the path where the deer must come through, while your teammates are making their way to the opposite side of the deer, intending to shoot and scare them right into your area. You hear the gunshots of your associates, and begin to hear running noises. Do you just begin shooting, sure that your plan will eventually put deer in your path or do you wait until you actually get a deer in your sights before pulling the trigger? Naturally, you'll want to wait until you have your target in your sights before shooting.

And to trade with both low-risk and decent reliabilities, you'll also want to begin to see what you are looking for the market to do—establish a strong trend in the direction you are anticipating—before actually pulling the trigger on committing precious capital to that trade.

Here's a quick story of a hedge fund manager/investor associate of mine and how not taking such precautions led him into trouble. This investor/money manager correctly perceived back in 1983 that the Japanese market would begin a sustained period of outperformance versus both the U.S. market and global market indices, and he invested over 70 percent of his total capital behind this idea by buying selected blue-chip and smaller-cap Japanese stocks. At this time, the Nikkei Index (an index of Japanese stocks similar to the S&P 500) was just approaching the 10,000 level. Over the next six years, the investor's vision came to fruition nicely as the Nikkei moved up almost 300 percent from 1983 levels (to around 38,000), and my associate's Japanese equity investments more than quadrupled. This investor had done an excellent job of finding a situation loaded with Austrian Liquidity Cycle (ALC) fuel—and had done some good stock-picking to outperform the soaring Nikkei during the bull run.

Now this investor realized that the Japanese market had gotten out-of-kilter valuation-wise, and he did take some profits in many equities; but because he also felt that on any serious setback the Japanese would lower rates and send the market back to new high levels, he kept the bulk of his Japanese investments intact. The Japanese equity/property bubble begin to crack in 1989 and by late 1990 the Nikkei had fallen back to the 20,000 level and was bouncing between 20,000 and 26,000. During the similar 1983 to 1990 period, the S&P 500 roughly doubled in price, while our investor was still up over 150 percent so that he had outperformed U.S. markets quite handily on a total return basis despite this enormous setback.

Sure enough, just as our investor had anticipated, in 1990 with the market down substantially, the Japanese central bank lowered interest rates rather aggressively. In addition, industrial production was down, Leading economic indicators were dropping to previous market-bottom levels, the current account and merchandise trade surpluses were down sharply, net exports were down heavily, price and wage inflation had dropped abruptly, and capacity utilization rates were down to levels reached in prior economic troughs. Even stock valuations had dropped to more "normal" levels for Japan (normal levels for Japanese stocks were out of the stratosphere for any other market on earth), while sentiment was wildly negative (another positive). In other words, from a liquidity and macroeconomic perspective, it appeared that the Japanese market might be at a buying point.

I had a lunch meeting with this associate at this time, and he was extremely excited about the prospect of a resumption of the wild bull market in Tokyo in late 1990. We had been discussing the markets periodically for many years, and he knew that we both looked at similar gauges of liquidity and that my models had overweighted Japan from 1982 to 1986, but that my valuation gauges had prevented me from investing in Japan thereafter. He was curious to know if I was jumping in aggressively again as well. I told him that although I was also intrigued by what appeared to be a possible Liquidity Cycle trough, our valuation gauges still were a little troublesome, I was concerned about a historic speculative bubble being popped, and that regardless I definitely couldn't reallocate to Japan until our technical models gave the "okay." He was intrigued by this idea and we discussed at length exactly what type of price action was needed to reconfirm the Japanese bull market technically. Interestingly enough, we agreed on many of the different technical criteria that would be necessary.

While he agreed that good breadth, stronger momentum, taking out some resistence levels, and strong global relative strength rankings would definitely prove a resumption in the Japanese bull market, he also felt that one would be missing a lot of the move if one waited for such occurrences. My reply was the same as the famous Baron von Rothschild's: "You can have the first 30 percent and last 30 percent of any move, just give me that safe 40 percent in the middle." This philosophy is in fact the essence of our approach: we wait for trends to establish and for safe and reliable moves to reveal themselves before risking capital. My associate's answer to this idea was that my models had been overly cautious from 1987 to 1990 (which was true from the perspective of trying to catch every last drop of a move) and that they were missing some good opportunities now. He ended the lunch meeting by declaring that he had leveraged his 60 percent position in Japan to the hilt—and was now over 100 percent invested in Japanese equities at what he perceived to be a cyclical bottom.

The Japanese market underwent a technically pathetic rally to around the 27,000 level in 1991 before collapsing to new lows, reaching under 15,000 by 1992. Significantly, Japanese equities never flashed any of the technical indications of bullishness we had discussed at lunch. By this point, my friend was feeling pain. He had achieved a negative return in 1991 and half of 1992 during a period in which the U.S. and global markets had moved up dramatically. He was now underperforming U.S. and global markets since 1983, and he was losing clients quickly. A 400 percent gain in six years had evaporated into a 50 percent gain in nearly a decade. What started out as a rather brilliant insight into a market destined to outperform on a long-term basis had turned into a career-threatening blunder. His assets under management fell from over $100 million in 1989 to under $10 million by late 1992, and neither his performance nor his assets under management recovered until he finally threw in the towel on Japan in late 1993 and began to reglobalize his portfolio.

Now certainly this associate made a number of mistakes over the course of time. He leveraged and plunged into a single market (as so many investors are doing in the United States currently). But if this investor had simply waited for the technical strength of the market to prove what he was anticipating and had respected the weakness of a decline of over 45 percent between 1989 and 1990 with some sort of technical trailing-stop risk reduction method, he would have been okay despite his dogmatic belief in the Japanese markets.

TAKING A WIDER VIEW

Many times, investors make the mistake of becoming enamored with a particular market and focus in on it too heavily. "How have the funds you consult for done versus the S&P this year?" is a question I hear often that is a tip-off toward this overly biased perspective. How a strategy does that is closely correlated with a U.S. index compared with the S&P is certainly a valid question. But that is not really what we are trying to do with our strategy at all. As discussed earlier, the long-term risk posture of the S&P is far too high-risk for most investors. What we are trying to do with the strategy we are building is allow investors to capture some of the tremendous gains in U.S. and global equities during favorable times, while avoiding (and investing in other favorable asset classes during) negative periods that can be so devastating to capital. If you really cannot tolerate losing 50 percent in a two-year period or 70 percent after inflation in a 17-year period, then how the S&P does in a particular year is irrelevant, because a 100 percent investment in the S&P is too risky for your portfolio:

If losing 50 percent in two years or 70 percent after inflation in 17 years is too risky for your portfolio, then the real question is how to capture acceptable levels of average annual profit while cutting that risk level to an acceptable level on a long-term basis.

To accomplish that feat, the investor may have to look at many different types of investments that may be uncorrelated to the S&P or even the world index. Investing in a diversified portfolio of these assets will definitely create a performance chart that is dissimilar to the S&P. But so what? What is important is to achieve decent long-run returns similar to (or higher than) the S&P's, while keeping risk to tolerable levels long-term.

Investors will find that the approaches we are advocating and building in this book have produced and are likely to continue producing average annual gains even higher than the S&P's over the long run with significantly less risk and less volatility. In addition, these strategies produce significantly less variability in annual returns than the S&P and world index. Thus while the S&P can be up more than 30 percent in several years, it can also be down over 30 percent in a year.

An uncorrelated strategy with smoother performance will likely achieve 15 percent to 18 percent or more on average, but may have a good, average, or bad year at the same time the S&P is having a great year, for example. A better question than how a strategy has performed in a given year versus the S&P is how that strategy's returns and risks have compared with the S&P over a prolonged period. If, over the next decade, the S&P returns an average gain of 12 percent per year with two years up over 30 percent, one year down over 20 percent, one year down 7 percent, one year down 3 percent, two years up around 5 percent, and three years up over 20 percent, and a maximum drawdown of 30 percent (percentages based on a fairly typical decade), and you, by following the strategy in this book, are up an average of 17 percent with a 14 percent maximum drawdown, will you be disappointed and concerned because you underperformed the S&P in three or four of its five strong years?

For many investors, it is difficult to pull away emotionally from aligning their performance with a single domestic equity index. But to cut risk and improve return, this difficult separation must take place. Technical tools are a key component helping investors to choose profitable and reliable trends as well as avoid larger risks.

Technical tools like trend models, relative strength, runaway market characteristics, and trailing stops can also allow an investor to impartially view a wide array of global markets and asset classes, giving one a much better ability to "read" what the markets are saying and invest in areas where the market is showing top gains that are likely to continue.

While many analysts feel that fuel concepts like the ALC and valuation gauges provide an adequate method of anticipating bull market moves, the goal of profitable low-risk investing is simply to locate and invest in top trends, not to catch bottoms or tops in any one market. With many markets to choose from, you can simply shift from reliable trend to reliable trend without needing to catch even the majority of any move—as long as you are invested in trends that are reliably developing when you are in them. To catch part of a trend means having the discipline to wait for the markets to confirm the move you are anticipating before you invest significant amounts of capital and risk in them. Wait for trends to develop clearly before jumping on board. You will make up for missed opportunity in enhanced reliability and reduced drawdowns. And it is the return in relation to the risk assumed that we try to optimize as risk-averse investors.

USING TECHNICAL ANALYSIS TO CONFIRM TRENDS

A big part of what technical analysis lets you do is to make sure that the market is confirming your analysis. If there is fuel and a catalyst for a market to be revalued and reliquefied, technical tools can help you wait until the market is beginning to appreciate the same: that is when you get the biggest price moves. A strong trend can last many years so it does not pay big dividends to hunt for potential winners that are yet unrecognized by market forces. Hunt instead for big winners in reality that have the potential to remain big winners in the period ahead.

An incredibly large percentage of value-oriented and fundamentally oriented investors place technical analysis in the same category as voodoo and tea leaves. Many of these investors come from an investment banking background, where they are taught to look for good companies to buy or sell with the stock being a quick access to ownership in those companies. Looking at a company's fundamentals and real value as an entity is very different from monitoring how its price is jiggling up and down; and since these jiggles have little impact on the type of company analysis that investment bankers do, investors with this training often dismiss the usefulness of technical analysis. Probably adding to the distrust of technicals is the classic Graham and Dodd type of disdain and distrust for "Mr. Market" who will pay far more than a company is worth one day, and far less than it is worth for a company the next. And indeed there is much truth to the whimsical nature of market psychology. Since market psychology is a large part of what determines the price of an asset, however, we need to use tools that take advantage of market psychology in a rational manner via proven technical methods.

In fact, technical analysis is simply a method of letting the market confirm that the catalyst toward revaluing a company or market is starting to be realized by the markets—which is precisely what you are waiting for as a value-oriented or fundamental investor. Why invest in something that is undervalued if the market is not appreciating that undervaluation? After all, if Mr. Market is not beginning to recognize that a company is worth more than its current price, you might have to wait a long time for such a realization. Instead of tying up your money in an asset that is not appreciating, you will do better to wait until the market begins to understand the undervaluation and correct it.

What is astounding is that to this day most economic and business schools teach that technical analysis is not robust. This is particularly amazing because a thorough study of history shows some technical tools to be among the most robust of any independent variables. An analysis I performed with Stanford Ph.D. Tom Johnson covering the early 1900s to the mid 1980s showed that the single most reliable independent variable for determining the strength of individual equities over the following six-month period was relative strength. Recently released research by O'Shaughnessy (in his book *What Works on Wall Street*) shows similar results for the next year's performance. Relative strength seems to outperform such significant independent variables as price/sales ratios, P/Es, recent earnings growth, P/E growth rate, and all the other classic valuation and fundamental criteria we could test. Relative strength basically tells you how strong a particular instrument is in relation to others over a defined period of time. In equity markets, the strong often get stronger, while the weak often get weaker.

Technical analysis tools are certainly not voodoo and tea leaves; they are in fact the basis of some of the most rigorous and robust single variables for determining top investments.

Some of the people who claim not to use technical analysis must define it differently than I do. The legendary George Soros claims not to use technical analysis. Yet Soros also favors starting with a small position and building a larger one as the market moves in his favor. By my perhaps different definition of technical analysis, this is a combination of technical confirmation and money management. Thus real price performance often does matter even to those who choose not to define such as technical analysis.

READING THE MESSAGE OF THE MARKETS

I also personally find that technical tools such as trend, momentum, relative strength, and pattern recognition are incredibly helpful in allowing me to read and understand the message of the markets. Here are two real-life examples where being able to follow and understand the implication of technical factors led to our being able to quickly anticipate and position in future significant trends.

In mid-1995, about three weeks before a critical European Monetary Union meeting, within a two-day period the bond markets of Spain, Italy, and Sweden all broke out of consolidating trading ranges to new highs on large gaps—one of the more reliable patterns for further gains, as will be described in subsequent chapters. In addition, all three periphery countries' bond markets moved up to among the top 10 global bond market relative strength rankings. The message of the market was consistent and clear—the meeting would result in sticking to the master EMU criteria for entry while the possibility of early entry for periphery European countries would be kept open. This would tend to favor periphery higher yielding bonds over other markets—and our reading of this unanimous message allowed us to position in Spanish and Italian bond markets as well as spreading them versus the German bunds for tremendous profits over the next six months.

A similar reading of the technicals allowed us to get a big jump on the exploding base metals moves of 1993. In early 1993 within two weeks of each other, zinc, lead, copper, nickel, and aluminum all broke out strongly of long-term basing patterns on gaps or thrusts (large-range days with high volume) on huge volume. Very quickly, these base metal markets came to dominate the commodity and even global relative strength rankings:

> Whenever you get all the members of a group telling you the same technical message in a short period of time the reliability of the continuation of such a trend is significantly enhanced.

We were able to position in the strongest members of the base metals, which went on to have one of the most spectacular years since the 1979–1980 period—and anyone participating in just this one trade could hardly help but have had outstanding results in 1993.

In later chapters, we discuss in detail how to use technical action to understand what the market is saying. For now, investors need only to realize that technical analysis can be critical in vehicle selection, in money management, in finding top trends, in determining the strength of a trend, and in being able to read what the markets are telling us across a broad variety of instruments and countries.

It is difficult for me to imagine using the ALC or valuation tools without technical analysis. It is one thing to see the money supply figures moving up and the Fed beginning to cut rates—it is quite another when the long-bond actually begins to establish a trend higher. Similarly, the lag between bond price movement and equities can fluctuate wildly from weeks to many months to even more than a year. How do you know when the bond market's action is finally beginning to hit the equity market? Technicals! When breadth- and trend-following tools signal a change that in and of itself is historically reliable, investors can be much more confident that the next phase of the ALC is indeed developing.

Conversely, how does one know when the economy is headed for overheating? Technicals—or price action. Sure you know further growth is going to soon begin impacting inflation numbers when economic gauges like capacity utilization, industrial production, and unemployment numbers begin to heat up sharply— but you also need to wait until industrial commodity prices begin to move up and bond prices begin to move lower before assuming that the Producer Price Index (PPI) and the Consumer Price Index (CPI) are starting to be impacted enough for the markets to take notice.

In part, the beauty of being able to read the markets by monitoring the movement of all kinds of asset classes and markets is that you do not need to be a genius to anticipate where the markets are heading—you simply need to be able to monitor their concerted movements in terms of trend, relative strength, momentum, price action, and around important support and resistence levels. It is far more important to be able to understand what the whole realm of markets are saying than to be able to pick the correct upcoming scenario. If you can read what the markets are saying, they will generally tell you the likely upcoming scenario and will often be ahead of inevitable temporary shifts and changes in that scenario.

OVERVIEW OF TECHNICAL ANALYSIS

In this section, we briefly look at some of the main concepts of technical analysis and provide examples of how investors can use these concepts specifically to improve their investing results. Major areas that we have found to be relevant in our testing and that we define as technical are trend-following and momentum tools, breadth analysis, sentiment gauges, pattern recognition and price action analysis, support and resistence levels, accumulation and distribution studies, volatility tools, and relative strength.

Trend-Following and Momentum Tools

The trend-following and momentum tools seek to analyze price movement over a specific period of time. The 40-week moving average (MA) used in prior chapters to help cut risk and increase annual return in global investing methodology is an excellent example of a simple trend-following tool. In this case, we are simply waiting for this trend tool to confirm that the equity and bond or bill markets are trending in the right direction before we commit investment capital.

Momentum tools usually measure price change over a specific period. Oscillators that compare price changes over different time periods in some way are tools such as stochastics, RSI (Relative Strength Index), MACD (Moving Average Convergence Divergence), and others. The following simple, yet effective momentum tool can improve investing results.

OTC Index 7.9 Percent Momentum Model.   Simply keep track of daily over-the-counter (OTC) index closes. When a close drops 7.9 percent or more from a peak close, a sell signal is given. Conversely when a close is 7.9 percent or more above a trough daily close, a buy signal is given. So simple, and yet, it beats buy-and-hold (BH), even when transaction costs are considered. Since 1963, BH has returned 11.76 percent compound annual rate with a 59.5 percent drawdown in the NASDAQ OTC index. This simple momentum model has returned an astonishing 18.2 percent compound annual rate of return since 1963 with a 22.4 percent maximum drawdown (which is a bit too high for us to stop here). This system's trades were profitable 61 percent of the time. The NASDAQ index was profitable 70 percent of years, while this system was profitable 91 percent of years, although it had back-to-back small losses in 1993 and 1994. Traders willing to risk larger drawdowns should consider this system as a whole or as a component of an aggressive trading strategy. Both shorts and longs were profitable (see System Spreadsheet 4.1).

Breadth Analysis

Breadth Analysis is the study of the internal dynamics of a broad market including variables such as advances and declines, new highs and new lows, advancing and declining volume, based on the individual components of a market index. The idea is that if one can determine what the broad market is doing, eventually the indexes based on that market will follow what the majority of stocks within it are doing. The following examples of ways to improve investing utilize breadth models.

System Spreadsheet 4.1 **OTC MOMENTUM MODEL**

System Description: Buy OTC Index when the OTC Index closes 7.9% higher than a trough value (low close since entering a short position). Sell when the OTC Index falls 7.9% or more from its peak (the high close since entering a long position).

Significance: Simple percentage momentum reversals can reduce risk and enhance market profits.

Data Used: Daily OTC close.

From: 8/23/63   To: 10/27/97

								Cumulative Return on $100 Investment	
Entry Date	Entry Price	Exit Date	Exit Price	Profit/ Loss	Days in Trade	Percent Change	Position	OTC % Model	OTC Buy and Hold
								$ 100.000	$ 100.000
8/23/63	$ 34.95	6/10/65	$ 47.58	$ 12.63	470	36.1	Long	136.137	136.137
6/10/65	47.58	7/16/65	49.02	(1.44)	27	−3.0	Short	132.017	140.258
7/16/65	49.02	5/17/66	55.48	6.46	218	13.2	Long	149.415	158.741
5/17/66	55.48	6/15/66	59.30	(3.82)	22	−6.9	Short	139.127	169.671
6/15/66	59.30	8/22/66	55.01	(4.29)	49	−7.2	Long	129.062	157.396
8/22/66	55.01	10/28/66	52.63	2.38	50	4.3	Short	134.646	150.587
10/28/66	52.63	2/14/68	81.53	28.90	339	54.9	Long	208.582	233.276
2/14/68	81.53	4/5/68	85.66	(4.13)	38	−5.1	Short	198.016	245.093
4/5/68	85.66	2/24/69	98.30	12.64	232	14.8	Long	227.235	281.259
2/24/69	98.30	9/16/69	92.58	5.72	147	5.8	Short	240.458	264.893
9/16/69	92.58	1/30/70	99.78	7.20	99	7.8	Long	259.159	285.494
1/30/70	99.78	6/1/70	75.25	24.53	87	24.6	Short	322.870	215.308
6/1/70	75.25	7/1/70	72.75	(2.50)	23	−3.3	Long	312.144	208.155
7/1/70	72.75	7/17/70	76.67	(3.92)	13	−5.4	Short	295.325	219.371
7/17/70	76.67	8/17/70	70.91	(5.76)	22	−7.5	Long	273.138	202.890
8/17/70	70.91	8/28/70	76.78	(5.87)	10	−8.3	Short	250.527	219.685
8/28/70	76.78	8/4/71	103.26	26.48	244	34.5	Long	336.929	295.451
8/4/71	103.26	12/10/71	108.81	(5.55)	93	−5.4	Short	318.820	311.330
12/10/71	108.81	2/5/73	126.00	17.19	302	15.8	Long	369.188	360.515
2/5/73	126.00	7/20/73	107.68	18.32	120	14.5	Short	422.866	308.097
7/20/73	107.68	11/12/73	105.08	(2.60)	82	−2.4	Long	412.656	300.658
11/12/73	105.08	1/17/74	95.95	9.13	49	8.7	Short	448.510	274.535
1/17/74	95.95	4/23/74	88.47	(7.48)	69	−7.8	Long	413.546	253.133
4/23/74	88.47	10/11/74	60.42	28.05	124	31.7	Short	544.663	172.876
10/11/74	60.42	11/19/74	60.93	0.51	28	0.8	Long	549.260	174.335
11/19/74	60.93	1/10/75	63.69	(2.76)	39	−4.5	Short	524.380	182.232
1/10/75	63.69	8/4/75	80.98	17.29	147	27.1	Long	666.734	231.702
8/4/75	80.98	1/6/76	80.27	0.71	112	0.9	Short	672.580	229.671
1/6/76	80.27	10/19/78	127.22	46.95	728	58.5	Long	1,065.972	364.006
10/19/78	127.22	1/4/79	120.66	6.56	56	5.2	Short	1,120.938	345.236
1/4/79	120.66	10/10/79	139.31	18.65	200	15.5	Long	1,294.198	398.598
10/10/79	139.31	11/28/79	143.53	(4.22)	36	−3.0	Short	1,254.994	410.672
11/28/79	143.53	3/6/80	148.64	5.11	72	3.6	Long	1,299.675	425.293
3/6/80	148.64	4/2/80	135.80	12.84	20	8.6	Short	1,411.945	388.555
4/2/80	135.80	12/11/80	188.75	52.95	182	39.0	Long	1,962.478	540.057
12/11/80	188.75	1/5/81	204.17	(15.42)	18	−8.2	Short	1,802.153	584.177
1/5/81	204.17	8/24/81	200.76	(3.41)	166	−1.7	Long	1,772.054	574.421
8/24/81	200.76	10/8/81	191.01	9.75	34	4.9	Short	1,858.114	546.524
10/8/81	191.01	1/25/82	183.52	(7.49)	78	−3.9	Long	1,785.253	525.093
1/25/82	183.52	4/16/82	182.25	1.27	60	0.7	Short	1,797.607	521.459

System Spreadsheet 4.1 *(Continued)*

Entry Date	Entry Price	Exit Date	Exit Price	Profit/ Loss	Days in Trade	Percent Change	Position	Cumulative Return on $100 Investment OTC % Model	OTC Buy and Hold
4/16/82	182.25	6/8/82	173.28	(8.97)	38	-4.9	Long	1,709.132	495.794
6/8/82	173.28	8/24/82	172.23	1.05	56	0.6	Short	1,719.489	492.790
8/24/82	172.23	8/1/83	302.08	129.85	245	75.4	Long	3,015.870	864.320
8/1/83	302.08	8/3/84	246.24	55.84	265	18.5	Short	3,573.358	704.549
8/3/84	246.24	9/17/85	281.07	34.83	293	14.1	Long	4,078.800	804.206
9/17/85	281.07	11/8/85	300.02	(18.95)	39	-6.7	Short	3,803.804	858.426
11/8/85	300.02	7/28/86	374.78	74.76	187	24.9	Long	4,751.649	1,072.332
7/28/86	374.78	1/7/87	372.49	2.29	118	0.6	Short	4,780.683	1,065.780
1/7/87	372.49	10/16/87	406.33	33.84	203	9.1	Long	5,214.998	1,162.604
10/16/87	406.33	10/30/87	323.30	83.03	11	20.4	Short	6,280.638	925.036
10/30/87	323.30	12/3/87	298.75	(24.55)	25	-7.6	Long	5,803.713	854.793
12/3/87	298.75	12/16/87	319.25	(20.50)	10	-6.9	Short	5,405.467	913.448
12/16/87	319.25	12/15/89	443.84	124.59	523	39.0	Long	7,514.996	1,269.928
12/15/89	443.84	5/17/90	445.74	(1.90)	110	-0.4	Short	7,482.826	1,275.365
5/17/90	445.74	8/2/90	428.89	(16.85)	56	-3.8	Long	7,199.958	1,227.153
8/2/90	428.89	11/12/90	351.46	77.43	73	18.1	Short	8,499.808	1,005.608
11/12/90	351.46	4/2/92	593.82	242.36	364	69.0	Long	14,361.110	1,699.056
4/2/92	593.82	9/14/92	594.21	(0.39)	118	-0.1	Short	14,351.678	1,700.172
9/14/92	594.21	2/22/93	652.42	58.21	116	9.8	Long	15,757.597	1,866.724
2/22/93	652.42	5/20/93	697.43	(45.01)	64	-6.9	Short	14,670.492	1,995.508
5/20/93	697.43	4/4/94	727.41	29.98	228	4.3	Long	15,301.123	2,081.288
4/4/94	727.41	8/24/94	751.72	(24.31)	103	-3.3	Short	14,789.761	2,150.844
8/24/94	751.72	7/8/96	1,148.82	397.10	489	52.8	Long	22,602.529	3,287.039
7/8/96	1,148.82	8/2/96	1,124.92	23.90	20	2.1	Short	23,072.751	3,218.655
8/2/96	1,124.92	3/18/97	1,269.34	144.42	163	12.8	Long	26,034.887	3,631.874
3/18/97	1,269.34	5/2/97	1,305.33	(35.99)	34	-2.8	Short	25,296.712	3,734.850
5/2/97	1,305.33	10/27/97	1,535.09	229.76	127	17.6	Long	29,749.358	4,392.246
		Maximum Drawdown						22.4%	59.5%
		Compound Annual Return						18.2%	11.8%

Five-Day Moving Average of Advancing Volume over Five-Day Moving Average of Total Volume. Here you are simply taking the five-day moving average of advancing volume and dividing it by the five-day moving average of total volume. Whenever the five-day moving average of advancing volume is 77 percent or more of the five-day moving average of total volume, an extremely strong breadth situation is developing into a very strong buy signal. Three months later, the S&P is up at an average annual rate of 25.3 percent—this is the time to get aggressively long (see System Spreadsheet 4.2).

Eleven-Day A/D Ratio. Simply take the 11-day moving average of advances and divide it by the 11-day moving average of declines (see System Spreadsheet 4.3). This gets bullish on moves

System Spreadsheet 4.2 UP VOLUME > 77% OF TOTAL VOLUME

System Description: Buy S&P when the 5-day moving average of the percent of total volume that is up volume > 77%. Exit after three months.

Significance: When up volume swamps down volume, stocks move up substantially in the near future.

Data Used: Daily NYSE Up Volume and Down Volume and daily close of S&P 500.

From: 1/4/43   To: 12/31/97

Annual Rate of Return: 25.3%

Entry Date	Entry Price	Exit Date	Exit Price	Profit/ Loss	Days in Trade	Percent Change
10/16/46	$ 15.24	1/20/47	$ 15.02	($ 0.22)	69	−1.44%
1/28/47	15.47	4/29/47	14.40	(1.07)	66	−6.92
7/8/47	15.67	10/6/47	15.28	(0.39)	65	−2.49
3/23/48	14.70	6/22/48	16.76	2.06	66	14.01
7/6/49	14.52	10/4/49	15.75	1.23	65	8.47
7/20/50	17.61	10/19/50	20.02	2.41	66	13.69
11/14/50	19.86	2/15/51	22.00	2.14	68	10.78
9/5/51	23.42	12/7/51	23.38	(0.04)	68	−0.17
1/18/54	25.43	4/19/54	27.76	2.33	66	9.16
11/8/54	33.02	2/7/55	36.96	3.94	66	11.93
2/24/56	45.32	5/24/56	44.60	(0.72)	65	−1.59
9/29/59	57.51	12/30/59	59.77	2.26	67	3.93
7/3/62	56.49	10/2/62	56.10	(0.39)	66	−0.69
11/2/62	57.75	2/5/63	66.11	8.36	68	14.48
6/2/70	77.84	8/31/70	81.52	3.68	65	4.73
12/1/71	95.54	3/1/72	107.35	11.81	66	12.36
1/7/76	93.95	4/6/76	103.36	9.41	65	10.02
10/6/80	131.73	1/7/81	135.08	3.35	68	2.54
8/23/82	116.11	11/19/82	137.02	20.91	65	18.01
8/6/84	162.60	11/2/84	167.42	4.82	65	2.96
1/7/87	255.33	4/7/87	296.69	41.36	65	16.20
12/27/91	406.46	3/27/92	403.50	(2.96)	66	−0.73
5/5/97	830.24	8/4/97	950.30	120.06	66	14.46
Total				$234.34	1,522	153.70%

Percent of Days Invested	11%
Annual Rate of Return	25.3%
Average Percent Gain	6.7%
Percent Profitable	71.9%
Maximum Drawdown	10.5%

over 1.9. Three months later, the S&P is up at an average annual rate of 29.2 percent—another breadth signal that shows you when to become aggressively bullish.

One of the main problems with breadth analysis is that as yet many global markets outside the United States do not publish or

---

System Spreadsheet 4.3 **11-DAY ADVANCE DECLINE RATIO > 1.9**

System Description: Buy when the 11-day average of the advance/decline ratio > 1.9. Exit three months later.

Significance: Strong breadth periods lead to substantial gains in the period ahead.

Data Used: Daily NYSE advances, daily NYSE declines, and the daily close of S&P 500.

From: 1/29/43   To: 12/31/97

Annual Rate of Return: 29.2%

Entry Date	Entry Price	Exit Date	Exit Price	Profit/ Loss	Days in Trade	Percent Change
4/1/43	$ 11.59	7/1/43	$ 12.36	$ 0.77	66	6.64%
5/31/44	12.35	8/29/44	12.84	0.49	65	3.97
4/23/45	14.63	7/23/45	14.51	(0.12)	66	−0.82
9/5/45	15.53	12/7/45	17.54	2.01	68	12.94
7/11/47	15.87	10/9/47	15.26	(0.61)	65	−3.84
4/1/48	15.12	6/30/48	16.74	1.62	65	10.71
7/14/49	14.79	10/13/49	15.97	1.18	66	7.98
8/1/50	18.02	10/31/50	19.53	1.51	66	8.38
1/26/54	26.09	4/27/54	27.76	1.67	66	6.40
7/11/62	57.73	10/9/62	57.20	(0.53)	65	−0.92
11/12/62	59.59	2/12/63	65.83	6.24	67	10.47
1/17/67	85.24	4/18/67	91.86	6.62	66	7.77
12/4/70	89.46	3/8/71	99.38	9.92	67	11.09
12/10/71	97.69	3/10/72	108.37	10.68	66	10.93
1/9/75	71.17	4/10/75	83.77	12.60	66	17.70
1/7/76	93.95	4/6/76	103.36	9.41	65	10.02
8/24/82	115.35	11/22/82	134.22	18.87	65	16.36
1/21/85	175.23	4/22/85	180.70	5.47	66	3.12
1/15/87	265.49	4/15/87	284.44	18.95	65	7.14
2/5/91	351.26	5/7/91	377.32	26.06	66	7.42
Total				$132.81	1,317	153.46%
			Percent of Days Invested			9%
			Annual Rate of Return			29.2%

even compute data based on the variables required to compile breadth tools, particularly in emerging markets, but also in some more developed ones. Therefore it is difficult globally to apply breadth models that work on readily available U.S. statistics because these same statistics are not available across international markets. Nonetheless where such statistics are available, breadth analysis can pay big dividends.

Sentiment Gauges

These gauges look at variables that attempt to measure investors' attitudes and psychology over time. Generally when sentiment is strongly bullish, Mr. Market is overly euphoric and is at least in the short term likely to be paying too much for an asset; whereas when sentiment is strongly negative, Mr. Market is overly pessimistic and likely to be dumping decent short-term value. Marty Zweig did much to legitimize such analysis with his famous *Barron's* articles in which he revealed his now classic put/call ratio concept. The idea is that once enough investors become bullish, everyone who is likely to buy already has and there is little demand left to push up prices, meaning any negative will trigger a decline. Conversely when enough investors become bearishly inclined, everyone who is likely to sell already has and the market is ripe for a recovery in prices on the appearance of even a minor catalyst. Sentiment gauges in general are much shorter-term indications of price movement than most other technical tools. Following are some examples of sentiment-based models that can improve investment performance.

Consumer Sentiment Index. When this index of consumer confidence goes to a euphoric level above 99.5, the S&P has moved down at a −2.5 percent annual rate. When the consumer sentiment index is below or equal to 99.5, however, the S&P has moved up at a 14.2 percent annual rate. System Spreadsheets 4.4 and 4.5 show these patterns.

Help Wanted Advertising Index. The help wanted advertising index attempts to measure the amount of advertising business does to get new labor. Thus when businesses are euphoric, they advertise heavily for new people to hire; whereas when businesses are

System Spreadsheet 4.4 **CONSUMER SENTIMENT > 99.5**

System Description: Buy S&P when the consumer sentiment index is > 99.5. Exit when ≤ 99.5.

Significance: When consumer sentiment is overly optimistic, stock prices perform poorly.

Data Used: Monthly Consumer Sentiment Index and monthly close of S&P 500.

From: 1/31/57   To: 12/31/97

Annual Rate of Return: −2.5%

Entry Date	Entry Price	Exit Date	Exit Price	Profit/ Loss	Days in Trade	Percent Change
1/31/57	$ 44.72	5/31/57	$ 47.43	$ 2.71	87	6.1%
2/29/60	56.12	5/31/60	55.83	(0.29)	67	−0.5
2/28/62	69.96	5/31/62	59.63	(10.33)	67	−14.8
8/31/64	81.83	5/31/66	86.13	4.30	457	5.3
1/31/84	163.41	2/29/84	157.06	(6.35)	22	−3.9
3/30/84	159.18	4/30/84	160.05	0.87	22	0.5
9/28/84	166.10	10/31/84	166.09	(0.01)	24	0.0
Total				($9.10)	746	−7.3%
			Percent of Days Invested			7%
			Annual Rate of Return			−2.5%

pessimistic, they cut back on all advertising to hire new people. When the 17-month Rate of Change in the Help Wanted Advertising Index is less than or equal to −21 percent, the S&P has moved up at very brisk 27.8 percent annual rate (see System Spreadsheet 4.6). And when the 16-month rate of change in the Help Wanted Advertising Index moves above 24 percent, the S&P has moved down at a −2.1 percent annual rate (as shown in System Spreadsheet 4.7).

Other Useful Tools—Pattern Recognition, Support and Resistence, Accumulation and Distribution, Volatility

Pattern Recognition and price action tools take a close look at "how" prices are moving and attempt to define the movement in terms of predefined patterns that are suggestive of future action, based on historical review of similar patterns in other

System Spreadsheet 4.5 **CONSUMER SENTIMENT ≤ 99.5**

System Description: Buy S&P when the consumer sentiment index is ≤ 99.5. Exit when > 99.5.

Significance: When consumer sentiment is not overly optimistic, stock prices perform better than average.

Data Used: Monthly Consumer Sentiment Index and monthly close of S&P 500.

From: 1/31/57   To: 12/31/97

Annual Rate of Return: 14.2%

Entry Date	Entry Price	Exit Date	Exit Price	Profit/ Loss	Days in Trade	Percent Change
5/31/57	$ 47.43	2/29/60	$ 56.12	$ 8.69	717	18.3%
5/31/60	55.83	2/28/62	69.96	14.13	457	25.3
5/31/62	59.63	8/31/64	81.83	22.20	588	37.2
5/31/66	86.13	1/31/84	163.41	77.28	4,611	89.7
2/29/84	157.06	3/30/84	159.18	2.12	23	1.3
4/30/84	160.05	9/28/84	166.10	6.05	110	3.8
10/31/84	166.09	2/28/97	790.82	624.73	3,218	376.1
Total				$755.20	9,724	551.9%
			Percent of Days Invested			91%
			Annual Rate of Return			14.2%

instruments. Investors should certainly familiarize themselves with classical patterns found in technical textbooks such as Edwards and McGee's *Technical Analysis of Stock Trends.* Our favorite technical patterns (defined more rigorously in later chapters) are breakouts from long consolidations. Consolidations are periods when a stock or market trades in a relatively tight range. A breakout occurs when prices move sharply beyond the tight range they have traded in for a prolonged period. A pattern that we use most often is called a "flag pattern." Prices rise sharply for many weeks and then trade within 15 percent or so of their high for four weeks or longer in a tight trading range. Once prices break out to new highs from this pattern, an investor can buy with good reliability and put a open protective stop loss (a sell stop below the market price that can protect one from taking a bigger loss than this predefined level) below the low of the consolidation level. In

System Spreadsheet 4.6 **HELP WANTED 17-MONTH ROC ≤ –21%**

System Description: Buy S&P when the 17-month rate of change of the Help Wanted Index ≤ –21%. Exit when > –21%.

Significance: When business sentiment is poor, stock prices rise extremely rapidly.

Data Used: Monthly Help Wanted Index and monthly close of S&P 500.

From: 1/31/51   To: 12/31/97

Annual Rate of Return: 27.8%

Entry Date	Entry Price	Exit Date	Exit Price	Profit/ Loss	Days in Trade	Percent Change
1/31/51	$ 21.66	6/30/52	$ 24.96	$ 3.30	369	15.2%
11/30/53	24.76	2/28/55	36.76	12.00	326	48.5
10/31/57	41.06	12/31/58	55.21	14.15	305	34.5
12/30/60	58.11	5/31/61	66.56	8.45	109	14.5
6/30/61	64.64	7/31/61	66.76	2.12	22	3.3
6/30/70	72.72	8/31/71	99.03	26.31	306	36.2
10/31/74	73.90	1/30/76	100.86	26.96	327	36.5
5/30/80	111.24	11/28/80	140.52	29.28	131	26.3
1/30/81	129.55	4/30/81	132.81	3.26	65	2.5
3/31/82	111.96	5/31/83	162.39	50.43	305	45.0
9/28/90	306.05	3/31/92	403.69	97.64	393	31.9
Total				$273.90	2,658	294.4%
			Percent of Days Invested			22%
			Annual Rate of Return			27.8%

so doing, an investor is often taking very low risk and can position in a vehicle likely to move up many times this initial risk in terms of percentage points. We will discuss this pattern in detail in Chapter 7. In the chapters ahead, we also look at "runaway market characteristics" a particular equity or market index has exhibited over a defined period. Runaway market characteristics are short-term price actions like gaps and thrusts that show unusually aggressive buying or selling power. When a vehicle exhibits 10 or more of these characteristics in a 21-bar period it shows that the vehicle is being bid-up aggressively by buyers or sold aggressively by sellers—and can help identify a potentially explosive situation.

System Spreadsheet 4.7 **HELP WANTED 16-MONTH ROC > 24%**

System Description: Buy S&P when the 16-month rate of change of the Help Wanted Index > 24%. Exit when ≤ 24%.

Significance: When business sentiment is optimistic, stock prices do not beat cash returns.

Data Used: Monthly Help Wanted Index and monthly close of S&P 500.

From: 1/31/51   To: 12/31/97

Annual Rate of Return: –2.1%

Entry Date	Entry Price	Exit Date	Exit Price	Profit/ Loss	Days in Trade	Percent Change
5/31/55	$ 37.91	7/31/56	$ 49.39	$11.48	306	30.3%
8/31/56	47.51	9/28/56	45.35	(2.16)	21	–4.5
4/30/59	57.59	4/29/60	54.37	(3.22)	262	–5.6
4/30/62	65.24	9/28/62	56.27	(8.97)	110	–13.7
2/26/65	87.43	12/30/66	80.33	(7.10)	481	–8.1
5/31/72	109.53	6/30/72	107.14	(2.39)	23	–2.2
7/31/72	107.39	12/31/73	97.55	(9.84)	371	–9.2
7/30/76	103.44	10/29/76	102.9	(0.54)	66	–0.5
12/31/76	107.46	2/28/79	96.28	(11.18)	564	–10.4
10/31/83	163.55	4/30/85	179.83	16.28	392	10.0
1/31/94	481.61	3/31/94	445.77	(35.84)	44	–7.4
5/31/94	456.50	6/30/94	444.27	(12.23)	23	–2.7
7/29/94	458.26	9/30/94	462.69	4.43	46	1.0
10/31/94	472.35	1/31/95	470.42	(1.93)	67	–0.4
Total				($63.21)	2,776	–23.6%
			Percent of Days Invested			23%
			Annual Rate of Return			–2.1%

Support and resistance levels are price areas where a market or vehicle has encountered buying power that has pushed prices up from that level numerous times (support) or selling power that has pushed prices down from that level numerous times (resistence). A vehicle that can consistently plow through important resistance levels in dramatic fashion is showing an ability to absorb selling pressure completely and indicating that aggressive buying power is very strong.

Accumulation and distribution tools are indicators formed from taking prices and volume (and open interest in the case of futures) and trying to derive the amount of shares (or contracts) that either were accumulated in a day (in the case of rising prices) or sold off and distributed in a day (in the case of falling prices). By running a cumulative total of this estimate of accumulation and distribution, investors can often get advance notice that a big move in a particular direction may be imminent. If a vehicle is in a long trading range (another name for consolidation) but accumulation indicators are soaring, it is likely to move higher; and when it breaks out above resistence, it is much more likely to move higher than a vehicle without strong accumulation indicators. Examples of this concept are on-balance volume, money flow indicators, and Lowry's Buy Power and Sell Power market timing tools.

Volatility tools are indicators like Bollinger bands, which seek to determine the standard deviation of a stock or index and put bands around prices roughly two sigma away from a daily adjusted mean. When prices hit these bands, they usually revert to the mean, particularly on countertrend moves. Volatility bands can help one determine support and resistence levels as well as see when a trend is so powerful that it is pushing prices beyond "normal" levels. Another great volatility tool was developed by hedge fund manager Larry Connors. This volatility analysis looks for strong stocks in which a shorter-term volatility average has declined to below 50 percent of longer-term volatility measures. The tendency for volatility to revert to the mean in this situation implies that a larger than normal move is likely to occur; and a breakout in one direction can help an investor jump aboard what is likely to be an explosive move. We use this tool to help key in on trading ranges that are about to lead to a big move.

Relative Strength

Of all the quantitative testable tools we tested over many decades of both bull and bear market history, relative strength (RS) has proven to be the most robust independent variable. This is also the tool we will apply to our global investing model to help improve our risk/reward in this chapter. Relative strength is a very simple concept. It simply looks at the percentage change of a vehicle over a defined period and compares that change to the change of other vehicles. Thus the stock with the highest six-month relative strength ranking out of 100 you are watching is simply the stock that has moved up the most percentage points in the past six months. William O'Neil popularized his own version of relative strength ranking of the more than 10,000 stocks that he monitors using his own front-end weighted average of 3-, 6-, 9-, and 12-month relative strength figures.

ANSWERING CRITICISM OF TECHNICAL TOOLS

A major criticism of technical tools is based on this observation by some money managers. If technical analysis is so good, how come there are few money managers with real-time long-term track records using technicals to produce superior returns? While it is true that as yet no public figure at the pinnacle of investment success (e.g., Soros, Templeton, Lynch, Buffett) relies heavily on technical analysis, nevertheless there are excellent public and private examples of long-term investment success by investor/managers who focus on technicals. Marty Zweig and Ned Davis use technicals extensively and Marty has logged a long-term consistent record of outperformance with significantly lower than market risk. Here is someone managing billions of dollars who is consistently beating the market on a risk/reward basis while using technical tools as a primary part of his decision-making process. Dan Sullivan, publisher of the *Chartist,* is another example of someone who has publicly produced decades of an exclusively technical track record that shows both better than market returns and substantially less than market risk. William O'Neil and David Ryan are managers who use technicals as a trigger to tell them when to enter the type of stocks their other screens identify (one of their main screens, relative strength ranking, is also technical).

Early in my career, I kept an open mind toward technical analysis. On one of my earliest trips to Europe in the mid-1980s, I met an elderly man who had achieved an incredible track record of long-term returns with extremely low risk since the 1950s. Although this private money manager was still managing billions of dollars, he was in failing health. Seeing that I was young, enthusiastic, and thirsting for ideas that would produce top investment returns consistently with low risk, he shared much of his work with me. He expressed the hope that it would live on beyond him.

Although he asked to remain anonymous, much of my work on relative strength and global relative strength is based on the ideas we discussed and the track record he achieved using this concept. This private European money manager had shown average annual gains of over 19 percent since the mid-1950s without ever having a drawdown greater than 20 percent, and with only one negative calendar year (–5% in 1974) in over 30 years of managing money. He managed money for a small number of extremely wealthy clients and kept the lowest profile of anyone I have yet known. His methodology was almost purely technical—and was astonishingly simple.

Although Dr. Tom Johnson, Dr. Paul Sutin, and I have done a large body of research on many similar methods and have thereby made some historically improved adjustments, the concept has remained essentially the same. What this manager did was simply keep a relative strength table for as many global market indexes as he could monitor, along with relative strength rankings for each of these country's bonds and short rates. Just as in the system we have been building in the past several chapters, he only looked at those countries with positive trends in stocks, and bonds or short rates, via their reading versus a 40-week moving average. Next, he created a global index and global interest rate relative strength ranking. In the original version, he simply used a six-month RS of all stock indexes above their 40-week moving averages. He also kept a six-month RS of all bonds and bills (short-rate prices), which he then averaged to get an interest rate RS ranking for each country with positive interest rate trends (30-day bill or 10-year bonds over 40-wk MA, or yields under 40-wk MA). Finally, he averaged the stock index RS ranking with the interest rate RS ranking for each country to get a combined stock and interest rate RS rank. Any time a country's stock index, or bond and bill (short rate) prices both fell below their 40-week moving average on a weekly close, that country was eliminated from the combined interest-rate/index RS rank table.

To use this table, this top manager simply invested 20 percent in each of the top five markets ranked in the combined interest-rate/index table. If there were fewer than five countries in the table (meaning most countries had negative trends in stocks, or bonds and short rates), he would invest a maximum of 25 percent in each market on the table and put the residual in T-bills (or later a money market fund). Thus if there were only three markets with positive trends in interest rates and indexes, he would invest 25 percent in each of the three with the residual 25 percent in T-bills. If there were only two markets, he would invest 25 percent in each of the two with the residual 50 percent in T-bills, and so on. In addition, every six months (January 1 and July 1), he shifted the portfolio to adjust to the new top-ranking countries in the table as necessary. And if a country invested in was dropped from the table, he would exit that country and reinvest in another country of the highest rank that was not invested in at that time (or in T-bills if no country fit that criterion).

Originally, our investor bought the top eight RS stocks (six months) that were among the bottom half of P/E ratios in a country index to try emulating the index easily; later he shifted to open-ended mutual funds in countries where those funds were available. The point is that he was not trying to vastly outperform the country index, merely to create similar performance. Although he experimented with selection criteria, he stuck mostly to the largest cap stocks in a country so that he could have 40 to 50 stocks in his total portfolio along with enough liquidity for the large amounts he was managing (the selection of stocks within a chosen country is discussed in intricate detail in Chapter 7). In general, the performance of this methodology was not based on stellar stock selection—selection basically matched the underlying index over the long run. Thus the system was easily tested and analyzed using indexes as a proxy.

Dr. Johnson and I did extensive work on this system in particular. Even as defined here, it produced compound average annual returns in the 13 percent range since World War II, while slicing drawdowns from 52 percent to around 19 percent and improving reliability and consistency considerably. The manager had used some money management strategies in addition to this system that had helped him boost his performance above these numbers (and we will also discuss such money management strategies later in this book). The point though is that the basic system was very good at cutting drawdown substantially while improving average annual gain and reliability. In our testing, we found that the moving average could be adjusted widely, as could the period of relative strength. Short term traders could improve results going to as low as eight-week RS (with quarterly portfolio adjustments), while longer-term investors could widen the RS to as far as one year, still with substantial improvements in returns and risk. We settled on one of the lower risk parameters which turned out to be a weighted average RS (similar to O'Neil's but slightly shorter in average duration). The exact formula is $(2 \times (1\text{-wk RS} + 5\text{-wk RS} + 8\text{-wk RS} + 13\text{-wk RS}) + (26\text{-wk RS} + 40\text{-wk RS} + 52\text{-wk RS})) / 11$, which gives one an average of about 16 weeks, but is heavily front-end weighted.

The results from applying this RS ranking to the combined interest-rate/index table in the manner described in the original methodology in this chapter as well as the valuation screen described in Chapter 3 are shown in Figure 4.1.

Figure 4.1 **40/40 RS GLOBAL PORTFOLIO SELECTIONS SINCE WORLD WAR II**

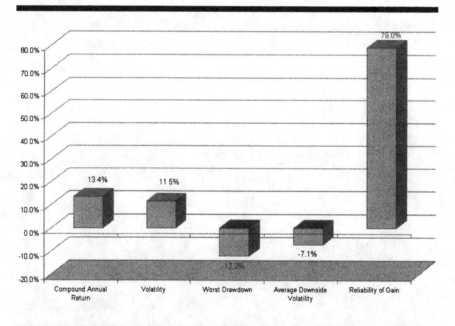

SUMMARY

Investors should take note of what we are doing by using the four simple concepts of (all) interest rates, (technical) Relative Strength (RS), trend, and valuation: we have developed a methodology for investing in global markets that beats buy and hold in terms of compound annual return by more than 4 percent per year, cuts volatility, increases reliability from 65 percent to almost 80 percent, and most significantly, slashes maximum drawdown from a totally unacceptable 54 percent (and 70% + after inflation) to a more tolerable 12.2 percent. This system can become the blueprint for investing in global markets with relatively low risk.

Containing Risk—Sound Strategy and Money Management Methods and the Principles of Character Necessary to Achieve Them

Strategy and money management are the basic fundamentals that underlie all trading success. You can have a nearly perfect analysis of the liquidity environment of a situation, find a vehicle loaded with fuel, wait for a perfect pattern to enter, and be almost perfectly correct in your expectation of what that vehicle will do; and yet you can still lose money if you do not use proper risk management and money management. As Stanley Kroll once said, "It is better to have a mediocre system and good money management than an excellent system and poor money management."

Top investors understand that money management is the most important and critical element in producing long-run investment success. This is the area where most investors make mistakes. After completing each trade, you should review the rules in this chapter to make sure you are consistently following them in your

151

trading. All investors need to remain in sync with these money management rules to assure success.

MONEY MANAGEMENT RULES

Individual Position Risk Containment

Rule 1: Always Use Protective Stops.   Use an open protective stop when you enter a new position to limit your theoretical risk on each position to a measurable amount. Theoretical risk is the distance between your entry price and your OPS. Thus if you buy a stock at 10 and use an 8 OPS, your theoretical risk is $(10 - 8) = 2$ points. Investors wanting to keep drawdowns less than 25 percent should strive to keep theoretical risk on each position at 2 percent of capital or less. For example, if you have a $1,000,000 account, you should only risk $20,000 per trade in theoretical risk. So if you buy a stock at 10 with an OPS at 8, you can buy no more than 10,000 shares because 10,000 shares × 2 points theoretical risk is $20,000. Otherwise, you would be taking excessive theoretical risk on this position.

Rule 2: Use Trailing Stops to Lock in Profits as a Trade Moves in Your Favor.   When a trade moves significantly in your favor, makes a consolidation or reaction, and then follows with a new high, move your OPS up to below the last strong support level so that you are protecting profits as a market moves up just as you were protecting initial risk when you first entered the trade. We describe specific methods for doing this later in this book.

Rule 3: Always Let the Market's Own Price Action Determine Where an Open Protective or Trailing Stop Is Placed by a Specific Rule.   The investor should not just randomly put an OPS at a level; that level should be chosen because of the market's own price action.

Rule 4: Use Creeping Commitment.   Start with a small position and build to a larger one as your trailing stop eliminates your risk to initial capital. Suppose we bought a stock at 10 with an 8 OPS, and that stock moves up nicely to 15, where it consolidates for many weeks between 13 and 15 before breaking out to new highs on a valid flag-pattern buy signal again. As long as the stock is not overvalued or overowned (defined rigorously in our vehicle selection criteria in Chapter 7), we can add to the position to build up a larger position in that stock as long as our new OPS is above the entry price of the last position so that we have no theoretical risk on the prior position. Thus our commitment to a stock can creep higher only in those stocks that show strong profits and continue to meet our criteria.

Rule 5: Never Allow Creeping Commitment to Cause You to Invest More than 25 Percent of Your Portfolio Capital in One Issue.   Begin divesting when an issue grows beyond 33 percent of your portfolio. In our example of a stock bought at 10 with an 8 OPS, we bought a maximum of 10,000 shares, representing a $100,000 investment, or 10 percent of capital. When it broke out again at 15.5, using a 12.75 OPS, we had a roughly 3-point risk assuming slippage and commissions, meaning we could only buy 6,600 (rounding down 6,667) or so additional shares with a $20,000 (2%) risk, which would increase our total investment to $202,300 or 20.2 percent via our risk control rule. Note that with 16,600 shares, the stock becomes more than 33 percent of our whole portfolio at a price of 19⅞. Not only would we not add to the stock at prices close to this, but we would begin a monthly monitoring of the price of this stock whereupon we would sell off enough of it to get it down to under 33 percent of our portfolio each month. This rule relates to extremes allowed, not normal positions.

Country and Sector Risk Containment

Rule 6: Limit Your Sector Allocations of Portfolio Capital.   Never allocate more than 25 percent of portfolio capital to any one sector, nor allow any one sector to grow to more than 50 percent of portfolio value. Thus in the stock example described earlier, if when the stock broke out a second time at 15.5 we had another stock in our portfolio in the same general market sector, then we could not pyramid our purchase with a second round of buying unless we sold off enough of the other stock in that sector to not violate the 25 percent rule. In addition, if we had two or more stocks in one sector, we would begin selling off monthly to keep our total value in those single sector stocks below 50 percent of the total value of the portfolio.

Rule 7: Use Creeping Commitment to Scale-In to Sectors without Adding Risk to Initial Capital.   The stock in our initial example is stock ABC. We bought ABC at 10 with an 8 OPS initially, and it moved up quickly to the 15 level. As it did so, our trailing stop methodology had allowed us to move our OPS up to 11, so that theoretically we had locked in a profit. At that point if we got a buy signal in another stock, called DEF, in a similar sector, we could add to DEF and slowly build allocation to that profitable sector without increasing the risk to our original portfolio capital. We thus reallocate our initial risk whenever we have a profit locked in on the sector so that we are building more allocation as quickly as allowed to sectors showing the most profit. But we make sure we are not violating Rule 6 when we add to a sector.

Rule 8: Limit Theoretical Risk to Any One Country to 6 Percent in Most Cases and 10 Percent in Extreme Cases.   Thus if we were wildly bullish on the U.S. market, we would only want to start with five positions of 2 percent maximum risk (or 8 positions of 1.25% risk each if we wanted higher diversification). We would then add to positions in this country only when one of our initial positions allowed us to move its trailing stop to break-even or better, so that we could take a new position without adding to theoretical risk to that country from all positions.

Rule 9: Diversify among Two to Six Instruments in Any One Country or Sector.   Unless market risk and uncertainty are unusually high, do not "de-worsify" among more than 10 instruments. You get most of the benefits of diversification with a portfolio of 6 to 10 stocks. In addition, if you select stocks very likely to outperform, you will usually want some degree of concentration.

Rule 10: Let Your Profits Run on Any Position, Sector, or Market until It Is Either Overvalued, Overowned, or Stopped Out via Trailing Stops.   Many times, a stock, sector, or country market will run a far longer trend than an investor might have initially suspected. Your goal should be to stay invested in strong trends for as long as they run, assuming chronic overvaluation or overownership does not exist (we deal with specific exit criteria more thoroughly in Chapter 7).

Rule 11: Never Average a Loss in Any Sector or Country.   If you have two or more positions in any one sector or country that are showing a net loss, do not add to this sector or country until you show a net profit on prior positions. You want to build positions in countries showing good profits that have continued strong prospects, not in ones showing losses.

Portfolio Risk Containment

Rule 12: Always Diversify among at Least Three Countries in Your Total Portfolio.   At times, you may want to concentrate heavily in one country, but you should always keep at least some portion of your portfolio in at least three different countries short or long.

Rule 13: At All Times, Diversify among at Least Three Asset Classes in Your Portfolio.   While the global liquidity cycle may strongly favor one asset class, and you may have a high concentration in one asset class at particular times, you should always have at least some diversification among asset classes in your portfolio, short or long. We will be discussing investment in other asset classes later on in the book, including stocks, bonds, currencies, futures, commodity-trend correlated commodity funds, noncorrelated commodity funds, distressed bonds, junk bonds, emerging market debt, gold and gold stocks, REITs, oil and gas, futures trading, arbitrage funds, hedge funds, short sales, and others.

Rule 14: Limit Your Portfolio Risk to 20 Percent Maximum If You Were Stopped Out of Every Position in Your Portfolio at Any One Time. You should always be asking yourself this question: If there were some catastrophe and I was stopped out of absolutely every position in my portfolio, what would be my total risk? In uncertain times, this should be kept to 15 percent or less, and in more clear environments do not go above 20 percent at any one time. This will help keep your potential maximum drawdowns to less than disastrous levels.

General Rules

Rule 15: When in Doubt, Stay Out or Get Out; Do Not Get Back in until You Are Sure about a Position.   Only enter a position when technicals, Austrian Liquidity Cycle, valuation, and a host of other methods show good reliability and strong profit potential in relation to risk. There is nothing wrong with sitting heavily in cash or bonds while waiting for the right combination of reliability, risk/reward, and technicals to show up.

Rule 16: Concentrate Most of Your Time and Effort on Vehicle Selection.   Seek to spend your effort finding reliable trends in top vehicles where low-risk, reliable trades are developing. Many traders spend more than half their time on arcane theories designed to help them pinpoint exact high and low points for the market as a whole. These traders and investors are putting too much of their valuable time on an area that actually has much less impact on their profitability than does vehicle selection. You want to spend most of your time and effort on the areas that have the greatest effect on your performance—and that means you must concentrate heavily on vehicle selection, where the bulk of profits come from.

Rule 17: Remember That Markets Are an Odds Game—They Are Not Predictable.   The most brilliant analyst on earth is in trouble if he is long Tokyo heavily and a historically catastrophic earthquake rocks Japan. Many events that affect the markets strongly are not predictable, while even those events that appear predictable don't work every time. Therefore strive to follow the markets and let them confirm your analysis before investing heavily, and use our risk containment rules just in case you are hit by an unforeseen market-jolting event. Also, investors need to be prepared to be wrong periodically, even when they are very sure about a particular trend continuing. Being wrong is part of the odds game. Take your lumps and move on. Even the best quarterback throws an occasional interception—that is part of the process and you must learn to accept it and not let mistakes detour you from your goals and strategy. One of the things that differentiates a great quarterback from a mediocre one is his ability to throw a disastrous interception and then on the very next play, throw another gutsy pass. It is the same with trading.

Rule 18: Start Out with Small Positions in a Given Market. Build up to big positions and exposure only as that market moves in your favor; do not violate our risk containment rules in any way. Rule 4 focused on the same concept in terms of individual positions, and Rule 7 dealt with it in terms of sectors (we use creeping commitment to add to individual positions or sectors only when we can do so without adding to theoretical risk to initial capital). Use the same concept when allocating to a given country or market. For example, if you're very bullish in the U.S. market, you will build up around five positions in individual equities of the United States with 2 percent risk each, and you will not add more allocation to the United States until at least one of those positions has moved up enough to allow a theoretical break-even or better OPS. You can then add to existing or new U.S. positions without increasing theoretical risk to initial capital. While we don't have any limits to allocation committed to a particular country or market as a percentage of capital if built up in this way, be sure to have other positions and asset classes in your portfolio.

Rule 19: Only Recapitalize Your Profits When You Have Earned Enough to More than Cover Your Expected Maximum Drawdown. Recapitalization is the process whereby investors use profits to resize their portfolio risk parameters. If you start the year with $1,000,000 and build 35 percent profits by year-end, then during the next year you can base your risk rules on a $1,350,000 portfolio starting point only when your maximum drawdown is expected to be less than 35 percent. A good rule of thumb for maximum drawdown estimates is 1.5 times whatever maximum portfolio risk you have assumed. Thus, if you follow our 20 percent maximum portfolio risk rule, you should only recapitalize once you have achieved a 30 percent or greater profit.

Rule 20: Consistently Devote Time and Effort to the Study of Market and Economic History. In this way, you will build your understanding over time. As the Bible reminds us, "There is nothing new under the sun." Most market events and environments have many parallels to similar environments in the past—though there are rarely completely identical situations. For example, if you understand how the markets reacted to a deflationary environment in the 1930s, you may better comprehend how the Japanese market is likely to react to deflation in the 1990s. History is rich with wisdom that will give you perspective and add to your insight today and tomorrow: tap its wealth.

Rule 21: Keep a Trading Journal and Review and Evaluate Your Trades and Decisions Periodically.   A trading journal should have a "before picture" and an "after picture" of every trade and major decision you make. Every 30 trades or so, every quarter, or at least twice a year, you should review that journal and the decisions of the latest period. Make sure you are following the plan you devised for investing and note periodic mistakes and tendencies. Then make a plan for compensating and correcting your errors and common weaknesses. Investors tend to look for new strategies outside themselves when they have poorer than desired performance. Usually the problem is not with their strategy, but with their execution of it: the problem is internal, not external (when this is true, no new strategy will ever solve their problem, it will instead merely allow them to shift the blame). Almost all the great traders we have studied use a trading journal; it allows them to correct internal problems, and to evaluate and get feedback. This is one of the most important rules. Few traders and investors who have kept a journal religiously for more than a few years remain market losers.

Rule 22: Learn to Walk before You Run.   Start out trading stocks and bonds, and as you build consistent proficiency, then build up to leveraged stocks and bonds. Again build proficiency in using 50 percent leverage for years before moving to higher leverage vehicles such as futures and options. Build the experience necessary before moving to highly leveraged vehicles. Learn to trade intermediate-term trades and long-term trends before trying to move to short-term trading, where your weaknesses are exposed quickly and ruthlessly. So many traders I talk to are trying to make 40 percent annual gains using short-term trading strategies, without ever having invested for longer-term periods successfully. A huge percentage of these traders fail even to make money over the long term. They could as easily be trying to perform successful heart surgery before even attending medical school. Good Luck. On the other hand, patient investors are willing to commit many years to the study of market action and successful investing. These investors start with stocks and bonds and when they are satisfied with their intermediate-term trading, they move slowly on to leverage and short-term opportunities. The irony is that after five or six years, these patient investors often achieve the average annual returns the short-term traders seek but never find. Learn to walk before you try running!

Rule 23: Markets Normally Move in Trends with Three to Five Sections or Legs. Try to know the secular trend (many years over many Liquidity Cycles), cyclical trend (usually 3–6 years in a Liquidity Cycle of recession to expansion), intermediate trend (many months), and short-term trend (days to weeks) in any market or sector you contemplate investing in.

Rule 24: In Investing, the Trend Is Your Best Friend. Once you know the trend in different time frames, strive to always be in sync with the time-frame trend and next longer time frame that you are trying to invest in. Thus if you're trying to invest for many months to years, make sure the intermediate and cyclical trends are in your favor.

Rule 25: Go Where the Oil Is. Trends are to traders and investors what oil is to the wildcatter. As J. P. Getty once noted: "The best way to find oil is to go where other people are finding it." And similarly, the best way to find market profits is to go where strong trends and strong potential exists. Constantly seek to analyze where the strongest trends on the globe are among all asset classes and sectors, as well as where the strongest potential trends lie. Do not invest in any stock or market unless you believe you are investing in one of the top 20 strongest trends available on the planet at that time. You must strive not just to find trends, but to position yourself in the very strongest trends on a consistent basis.

Rule 26: Buy Strength and Sell Weakness. Since you are looking to position in the strongest trends, you will not bottom- or top-pick in any market or vehicle. Your goal is to find exceptional strength where there is still room on the upside or to find exceptional weakness where there is still room on the downside. Positioning in strong trends allows you to improve the reliability of your trading. It does not limit the upside, however. In fact, catching a reaction or breakout in a strong trend is usually far more profitable on a risk/reward basis than is catching the bottom or top of a market.

Rule 27: Let Your Profits Run and Cut Your Losses Short with Open Protective Stops and Trailing Stops.

Rule 28: Remember That Price Makes News, News Does Not Make Price. Markets are discounting mechanisms and leading indicators. As such, they strive to anticipate the next 6 to 12 months of economically relevant action. News is only important in how it changes expectations of the future outlook.

Rule 29: Scrutinize How a Vehicle or Market Reacts to News That Should Be Construed as Positive or Negative. When a market or vehicle reacts negatively to positive news, it is telling you that such news is less than prices have already expected and that such a market or vehicle is particularly vulnerable. In this situation, immediately lighten up on your long positions. Similarly when a market or vehicle reacts positively to bearish news, it is particularly susceptible to short-covering or accumulation; cut back on shorts in such a vehicle or market. A strange reaction to news is telling you what expectations have already been built into price. It is therefore a warning sign that prudent investors should heed.

Rule 30: Invest with Fuel on Your Side. In the long run, it is increased revenues and earnings that propel stock prices higher. Using our criteria (explained in Chapter 7), make sure that revenues and earnings look poised to move dramatically higher before investing on the long side.

Rule 31: Remember to Use Both Market and Vehicle Valuation Tools. You should only be buying a stock when its P/E is 70 percent or less of its long-term growth rate (5 years), its last two quarterly earnings gains (over similar year earlier quarters), and its expected earnings growth over the next two to three years. Even if you find stocks like this, you must be particularly cautious if those stocks are trading in a country where the overall index is excessively valued. Corrections in valuations of a whole markets rarely leave any stock unaffected. Similarly, look for overvaluation for shorts, and try to be cautious in selling short stocks in undervalued countries.

Rule 32: Recently Inverted Yield Curves Need Special Attention. In any country where a recently inverted yield curve is followed by evidence of economic slowdown, watch carefully for a strong bond market trend as a signal to go long bonds. This combination often leads to the longest and strongest bond bull moves. Such signals are usually heralding the beginning of the end of a recession, growth recession, or soft landing.

Rule 33: Put the Value-Added Wealth Equation on Your Side.   To increase wealth, you must increase your skills, ability, intelligence, and specialized knowledge, which leads to: increased balance, ability to learn, adapt, grow and produce; *which leads to* increased confidence, skills, and ability to contribute; *which leads to* increased happiness and contribution, *which ultimately leads to* increased wealth and well-being.

PRINCIPLES OF CHARACTER

After decades not only of studying the most successful investors but also of teaching investors how to improve their performance, I have learned that certain key concepts or principles of character are critical in allowing investors to reach their maximum potential. While developing discipline is such an important investment skill that it would require its own book-length discussion, in this chapter I want to at least identify basic concepts that investors should use to develop the winning character necessary for long-term success in the investment markets.

Ultimately, your trading performance and your life are nothing but a mirror of your consistent thoughts and beliefs, reflections of your values and your character. While strategies, rules, and selection methodologies are important components of trading/investing success, they are just the first giant step toward investment success. Perhaps even more important is the process you develop for systematically evaluating your success and mistakes in order to learn, grow, and improve your trading and self. These principles are based on some of the top beliefs found in top traders throughout history.

Key Principles

Principle 1: Concentrate on the Process, Not the Result.   Strive to trade at your top level every day and to consistently improve your understanding, level of expertise, and skills, and you will win big. Don't concentrate on winning; concentrate on the process that creates winning.

Principle 2: Make Money and Decisions from Your Skills, Not Your Ability to See through a Crystal Ball.   Do not try to predict the markets; try to learn how to locate runaway trending instruments, and to exploit low-risk, high-reward opportunities for entering with those trends. Don't waste time predicting the environment; invest time developing the skills and abilities necessary to profit from any environment.

Principle 3: It Is Never the Markets—It Is Always You.   Statistics and society may predict, but you alone determine whether you will succeed or fail. You alone are in control; take responsibility for your performance and your life. There are always tremendous opportunities in the markets. It is not what happens; it is what you do with what happens that makes the difference between profit and loss.

Principle 4: Every Event Holds the Seed of a Positive Message or Meaning.   Eventually every trader will face a larger than desired series of losses, or drawdown. How you react and what meaning and lessons you take from that challenge will determine how successful a trader you become. People's greatest changes, ideas, and improvements come from challenging adversity, and a trader's greatest improvements usually come from drawdowns. Seize each day and each loss and mistake as an opportunity to learn, and grow, not as evidence of your inadequacy.

Principle 5: Seek to Embody the True Spirit of Competition.   The Latin root for competition means "to conspire together." The idea is not to try to beat your opponent. It is to pit yourself against a competitor so that you both improve faster and perform at a higher level than you would alone. Coach John Wooden said it best: "Never try to be better than someone else, but never cease to try to be the best you can be."

Principle 6: Treat Investing as If It Were Farming, Not Cramming.   Long-term trading success is like farming—there are no easy shortcuts. Seek to study new methods and tools for farming your skills and understanding, not tips and predictions.

Principle 7: Develop a Love and Respect for Trading, Free Markets, and Individual Liberty and Initiative. Profits are just the gravy. This is also a key to giving you the sense of purpose required for true success. When they test a group of traders, one of the traits that almost all successful traders and investors share is a deep understanding of how trading and investing is part of the process that allows humankind to progress. Even day-traders provide critical liquidity that allows others to hedge, companies to raise capital, and investors to invest with limited risk. Stock selection allows investors to become second-level venture capital firms, with their demand helping provide access to financing in areas where the people need capital most. The more you understand the remarkable way in which freedom and free association work to produce economic gain and real progress for humankind from new innovations and technologies, the more likely you are to feel a strong sense of purpose at being a part of such an incredible system. And the stronger your sense that your efforts are creating something good that is bigger than yourself, the more committed, enriched, excited, and innovative you will become.

Principle 8: Become a Voracious Learner, Reader, and Knowledge Seeker. The more you learn, the more you earn. It is what you learn after you are sure you know everything that really makes you successful.

Principle 9: Do Not Seek Riches, Seek "Real Wealth." Real wealth is not money or material goods, it is the creative and productive force, the indomitable spirit inside everyone. People possessing real wealth can experience life with an unbridled capacity for joy regardless of their financial condition. Real wealth is contained in the knowledge that what you have inside you is the source of your happiness and success and that no matter what life tries to throw at you or take away, you will only become stronger—for that feeling of certainty, confidence, abundance, and security is wealth.

You can never get true feelings of security, happiness, abundance, success, or wealth from material goods, for feelings come from within you, not from outside. But if you develop the inner feelings and knowledge that security, happiness, abundance, success, and wealth come from within you, you can create all the riches you desire. It is not what you get in life, it is what you become that matters. A person who becomes happy, dynamic, enthusiastic, energetic, growing, producing, and contributing will create wealth and grow rich. A person who focuses on negative circumstances may win the lottery but will only experience misery in style.

People who can learn and grow because of the circumstances in their lives are wealthy. They may be temporarily broke, but they are never poor. Those who let circumstances depress and control them are poor. Even though they temporarily acquire riches, they will lose them or never enjoy them fully. The key to real wealth is not the circumstances we find ourselves in, but the meaning we take from them.

People who get their feelings of adequacy from the environment will only feel brief illusions of adequacy because we cannot control the world we live in any more than we can control the markets we trade in. And who would want to anyway! How exciting and illuminating would trading really be if we knew in advance the high, low, and close, every day. It would be completely dull, virtually dead. Life itself is the process of growing and adapting as an organism to new input and situations, not trying to re-create the situations we have already experienced.

Seeking money as a result of working to provide products or services of value to others is a noble pursuit that can lead to feelings of true abundance, happiness, confidence, and self-worth, but seeking money by trying to take advantage of or cheat others cannot produce anything but feelings of inadequacy.

And people do not get rich and the money suddenly changes their lives. It is the other way around. Wealth is a result of successful living, not the source of it. Developing a character and value structure that is consistent with happy, productive living is the process that produces real wealth and abundance.

Principle 10: Understand and Believe That Investing and Trading Create and Add Real Value to Humankind.   Traders and investors are in the business of directing the force of the lifetime accumulation of our unconsumed productivity (savings, capital) to the areas that will most benefit society. Investing can entail assuming the risk of wheat price declines from a farmer; eliminating currency risk for a multinational company; increasing the ease at which a company can acquire the capital to develop new factories, products, and innovations; helping to produce an efficient set of rewards and punishments for successful or unsuccessful management of a company; or simply increasing the liquidity of the structure that allows all the preceding transactions to occur. In each case, the result is the most efficient process that we have found for linking capital to its most productive uses, as indicated by demand.

The Essence of Consistent Profits—Understanding

> As an investor as long as you understand something better than others, you have an edge.
>
> —George Soros

Thus far in this book, we have focused on developing models and tools that are useful in determining investment allocation and individual equity selection. These models and tools can help investors generate above-average returns with relatively low risk in the market environments of the future.

It is foolhardy, however, for any investor to use a model or set of tools without learning how and why those variables have worked in the past, and what is necessary for those variables and models to work in the future. Furthermore, it is much more important for investors to understand the dynamics behind a model or set of tools than to follow a set of historical rules of thumb based on those models. *Understanding is much more critical to your investment success than the models you use.*

So although we have developed simple models in the preceding chapters, along with rules of thumb for their application, investors who want to achieve consistent low-risk investment success still must gain true insight and understanding into how markets work and what factors lie behind profitable investments.

In this chapter, therefore, I present critical components for developing true understanding of the global investment markets. The investment novice may simply take the models we develop in this book and apply them; the investment professional or aspiring master will spend much more time in analyzing this chapter's sections than those that build mechanical models. The novice is looking for quick tips that can improve short- to intermediate-term trading results; whereas the master is striving to develop the skills and knowledge necessary to understand and achieve top investment performance consistently. The novice angler simply wants to know where the good fishing hole is now, where the fish are plentiful and hungry. The master angler wants to learn how to find good fishing holes consistently throughout a lifetime. The novice seeks Holy Grails and shortcuts; the master knows there are no shortcuts and that the constant effort and the never-ending search for knowledge required of true mastery provide their own reward. The master realizes that to act wisely one must first become wise—and that wisdom is a lifelong pursuit. My hope is that this chapter will help many would-be novices begin the journey toward mastery.

If you understand the Austrian Liquidity Cycle (ALC), valuation tools, the importance of technical analysis, and how to pick winning (and losing) stocks, you have a sound foundation for judging the potential of different markets. In this chapter, we discuss several other concepts that investors can use to help understand how to best profit from current and future market environments with a minimum of risk.

Because so few investors understand even the very basics of economics that underlie all market success, we devote considerable space in this chapter to an economic concept every investor should understand—a theory we call Austrian alchemy. We then explore the components behind long-term economic growth rates and investment growth rates and see the implications of different government policies on investments and long-term growth. We also discuss how investors should view and respond to media hype. In addition to describing the broad economic secular themes and trends that may develop in the decades ahead, we show investors how to identify those themes and trends that can propel profits higher. Throughout this analysis, we explain the mechanisms that lie behind gains in different asset classes and specific investments.

AUSTRIAN ALCHEMY

One of the greatest philosophers and economic thinkers in history was Ludwig von Mises, the founder of what is today referred to as Austrian economics. Mises' work on free-market-oriented economics was expanded on and popularized by such Nobel Prize winning economists as Friedrich A. Hayek and Milton Friedman. Austrian economics is based on the simple idea that one must first analyze individual human action to gain any understanding of economics—in Mises' view, economics is simply a branch of the study of human choice (praxeology). It is one of the great tragedies of history that largely because Austrian economics did not give government an excuse to empower itself further (and did not put budding economists in power or policy-making roles), it was trampled by the Keynesian economics that has been and still is taught in our schools.

From the perspective of being able to properly anticipate future events and economic forces, Austrian economics has an almost unbelievably prescient forecasting record, whereas Keynesian economics has an almost equally poor one. Mises' economic theory allowed him to foresee and predict (between the early 1900s and the 1960s): the collapse of the Ottoman Empire because of failed socialist policies, the rise and downfall of fascism, the failure of Communism and Socialism, as well as the failure of U.S. (1960s) redistribution policies to positively impact poverty rates. Unlike Keynesian economics, which utilizes theoretical curves with unrealistic assumptions to give hypothetical results that have little bearing on real-world phenomena, Austrian economics is rooted in the real world—its predictions and analysis tend to be much more valid, realistic, and useful than those of other branches of economics.

The classic joke applied to the field of economics is of three people stranded on a desert island who find a case of canned food that has floated ashore from their shipwreck. Now they must figure out a way of opening the cans to avoid starvation. First, the engineer tries to estimate exactly how high a cliff they will need to drop the cans from to open them: he tries but either fails to open the can or else splashes its contents all over the ground. While working on another solution, he asks the artist and economist to help solve the problem. The artist spends hours sculpting a wooden can opener, which breaks when they try to use it. Frustrated, the artist and engineer turn to the economist. The economist is bewildered at his frustrated companions. "It's so elementary," the economist exclaims, "you simply *assume* a can opener." Such a hypothetical solution so out of touch with reality often works in Keynesian economic literature—but happily this is not a fair criticism of Austrian economics.

Mises, in his brilliant work *Human Action* (Chicago: Henry Regnery Company & Contemporary Books) starts with the simple concept that human beings tend in general to act purposefully and in a way that they perceive as being in their self-interest, and then moves to more profound implications of this concept. If indeed individual actions determine how the mass of humans will behave, and individuals act to benefit their own perceived best interest, then one must analyze carefully how individuals themselves will derive benefits to determine a likely course of events.

Mises developed his theory as a result of being hired by the Austro-Hungarian government to do a multiyear study. His assignment was to find out why the world's first-ever welfare policies were failing not only to pull the people of the Austro-Hungarian Empire out of poverty, but also were costing more and more each year and beginning to lead to economic difficulties. It was in objectively studying the impact of such bureaucratic solutions to poverty that Mises formulated his theory of human action. It is fascinating study to read Mises' book *Bureaucracy* (written in 1944, but based on the concepts developed in his 1922 book *Socialism*) and then read UCLA professor Wilson's book, also entitled *Bureaucracy*, which analyzes the effect of different bureaucratic agencies in the United States during the 1980s. The authors describe the exact same picture and result from nearly identical policies created in totally different eras and countries—and draw many of the same conclusions. Both Wilson and Mises, by studying failed policies, gain much insight into human behavior, policy implications, and economic repercussions of distorting free market processes.

Key Principles of Austrian Economics

We have in a sense, already used some Austrian economics in our earlier discussion of the Austrian Liquidity Cycle and our desert-island example in Chapter 2. Starting with a base of a totally free market and moving forward to understand the implications of every distortion to it is one of the most important methods of analysis an Austrian alchemist can use. The following Austrian-derived principles are key in understanding how a distortion or policy change will impact economic forces:

- First, as mentioned earlier, start with the *base of a totally free market* situation (e.g., desert island). Then look on any law or impediment as an artificial distortion.

- Next, analyze what *effect* those *distortions have on* the *incentives* of individuals within that economy. In Austrian economics, incentives are key determinants of changes in actions. Because changes in incentives affect behavior consistently, they are usually more important than the direct results of a distortion or policy change. Behavior changes reflect changes in decisions about production, capital investment, and labor utilization. Take, for example, the policy of stealing crops from farmers to feed the poor. While the temporary result might be food distributed to more people, the long-run result of doing so would be different. The farmer would have little incentive to produce efficiently or with more labor-effort because the results of his increased labor would not benefit him (in fact, the less he labored producing, the less effort he would be wasting); therefore, he would begin to produce less food. Over the long run, total production would dwindle so much due to this lack of incentive that there would be far less food for everyone in the society. If you doubt this, take a look at farm production in the former Soviet Union, or at the difference in the farm production of Guangdong's farms in China before and after farmers were allowed to sell their excess crops themselves (production rose more than 100% in just three years). When you steal from the producers, the poor are temporarily enriched, but in the long run everyone is impoverished. As Socialism and Communism were becoming popular in the 1920s, Mises used this theory to predict their future failure. He showed how poor incentives created by Communism and Socialism would eventually lead to such dismal economic growth rates and widespread relative poverty that these statist systems would fall apart of their own weight. Thus 70 years ago, Mises predicted the collapse of Communism that we have witnessed in Russia and China.

- Once you have analyzed the change in incentives for individuals due to a distortion, you can recognize that *whatever a distortion taxes it punishes economically and thereby gets less of.* If you tax capital investment for instance, you will get less of it because you have eroded the risk/reward on which capital risk is based. A shrewd investor, as discussed, measures the potential reward of an investment and then compares that reward with the potential risk. When you tax the gains of investment, you erode the potential gain, and increase the potential risk.

- Similarly, *whatever you are subsidizing with a distortion, you will get more of.* When asked what the expected results would be of the Johnson "War on Poverty" welfare programs, Mises once quipped that it would create a great expansion in the number of people seeking assistance, and specifically create an explosion in unwed single mothers with multiple children because that was the highest paid category on the welfare system. Since then the number people seeking assistance is up more than 20-fold, while the number of unwed mothers with multiple children on welfare has increased by over 1000 percent, and the poverty rate has moved higher (as we shall explore in more depth).

- To assess likely outcomes, always *look for those who directly or indirectly benefit economically* behind the scenes. Try to analyze what people are really paying for in economic transactions, instead of just looking at the surface. Years ago, people in the United States wondered why the Bosnian war continued for so long, and why Western Europe did not take a stronger role in containing the conflict. However, those who analyzed the economic forces behind the scenes would have discovered that German military manufacturers were selling to two sides of the conflict and profiting from a continuance; hence a less than all-out German effort at resolution. Another example of the concept of understanding what people are really purchasing is in the difference between Mountain View, California, housing prices and Los Altos, California, housing prices. Houses on the exact same amount of land with the exact same layout, builder, and square footage across the street from one another sell for $200,000 difference in price. The reason: one house is in the prestigious Los Altos school district, whereas the other is in the more mediocre Mountain View school district. People are not paying $200,000 more for any difference in the house: they are paying to educate their children in a top school district versus an average one. It is not surprising then, that the speculator who put big money into trying to make the Mountain View houses be of better quality than the Los Altos houses (and therefore pricier) is having little profit success. He failed to understand what people were really purchasing was not so much a house as it was entrée to a first-rate school district.

- Bureaucracy is a more inefficient and ineffective organizational structure than a profit-motive structure. In a for-profit structure, companies profit by providing a better product or service; their individual benefits are thus somewhat aligned with the goal of their effort (the benefits of the customer). In a bureaucracy, however, the bureaucrat does not benefit individually by solving or helping a problem assigned to the agency. Further, those at the top want to control the bureaucracy so they create rigid rules, forms, and red tape to determine what the actual bureaucrats are doing. Those at the top (usually Congress or the state or county equivalent) are the furthest from seeing the actual problem and the actual result of the policies and red tape they implement. Bureaucrats are thus inevitably turned into forms pushers and procedure followers instead of thinking, acting participants in a system from which they can derive benefits.

Although many more insights can be derived from Austrian economics, the preceding ones are among the most useful. Here are some brief corollaries:

- To get more of a good or service, you must either reward it more or punish it less.

- How a program, plan, or policy is implemented is more important than the goal of that plan. Thus while welfare may have had a goal of ending poverty, the implementation encouraged unwed motherhood, pulled resources from the very components fostering job growth, and helped create a permanent dependent underclass.

- To change an individual's behavior, it helps to provide a model showing that behaving differently produces more desirable results. Thus packing all the poor into public housing where there are few models of true success created slums of hopelessness where models of success were most needed.

- To assess a proposed plan's potential for success or failure, look at examples of similar plans and policies that were initiated in the past or in other countries. In addition, when you see one or two countries develop similar programs that are successful, analyze what elements of human action made them successful and see if you can emulate those components (we will do this later on when we look at Chile's pension reform program and Singapore's medical insurance system).

- Economic growth is the main element that has historically and consistently led to a decline in poverty rates across countries. Therefore programs that foster growth lead to poverty alleviation and those that punish growth (tax increases) lead to increases in poverty. Remember that the cure for unemployment is employment—and jobs are created by entrepreneurs, not governments. Taking resources away from entrepreneurs and putting them into the hands of politicians is therefore unlikely to create any positive economic effects. It would be like taking seed corn from a farmer just before planting and giving it to the mayor of the town nearest to the farmer's fields. Would that solve the food shortage in the town?

Summary of Principles and Corollaries

If we start with the model of a totally free market and then assume all impediments to that free market are distortions, we can analyze the effect of those distortions. One of the main effects of a distortion is a change in the critical incentive structure of the system. How an incentive structure changes is important because individuals usually behave in a way that they perceive as being in their self-interest. Distortions either punish or subsidize some group—and this change in incentives (and therefore self-interest) will create different behavior that is not aligned with free market forces. The incentive effect created by the specific implementation of a policy or distortion is more important than the goal because it is the actual implementation that changes incentives. To determine how underlying benefits are really being distributed, investors must look behind the scenes for the actual beneficiaries of a distortion.

Because individuals tend to act purposely and in their own interest, a system that aligns individuals self-interest with the outcome desired is much more likely to be successful in achieving that outcome than a system in which an individual's self-interest is not aligned with the outcome. Thus a profit-motive system is more likely to produce results in concert with the customer's desired outcome than a bureaucracy, which inevitably creates red tape, forms, process-pushers, and a lack of connection between desired result and action.

To change behavior, one needs to show concrete models and examples to people of how behaving differently produces better results. One should also look to history and to international models of successful (or unsuccessful) policies and analyze these examples. Finally, lower poverty rates are fundamentally caused by economic growth; historically, poverty rates correlate inversely with economic growth rates in any country analyzed. We will explore the implications of many of these statements later on in the chapter.

ALCHEMY VERSUS ECONOMICS

The second part of the term Austrian alchemy is the word *alchemy*. While Mises himself was what I would term a philosophical alchemist because he realized that humans could produce with labor what did not exist before, modern economists like Paul Pilser have done some excellent work on economic alchemy, which melds well with Austrian economic principles to explain our dynamic technological world in terms that people need to understand.

Alchemists were firm believers in the philosophy that a true God would not put us in a scarce environment, and that there therefore must be a way for individuals to create wealth through individual action. In seeking to make gold from lead, they invented metallurgy, chemistry, pharmacy, medicine, and much of modern science technology. This made many of them wealthy. Ironically, had they succeeded instead in turning lead to gold, the increase in gold supply would have simply forced the price of gold lower.

While the classic definition of economics is "how a society allocates scarce resources," and economics thereby promotes that the way to achieve wealth is by controlling those scarce resources, alchemists believe that one achieves wealth by creating value for others. As Pilser points out in his book *Unlimited Wealth* (New York: Crown Publishers), if economics were valid then the richest country in the world would be the one with the most natural resources, while the poorest would be the one with the least. Of the major economies in the world, Russia has the most natural resources, while Japan has the least. Yet by any measure, Japan is richer today than Russia. The wealth of a nation is not in its physical resources, but in what the people know how to do and the capital infrastructure they have at their disposal to do it. We live in an alchemic world where wealth comes from adding value, not from controlling "scarce" resources.

The Concepts of Alchemy

The Role of Technology.   *Technology* is a major determinant of wealth because it determines the nature and supply of resources. With the technology to create silicon chips, what was once worthless sand becomes an invaluable resource, silicon. In the 1600s, Native Americans lacked farming technology. To them, land was simply a place to find wild game to eat. The American Indians often hunted a piece of land until it had no further hunting prospects and then traded it to the White settlers. Indians did not recognize the worth of the land itself. But to farmers with a steel plough technology, the land was an invaluable resource that would allow them to produce huge amounts of food and wealth. Technology defines what we call a resource. What the farmer was doing by using the plough on new land was filling a technology gap.

Filling the Gap. A *technology gap* is a better way of doing something. The backlog of unimplemented technological advances (the technology gap) is a *main determinant* of long-term economic growth potential for a society. The speed at which technology gaps are implemented and their effect on productivity are major determinants of economic growth within a society. In an environment of accelerating technological change, *capital investment and the ability of the labor force to implement new technologies* purchased with capital investment determine how fast technology gaps are filled and how much *growth* exists in an economy.

Speed—A Critical Component. The speed at which we exchange information acts like a grease in determining how fast technology advances. Just as the advent of the printing press 500 years ago enabled quicker implementation of new ideas and techniques because they could be distributed to more people more quickly, the personal computer and the Internet communication revolution are causing a new burst of quicker technological advances that can ripple through the economy at faster rates. Because technology gaps are a major determinant of economic growth, the speed at which we ourselves learn and adapt to new technologies is an overriding determinant of our own individual success. Essentially, an individual adds value by exploiting a technology gap.

The Free Exchange of Ideas. The *free interaction* among independent-thinking individuals is the true source of wealth because ideas are the source of innovation behind technology gaps. Communication is the source of technology gap implementation. Whatever interferes with free interaction and communication stunts growth in individuals and societies, while broad and free communication enhances and releases untapped growth potential. The invisible hand of prosperity lies in freedom.

The Myth of Scarcity. There are no scarce resources in the long run because technology can create a substitute for almost everything. History is filled with examples of perceived crises that were disguised opportunities for the innovator who came up with a substitute for the good perceived to be in shortage. People thought they would run out of iron near the end of the Iron Age, of whale oil and then coal energy in the 1800s. Oil became the next opportunity—a form of energy from what was formerly a by-product. In the 1970s, the Club of Rome published reports saying that there were only 30 years of oil left on the planet. Technology improved our usage and our discovery process and today it is projected that we have nearly 200 years of oil left. When oil becomes expensive and in shorter supply, a new form of energy will be developed. Innovation can turn sand into gold and create abundant resources out of things we cannot yet imagine.

Relating Demand to Technology. Technology is part of what determines both the quality and quantity of demand. The demand for new significant technological breakthroughs in products is nearly unlimited. In the 1950s, it was ridiculous to imagine a family having more than one black-and-white television set. As technology made improvements in quality (color and size), quantity, and price, demand soared so that today the average family purchases more than four TVs. As the prospect for HD TV is contemplated, producers don't look just to sell to the top end of the market, but, eventually to virtually replace the entire existing supply of television receivers.

Replacing Labor with Technology. When technology replaces labor it is a long-run benefit to society because it frees up resources for other things. This concept is so misunderstood by most people that it is worth elaborating on. The desert island example is helpful here. Suppose that of the 10 stranded people, 2 are working at fishing. One day, one of the fishermen decides to spend some savings on the day's subsistence and forgo fishing; instead, he tries to build a fishing net that would allow him to catch more fish. After several false tries that bring him near the brink of starvation, he finally comes up with a brilliant raft-net combination that increases 10-fold the number of fish he can catch in a day. Suddenly, the price of fish plummets in response to the new supply, and the other fisherman can no longer live on the returns from his outmoded one-pole fishing methods. The second fisherman may face a difficult period ahead in trying to find some other task that will benefit the other islanders enough to pay his subsistence, but in fact, the society's benefit from the new innovation is not just the 10-fold increase in new fish on a daily basis, but is also the new productivity from the extra laborer who is occupied adding value in another way.

Imagine what might happen to island productivity if, out of a heartfelt sympathy for the second fisherman, the islanders elect to steal (tax) 50 percent of the net-innovator's fish and just give them to the other fisherman so that he can keep on fishing the way he has been and still receive enough to survive. Notice what this distortion does to the innovator's incentives. The net-maker had discovered that getting up before dawn optimized the number of fish caught with his net, but when he personally only benefited by half of his increase in productivity, he decided it was hardly worth the extra effort. And since the second fisherman was really only catching about a fifth of the fish he sold, he often spent time playing gambling games with the other islanders instead of working; his own work made up such a small amount of his own wage that it was hardly worth the effort. In addition, one of the berry-gatherers had thought of spending some of his savings to try building a special berry-picking rake tool, but when he calculated his probable gain after the tax he was likely to be hit with to compensate the other berry gatherers, he decided the potential reward was not worth the risk associated with spending all his savings on the project, which might not pay off anyway. After just a brief period, the island's overall productivity is significantly less with the tax distortion than it would be without it. The innovator's production is less, the second fisherman's production is less, and the potential of new technologies is less. How much better the island economy would be if the second fisherman could quickly find another task that added value to the island and the free-market incentives of risk to innovation remained intact.

Since the 1920s, the West has taxed the net-maker—essentially applying economic solutions (how to allocate resources) to problems that require alchemic solutions (how to get the second fisherman to add value in a new way). The result of these distortions is substantially less growth than is possible, less innovation, less risk-taking, less capital investment, higher poverty rates, and a destructive subsidization of the underskilled. In the United States, in fact, we have created with these distortions a third-world country within our own country, a permanent underclass that is falling further and further behind the soaring top 20 percent who dominate the world in terms of productivity. Tax rates for the very people who are creating the new jobs needed to solve the problem have thus soared from 0 percent (pre-World War I) to as high as 90 percent in 1980 and around 60 percent total in California and New York today. We will explore this issue in more detail later on in the chapter, but the theoretical implications should be clear.

Investors should realize that in a developed country like the United States, only about 5 percent of what we produce feeds, clothes, and shelters us (economic), whereas 95 percent of what we produce is alchemic—goods beyond subsistence resources that did not even exist 50 years ago.

In addition, technology tends to magnify the skill-set of laborers and the importance of labor being able to work together as a team and to adjust to constantly changing technologies. The ability to learn and adapt to new technologies and acquire new skills quickly is the ultimate advantage of labor today. Time Warner is an example of a company bought for billions of dollars, whose main assets were almost entirely the intellectual skills possessed by the labor that company had assembled.

Alchemic laws impact investors who are fundamentally in the business of assisting entrepreneurs to initiate the business of change. Investors control the capital that is the catalyst for filling a technology gap. A top investor must always be on the lookout for what is coming next technologically and realize that each change in technology is a new link in a continuing chain of innovation, as well as a profit opportunity. *To find top growth opportunities, investors must seek companies that are applying new technologies or exploiting technology gaps.*

The company innovating a product is not necessarily the one that profits most from it; instead, the company that profits is the one bringing the product to customers in a way that spurs demand. Seiko, for example, did not invent digital watches—it merely contracted the technology from Swiss watchmakers who did not see the potential. But it was Seiko who made the most money from digital watch sales. Similarly, Sony did not invent transistors, and Ford did not invent cars, but these were the companies that utilized new technologies to bring desired products to the consumer.

THE LONG-RUN GROWTH PARADIGM

The long-run growth paradigm is an implication of the combination of Austrian economics with Economic alchemy that investors need to understand, particularly when trying to determine allocation among countries that may have similar ALC, valuation, and technical models. Investors need to constantly be on the lookout for investment opportunities:

> The ideal equity investment occurs during a recession when long and short rates are both dropping, stocks are undervalued, capacity constraints are low, technical models are positive on bonds and newly positive on stocks, and the long-run growth potential of a country looks excellent.

This is an environment where an investor can begin to build a long-term position up slowly over a three- to four-year period during the entire budding expansion phase. Over an economic cycle, the vast majority of an investor's profits may come from such ideal-time investments. Most times, such an ideal environment doesn't exist in total and an investor must do the best possible with what the market is giving, but one must be on the lookout for such investments and strive not to miss out on an opportunity for triple-digit multiyear profits in the making.

Thus investors must be able to assess the long-run potential of a particular market and country's growth rate. The following algorithm will help investors to determine the superior growth potential of both country and market.

The long-run growth algorithm goes like this:

Increased savings leads to increased capital;

Increased capital leads to increased capital investment;

Increased capital investment + the size of technology gaps (created by new innovations) lead to

Increased marginal productivity of capital, which leads to

Increased productivity.

Increased productivity leads to

Increased growth + increased wages + increased employment + decreased poverty rates.

Working backward, we can see how this long-run growth paradigm operates in the real world. The more you can understand the forces that create major market moves, the more on top of the market you are likely to be. There are so many important points (and several Nobel Prizes in economics) contained in this algorithm that understanding it is critical for investors. One of the most critical is the impact and importance of Productivity. Figure 6.1 shows the impact of productivity on a number of variables.

The ideal economic environment is strong economic growth, increasing employment, increasing real wages, and decreasing poverty rates. This is also the type of environment where corporate profits grow the strongest, and therefore potential stock gains are the greatest. Strong growth and high per capita income countries also tend to have the lowest pollution problems and the smallest social problems, largely because they are best able to afford to take care of any problems that arise. What factors go into creating this nirvana environment on a prolonged basis?

Figure 6.1 does a good job of showing the strong correlation between productivity gains and gains in real average hourly earnings (real wages), gains in corporate profits (earnings and long-term stock appreciation potential), and total employment (job growth directly cutting unemployment and poverty). Notice on the top chart that since World War II whenever productivity gained consistently, real average hourly earnings (real after-inflation wages) gained soon thereafter. In addition, whenever productivity declined consistently, a decline in real wages soon followed. There is clearly cause and effect here. A recent economic Nobel Prize was given basically for proof that productivity is the long-run determinant of wages (not government increases in the minimum wage rate). It makes sense. When an individual worker is suddenly producing more, a company's ability to pay that worker more increases—and eventually it will do so.

The second panel of Figure 6.1 shows the similar leading nature of productivity versus corporate profits as a percentage of gross domestic product (GDP). Again, every major increase in corporate profits is led first by an increase in productivity and every major decrease in corporate profits is led by a decrease in productivity. This is logical—companies can make more when each worker is producing more—some of those productivity gains will eventually lead to increased wages, and some will remain in the

Figure 6.1 **THE IMPACT OF PRODUCTIVITY**

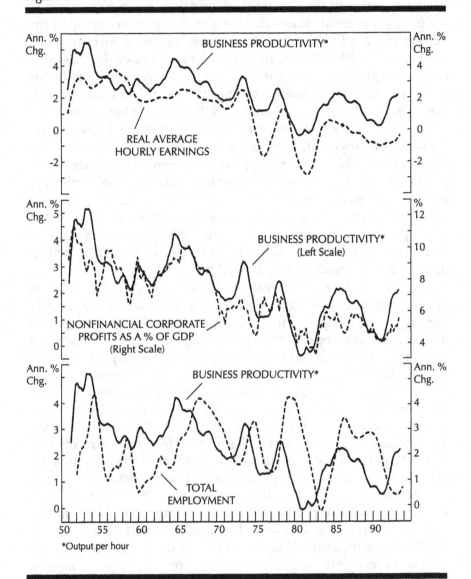

Note: Productivity, employment, and hourly earnings are all shown as 3-year moving averages.

Source: Reprinted by permission of the *Bank Credit Analyst.*

profit coffers of corporations who have supplied the capital allowing labor to produce more.

The bottom panel of Figure 6.1 shows the lagging but still strong correlation between productivity and total employment. Again this is logical. Once corporations are reaping the higher profits from increased productivity, they will first increase wages and then they will begin hiring more workers. Employment lags productivity gains because corporations are reticent to hire new people until they are sure that demand will remain strong and profits are continuing to stay strong enough to allow for higher baseline costs. Higher employment usually means lower unemployment and lower poverty rates as a higher percentage of the population have gainful occupations. These charts show that we had two really consistent increases in productivity—one from the early 1960s to the mid to late 1960s and the other from 1982 to the mid to late 1980s. These were also the two main periods when the government's own poverty rate measure showed dramatic declines from its uptrend since the late 1950s.

The bottom line is that productivity gains lead to higher employment, higher wages, and higher corporate profits because when employees can produce more with their time, corporations make more money from that time. In making more money, corporations are then able to expand their operations and to pay higher wages for employees already producing more per hour. Productivity simply measures how much is being produced per unit of time.

One point people often confuse is the concept of wages per productive unit of time. For example, in the early 1990s NAFTA debate, it was often stated that it would be impossible for U.S. workers to compete with people earning one dollar per day or less. But such comparisons of average wages totally ignore the productivity of the labor involved and so are not a real comparison.

As an analogy, suppose you are in the grave-digging business and for some tragic reason there is a sudden surge in demand for your services so that you must hire more people.

You have a choice. You can hire a person for 50 cents per hour who digs with his fingernails and takes 20 hours to dig a single grave. As a potential employer, you are not so much concerned with the wage as with the cost per grave (the wage per productive unit). At 50 cents an hour, the 20-hour grave will cost you $10. You can also hire another person who digs with a shovel for $1.50 per hour and can dig two graves in 10 hours. His per grave cost is actually $7.50 per grave, which is cheaper than the man who costs a third as much per hour. Finally, you can also hire a highly skilled bulldozer operator who can make 40 graves in an 8-hour day, but costs $10 per hour. The highly skilled worker costs $2 per grave and is therefore actually the cheapest worker when productivity of graves is taken into account.

How can American labor compete with Chinese labor costing $1 per hour? Actually when one accounts for the per unit productivity rate, American labor is some of the cheapest and most competitive in the world. So remember the importance of productivity in the wage comparison equation.

Also study Figure 6.1 carefully because its implications are profound. Productivity is the key to economic growth, rising corporate profits and stock values, rising wages, rising employment, and declining rates of poverty. It is also what allows us to deal with other problems such as pollution. So a society that robs resources from productivity gains is merely stripping itself of future progress.

If productivity is central to creating the economic environment that everyone desires, the next question becomes, How do we get increases in productivity? As already discussed in the alchemy principles, innovation and the new technologies it spawns create potential technology gaps; and capital investment putting those new technologies at the fingertips of workers fills those gaps. Therefore, if you take International Monetary Fund (IMF) data on investment as a percentage of GDP and correlate that across countries to their average annual GDP growth per capita, you will find that in general the countries with higher investment get higher growth. Figure 6.2 does just that, and it also takes this scatter diagram of countries' growth versus investment and regresses it to show the regression line. This regression line shows a close correlation between a country's investment rate and its growth rate per capita; as investment increases, the regression of all countries shows a sharp increase in GDP per capita growth rate (the line is upward sloping).

In our grave-digging analogy, it is easy to understand why investment is so important. What determined the productivity of

Figure 6.2 CORRELATION OF INVESTMENT AND PRODUCTIVITY

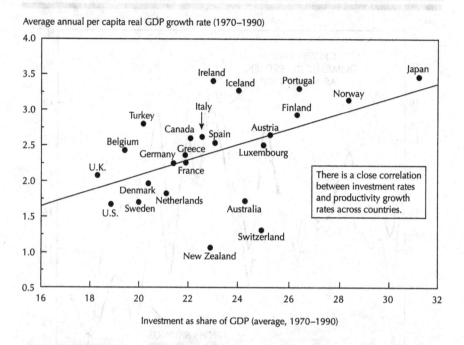

Average annual per capita real GDP growth rate (1970–1990)

There is a close correlation between investment rates and productivity growth rates across countries.

Investment as share of GDP (average, 1970–1990)

Source: International Monetary Fund. Reprinted by permission of the *Bank Credit Analyst.*

each grave digger's production was the amount of capital invested in the tool being used. A shovel allowed for higher production than bare hands, whereas an expensive bulldozer allowed for much higher productivity. While there was a slight skill difference in these laborers, the major difference was the amount of capital that had been invested in their tools—the higher the capital invested, the higher productivity became.

If capital investment and the size of the technology gap that investment is made in are major elements of that all-critical productivity, then the next question is, What determines capital investment? As Figure 6.3 illustrates, in the long run domestic savings correlate highly with investment. While there is often foreign investment as well, domestic savings still make up a large percentage of the new capital that can be invested. And we

Figure 6.3 **SAVINGS AND INVESTMENT**

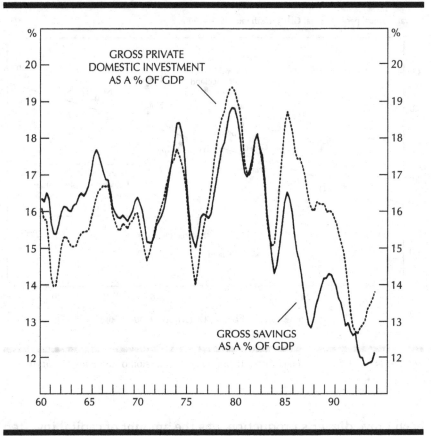

Note: Both series are shown as 4-quarter moving averages.

Source: Reprinted by permission of the *Bank Credit Analyst.*

can be confident that where high savings exist, capital investment is also likely to be high.

Two things should jump out at you from the saving/investment chart shown in Figure 6.3. The first is the incredible correlation between savings and investment since the 1960s. The second is the large decline in savings the United States has witnessed since the late 1970s. In addition to capital gains taxes, which punish critical savings and investment, in the 1970s the United States created several distortions that produced a disincentive to save.

The combination of negative real interest rate in the late 1970s and tax deductibility of debt made debt assumption (which is essentially dissaving) not only profitable but even tax deductible. While the early 1980s adjustment to tax policies made a temporary dent in the decline in domestic savings rates, it did not change the deductibility of mortgage debt, and its impact declined when tax rates were quickly raised again. The result was a temporary blip in savings rates that continue dropping to lower and lower levels even today—which is disastrous for the potential growth of the economy as a whole. Thank goodness, foreign investment in the United States is quite high in the 1990s!

In the late 1980s and early to mid 1990s, two things saved the United States from facing a decline in productivity concurrent with the decline in domestic savings rates. As discussed earlier in this book, the first was strong foreign investment in our debt markets, in particular from Japan and the rest of Asia as their sterilization programs forced them to basically pay for our domestic deficits and much of our current account deficit as well. Even more significant has been the impact of the personal computer—a new technology that has led to one of the largest technology gaps ever encountered in world history. Figure 6.4 illustrates well the effect of the PC on the marginal productivity of capital, or the increase in productivity from adding additional capital. This is partly a measure of the size of the technology gap, which began to skyrocket in 1983 and continues to explode. In fact, the marginal productivity of capital has risen so dramatically in response to new computer technologies that we have been able to see an increase in productivity despite lower domestic capital investment and savings. To spur productivity rates higher over the long run, however, we cannot count on marginal productivity gains to be nearly so high and must attack our low savings problem by eliminating the artificial barriers and punishments to savings and investment. Domestic savings comprise personal savings of individuals, business retained earnings, plus government surpluses or minus government deficits. Therefore, a prolonged decrease in government outlays is pivotal in increasing our domestic savings rates.

Figure 6.4 finishes our proof of the long-run growth paradigm. Figures 6.5 and 6.6 complete the picture and help investors understand the implications of the paradigm. Over the long run, the S&P's gains correlate closely to gains in GDP and to gains in

Figure 6.4 **INVESTMENT TRENDS AND MARGINAL PRODUCTIVITY OF CAPITAL**

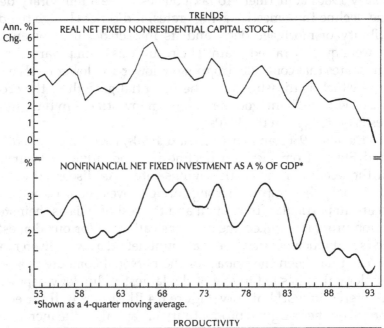

*Shown as a 4-quarter moving average.

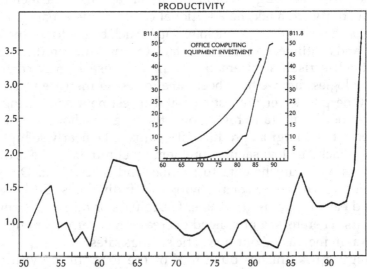

*3-year change in GDP divided by 3-year change in net stock of nonresidential fixed capital.

Source: Reprinted by permission of the *Bank Credit Analyst.*

Figure 6.5 **STOCK MARKET AND THE ECONOMY**

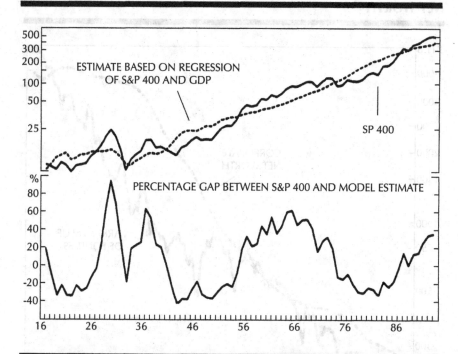

Source: Reprinted by permission of the *Bank Credit Analyst.*

corporate net worth. As mentioned before, earnings gains ultimately lead to increases in the value of equities, and one cannot get
consistent earnings growth without corresponding GDP growth
and corresponding corporate net worth growth.

Using the main principles of Austrian alchemy and the concepts behind the long-run growth paradigm, we can begin to look
for the investments and policies that encourage high productivity-
led growth to propel stock prices higher. Investors must grasp
this key point: If you understand the forces behind a strong
growth, high-profit-producing economy, you are much better able
to focus your investments on such situations when choosing
different countries and companies to invest in. Therefore the following section focuses on the effect of differing policies on the
growth and investment potential of a country using the principles covered thus far.

Figure 6.6 **MARKET VALUE OF EQUITIES VERSUS CORPORATE NET WORTH**

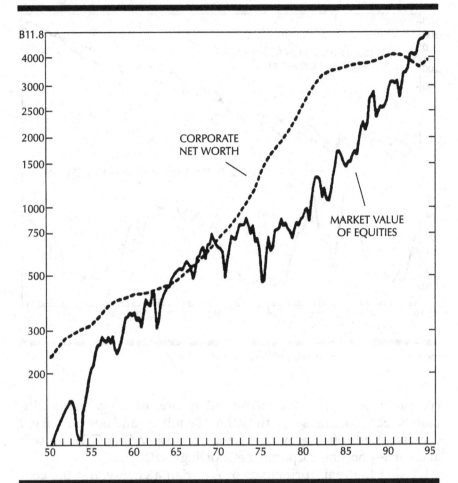

Source: Federal Reserve Flow of Funds. Reprinted by permission of the *Bank Credit Analyst.*

NEGATIVE TAX POLICIES

One of the principles of Austrian economics is that a tax acts as a punishment incentive-wise, creating less of whatever is being taxed than would exist without the tax. What then would be the theoretical effect of taxing corporate profit returns from manufacturing in a given country? Our theory would hold that in general those countries with lower tax rates would be able to generate higher returns, whereas those countries with higher tax rates would be able to generate lower returns, all else being equal. In reality, all else is never equal, but Table 6.1 shows that the profit returns on manufacturing assets conform remarkably well to this theory.

Though not 100 percent identical, those countries with the highest tax rates tend to show the lowest returns on manufacturing assets, whereas those countries with the lowest tax rates tend to show the highest returns on manufacturing assets. For example, you are much more likely to get more profit from investing in a manufacturing company that is Singaporean, Dutch, or Irish than one that is Swedish, at least over the long run. The corporate tax does a good job of literally taking profits away from investors, and putting it in the hands of government. The corporate tax also stifles the growth of corporations' net worth and therefore ultimately cuts down GDP growth and the potential growth of the economy and the stock market based on that economy. Look for countries with low corporate taxes for top investment potential.

Figure 6.7 shows the effect of what has to be the stupidest tax on earth—the capital gains tax. Remember that capital investment

Table 6.1 **TAX RATES**

(1988 pretax average return on manufacturing assets and 1986 average effective tax rates)

Country	Return	Taxes
Ireland	28.6%	4.3%
Singapore	20.2	4.9
Netherlands	26.7	9.0
Taiwan	14.8	11.2
Canada	7.8	37.8
France	6.8	40.0
Germany	7.1	45.2
Japan	8.6	50.6
Sweden	7.8	54.5
All countries	8.4	30.5

Source: U.S. Department of Commerce and *Investor's Business Daily.*

Figure 6.7 **TRADE-OFF**

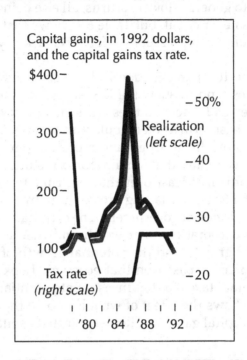

Capital gains, in 1992 dollars, and the capital gains tax rate.

Source: International Revenue Service and *Investor's Business Daily*. Reprinted by permission of *Investor's Business Daily*.

is what fills technology gaps and puts more productive tools in the hands of labor, directly enhancing that Rosetta Stone of desired economic effects—productivity. Imagine the effect of punishing capital investment on a society: essentially such a tax punishes the very productivity gains required to create economic gains. This tax is a direct attack on growth of profits, employment, and wages, and hence on poverty reduction. Governments may need revenue, but this is not the place to get it unless they are looking for slower growth, lower wages, lower profits, higher unemployment, and more poverty.

We mentioned earlier the long-term negative effects of stealing the farmer's crops to feed the poor. A capital gains tax essentially steals the seed corn the farmer must plant before any crop can grow. Moreover, higher capital gains taxes immobilize capital. Under a high capital gains tax, investors tend to stick with their investments because they hope for more gains down the road and want to avoid a sure loss of the tax rate on profit taking. This locking up of capital holds back the continual reinvestment in new technologies needed to fuel optimum productivity gains. Figure 6.7 shows how sensitive this lock-in of capital effect is in the United States. As Reagan cut the capital gains tax rate from 50 percent to 20 percent, the realization of capital gains literally exploded, rising over fourfold within two years after implementation. This is capital that wanted to go to new investment areas but was punished for doing so by the higher tax rate. As soon as the tax rate was raised to 28 percent again realizations dropped off dramatically once more.

While one could argue that the lower tax rate of the early 1980s actually produced more revenue than the higher tax rate ($400 million × 20% is > $100 million × 50%) because of soaring realizations, it should be evident that taxing the seed corn before it even produces anything at any rate at all is sheer lunacy for a society desiring the positive economic effects of higher productivity. The only sane capital gains tax rate is 0 percent in a society desiring higher profit, higher employment, higher growth, higher stock values, and lower poverty rates. And as Table 6.2 shows (rates of early 1990s), many developed countries and most of the fastest growing countries on earth have already figured out the stupidity of a capital gains tax and have made such gains exempt from taxes of any sort. Countries with the lowest capital gains taxes make more favorable investments because they are likely to face higher productivity gains and therefore higher profit growth.

There is an additional huge cost to investors from the capital gains tax rate, which is illustrated in Figure 6.8. That cost is the direct loss of investment profits, which when compounded over an investment lifetime, is an astronomical cost. As the figure shows, the U.S. investor paying the top capital gains tax rate, starting off with $100,000, and achieving a high 20 percent annual rate of return ends up with only $800,000 after 40 years, whereas the Hong Kong investor with no capital gains taxes takes the same $100,000 and earns the same 20 percent annually for 40 years and ends up with $10.6 million—more than 13 times as much money. The only difference is that one government was

Table 6.2 **CAPITAL GAINS TAX RATES**

Country	Maximum Long-Term Rate (%)	Maximum Short-Term Rate (%)
United States	34	34
United Kingdom	35	35
Sweden	18	40
Canada	17.51	17.51
France	15	42
West Germany	Exempt	50
Belgium	Exempt	Exempt
Italy	Exempt	Exempt
Japan	Exempt	Exempt
Netherlands	Exempt	Exempt
Hong Kong	Exempt	Exempt
Singapore	Exempt	Exempt
South Korea	Exempt	Exempt
Taiwan	Exempt	Exempt
Malaysia	Exempt	Exempt

smart enough not to tax the seed corn of growth. Think for a minute about the long-term ramifications to your children and grandchildren of allowing your government to tax capital gains so highly when most high-growth countries do not. Which country will be able to buy the other down the road?

Taxing savings and capital gains directly has a negative influence on productivity and therefore growth, but what about an indirect tax on the source of most savings, a tax on income? U.S. history has only two examples of broad-based income tax cuts, those of the Kennedy administration in the early 1960s and those of the Reagan administration in the early 1980s. Our long-run growth algorithm would lead us to conclude that anything that cut potential savings (and savings come from excess income among other things) would also lead to lower growth and general economic performance. Similarly any cut in income taxes would tend to cut the punishment for savings and should help indirectly to boost growth.

Figure 6.8 **AFTER-TAX WEALTH**

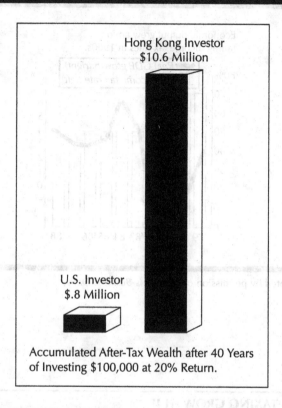

Hong Kong Investor
$10.6 Million

U.S. Investor
$.8 Million

Accumulated After-Tax Wealth after 40 Years
of Investing $100,000 at 20% Return.

Figures 6.9 and 6.10 show GDP growth rates along with the cuts in income taxes during the Reagan and Kennedy tax cut programs. The GDP growth following these tax cuts averaged among the highest rates for the longest periods in this century. Not shown but also consistent was the drop in GDP growth rates when these tax cuts were erased by later income tax hikes. Perhaps our Founding Fathers and the Supreme Court of the Civil War Era were farsighted in finding the income tax to be unconstitutional. In any event, investors looking for solid long-term economic performance should favor countries with low income taxes as well as low or zero capital gains taxes and low corporate taxes.

Figure 6.9 **TAXING GROWTH I**

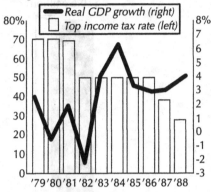

Economic output grew amid
falling income tax rates in 1980s.

Source: Reprinted by permission of *Investor's Business Daily.*

Figure 6.10 **TAXING GROWTH II**

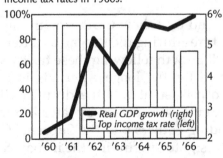

Economic output grew amid falling
income tax rates in 1960s.

Source: Reprinted by permission of *Investor's Business Daily.*

On the subject of income taxes, the media have been touting revisionist history about the Reagan tax cuts (the Kennedy tax cuts apparently were okay but Reagan's were bad). The fallacy being propagated is that the tax cuts were responsible for the soaring deficits of the late 1980s. There are two points investors need to understand about the tax cuts of the 1980s. The first is that the year following the tax cuts, 1983, government revenue from taxes actually began climbing consistently above the level of the prior years, which had higher tax levels. The so-called Laffer curve worked—GDP increased enough from lower taxes that even though tax rates were lower, they were being applied to enough higher output levels that tax revenues did not go down. What made the deficit rise (as explored in more detail later in this chapter) was that spending grew by more than the increase in revenue. If spending had been kept flat, deficits would have actually dropped in nominal dollars. Spending however exploded, slightly from higher defense spending, but mostly from out-of-control skyrocketing entitlement outlays.

The second point that investors should realize about the Reagan tax cuts and deficits is that deficits as a percentage of GDP actually declined sharply following Reagan's tax cuts as illustrated in Figure 6.11, showing tax rates versus the deficit as a percentage of GDP. It is far more instructive to view both government spending and the government surplus or deficit as a percentage of GDP than as a nominal number. When you compare spending versus GDP and deficits versus GDP, you can look across different countries and quickly identify whose spending is out of line with its ability to pay for that spending. As Figure 6.11 shows, one year after Reagan's initial tax cuts, the deficit as a percentage of GDP actually began a sustained decline and was cut in half before Reagan left office. Further notice that the deficit as a percentage of GDP did not rise materially again until Bush began to institute higher tax policies once more. Government spending as a percentage of GDP also fell during Reagan's tax cut era even though annual expenditures on entitlement programs grew from less than $350 billion a year when Reagan took office to over $500 billion a year when he left office (taking up over ½ of the entire budget). The point here is that lower taxes do not necessarily mean lower revenues, nor do they mean higher deficits in relation to GDP.

Figure 6.11 **TAX AND SPEND?**

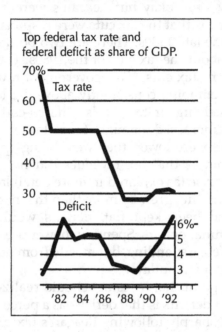

Source: Reprinted by permission of *Investor's Business Daily.*

Note that we are using U.S. figures merely for data convenience purposes. The U.S. example is not isolated, though few countries change rates and policies as frequently as does the United States. Huge tax cuts in countries such as Great Britain, Chile, Hong Kong, Argentina, New Zealand, and much of Asia have led to higher government revenues accompanied by higher growth. So investors need to look for low-tax rates, first on capital, then on corporations, and then on income to zero in on top long-term growth potential countries.

DISASTROUS SOCIAL PROGRAMS

Question: What is the most costly war ever undertaken in the human history? No, not World War II—but the so-called War on

Poverty undertaken by the United States since the mid 1960s. Imagine if the United States had been at war with an enemy for over 30 years, had spent literally over 5 trillion dollars on the effort (so that spending on the war now took over half of the entire federal budget), and after all that spending and effort, was still losing the war rather consistently. Would you want the United States to continue if this war were on foreign soil? What if every other government that attempted to fight this enemy directly had faced similar failure?

Since the mid-1960s, anti-poverty programs and other wealth transfers have continued to explode in cost and yet the poverty rate continues on a long-term rising rate. Figure 6.12 shows that there is absolutely no correlation between increased spending on antipoverty programs and the poverty rate itself. In fact the only two periods where poverty rates dropped for a sustained period were

Figure 6.12 **A POOR EFFORT**

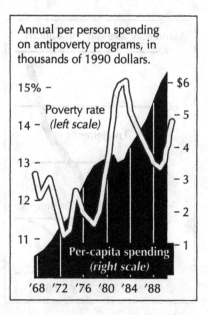

Annual per person spending on antipoverty programs, in thousands of 1990 dollars.

Poverty rate (left scale)

Per-capita spending (right scale)

Source: U.S. Census Bureau, The Heritage Foundation. Reprinted by permission of *Investor's Business Daily.*

following the Kennedy tax cuts and ensuing higher growth in the 1960s, and following the Reagan tax cuts and ensuing higher GDP growth from the early to late 1980s. Today, the poverty rate is approaching prior highs, up substantially from the rate when the antipoverty programs were started, although we have spent trillions of dollars on these programs and continue to spend over half the federal budget on such entitlements (see Figure 6.13).

This is pretty much the same phenomenon found by Ludwig von Mises when he studied the effects of the first socialist antipoverty programs on the Austro-Hungarian Empire, which ultimately crumbled under the weight of spending on these programs (among other things). And the reason for this dismal failure is the same as it was then: the incentives to growth that are punished by the tax are far more wide-reaching than the effects of the initial redistribution. The punishment of work, risk, and innovation retard

Figure 6.13 RAMPING UP

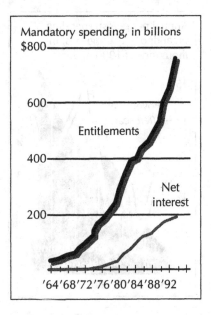

Source: Tax Foundation and Joint Economic Committee. Reprinted by permission of *Investor's Business Daily.*

growth while the subsidization of not-working and of single-mothering has created a chronic underclass that is essentially on strike against a system that keeps them from being able to access the growth they need to become fully employed. We have pulled rocks from the bottom of the dike to help stop a leak near the top only to find that the holes in the foundation let far more water through than any leak on the top ever could.

For more than 30 years, the U.S. government has instituted the most expensive beggar-thy-neighbor policies ever tried, stealing seed corn from the crop producers and then wondering why crop production does not rise enough to feed the hungry. No wonder poverty rates are higher today (even though the federal government keeps fudging with these statistics). Among the results are exploding crime rates as the underclass attempt to fight back against a society that offers them little hope of embetterment; trillions of dollars of spending doing more harm than good; substantially less growth, employment, innovation, savings, risk taking, and capital investment than would occur normally; and the creation of such high tax rates to keep the ballooning entitlement spending going that the very people responsible for creating new technologies and jobs have become tax-slaves to the government. Meanwhile, the government's primary function has become to serve as a wealth-transfer agent (with ⅔ of spending going to wealth transfers today).

Tragically, many Western European governments have emulated the U.S. social programs with their own unique brands of wealth-transfers. In no case has the policy been successful in accomplishing its goal of cutting poverty rates significantly. European social programs are used and paid for more by the middle class than the U.S. brand, the bulk of which is paid by the top producers. However the results to incentives are similar though slower, and Europe has had a decade of very slow growth partly as a result of spending problems associated with transfer programs.

The Asians regard social programs as one of the "poisons of the West" which along with drugs (the other poison), they remain determined to avoid. While Asia has its own distortions (mostly authoritarian regimes with currency-system distortions that have created credit bubbles and overcapacity problems), its ability to avoid damaging government antipoverty programs has helped it to more than double the growth of the West over the past decade.

Certainly a yawning technology gap created by years of statist governments that prevented free-market technologies from being applied in market-friendly environments also helped fuel economic gains once such preventions were released. But the point is that investors must seek countries with minimal socialist antipoverty programs and costly wealth transfers when looking for optimum growth opportunities.

Investors should also be cognizant of the effects of such policies, especially programs like Medicare and Social Security which are set up for demographic catastrophe over the next 10 to 20 years (to be discussed in more detail later).

Investors must understand the chains on a country's growth rate to correctly assess potential growth among different countries so that they can place capital in the path of future high-growth opportunities.

MINIMUM WAGE POLICIES

One more clear negative for growth about which there is much misinformation concerns minimum wage hikes. All honorable people want to see everybody as well off as possible, and alleviating poverty everywhere is critical for the survival of humankind. That is not the question. The question is *how to achieve lower poverty rates*. The long-run growth paradigm states that to significantly increase real wages on a long-term sustainable basis, it is necessary to enhance productivity. Think about it. If you artificially and arbitrarily raise wage prices without a corresponding increase in productivity, all you are doing is transferring money from corporations (and stockholders) to employees. The money you transfer is taken out of potential new capital investments that are needed to actually boost future productivity and is instead given to labor. Again, we are chopping away at the very source of long-term higher future real wages for the benefit of an artificial decree made today. Nor does the minimum wage hike improve the lot of the poor, as is commonly argued. For in addition to cutting the corporate profits, which are often reinvested in new capital investments, minimum wage hikes force corporations to reassess whether the labor they employ can produce enough beyond the higher wage to achieve profits for the company. Lower skilled (poor, young, and uneducated mostly) labor who are not yet producing at the new higher wage rate must either be more quickly brought up the skill-productivity chain or else fired. Figure 6.14 illustrates this phenomenon well. Notice that each time the minimum wage rate is hiked, a surge in black teenage-male unemployment follows. It should also be noted that virtually every significant decline in black teenage-male unemployment came following a period of stable minimum wage rates and after the two strongest growth periods since World War II, following the Kennedy tax cut and the Reagan tax cut.

A higher minimum wage rate does not put a floor under wages, as its advocates surmise, but it puts a ceiling on low-skilled labor employment levels. Those who do not already have the skills to produce above the new higher minimum level are simply cut out of the job market entirely. What is fascinating is that many politicians and the liberal media fail to understand

Figure 6.14 **WHO BENEFITS?**

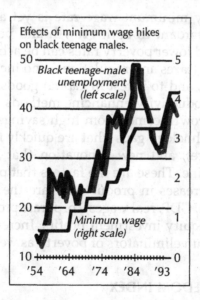

Source: Economic Report of the President, 1994; *Investor's Business Daily.* Reprinted by permission of *Investor's Business Daily.*

what both liberal and conservative economists alike have come to agree is negative policy.

Thus even Nobel laureate James Tobin, a liberal Keynesian economist, comments in regard to raising the minimum wage:

> People who lack the capacity to earn a decent living need to be helped, but they will not be helped by minimum wage laws, trade-union wage pressures or other devices which seek to compel employers to pay them more than their work is worth. The more likely outcome of such regulations is that the intended beneficiaries are not employed at all. Instead of a higher minimum wage, I'd rather see people with jobs.

More conservative economist, Nobel laureate Milton Friedman agrees:

> Many well-meaning people favor legal minimum wage rates in the mistaken belief that they help the poor. These people confuse wage rates with wage income. It has always been a mystery to me to understand why a youngster is better off unemployed at $4.75 per hour than employed at $4.25 an hour.

A compulsory minimum wage rate is yet another distortion that acts as a retardant to both growth and poverty alleviation. Higher wages and lower poverty rates can be achieved by lowering the impediments (taxes and regulations) and increasing the incentives to innovate, and to invest in capital goods, education, training, and other productivity-enhancing methods.

Long-term growth comes from high savings, large capital investment, big technology gaps (that are quickly fillable with existing infrastructure), and new innovation that keeps technology gaps in the pipeline. These are the factors that propel increases in productivity. Increases in productivity are the fuel of long-term growth in wealth, GDP, real wages, corporate profits, employment, and ultimately, equity investment profits. Increases in productivity are the long-run eliminators of poverty as well.

ECONOMIC FREEDOM INDEX

There is one fertile environment that seems to spawn innovation (creating technology gaps) and capital investment. That environment is economic freedom and a developed capital market infrastructure. Periodically, the Heritage Foundation releases its latest global study, which rates each country in terms of both growth and economic freedom. When the people in a country can do whatever they want with the money they earn by taking it out of the country, and by investing it in whatever they choose, their country is rated highly on the economic freedom scale, which also measures the degree of free-market infrastructure. Figure 6.15, which plots the results of a Heritage Foundation study, shows that those countries with the highest degree of economic freedom tend to have the highest per capita income for

Figure 6.15 **HERITAGE FOUNDATION GLOBAL ECONOMIC FREEDOM VERSUS WEALTH STUDY**

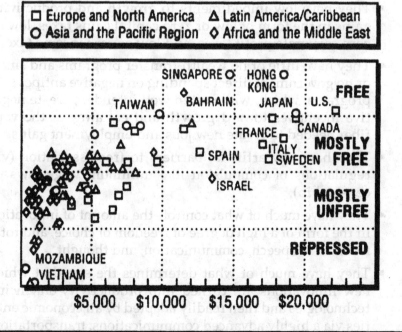

Source: Index of Economic Freedom used by permission of The Heritage Foundation/*The Wall Street Journal.*

206 THE ESSENCE OF CONSISTENT PROFITS

their region of the world; those mostly free have slightly less per capita income than those countries that are freer in their region; and those countries that are mostly unfree or repressed economically all have among the lowest per capita income in both their region and in the world.

WHEN INVESTING, LOOK FOR COUNTRIES WITH LOW IMPEDIMENTS TO GROWTH

If there are many countries that have positive liquidity environments, good technicals, not overvalued markets, and relatively similar relative strengths, top global investors should try to invest among the countries that have the following long-run growth steroids:

- They are the most free or are in the process of moving toward economic freedom in a significant way.
- They have low impediments to growth and productivity gains in the form of low or zero capital gains taxes, low or zero corporate profit taxes, and low or zero income taxes.
- They have little or no wealth-transfer programs and small or no government direct spending on negative antipoverty programs, which, while often well intended, create negative incentives toward growth and eat away at the very fiber needed to create new jobs and employment gains.
- They have low artificial barriers to free association (via regulations of compulsion like minimum wage laws or censorship).
- They have much of what controls the amount of innovation in the form of a high degree of freedom of choice, and total freedom of speech, communication, and thought.
- They have much of what determines the speed at which new innovations are turned into productivity-enhancing technologies and then readily adapted by all economic entities via a highly advanced communications, transportation, and capital market infrastructure.

PROFITING FROM UNDERSTANDING DISTORTIONS

One of the major benefits of understanding Austrian alchemy and the long-run growth paradigm is knowing what underlies long-term growth in countries and companies.

Beyond this, however, understanding these economic principles is also helpful in evaluating the relative investment risks, rewards, hot spots, and cold spots that each country's peculiar distortions are likely to create. Free-market distortions usually lead to volatile boom-bust periods in markets. An investor can clean up on the booms on the long side and the busts on the short side only by having a very clear understanding of the processes creating those booms and busts.

For example, the investor understanding the distortions of excess savings incentives, current-account surplus sterilization, and artificially low interest rates in Japan could and will have a real jump on competing investors. Excess savings incentives and artificially low interest rates in the mid to late 1980s created a credit bubble that funneled excessive investment into financial markets, real-estate markets, and capital goods. Current-account surplus partial sterilization helped pour capital into creating even more excessive export capacity.

When interest rates are negative, investors should see lights flashing in their heads alerting to buy real estate, real assets, and companies associated with such (as runaway technical tools highlighted in the next chapter dictate). Credit bubbles usually lead to runaway financial asset inflation. Once these policies in Japan became clear in the early 1980s, an investor understanding the forces created by them could have foreseen the wild bull market of Tokyo and the bust that would inevitably have to follow.

One can often jump aboard the distortion wagon, but keep in mind that such booms must ultimately end in bust and it is better to get off the bubble before the bust begins. When a bubble is being created, generally as long as a market is not very overvalued, the game is still on and one can participate in it. What ends a bubble? First values get chronically and wildly out of line. Then economically ill-advised investments begin to proliferate. Some sort of catalyst eventually pops the bubble. This catalyst is often a monetary policy that turns less stimulative (in the form of rate hikes) but it may also be other influences such as a softening of economic growth to a low enough level that ill-advised investments begin to lose money and the credit bubble turns into a negative cycle. Exogenous shocks can also be a catalyst forcing investors to realize that they have bid up prices to unrealistic levels, discounting far more growth than is realistically feasible.

Once the bubble pops, investors can look for the primary recipients of the bubble for potential short sales. Those sectors that benefited more heavily from the bubble are the very ones that will be deflated the most as it unwinds. If the bubble is popping due to rate hikes, those most leveraged will unwind the fastest. If the bubble is popping due to lower growth making interest rate payments impossible for many debtors, then banks and real estate may be big recipients of the deflation. When an exogenous shock is the catalyst, the sector that takes the big price hits will be the one that was benefiting from the credit bubble and that is most surprised by the shock. It is best to try to avoid both the final upmove and the initial downmove of a bubble.

While the final phase up is often wildly profitable, it usually starts from a high degree of overvaluation and culminates in a ridiculous one. It is often extremely difficult to exit before the party is over. The first phase of decline can be violently sharp and occur in a very short period. However, wildly speculative markets often have sharp volatile corrections that can fool would-be bears. Many an astute global investor got trapped prematurely short in the wild Japanese market of the late 1980s before the market finally caved in.

Overvaluation is fine to sell short, but the low-risk investor is best served waiting until the trend is clearly down before beginning such an undertaking. You will miss out on much of the profits, but catch enough of the downmove to make good returns.

What popped the bubble in Japan was a classic reversal of stimulative central bank policy, via interest rate rises. The Japanese central bank finally figured out that it had fueled an asset mania and began raising rates; by January 1990, the Tokyo market started declining in earnest. With a non-negative real interest rate, many Japanese ventures started to go bad quickly, and the interest rate increases had a large impact on a wildly overvalued real estate market (see Chapter 2). Some of the primary beneficiaries of the credit boom, like the brokers, have declined by over 95 percent since their late 1980s peaks.

SOME U.S. DISTORTIONS

Many pronounced distortions in the United States markets easily and quickly come to mind: incentives to undersave, reserve currency status, frequent policy shifts, sky-high corporate/capital gains/income tax rates, minimum wage distortions, historically expensive transfer payment programs, skyrocketing antipoverty program costs, unsound retirement and medical transfer systems set to explode in the next two decades, importation of the Japanese credit bubble, the world's largest unified marketplace, and by far the most advanced communications/transportation/capital market infrastructure in the world. The United States economy also has the strong cultural values of independent thought and free expression that spur the highest innovation rate anywhere.

Incentives to undersave create chronic undersavings and the need to import capital for capital investment (hence we have become a debtor nation). Our reserve currency status meant that foreign governments were loathe to punish our central bank for overly inflationist policies in the 1970s which allowed the problem to get out of hand. Frequent policy shifts lead to an unstable long-term policy environment, short-term focused investment and corporate activity, distrust of government policy, and a higher than otherwise real interest rates as investors must allow for negative potential tax changes in the future on long-term bond interest risk evaluations. Sky-high tax rates and free association limitations of all kinds mean much lower growth, employment, real wages, and higher poverty rates than are necessary, along with far too high a percentage of GDP eaten up by government and the attempt to conform to government edicts. Transfer and antipoverty programs take seed corn away from producers and do destructive things with it, hurting everyone in the process. Combine massive transfer programs with a media-dominated culture and you get a central government with so much favor-peddling power that government positions are more or less sold to the highest campaign-funding bidder with the proceeds going to buy the media attention necessary to win elections. Such a system favors incumbents by 96 percent despite massive public dissatisfaction with government, limits potential third parties, and is probably more accurately described as an "auction-ocracy" than the democratic republic originally created from the Constitution.

A sound retirement system takes money from each individual's contributions and invests them for later use in retirement. Social Security is not sound. A brief discussion of Social Security and Medicare is needed here because they are time bombs that could destroy the United States' waning growth potential significantly in the decades ahead.

The Social Security Time Bomb

In 1935, Social Security was sold to the public with Franklin Roosevelt's promises that it would provide "social insurance," "retirement," and "full employment." None of these promises has been even remotely fulfilled.

In fact, calling Social Security "insurance" at all is a fraud. Insurance takes premiums from a large pool of people with similar risk profiles and holds the funds to draw on when the small percentage of the pool population faces the risk that is being insured against. Social Security, on the other hand is a Ponzi-scheme—it takes from one group (workers) and gives directly to another group (retirees). There are no funds at all to draw on. An IRA or retirement annuity, by contrast, takes an individual's premiums as tax-free savings and builds a large fund for that person to draw on at retirement—a true type of pension. Several years ago, a group of Harvard Law School professors estimated that if a private company were to create an "insurance" or "pension" product exactly the same as Social Security, it would be guilty of so many counts of fraud and other crimes that its board would be up for possible penalties of life sentences. But who is there to protect us from government fraud and abuse?

Social Security initially appeared to be working because there was a multiyear period of payment prior to any distributions, and because at the time there were over 50 taxpayers for every beneficiary. Today, there are fewer than 3 taxpayers per beneficiary; in the next two decades that ratio will fall below 2 to 1; and by 2050 there will be fewer than 1.3 taxpayers per beneficiary. Even the most optimistic government forecasts show Social Security failing by 2030, with Social Security tax rates alone needing to soar an additional 48 percent to 63 percent just to pay minimal benefits. Social Security taxes have already climbed from 1 percent to almost 15 percent today—after over 18 direct and indirect Social Security tax increases.

Today Social Security has over 10 trillion dollars of completely unfunded liabilities. But even after trillions of dollars of spending (it is the most expensive single government program in history), the poverty rate among people over age 65 is only a very small fraction lower than where it was when the program was launched—and the overall poverty rate has not dropped either. The program is arguably the largest fraud ever perpetrated on a people. Its goal has never been even remotely reached, while its costs have been astronomical.

Yet the misunderstanding of the degree of abuse of this system is still hardly fathomed by the American populace. It is still commonplace for those plundered to thank the criminals who robbed them. Many people in their retirement years say things like, "I don't know where I'd be without my $1,200 a month Social Security check." It is absolutely astounding how many retirees know that their children and grandchildren are being cheated by Social Security, but think that they were spared. Although retirees are not getting nearly the rip-off today's workers are assured by Social Security, almost everyone who has ever paid Social Security taxes is not getting fair value. In a 1997 *San Francisco Chronicle* article, a 76-year-old man claimed Social Security was a "lifesaver" for him. However when an accountant sat down and showed this man that if he had simply invested the same amount of taxes he paid over his life in T-bills he would be getting over $2,000 a month instead of $1,200 and that if he had invested in stocks and bonds, he would be getting over $3,500 a month—all by receiving only interest payments without tapping his principal—the man was "shocked."

If a 20-year-old earning minimum wage began putting his Social Security tax amount into T-bills (5% assumed) every year instead of government boondoggles, he would retire a millionaire by the time he was 65. Or if the average income earner put just three years of Social Security taxes into the stock market during his first three years of work, he would be able to retire with more than $300,000—and achieve an interest-only monthly payment of twice what Social Security now pays monthly (assuming 10% average annual gains). Instead, Social Security steals this amount every year of this person's life and it will end up bankrupt in 20 to 30 years. More of Generation X believe in UFOs than in the viability of Social Security in the twenty-first century. Investors note: in our opinion nobody retiring more than 10 years from now should count on receiving one penny in benefits.

Is there any solution to this boondoggle? Absolutely—Chile, Peru, Singapore, and others have all come up with brilliant free-market-oriented privatizations of their pensions that have worked wonders and brought some of them out of even worse straits than America faces on a per capita basis.

Chile replaced a government pension entitlement with a radically new entitlement that Americans should heed—that people are entitled to use the money they earn. In the Chilean Model, middle-aged or younger workers could opt out of the government pension program—but to do so required that they pay a minimum of 10 percent of income to a private retirement plan similar to IRAs here. Existing retirees or those within a few years of retirement remained untouched, and a safety net was set up for those in dire poverty. Today over 93 percent of the populace is utilizing the private retirement option. Taxes on investment were also slashed. Of course, 10 percent was only a minimum; with new incentives and lower taxes, savings soared from under 5½ percent to over 26 percent of GDP in just the past decade. During this period, Chile has had one of the fastest growing economies on earth, rivaling the growth of many Asian nations.

Salvador Valds-Prieto, an MIT-trained economist in Chile, has come up with a U.S.-refined phaseout plan for Social Security with many of the positive elements of the Chilean Model. First, cut and phase out completely over time the Draconian Social Security tax. The second element is to convert all benefit promises to those with less than 10 years to retirement (and phase out partial obligations for those with up to 20 years to retirement) into long-term government bonds. On an individually managed basis, replace lost payroll taxes with mandatory contributions to the new individual private accounts investing in stocks, bonds, and so on. Next, use phased-down payroll taxes and general revenues to supplement pensions of the transition generation and to continue paying obligations of current retirees. Finally, allow an option for current retirees to continue receiving benefits or to instead be able to withdraw from their current IRAs or pensions without incurring any withdrawal tax.

This solution costs every generation some, but also gives benefits to each generation. And it phases out the biggest fraud in history. The subject of privatization is finally getting some recognition from even the establishment media. In late 1995, *Time* and *Newsweek* ran articles favoring privatization of Social Security. Even local newspapers are starting to question whether privatization will work. U.S. investors need to protect their wealth by encouraging a phaseout of this behemoth money-grabbing program and to start understanding that each individual's retirement is a personal responsibility.

In the year 2000, Social Security will reach age 65. Let's hope for the sake of all peoples that U.S. citizens and their government develop the courage, common sense, and intelligence to retire Social Security itself by that time.

U.S. Medicaid/Medicare Problem

Figure 6.16 illustrates how far off the mark government has been in assessing the price of Medicare and Medicaid programs, which have cost over 100 times their estimated budgets as of 1997. What government failed to realize is that when you open a soup kitchen and give out free or extremely low-cost meals every day, pretty soon your line starts to grow and grow and grow. It is the same thing with giving out free or very low-cost medical care. Today even wealthy Americans use these programs simply because doing so is cost-effective.

Medical care is like food, housing, legal services, or any other good or service provided in an economy. The more the free market links customers' demands and providers' supply, the better the service. The labor shortage following World War II combined with wage-price controls instituted during and after the war economy, led companies to offer health-care "insurance" as an inducement to get around wage-controls and increase benefits without legally hiking wages to attract better labor. The result was the proliferation of third-party payer systems, whereby the patient indirectly pays insurance premiums and the insurance pays the medical

Figure 6.16 **COSTLY OVERRUN**

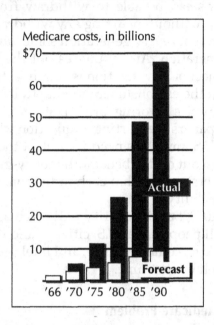

Source: Federal Hospital Insurance Trust Fund. Reprinted by permission of *Investor's Business Daily.*

provider. The linkage between supply and demand is thus distorted, and all sorts of problems appear in the system. Medicare and Medicaid make up two government-subsidized systems of third-party payment systems.

The third-party payer system uses insurance to cover things that shouldn't be covered by "truly economic" insurance. Truly economic insurance is meant to pool similar risk exposures for areas where only a fraction of the pool will face high-cost risks. A prepaid medical savings plan would allow for payment on an individual basis to an account designed to cover normal medical costs, and is best administered by each individual who will optimize his or her own costs. Medicare and Medicaid however, take from one group (young and healthy) and redistribute to another group. There is no savings pool or individual choice in garnering health services. Today "insurance" pays over 80 percent of all health care costs, compared with under 50 percent in the 1960s. Insurance's economic purpose fits in well with high deductible, catastrophic coverage, but causes massive third-party distortions when used for everyday care:

- Studies show that for every 10 percent decrease in out-of-pocket expenses, patient demand for health care goes up 4 percent.
- People who pay their own doctor bills or have high deductibles have better health yet spend almost half of what low-deductible, comprehensive coverage insured patients spend.
- People who rely on public insurance spend twice what those with private insurance do.
- Today 70 percent of the people in nursing homes are on Medicaid although only 12 percent of them are in poverty. Long-term private insurance only costs about $2,000 a year for a 65-year-old, yet only a fraction of the elderly have this coverage because they realize that the federal government will pick up the tab if they don't, and because they're uninformed about coverage.
- The average family pays only $2,400 a year for their own care, and $4,500 a year to pay for other people's care through Medicare and Medicaid taxes and private insurance subsidies.

Demographics make this trend even more frightening. *As the baby boomers grey, the population of the elderly will more than double over the next 30 years.* This is a major crisis. Yet tightening Medicaid, making a long-term care tax credit, combining a tax credit/deduction for medical savings accounts to cover costs under $3,000 per year along with tax credits for catastrophic care (over $3,000), and deducting the cost of private long-term care insurance from the Social Security premiums of those who do not get coverage would help solve much of the problem without the need for continuing the massive transfer of wealth from the young to the old that will cost over $2 trillion a year in two to three decades. It would also put choice and power back into the hands of patients, and responsiveness and care-decisions back into the hands of doctors and medical care providers, so that the demands of the customers and trade-offs of the service providers are linked directly without intervention from a random third party.

Insurance doesn't just reimburse hospitals for your bill, it pays hospitals a percentage of its working capital, equity capital, and its total costs. Thus hospitals incentives are not to hold down costs, but to build market share by being more state-of-the-art than other hospitals. This leads to what experts call "a medical arms race." Diana Elser, spokesperson for the Jackson Hole Group, a health care think tank, put it flatly, "What is driving inflation is overcapacity in hospitals and technology, and over-utilization."

As a congressionally authorized Rand study concluded, "The market forces controlling both price and output are not working in the medical sector because of the overriding presence of third party payers." As Jane Orient, President of the Association of American Physicians and Surgeons, put it, "The major reason we have big overhead is because insurance is used to cover things that shouldn't be covered."

Remember the Austrian principle that says bureaucratic organization creates loads of red tape and ineffective organization? A Louis Harris survey found Medicare and Medicaid imposed the highest administrative, paperwork, and red-tape costs in the U.S. health care system, followed by health maintenance organizations (HMOs) and preferred provider organizations (PPOs), and private comprehensive insurance. Lower on the cost list were high deductible catastrophic insurance and lowest of all, fee-for-service (where the patient pays the doctor himself). Studies show that if everyone had catastrophic health care insurance with $3,000 deductible, 88 percent of these costs would be eliminated.

Many people believe that the uninsured problem is a big reason for maintaining the current Medicaid/Medicare system. However only 19 percent of the so-called uninsured, roughly 7 million people are "chronically uninsured." Fully half of them are aged 19 to 24 when health care is least needed. Only 2.5 percent of the uninsured, fewer than 1 million people, are ever denied coverage because of a preexisting condition. This is not an expensive problem to safety net if only the truly needy are temporarily subsidized until they are able to get work and pay for their own care. And keep in mind that all Americans already have the legal right to critical and emergency health care regardless of their ability to pay; it is illegal for hospitals to deny care to such uninsured patients. Every year private insurance is forced to subsidize hospitals for "uninsured care" to the tune of $13 billion, while state governments pick up the rest of the so-called uninsured bill of $12 billion. The uninsured are a problem, but not nearly as large a one as we've been told, and we are already paying for their critical care.

Notice that virtually all the problems found by these studies are really symptoms of distortions and disruptions to a free market. The further we get away from a free market in this or any other sector, the worse our quality and costs will get. Is there an example of anyone who has tackled this program by restoring free-market forces with any degree of success anywhere in the world?

The Organization for Economic Cooperation and Development (OECD) and other global agency studies show that there is really only one country that is consistently improving the quality of its health care while keeping cost increases consistent with general inflation: Singapore.

Singapore basically uses a combination of catastrophic insurance plus the legal requirement that each person have a "medical savings account" worth around $3,000 to cover the first $3,000 in costs before the catastrophic insurance kicks in. Whatever isn't spent in one year can be passed to the next year, and what is spent must be replaced—it is literally deducted from salary. In this system, 94 percent of all costs come directly out-of-pocket from individuals (medical savings accounts). Doctors and hospitals compete on a cost basis for business, with published prices.

One of the main factors holding down costs in Singapore's system is the simple truth that people spend more wisely and prudently when it is their own money than they do when it appears to be someone else's money they are spending.

While the forcing of everyone to create a medical savings plan may be a bit authoritarian, the United States could accomplish the same thing through tax incentives via a "medical IRA," or medi-save. In fact, most companies that provide health insurance packages are actually now paying about $2,400 per employee more than the cost of both the $3,000 medi-save and catastrophic coverage for a family each year. Those extra costs consist mostly of inefficiencies and red tape caused by the third-party payment system, which is a leftover of wage controls long since eradicated.

Some mixture of tax credits or vouchers to phase in this type of plan would restore 88 percent of insurance claims to fee-for-service, with individuals spending their own money and policing costs. It would put the customers in charge instead of the federal government. Demand and supply would be relinked, cost would be an important determinant of demand, and competition would bring about cost containment by both doctors and hospitals. Private insurance subsidies would be cut. And it would be a first step toward restoring more market-oriented reforms to an already wildly overregulated industry.

There are several reasons for this discussion on Medicare/Medicaid: (1) to apply our economic alchemy principles to real problems to learn how distortions operate; (2) to highlight distortions in the U.S. system and their possible effects down the road; (3) to show investors that there are market-oriented solutions out there, and that our problems are solvable if we act quickly and courageously; (4) to get investors to analyze problems developing behind the scenes so that they can avoid shocks from economic disturbances caused by these underlying problems.

The implications of the Medicare/Medicaid and Social Security problems are serious. First of all, the era of balanced budgets in the federal government is likely to be relatively short-lived because of the twin transfer-system monsters. Costs of these transfer mechanisms continue to spiral higher and higher. As the baby-boom generation greys, demands on retirement funds and on funds for health care will explode. Anyone out there wanting to retire in the next 10 to 40 years should ponder the possible repercussions. These demographic and social-program issues exist throughout the developed world, not just in the United States. When the peak baby boomers have to begin drawing heavily on their retirement funds by selling stocks, will the markets be able to sustain their historically unprecedented valuation levels of today? Will the dumping of mutual funds and stocks required by a drawdown on retirement funds have a negative effect on the supply/demand picture for equities resulting in lower prices? If you want to be able to pull money out of the markets during these social and demographic trying periods, you might want to consider a diversification into asset classes other than equities or at least develop a flexible strategy for limiting the damage to your portfolio.

Other U.S. Distortions and Some Advantages

As discussed in Chapter 2, the Japanese yield-curve play has funneled money artificially into the U.S. financial system. What we have not yet discussed are the positive aspects rounding out the U.S. picture.

While I lament many of the retardants to growth caused by the distortions to our economy, the *United States is still host to many of the best investment opportunities in the world*. Whenever our models have confidence that the U.S. market is in a bullish trend, we try to have a larger than normal allocation to it. In part, this is because the data and information on U.S. stocks are so far superior to any other market on earth that an investor is taking a swing at non-U.S. stocks with one eye closed in comparison.

The United States is still the largest single unified marketplace in the world. And it has the most advanced and sophisticated communications/transportation/capital market infrastructure. This is significant because *infrastructure determines how quickly new technologies can be integrated* (as long as there is capital to invest in them). Our capital market infrastructure is so dominant that our domestic stock market has become quite globalized as foreign companies compete to access it. On U.S. exchanges, investors can find ADRs (American Depository Receipts of foreign stocks) from almost every country of the world. We have Spiders and Webs allowing investors to trade global indexes in the same manner they trade individual stocks. In the United States, a small company with a new innovative technology can raise more capital more quickly than in any other country in the world. And if a new technology or product really is a better mousetrap, our unified market and excellent infrastructure allow the company producing it to achieve sustained growth rates (triple-digit annual earnings growth for five years or more in some instances) unmatched around the globe.

Perhaps just as significant, the United States has uniquely strong cultural values of independent thought, free expression, and a pioneering risk-taking spirit that have made it by far the most innovative country in the world. And our cultural history is short enough that Americans welcome change much more quickly than people of most other nations. The innovations and new technologies created by Americans are so extraordinary that they have swamped our host of (distortion created) problems and allowed us to prosper despite a plummeting savings rate and a stifling tax and wealth-transfer system. If the United States did not have to work with one hand tied behind its back (by its government and the distortions it institutes), it could grow just as fast as any other nation on earth.

Unlike many emerging markets, the United States does not have huge gaping technology gaps caused by statist prevention of markets for decades. But what it does have is the highest proliferation of newly innovated technologies anywhere, and the fastest infrastructure for adapting them quicker than anywhere else. The main constraining force is capital investment, which we tax and punish, along with artificial barriers to savings and encouragement of debt (dis-savings). So far, the rest of the world has been happy to help us along by investing in us. And so we grow, albeit at a substantially suboptimal pace.

We have discussed Austrian alchemy and the long-run growth paradigm, seen how they help explain different policy results, and looked at some example distortions and their likely effects on growth and investment. By now, investors should have a strongly enhanced sense of what causes long-term growth opportunities and what effects policy distortions can have on growth. They should also now have a much better grasp of the importance of understanding economics, and of how policies, corporate profits, and the economic environment at any point in time are all closely linked. Investors should understand that when a country like France tries to "cure" its unemployment problem by mandating a shorter work week for all labor, they have really just increased the wage per productive unit and cut back the investment potential needed to create more jobs. In formulating our economic understanding model, we are trying to help investors learn how to evaluate economic effects on their own. Independent thought is a critical aspect of consistent investment success. Armed with the ability to understand the economic forces behind the scenes, and to evaluate events, investors need also to be able to filter the daily bombardment of the media.

EVALUATING GOVERNMENT/MEDIA HYPE

Global investors face the constant challenge of evaluating what is printed in the press of various nations, particularly the United

States. One of the things that we are striving to get readers to do is to *stop simply reacting to market events and looking to the establishment press to explain them, and to instead understand what is behind market events before or as they are happening.* Investors who understand the true forces that are creating market events can anticipate and profit from them. Investors who merely react to market events are mired in a fog of uncertainty that makes profitable investing extremely difficult and trying.

A good example of this developed in the global bond markets in 1993 and 1994. The 1994 bond market crash was one of the steepest on record this century. Starting in March 1993, subscribers to our monthly newsletter, the *Portfolio Strategy Letter* (PSL) received in-depth analysis of the massive liquidity infusion the Fed was instigating and the market spike in bond prices this would create in the United States. As the United States began to export liquidity via speculation in foreign equity and bond markets, those foreign markets became just as addicted to American liquidity-fueled speculation as our markets. Realizing the huge risk bonds entailed, investors who understood what was happening dumped bonds quickly on our October 1993 model sell signal.

But investors who did not understand the forces behind the market events did not see what all the fuss was all about. Those same investors were later confused and perplexed by the extent of the bond market decline in 1994. "The fundamentals just don't justify these bond rates" said those left holding bonds. "Buying bonds in the 7 percent yield area is an almost risk free investment" one prominent money manager declared in March 1994. Four months later, this same manager's fund was off 12 percent on the year and he was still cited as being "more bullish bonds more than ever" despite sitting on double-digit bond market losses. He did not understand what was happening in the markets at the time—and yet the press was quoting this manager.

When the economy began a more swift recovery in late 1993, banks began to loan money instead of buying bonds—following the liquidity curve. Demand for bonds collapsed thereafter. Japan also cut bond demand as it redirected more of its excess savings domestically. As rates rose in response to these factors, the equivalent of one of the largest margin calls in history hit market participants who had loaded up on leveraged bond market positions globally. Speculative excesses had to be erased regardless of economic conditions.

A similar "fundamental failure" developed in 1993 in European markets. Many European money managers watched in shock as, for the first time in post-World War II history, European stock prices took off while yield curves were still inverted. "The fundamentals just don't justify a significant rally," a European money manager stated in the *Financial Times* in early 1993. These investors failed to understand that the reason for the explosive rallies was almost exclusively U.S. investment into European stocks in anticipation of the same sort of recovery that had developed in the United States two years earlier. These same managers became bullish around the end of 1993 as "fundamental evidence of bottoming European economies finally justifies equity investment" the *Financial Times* quoted the same European money manager as saying. Next in 1994, these investors were horrified by the sharp declines in Europe of 15 percent and more as the yield curves normalized.

The main cause of their losses is that they do not understand the dynamics of government actions that create market events and thus can only react after the fact. So how can an investor stay on top of what is behind market events?

To maintain true market understanding, investors must stay on top of two of the prime forces that determine market action and create perceptions that are out of touch with reality: government and media. Any investor who harnesses a true and realistic understanding of these two opinion creators will be able to stay ahead of dominant investment trends and will understand when and why traditional fundamental relationships sometimes lead to false conclusions in financial market decisions.

Remember that investors, like everyone else in a free society who is not infringing on the rights of others or exploiting a public good or market distortion, can only profit by adding value. And one of the greatest values that investors can add to the markets is a realistic perception of the state of affairs and prospects for profit and growth. Fair-playing investors must seek and pursue the truth. In a financial sense, the truth will set you free.

To properly assess the veracity of any person's or organization's statements, one must first understand the self-interest of that individual or organization, which will tend to color its outlook, influence, and statements. This makes determining the fact from fiction and reality from hype exceptionally difficult, particularly where politicians and the media are concerned.

Understanding the truth regarding government influence is more critical than most investors realize. Fully 50 cents out of every dollar spent in the U.S. economy is either spent directly by government or spent on government mandates. This makes government the largest industry, employer, actor, and influencer in the markets.

Not only does the government control most of the spending, but it prints and distributes the currency, dictates that currency's value, heavily regulates banks and financial institutions, and regulates most other businesses. Can you think of a more powerful institution in the world? Imagine the power of being able literally to print money and spend it.

Most of the constitutional constraints that were designed to limit government spending and control have been abolished. With no gold standard constraint, government spending has predictably exploded. It is in the self-interest of every individual politician to try to expand his or her power base in the short term—and that comes at the expense of long-term good for society. This is why our founding fathers created the very constraints on government that have been abolished.

While the actions of government often literally shape global market events, the media and government combine forces to shape public opinion and create false perceptions that cause market losses. Here are some concepts investors need to keep in mind when sifting through media and government statements, articles, and broadcasts to find the small grains of truth and reality.

Both media and government act more as a weather vane of the mob than as reporters of facts or visionaries of the future. Politicians stick their fingers in the wind, determine what the public mood is and what the public wants to hear, and then try to figure out how to make it appear that they are addressing public concerns in the form of legislation or media interviews. As Paul Pilser has stated so well, politicians lead society much in the same way a dog leads its master on a walk—the dog looks to see what direction its master is heading and then quickly runs out in front so that it appears to be "leading." As soon as the master changes direction and the dog notices, he quickly runs in front of its master in the new direction. That's the essence of political leadership. Clinton is an expert at this type of "leadership."

So politicians will coauthor bills with catchy names, like "tax simplification bill" to make it appear that they are addressing public concerns although their bills are really designed to empower themselves by making the tax code less understandable and less "loophole ridden" so they can accumulate more tax revenues. It is very much Orwellian doublespeak.

The media follows the same pattern. They try to figure out how to tell the public what they want to hear by packaging it in catchy commercials, newsclips, articles, headlines, and sound bites. They latch on to the false portrayal of legislative bills' names because they believe they will sell more papers and get more viewers by telling the people what they want to hear than they will by thoroughly analyzing the substance of the bill and understanding its true effects. An interview is easier than an analysis.

Most people do not have the time to confirm the veracity of media representations, or politicians' statements. So most people, investors included, absorb only the story the media wants them to absorb. Many times the media does not understand the story they are reporting. A widely read example of this is the media's coverage of Hillary Clinton's commodity trading. It is impossible for her to have legitimately made the profits she declared—literally impossible. But commodity trading is a confusing business, and experts who only looked at a small fraction of the first brokerage statements said it looked possible to them. So instead of gaining an understanding of the subject matter and then evaluating it for themselves, the media dismissed the matter entirely. And the public followed. Disgusting to people pursuing the truth, but a beautifully accurate microcosm of how stories are reported on myriad subjects.

Other times, the media distort the truth purposely. Probably the best known example of this occurred in 1898 when William Randolph Hearst told politicians, "You supply the pictures and I'll supply the war" and his February 17 headline "The Warship Maine split in two by Enemies Secret Infernal Machine" had no basis whatsoever in fact or even evidence, but it ended up starting the Spanish-American War—and more than doubling his circulation.

The media sells stories by packaging them in hype. They do not care whether that hype is an accurate representation of the truth. They want to sell stories, and they know that the best way to do that is by stirring up people's emotions. If you walk by a newspaper stand and the headline is "Sunny Dry Weather Continues," are you going to buy that paper? Probably not—why would you? But if the headline reads, "Major Hurricane Could Destroy Local Area," whether the story is true or not, you may well decide to purchase a copy of the newspaper.

The problem is that most people can't differentiate between hype designed to sell stories and reality. This dynamic of government media and a public unable to distinguish fact from fiction creates market manias and acceptance of falsehoods.

First, the media and government discern a trend in opinion. They couldn't care less whether that trend is true or false. The politicians start talking about the perceived problem as though it were a crisis—and the media plays it up because it knows people are interested in the subject and will buy papers that feature it.

Second, people read what they have been thinking; and as they read it, they are confirming what they already thought. They become even more convinced that what they had been thinking is true, even though they never take the time to confirm the facts. A vicious cycle of reconfirming and more reporting of "experts" saying what people perceive develops, and pretty soon the perception becomes "reality" for people.

In markets, as more and more people become convinced of a trend, such as a bull market in stocks, everyone is buying mutual funds, which simply confirms what they already know—stocks have nowhere to go but up. Initially as more people accept this perception, the buying forces prices up, "proving" that the perception is true. A mania develops and feeds on itself, forcing stock prices to unrealistic valuations that discount far beyond the likely course of profits or earnings (Soros called this phenomenon "reflexivity" in his great book, *The Alchemy of Finance*). Advertisements and the industry report substantial profits over long-term periods, prompting rearview mirror investors to shift into obviously outperforming stocks. But these investors are not weighing future prospects—just past performance. Valuations are bid to extremes and greater-fool investing becomes the rule. Investors become "momentum investors" without regard for valuations, meaning that they simply buy stocks because they are going up.

The media feeds on people buying into the concept that everything that worked well in the past will work well in the future. The trouble is that the media lacks any macro or historical perspective in serving out its own self-interest. So does government.

Both government and media benefit from manias, and from the ensuing crisis that they create. So both government and media pretend current trends and events will continue indefinitely into the future. Whatever may be the hottest current trend, the media and politicians talk about it as though it will continue to happen forever. And the lazy public buys into what looks so obviously "true." It is easy and comfortable to agree with what everyone knows to be obvious, whether the world is really flat or not.

Not only do government and media profit from extending manias, but they also profit from the crisis that a mania creates. Once some event triggers a reanalysis of the facts, markets turn quickly. Panic declines develop. Government jumps in, pretending to be the defender of the public against the "profiteering" villain scapegoat that they choose this time around as the target to blame for the behavior they themselves have helped to create. Attacking the scapegoat allows government to expand its influence and power over that industry. And the attack fuels an emotionally charged story the media can exploit to sell more papers or get more viewers.

From 1929 to 1932, the target was not incredibly loose monetary policy (the real problem), but the "unbridled pursuit of banking profits." Government promptly destroyed the entire U.S. banking system by literally taking it over and regulating it to death. The villainous users of a new technology called the telephone which made information flows "much too fast for markets to handle" were also blamed and several bills in congressional committees proposed making the use of phones illegal in stock transactions.

In 1987, it was "program traders," those evil companies with the nerve to use computers to enhance returns. None of these "villains" really caused the market crashes they were blamed for, but the public was afraid and confused by these targets, so they were perfect scapegoats to take the blame for the manias created by the government and media.

A critical skill for investors therefore is the ability to sift hype from the truth and perception from reality. People don't often lose money by seeing the world as it really is. They lose money by seeing the world as they are told it is by people whose self-interest leads them to promote a perception that does not jibe with reality. And they lose money by not checking out facts and thinking for themselves. This is a tragically repeating cycle throughout market history. But the investors who profit from a deeper understanding of what is going on and from investing in the resultant long-term reality limit the acceptance of falsehoods and pave the way toward the eventual and more rapid realization of reality. As investor Doug Casey notes:

> When you understand what politicians are really doing, you will find it easy to anticipate government's next move. When you understand what the media is really doing, you will find it easier to tell the difference between marketing hype and reality. Understand both, and you are guaranteed to make better investments because you'll be able to anticipate what other investors will do next.

Investors must constantly monitor what government and media are doing and analyze why, and what phase of the Liquidity Cycle we are in to understand what underlies market actions. Government and media watching is thus a critical component of successful investing. You are not likely to hear about a market top on CNBC or read about it in a financial journal. Instead you are likely to hear how the decline is just temporary and the market will come back—and they will keep saying that most of the way down. Similarly at market bottoms, the media have finally capitulated and are filled with negative stories, making it so hard to be bullish that it can be painful to enter buy orders. *Watch the facts, filter what the pundits, media, and government say, and realize the game they are all playing.* Only then will you be independent enough to add true value to the markets and profit consistently.

SECULAR THEMES AND TRENDS

Secular themes and trends are yet another area that investors must watch to understand long-term investment potential. Determining the top investment themes and emerging global trends is a primary component of successful stock selection and asset-class allocation. Successfully positioning one's portfolio in runaway growth stocks that also appear to be part of some major social shift or theme gives one consistently higher returns than just finding top growth stocks, because these equities are likely to give significant returns for many years to come.

Our approach to using these trends in global stocks is fairly straightforward. We constantly look for major shifts and themes that will take years or even decades to be played out. We then note the companies that are benefiting from these trends. When they begin showing explosive growth in earnings, our analysis is confirmed. We buy them, in most cases, when they meet our emerging trends and our selection criteria (as defined in Chapter 7). That is where we can improve our odds of picking a really top winner—when a stock meets our growth, value, institutional, low debt, leading relative strength and earnings growth, strong balance sheet, bull market, and other criteria, and it also is benefiting from some of the emerging trends we foresee.

How do we develop/find/determine these emerging trends? As Warren Buffett once replied when asked what it took to be a top investor, "you have to do an enormous amount of reading" to understand what is going on in the world and the markets. You also need a good understanding of economics and human nature.

Most investors drive into the future with their eyes glued to the rearview mirror—a habit that causes frequent accidents. If instead you can see trends coming and anticipate major shifts and changes, you can profit from them. You can look ahead and position your business, life, and investments for what is likely to come. You can become a proactive person who is helping to make the shifts that will improve human society.

Many investors, corporate managers, and even CEOs are either reacting to yesterday's trends or are so overly concerned about the next quarter or two that they do not even think about what is going to happen 5 years or 10 years from now. Americans in particular, lose competitive battles largely because of failure to look ahead. And yet how can we create, build, and attempt to control the future if we cannot even see it or think about it? Therefore the first step in locating secular trends is to begin thinking about them and to scan your experience for possible long-term forces.

A trend is simply a definite, predictable direction or sequence of events. The key questions for determining whether a sequence of events is important and long-lasting are (1) What caused the trend? (2) Will it likely have significant effects? Basically, identifying trends is simply watching events, looking for a direction or sequence to them, analyzing the causes and effects of those events, and determining whether they have lasting economic, social, or political significance or impact. Are Austrian alchemy forces at work that will keep this trend rolling into the future for some time?

Always remember that the cause of a sequence of events rarely exists solely within a single field of study. This is why economic forecasting, market research, polling, and other single field studies often get blindsided. Econometric analysis did not predict or foresee OPEC's raising prices in the early and late 1970s, but many astute political analysts did foresee that. The investor who can keep abreast of many fields of study is thus much more likely to be on top of a situation than others.

Good trend tracking includes analyzing information from as many fields as possible, with the incorporation of economic, social, political, and other factors. You must learn to integrate data from many fields, and look at trends in many fields, to make cause-and-effect connections that will allow you to anticipate and become proactive.

The first step toward anticipating is understanding the present in relation to the past. That is one reason we have spent so much time on Austrian alchemy and long-run growth variables and where we are in terms of historical policies and distortions. If you know where you are, and how you got there, you are likely to have a good sense of where you are going. But to truly understand where you are, you must learn to screen out irrelevant information, and to distinguish reality from illusion. Much of the information distributed by the media is either totally irrelevant, or so warped in its viewpoint that it borders on illusion or propaganda.

To understand investment trends, you need to understand basic economics and human nature. The most important, helpful, and practical book on economics is Ludwig von Mises' *Human Action*. It will give you the finest framework I know of for interpreting both economic and political events. Other helpful books include *Unlimited Wealth*, by Paul Pilser; *Megatrends*, by John Naisbitt; *Thriving on Chaos*, by Tom Peters; *Innovation and Entrepreneurship*, by Peter Drucker; and *Clicking*, by Faith Popcorn. We have summarized the most important elements of these works in this chapter, but investors truly seeking mastery will want to study these works and come up with their own insights and conclusions.

Armed with a basic framework, an investor who wants to stay on top of emerging trends needs to constantly read sources of information such as *Investors Business Daily, Wall Street Journal, Barron's, Forbes, Daily Graphs,* and a host of newsletters (like our own *Portfolio Strategy Letter* among others) that discuss emerging trends. Be on the lookout for any interviews with top money managers, who often share their favorite themes and sectors. An excellent example of emerging trend discussion is the semiannual *Barron's Roundtable,* which reviews the outlook and some stock picks from a host of excellent investors/managers. If you read the *Roundtable* carefully, you will find that most managers in it spend considerable time discussing the themes they are trying to exploit in their portfolios. This is therefore an excellent place for investors to hunt for possible secular themes and trends for further research.

The new high list of 52-week new highs for each country is also a good place to look for new themes. Serious investors should always monitor the new high list. Whenever you find a number of stocks in a particular or new industry, that should be a wake-up sign that something is happening in that industry or sector. Is it a sustainable trend that will allow this sector or industry to continue being a top relative strength area? Is there fuel behind it? The new high list is also a good area to watch for stocks that might meet our selection criteria (described in Chapter 7).

Another good place to locate emerging trends is the list of stocks that meet our rigid high-growth, undiscovered, and underowned criteria. Investors should do further research on these stocks and industries to see if they can determine what is behind the growth rates shown by these companies, particularly companies that show greater than 50 percent growth for 18 months or more. An excellent example of a stock and trend we found via our selection screen is the network stocks of 1991 to 1993.

EXAMPLES OF SECULAR THEMES AND TRENDS

In this section, we describe two examples of significant secular themes and trends still in operation today, and explain how we used our knowledge of these trends to position in top companies in the past. Our goal here is not so much to lead you to good fish holes as to enable you to understand the forces that have led us to the best fish holes in the past so that you can learn how to find them yourself. Instead of listing dozens of today's better trends and themes, we are striving to show you how to find these themes yourself during any time, not just the immediate future. Two places to consistently locate excellent themes and trends are involved in these real-life examples: (1) the filling of technology gaps as a technology is beginning to be implemented but not yet widely utilized; and (2) a company whose business lies in the path of strong demographic trends.

The first example is one of the most profitable investments we ever made for funds we consult for: Cisco Systems, a company that was filling a huge technology gap.

Once the Gulf War conflict was leading to an easy victory in early 1991, a new bull market emerged in stocks. The bond and T-bill market moved above their respective 200-day moving averages in October 1990, while stocks followed in January 1991. Shrewd investors began looking for companies experiencing rapid earnings growth. A little-known stock called Cisco Systems met our criteria and intrigued us because it showed triple-digit earnings growth over the prior three quarters, and it was still relatively undiscovered, having just gone public the year before. As we looked further back in Cisco's history, we found that the company had actually experienced triple-digit quarterly earnings growth every quarter since late 1989! Certainly there had to be one heck of a story here.

We soon learned that the entire computer networking group had been growing at nearly triple-digit annual rates, that the group was a textbook example of a technology gap that needed to be quickly filled, that Cisco was the only major company that had gone public (Wellfleet followed in mid 1991), and that Cisco held a 45 percent market share. Cisco Systems, the leading network company, had introduced the router, linking together far-flung and incompatible data networks and directing data traffic between newly linked local-area networks. We checked with people whose companies were using Cisco's products and asked around to see what the reception was to networking products in general.

We learned that largely incompatible computer systems were a serious problem for almost every major corporation in America, and that routers and other new networking technologies were helping to solve this problem, but that they were just beginning to be implemented. This meant that not only was Cisco the leading company filling a huge technology gap, but that it fit almost perfectly the stage of technology life cycle that is optimum for safe but profitable investing. Figure 6.17 illustrates the technology life cycle.

Venture capitalists become experts at financing technology companies that are working on future technologies not yet developed into profitable products. Such stocks are in the *"future" initial phase*, where risk is fairly high (shown in Figure 6.17 on the left-hand side). We prefer to buy companies in the *"emerging" phase* where the company has *a profitable product that is beginning to be implemented* by a higher and higher percentage of the market. The company should potentially have room for three years or more of rapid growth while its product spreads to its entire potential market. In the emerging phase, the product is starting to

Figure 6.17 **TECHNOLOGY LIFE CYCLE FACTORS**

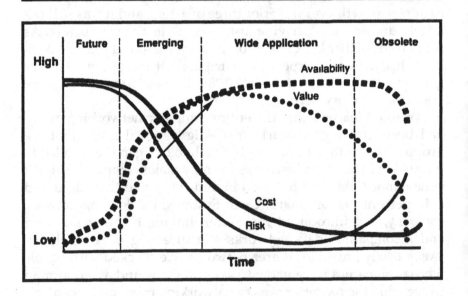

Source: From *The Great Boom Ahead: Your Comprehensive Guide to Personal and Business Profit in the New Era of Prosperity* by Harry S. Dent, Jr. Copyright © 1993 by Harry S. Dent, Jr., and James V. Smith, Jr. Reprinted with permission by Hyperion.

be recognized for its potential but it is *not yet in wide application*. The product should have strong potential for becoming widely applied, and the growth created by that rise in application should be a large enough market to fuel at least 50 percent earnings gains for the next few years. The arrow marked on the chart shows the ideal stage of application to look for when buying companies that fill potentially large technology gaps. Generally once the company's products begin to be more widely applied, the growth rate begins to slow down, and investors should begin cutting back on allocation and hunting for the next emerging theme, while keeping some investment in the former stock until it meets our exit criteria.

Our research told us that Cisco and the entire networking group met these criteria pretty much consistently from 1991–1992. Those who bought on Cisco's first buy signal in April 1991, and kept adding on new buy signals until a maximum amount of commitment (25%) was taken, saw the stock explode from 15½ to over 107 before faltering some in late 1993. Moreover, as chronicled in Chapter 7, investors following our techniques never risked more than 2 percent of capital (between entry and open protective stop) on the stock and yet it contributed more than 180 percent profits to 100 percent of the investor's portfolio! We aggressively added to Cisco up to our maximum allowable allocation because it continued to meet not only our selection criteria, but also our understanding of being a leader in a top emerging trend that exploited a large technology gap.

Cisco is a real-life example of how understanding technology gaps (Austrian alchemy), the technology life cycle, and where top investments occur on the technology life cycle enabled us to load up on a top stock meeting all our selection criteria in our funds and accounts (and in our letter to clients). Because we knew that the trend of implementing networking technology had a long way to go, and because we understood the potential growth that was always significantly higher than Cisco's P/E (until late summer 1993), we had the courage and foresight to load up on this stock on every pattern-breakout opportunity. Investors will often find that many of their top investments looked good from many perspectives at the time, and in retrospect look like blatantly obvious slam dunks. It is developing the patience to wait for such multi-positive blatant opportunities that is difficult.

Another example of how a secular theme and trend helped us key in on a top stock opportunity occurred during the post 1987-crash period. The theme was the demographic trend of home formation by the baby boomers, and the stock was Home Depot.

One of the biggest "waves" taking place in America is the movement in age of the baby boom. A clear analysis and understanding of demographic trends almost always suggests what areas are likely to benefit or be hurt by changes in population density among various ages. The baby boomers basically wreak change and havoc wherever they go as society must adjust to their sheer size and then readjust in their wake. Whole books have been written entirely on this subject, and I would suggest investors check out books such as *The Age Wave*, by Ken Dychtwald. Harry S. Dent also did a good job of analyzing some of the main demographic effects of baby boomers in his book *The Great Boom Ahead*.

Figure 6.18 **U.S. BIRTH RATES IN THIS CENTURY**

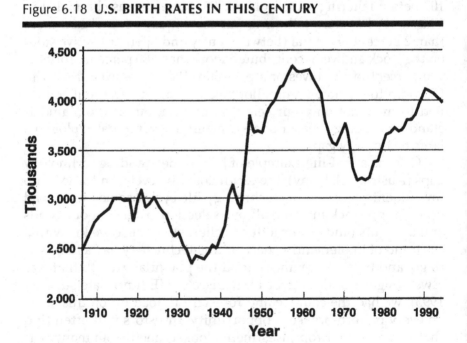

Source: Reprinted with the permission of Simon & Schuster from *The Roaring 2000s* by Harry S. Dent, Jr. Copyright © 1998 by Harry S. Dent, Jr.

Figures 6.18 through 6.20, from Dent's work, show some effects of the baby boomers.

As can be seen from Figure 6.18, there were three waves of baby boomers in terms of birth rates, which peaked just after 1960 in the United States. Investors should note that the baby boom was much less pronounced in Europe and Japan. Figure 6.19 shows average annual family spending categorized by 5-year age groups. One can see that spending peaks around age 46. It should also be noted that there is a spending spurt around age 25, when home formation begins.

Therefore, Figure 6.20 shows birth rates lagged by 25 and 45 years respectively so that one can see when peak spending waves are likely to develop from baby-boom generations. We can see that 25-year lagged birth rates began to shoot up in the mid to

Figure 6.19 **AVERAGE ANNUAL FAMILY SPENDING BY AGE**

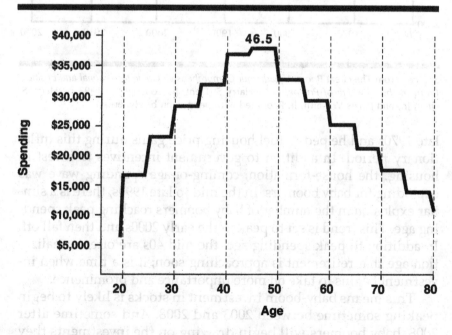

Source: Reprinted with the permission of Simon & Schuster from *The Roaring 2000s* by Harry S. Dent, Jr. Copyright © 1998 by Harry S. Dent, Jr.

Figure 6.20 **25 AND 44/46 BIRTH LAGS (FAMILY DURABLE GOODS CYCLES)**

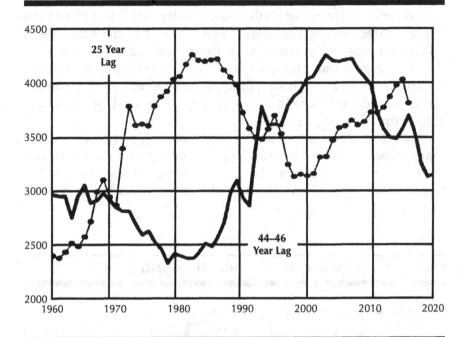

Source: From *The Great Boom Ahead: Your Comprehensive Guide to Personal and Business Profit in the New Era of Prosperity* by Harry S. Dent, Jr. Copyright © 1993 by Harry S. Dent, Jr., and James V. Smith, Jr. Reprinted with permission by Hyperion.

late 1970s and helped to fuel housing price gains during this inflationary period. In addition to government incentives to invest in
housing, the house-formation, coming-of-age spending wave was
exploding for baby boomers. In the mid to late 1990s, there is a similar explosion in the number of baby boomers reaching peak spending age. This trend is set to peak in the early 2000s and then fall off.
In addition to peak spending age, the mid 40s are often a realization age that retirement is approaching soon; it is a time when investment begins to take on more importance and prominence.

This means baby-boom investment in stocks is likely to begin
peaking sometime between 2003 and 2008. And sometime after
2008, baby boomers will begin drawing on the investments they
have made and may even become a drain on the financial markets for liquidity. It would not be surprising if the U.S. market

continued to remain relatively overvalued (and fluctuate between slightly overvalued and highly overvalued) until the baby boom demand begins to soften (unless there is a liquidity-led recession or global recession/deflation before that period). Demographically, at least, absent some reason to fear stocks, baby-boom investment in equities is likely to remain robust until between 2003 and 2008.

In addition, businesses catering to greying baby boomers are likely to face demographic pressure propelling their earnings and demand for their services in the future. And it will be important to watch for trends in the spending patterns of the 45-year-olds today, so that one can jump aboard companies with hot products that will continue to appeal to this group as it peaks in the decade ahead.

Here's an example of a situation where analyzing demographic trends helped us focus our portfolio on a stock that was a clear and blatant recipient of benefits from the demographic trends just described.

In January and February 1987, bond and T-bill trends turned negative by falling below their respective 200-day moving averages. Investors using our defensive approach had to turn to other markets and other asset classes throughout much of the year while U.S. stocks continued to soar ahead, reaching a peak in August 1987. From the February caution signal near the 300 level in the S&P, the market rose another 12 percent before reaching a peak on August 25, 1987, of 336.77. However from that August peak, the U.S. and global markets entered one of the quickest bear markets in history, and the S&P crashed in October 1987, reaching a trough of 223.94 on December 4, 1987: a decline of 33.5 percent basis the cash S&P index in just four months. Finally risk-averse investors were paid off for having favored other asset classes and markets since early 1987. Global investors who had sidestepped the debacle waited patiently for an opportunity to jump on bargains.

While the S&P moved above its 200 MA in June 1988, the bond and bill markets oscillated back and forth and did not move above their respective MAs until late 1988, with the S&P trading at the 270 level. A new Liquidity Cycle appeared to be just beginning.

At my company, we sought to quickly develop a list of some of the strongest secular themes and trends and try to match up the companies meeting our selection criteria to see if we could get any synergy. The concept illustrated in Figure 6.20 caught my attention because it was obvious that 25-year-olds were at the highest level in many decades and this is when home formation spending trends begin to surge.

One of the stocks meeting our rigorous selection criteria (as described in Chapter 7) was Home Depot, seller of building material and home improvement products. The stock had experienced phenomenal growth since going public in 1981, rising in almost perfect concert with our demographic chart of 25-year-olds. The stock had beautiful relative strength and had in fact made a new high in 1988, while the S&P was still 20 percent below its old highs. In early February 1989, Home Depot broke out of a flag pattern (and a cup and handle) to new highs for a relatively low risk trade. It then went on to give us three more opportunities to add positions by breaking out of new flag patterns in late March 1989, late July 1989, and March 1990, before breaking below our trailing stops in July 1990 (and just prior to the October 1990 caution signal

---

Figure 6.21 **HOME DEPOT STOCK BULL MARKET OF LATE 1980s**

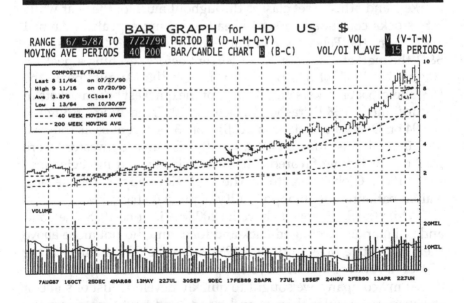

Source: Bloomberg Financial Markets. Copyright © 1998 Bloomberg LP. All rights reserved.

by bond and bill markets breaking below 200 MAs). During this brief time frame, Home Depot moved up by more than 300 percent and allowed us numerous entries to build a maximum position in the stock. And because we knew that Home Depot was in sync with a major secular theme of 25-year-old home formation spending, we were able to have the courage to build a significant position in the stock (see Figure 6.21).

The rewards of tracking emerging trends are immense! It takes time, effort, and some study, but it is worth it. In the age of information, trend tracking is potential power. Knowing how to use that information to position your capital in the strongest growth industries, is profit power.

SUMMARY

We have covered a large amount of information in this chapter. It is far more important to understand the forces behind growth than it is simply to come up with a method that retroactively finds good growth opportunities. We hope that this discussion helps investors understand many of the forces creating investment growth. And further, we hope that this chapter encourages many investors to seek investment mastery.

Equity Selection Criteria Long and Short—How Profits Are Magnified

In this chapter, vehicle selection criteria are outlined that can enable you to profit substantially from global stock markets and outperform indexes on both a nominal and risk/reward basis whenever you decide to build exposure in any particular market on the globe.

So far, we have explained how important timing tools such as valuation, the Austrian Liquidity Cycle, Technical Models, Austrian Alchemy and clear understanding, secular themes and trends, and other techniques can help an investor sidestep risk, locate excellent risk/reward opportunities, and concentrate on reliable market trends. The focus has been on money management and defense, as well as on identification of environments where an aggressive offense and allocation are warranted. Investors who use these techniques can avoid large drawdowns and locate the highest potential risk/reward markets.

After analyzing the preceding variables and choosing favorable equity markets (if they exist at the time), the investor's next question is, "What specific stocks do I select for my portfolio, and how and when do I buy and sell them?" The goal of this chapter is to answer that question.

MUTUAL FUNDS

First, however, a brief discussion of the mutual fund investor is in order. Could a mutual fund investor simply invest in some index-comparable fund for each country selected in our top five RS country allocation methodology and get above-average returns with below-average risk? Absolutely, the answer is yes. Many investors may not want to spend the time and effort selecting individual securities in the manner outlined here, even after they know the incredible advantages of doing so. If this describes you, that is fine. Nevertheless you should study this chapter because every investor needs to understand the variables that lie behind individual equity performance.

For the most part, mutual fund investors should avoid using closed-end funds. These funds trade a limited number of shares on the open market daily; they are much like a stock composed of a portfolio of equities. Because closed-end funds trade at market prices instead of their actual value (net asset value or NAV, which is the actual worth of the portfolio), they can cost an investor more than the portfolio is worth (in which case they trade at a premium to NAV), or even be trading for a price below their actual NAV worth (called a discount to NAV). This premium and discount vary wildly in most closed-end funds causing closed-end funds to correlate poorly with their underlying index. A typical example of this problem occurred in 1995: our models were strongly bullish on the Swiss market; and the Swiss index soared, returning over 42 percent. However, the closed-end Swiss Helvetica Fund rose under 13 percent for the year and actually declined from May to year-end, while the Swiss index returned over 19 percent. The reason was twofold: poor stock selection in the portfolio along with a premium turning into a discount. Global investors are much better off using WEBS (World Equity Benchmark Basket Securities), if available, for the country they are striving to invest in. WEBS, which are index funds that trade on the New York Stock Exchange (NYSE), are tradable intraday like a stock or a closed-end fund. They mimic indexes in the countries they represent, but they are so heavily arbitraged that they rarely trade at a premium or discount to their underlying index of more than 2 percent or so. They thus do an excellent job of mimicking their underlying index; in fact, they are the closest thing to buying that actual index. The only drawbacks to WEBS are that there are not enough of them and they represent too few countries.

Next in line would be top-ranked open-end funds (these purchase and redeem their shares depending on investor demand and trade only for their NAV) which tend to closely correlate with their underlying index, or preferably outperform on a risk/reward basis. Why would an investor prefer a WEB to an open-ended fund if that fund outperforms during both up and down market cycles? When an open-ended fund outperforms during good and bad environments, the investor probably should favor it; however, there are extremely few of these in the real world. The other problem with open-ended funds is that investors can only transact at the end of the day increasing their risk. If you are using WEBS and a news event hits that is likely to have a very negative effect, you don't have to sit through the rest of the day watching your investment value plummet—you can exit immediately at the market. There are very few highly index-correlated funds that outperform their respective index during both good times and bad by such a large extent that they are worth the extra end-of-day risk.

Be careful of mutual fund rating services, most of which rate funds on total return rankings, while ignoring the risk endured to achieve these returns. Rating services have sadly become the epitome of rearview-mirror investing. Don't get caught in the trap of thinking that a "diversified" portfolio in one country or sector is safe. Such funds do very well during roaring bull markets, and very poorly in bear markets in general. Try to find funds that outperform in both positive and negative environments; for a mutual fund manager, that approach is the definition of adding value. The Forbes ratings are the only ones that pay decent attention to how a fund performs in negative market periods.

It is actually quite difficult to find top-quality U.S. domiciled funds for many emerging markets without incurring huge load-fees. For this reason, I suggest global mutual fund investors get an offshore bank account, offshore annuity, or offshore company, any of which will allow them to trade offshore mutual funds, which tend to emulate indexes to create a vehicle not available in the United States (see Table 7.1). The other possibility is to take these countries off your potential investment list. However, the return from many of these top global areas is substantial making it worth the trouble to invest in good funds abroad. Another option is to try to use ADRs and GDRs—foreign stocks traded on U.S. or London exchanges as a surrogate for country indexes. If you use the patterns and monitor the criteria suggested in this chapter, then this will work. If this is too much work for you, then do not use ADRs and GDRs.

Brokers for Foreign Stocks

Banque Union de Credit
   ($20,000 min)
Rue de Mont Blanc 3
P. O. Box 1816
Geneva 1, CH-1211 Switzerland
011-4122-73207939
Fax 011-4122-732-5089
Contact: Camille Perusset

TD Greenline
Discount Canadian Stocks
Minimum Fee C$43
416-982-7686

Hong Kong and Shanghai Bank
Securities and Investments Dept.
8/F Edinburgh Tower
The LandMark
Central, Hong Kong
011-852-842-2280
Fax 011-852-845-5802

Century Capital ($1000/trade)
5 Century Drive #249
Greenville, SC 29607
1-800-752-3233

Anglo-Irish Bank of Austria
Rathastrasse 20,
P. O. Box 306
A-1011 Vienna, Austria
011-43222-43-6161
Fax 011-43222-42-8142

Charles Schwab & Company
101 Montgomery Street
San Francisco, CA 94104
1-800-648-5300
Fax 415-956-3212

Barry Murphy & Company
77 Summer Street
Boston, MA 02210
1-800-221-2111
Fax 616-426-9309

Bank of Copenhagen
c/o Ms. Finsen, 4-6
Ostergade DK-1100
Copenhagen, Denmark
011-45-33-11-1515
Fax 341-1393

Also, most mutual fund investors seem to think of mutual funds as savings vehicles, which they are not. Don't forget how "mutual funds" got their name in the United States. Closed-end funds are called investment trusts in most other English-speaking countries and used to be called investment trusts in the United States. More than 90 percent of them went out of business during

Table 7.1 BROKERS FOR FOREIGN FUNDS

Fund Company	Equity Funds	Bond Funds	Money Market Funds
Global Asset Management 11 Athol Street Douglas, Isle of Man, IM99 1HH British Isles 011-441-624-632632 Fax 011-441-624-625956	Australia, Brazil, France, Japan, Singapore/Malaysia, United Kingdom, United States	East Asian, ASEAN, European bonds, Latin American, United Kingdom, Swiss, German, Japanese	U.S. Dollar, British Pound, Swiss Franc, Deutsche, Mark Yen
Foreign and Colonial 47 Boulevard Royal P.O. Box 275 L-2012 Luxembourg 011-352-464-0101 Fax 011-352-46-36-31	Argentina, Brazil, Colombia, India, Japan, Mexico, Peru, Poland, Taiwan, United Kingdom, United States		
Fidelity Offshore Kingswood Place Tadworth, Surrey Kt20 6RB United Kingdom 011-44-1737-838317 Fax 011-44-1737-830360	ASEAN, Australia, Canada, China, Europe, France, Germany, Hong Kong, Indonesia, Italy, Japan, Latin America, Malaysia, Nordic, Singapore, Southeast Asia, Spain, Switzerland, Thailand, United Kingdom, United States	Sterling, Yen, U.S., Eurobond, Far East, International, Deutsche Mark short term	Australian Dollar, Canadian Dollar, New Zealand Dollar, Singapore Dollar, Swiss Franc, U.S. Dollar, Yen, Spanish Peseta, Deutsche Mark, Lire
Credit Suisse Neuschelerstrasse 1 P.O. Box 669 CH-8021 Zurich, Switzerland 011-411-212-161 Fax 011-411-212-0669	France, Germany, Italy, Japan, Korea, Latin America, Netherlands, Spain, United States	Australian Dollar, Canadian Dollar, Lire, New Zealand Dollar, Peso, Swiss Franc, U.S. Dollar, Yen	Canadian Dollar, Deutsche Mark, Lire, Swiss Franc, U.S. Dollar, Yen, British Pound, Dutch Guilder, Spanish Peseta
Barclays Gredley House 1-11 Broadway Straford, London E15 4BJ 011-411-081-534-5544	Australia, China, Euro Equity, Hong Kong, India, Indonesia, Japan, Korea, Malaysia, Philippines, Singapore, Southeast Asia, Spain, Thailand, United Kingdom, United States	Eurobond, Gilt, U.S. bond, Deutsche Mark bond	Deutsche Mark, U.S. Dollar, British Pound, Swiss Franc, Yen
Jardine Flemming 4th Floor Tardine House One Connaught Place Hong Kong 011-852-2843-8888	ASEAN, Asia, Australia, China, Europe, Germany, India, Indonesia, Japan, Korea, Malaysia, New Zealand, Pakistan, Philippines, Taiwan, Thailand	Eurobond, Far East bond, Global bond	Australian Dollar, British Pound, Canadian Dollar, Deutsche Mark, European Currency Unit, Hong Kong Dollar, Yen , Swiss Franc, U.S. Dollar

the Great Depression era, however, and investors lost all or most of their money. Likewise, open-ended mutual funds used to be called unit investment trusts in the United States, and they still are in most of the English-speaking world. Again, 90 percent of these trusts failed in the Depression. After World War II, the brokerage community itself lobbied for regulation to create a similar entity with a new name—"mutual fund." The reason brokers wanted a new name is that the term "investment trust" had such a bad reputation: almost everyone who had invested in one lost everything, and almost no investor would invest in them because they had such negative associations to them. The brokers' idea was to create a more regulated version of the same thing and re-name it for marketing purposes. While mutual funds today do not use the leverage employed by the investment trusts of the past, in a bear market they are not safe savings vehicles; investors should remember that one can lose money after decades of investment in a secular bear market.

INDIVIDUAL STOCK SELECTION

One of the money management principles stressed in Chapter 5 is that investors should spend most of their time on vehicle selection, because this is where the biggest payoff to effort exists. A famous CDA/Wiesenberger study using data from 1940 to 1973, and repeated using data from 1980 to 1992 highlights just how important equity selection is in the investment process.

The study is based on two fictitious investors, Mr. Selection and Mr. Timing. Mr. Timing can perfectly call every market swing of 10 percent or more, exiting at the exact high before every downturn, and buying at the exact low before every upturn of 10 percent or more. Mr. Selection simply invests 100 percent of his funds in the top-performing market sector each year. Who generates more profits? Most investors believe that the two fictitious investors would generate similar profit results. In fact, Mr. Selection beat Mr. Timing from 1940 to 1973, generating over 30 times as much profits. And again from 1980 to 1992, Mr. Selection generated over four times as much profits. While the results are fictitious, they illustrate that selection is more critical than timing in determining the profitability of your investments. The success of top traditional hedge funds, such as Julian Robertson's Jaguar funds, or Zweig's Zweig DiMenna fund, also shows that funds based almost solely on vehicle selection (both long and short) can outperform the market substantially and consistently in both their risk and return.

Once you find reliable moves through the other avenues covered thus far, getting the most out of those moves is accomplished through equity selection criteria and entry/exit methodologies based on research that I completed with Stanford Ph.D. Tom Johnson during the 1980s. In addition, the methodologies represent over a decade of real-time trading/fund consulting.

Dealing with the Risk of Meteors

There's an old market saw that goes: "In the financial world, there are many meteors, but few fixed stars." In other words, many stocks explode up in price, reach extreme overvaluation, and then plummet back into relative obscurity, while few stocks can consistently generate 40 percent earnings growth for more than a decade (along with commensurate stock gains).

If you look over the past century of data, you will find that each decade produces at least one bull move in stocks enough to produce many "meteors" whose stock prices explode up 300 percent or more in a one- to three-year period. These fad stocks start out by showing strong consistent or turnaround earnings growth (defined rigorously later in this chapter), then begin to take off in price and become strong relative strength stocks as they are starting to be discovered, and then in the final one third of their price movement they become "darlings" of Wall Street and get wildly overvalued and overowned by institutions prior to collapsing back into relative obscurity and fairer valuations based on much slower earnings growth. These are the meteors of the stock market.

However, you will also find historically, that each decade produces at least one bull move in which a handful of "fixed stars" develop. Just like meteors, these fixed stars start out by showing strong consistent or turnaround earnings growth (defined rigorously later in this chapter), then begin to take off in price and become strong relative strength stocks as they are starting to be discovered, and often also become popular with the Wall Street crowd. Fixed stars may become overvalued, but very rarely become wildly overvalued. What really differentiates fixed stars is that while their earnings growth slows some, they are still able to produce more than 40 percent annual earnings growth for over a decade. Because of their continued strong growth and lack of high overvaluation, these stocks do not collapse, they just begin to move up with more volatility and at a slower rate than their initial prepopularity phase.

Most of each decade's greatest equity opportunities lie in either its fixed stars or its meteors. The problem is that both exhibit similar characteristics in their early phases, and it is often difficult to determine which is which. Further, even if you were able to successfully cut out many faddish trends and themes, it is rare for an individual to be farsighted enough to have a very high hit rate on determining stocks that are going to be fixed stars. And, there are still some excellent opportunities over one- to three-year periods in meteor stocks—you just have to have a methodology that allows you to exit quickly when stocks become overvalued, overowned, overhyped, or weaken substantially in price.

Therefore, once one acknowledges that an investor striving to find the top growth opportunities is likely to get many meteors in his portfolio, the question becomes how can one participate in the run-ups in meteors while still limiting risk and avoiding much of their eventual collapse. The answer we came up with is to employ the following:

- Hunt for strong earnings growth and runaway characteristics (both of which we will be describing specifically ahead) in stocks Wall Street hasn't yet completely discovered.
- Trade these stocks (rather than invest, buy, and hold) using limited risk pattern recognition strategies for entry/exit/OPS (Open Protective Stop), and get out (at least partially) when institutions begin to dominate trading in the stock.
- Take partial profits when these stocks begin to get slightly overvalued and then tighten up trailing stops and look to exit completely on the first sign of serious weakness.

Meteoric Industries from Prior Decades

The following list of historical meteor industries gives some perspective on what they look like. Although in retrospect these industries seem obviously faddish, at the time most observers believed the trends that brought these industries to the forefront would continue for many years:

1910 Buggy makers and cigar stores.

1920 Aviation, oil, ice, and closed-end investment trusts.

1930 AT&T, higher yielding utilities, no-debt financials with earnings.

1950 Uranium, bowling chains.

1960 Conglomerates, recreational vehicles.

1970 Nifty fifty, OTC growth, oil, gold stocks.

1980 Junk bond promoters, REITs, Japanese stocks, discount distributors of goods, PC software, hardware, electronic supplies, pharmaceuticals.

1990 Medical, biotechnology, capital goods, software, telecommunications, communication software and hardware, health maintenance organizations (HMOs), financials, emerging markets and debt, Internet companies, cigar manufacturers.

Investors should understand that most "trends" do not have the power to propel an industry into the forefront of profit growth for more than a decade. However, if we can find and get aboard new meteors with limited risk in this and future decades, and then get out before they become too overvalued, we can still achieve excellent low-risk profits, and fixed-star portfolio performance. If we happen to catch a fixed star now and then in the process, it won't hurt either.

IDENTIFYING METEORS AND FIXED STARS

When we looked back over the past century of market data to formulate a successful equity investment strategy, Tom Johnson and I made some assumptions. The first was that J. Paul Getty's most important rule of wealth also applied to stocks. The rule is "Go where the oil is." In stock terms, we went where the strongest stock moves were to see if we could isolate some common characteristics so that we could focus our trading on the strongest trending vehicles. We believed that since strong trends were where most stock market profits came from, strong trends were the oil we were trying to find.

Therefore, we sought to historically locate both the meteors and fixed stars and see what characteristics they had in common. Dr. Johnson and I sought to keep an open mind as to what types of characteristics to analyze in looking for common traits. We also tried to review every similar study to be sure we weren't reinventing the wheel, and to see whether others had found characteristics we could start with. I try to advocate always standing firmly on the shoulders of greatness; thus we took a plethora of our concepts from other great investors who had done similar studies—William O'Neil, Frank Cappiello, Marty Zweig, Peter Lynch, Jim Rogers, W. D. Gann, Dan Sullivan, J. Paul Getty, H. M. Gartley, and many others. From a very early age, I had personally sought to voraciously read almost everything connected with building profits in the markets. We weren't trying to come up with original research necessarily, just find what worked.

I put hundreds of historical charts up on my office walls and ceiling of each of the top winning stocks of each era, along with many of the variables we could get historical data on. One of the first things I noticed was that a large percentage of the big winners exhibited what I like to call "runaway market" characteristics. Runaway characteristics are chart-evidence of extremely aggressive buying.

Runaway Market Characteristics

Just over 85 percent of the top stocks in the past 100 years displayed technical patterns that indicate extremely aggressive buying in the first third of their major move upward. In this section, we review some of the most important generic patterns signifying a runaway trend in progress. We start with "TBBLBG," an acronym for the terms *thrust breakout, breakaway lap,* and *breakaway gap.*

Moves above Previous Resistence Levels on TBBLBGs.   A previous resistence level is simply a price level that when hit, leads to a six-day or longer correction. Prior intermediate-term highs on a daily chart, prior short-term highs on a weekly or monthly chart, and all annual highs are examples of resistence levels.

A thrust breakout (TB in the acronym) is a move above resistence on a thrust pattern. A *thrust* pattern is simply a day in
which the range (high–low) is two or more times the average
range of the preceding 20 days; the volume is higher than the volume of the prior day; and the close is in the top 1/3 of the day's
range. While we have described it rigorously here for computer
programmers, the following simpler terms are probably just as accurate: a thrust is an unusually large range day where the close is
near the high and the volume is higher than the prior day. Any

---

Figure 7.1 **THRUST BREAKOUT UP (TB)**

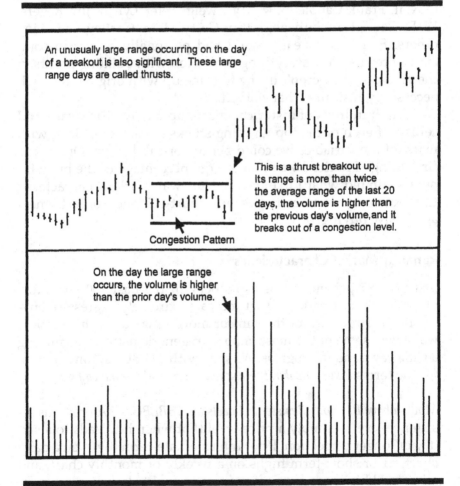

time you see a large range day on a chart, odds are you're looking at a thrust—just check out the volume and see whether the close is near the day's high. Figures 7.1 and 7.2 illustrate a thrust breakout above resistence and a thrust breakdown below support (in the case of a bear move).

The next component of TBBLBG is BL—breaklap. A breaklap is a move below support or above resistence on a lap day. On a *lap up day*, prices make a low that is greater than the close of the previous

Figure 7.2 **THRUST BREAKOUT DOWN (TB)**

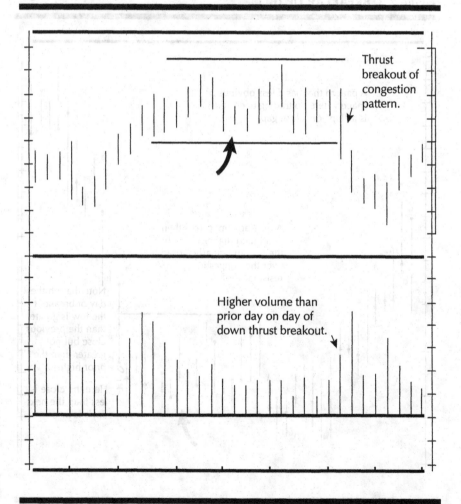

Thrust breakout of congestion pattern.

Higher volume than prior day on day of down thrust breakout.

day, but less than the previous day's high (a low above the previous day's high would be a gap, to be discussed). On a *lap down day*, prices make a high that is less than the prior day's close, but greater than the prior day's low. For those familiar with technical patterns, this is a "hole" in trading between the prior day's close and the next day's action that doesn't meet the criteria of the traditional "gap." On the day the lap occurs, we want a break of support or resistence. Figures 7.3 and 7.4 illustrate a breaklap up and

Figure 7.3 **BREAKLAP UP (BL)**

A pattern that has a less obvious space where no trading occurred is a "lap" or "close gap."

After "lap" up, prices then continued higher through the day and clearly closed over the congestion resistence.

Note that on the day of breakout the low is greater than the previous close but not greater than the prior high.

Here the close is less than the next day's low.

Figure 7.4 **BREAKLAP DOWN (BL)**

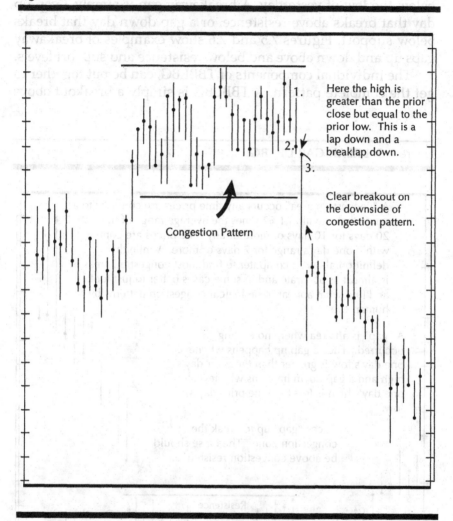

1.

Here the high is greater than the prior close but equal to the prior low. This is a lap down and a breaklap down.

2.

3.

Clear breakout on the downside of congestion pattern.

Congestion Pattern

a breaklap down. A lap is similar to a gap, except that the "gap" or empty space in price occurs between one day's close and the next day's high or low.

Finally, *BG* in TBBLBG stands for breakaway gap. A gap is really just an empty space where no trading occurred on a bar chart. A *gap up* occurs when the low of today is greater than the high of the prior day. The distance between yesterday's high and today's low is the actual gap size. Similarly, in a *gap down*, today's high is below the low of yesterday. A breakaway gap is simply a gap up day that breaks above resistence, or a gap down day that breaks below support. Figures 7.5 and 7.6 show examples of breakaway gaps up and down above and below resistence and support levels.

The individual components of TBBLBG, can be put together to get the complete pattern. A TBBLBG is simply a breakout above

---

Figure 7.5 **BREAK GAP UP (BG)**

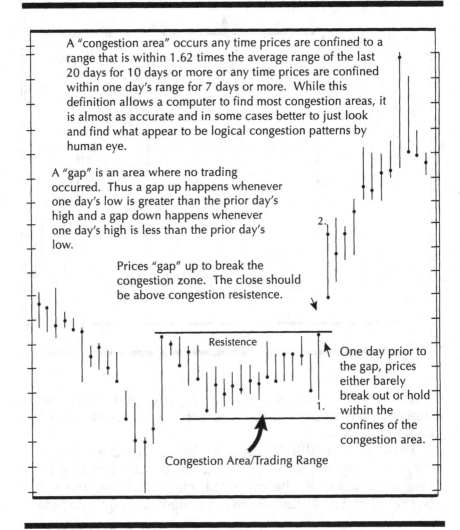

A "congestion area" occurs any time prices are confined to a range that is within 1.62 times the average range of the last 20 days for 10 days or more or any time prices are confined within one day's range for 7 days or more. While this definition allows a computer to find most congestion areas, it is almost as accurate and in some cases better to just look and find what appear to be logical congestion patterns by human eye.

A "gap" is an area where no trading occurred. Thus a gap up happens whenever one day's low is greater than the prior day's high and a gap down happens whenever one day's high is less than the prior day's low.

2.

Prices "gap" up to break the congestion zone. The close should be above congestion resistence.

Resistence

One day prior to the gap, prices either barely break out or hold within the confines of the congestion area.

1.

Congestion Area/Trading Range

Figure 7.6 **BREAK GAP DOWN**

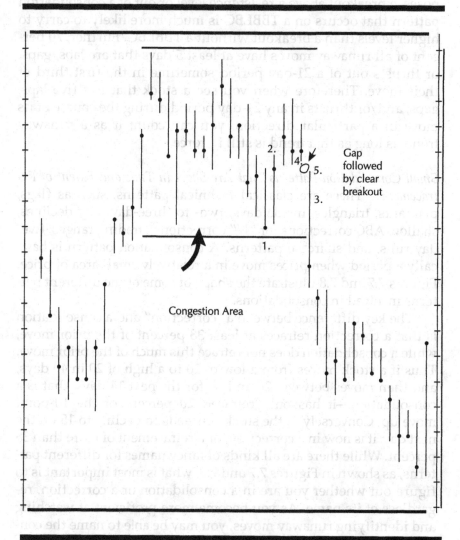

Gap
followed
by clear
breakout

Congestion Area

resistence or below support that occurs on a day that is a TB or a
BL or a BG (hence the name TBBLBG).

Most runaway moves contain many laps, gaps, and thrusts in
the direction of the strong trend. In addition, most runaway moves
up tend to break out above resistence levels on a TBBLBG most of
the time, while most runaway moves down tend to breakdown

below support on a TBBLBG most of the time. For trading purposes, a breakout above a resistence level or out of a consolidation
pattern that occurs on a TBBLBG is much more likely to carry to
higher levels than a breakout without a TBBLBG. Further, 70 percent of all runaway moves have at least 5 days that are laps, gaps,
or thrusts out of a 21-day period sometime in the first third of
their move. Therefore when you see a stock that has five laps,
gaps, and/or thrusts in any 21-day period during the course of its
move in a particular direction, you can count it as a runaway
trend as long as that trend is still in force.

*Small Consolidation Patterns That Are Short in Time and Extent of Re-
tracement.*   These are classical technical patterns, such as flags,
pennants, triangles, inside days, two- to three-day only declines,
shallow ABC corrections (or "N" corrections), trading ranges, five-
day runs, and staircase patterns. A consolidation pattern is basically a period when prices move in a relatively small area of price.
Figures 7.7 and 7.8 illustrate the shape of some of the different patterns involved in consolidations.

The key difference between a "correction" and a consolidation
is that a correction retraces at least 38 percent of the prior move,
while a consolidation does not retrace this much of the prior move.
Thus if a stock moves from a low of 10 to a high of 20 in 40 days,
and then moves between 20 and 18 for the next 14 days, that is a
consolidation—it has only retraced 20 percent of the 10-point
move up. Conversely, if the stock proceeds to decline to 15 on the
next day, it is now in a correction, or a retracement of more than 38
percent. While there are all kinds of fancy names for different patterns, as shown in Figures 7.7 and 7.8, what is most important is to
figure out whether you are in a consolidation or a correction, regardless of its name. As you become more proficient at watching
and identifying runaway moves, you may be able to name the consolidation pattern, but that is not critical. Here are two real-time
examples of runaway moves that show how to use the preceding
tools to identify them.

Figure 7.9 shows a runaway move in the November 1987 Soy-
bean futures market. Label the bottom bar (the day with the lowest low) on the chart as 0 and count forward. Day 1 is a gap up, as
are days 4 and 7. Day 7 is also a thrust, as is day 11, while day 14
is a breakaway gap. So we have six laps, gaps, or thrusts in just the

Figure 7.7 EARLY IDENTIFICATION OF RUNAWAY MARKETS

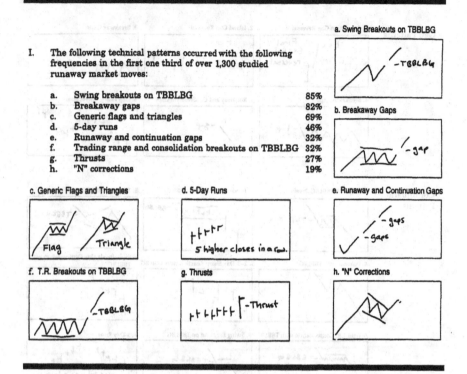

I. The following technical patterns occurred with the following
    frequencies in the first one third of over 1,300 studied
    runaway market moves:

a.	Swing breakouts on TBBLBG	85%
b.	Breakaway gaps	82%
c.	Generic flags and triangles	69%
d.	5-day runs	46%
e.	Runaway and continuation gaps	32%
f.	Trading range and consolidation breakouts on TBBLBG	32%
g.	Thrusts	27%
h.	"N" corrections	19%

a. Swing Breakouts on TBBLBG

b. Breakaway Gaps

c. Generic Flags and Triangles

d. 5-Day Runs

e. Runaway and Continuation Gaps

f. T.R. Breakouts on TBBLBG

g. Thrusts

h. "N" Corrections

first 14 bars off of a low. Certainly this qualifies as having five
laps, gaps, and thrusts in a 21-day period, because we have six in
a 14-day period. Thus we can see quickly that we're in a runaway
move, which continues to take prices substantially higher.

Figure 7.10 shows the decline in Halliburton stock in the
1981–1982 bear market. If we count days from the far left, on day 8
HAL makes a high. Day 9 is both a gap and a thrust, day 10 is a
gap, day 12 is a thrust, day 16 is a gap and a thrust—so just 8 days
after the high we have 5 or more laps, gaps, and thrusts, certainly
well within a 21-bar period. Now we can assume HAL is in a runaway move down, with likely substantially more downside to
come. Notice that during these moves neither HAL nor Nov '87
Soybeans ever corrects—they either explode in the direction of
the trend or they consolidate. This is the real key to finding explosive moves.

Figure 7.8 **RUNAWAY MARKET PATTERNS**

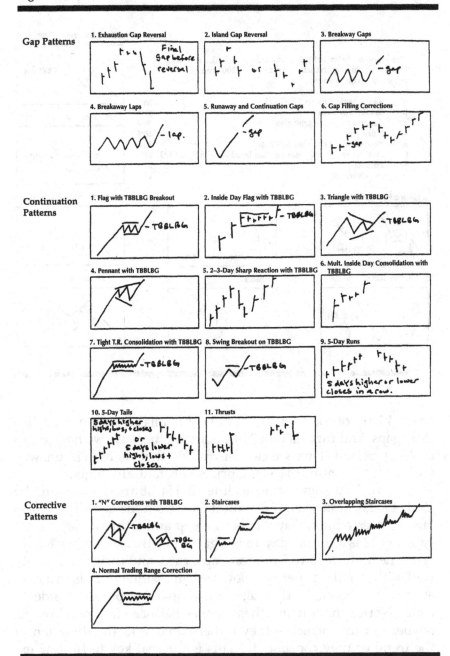

Figure 7.9 **SAMPLE RUNAWAY UP MOVE**

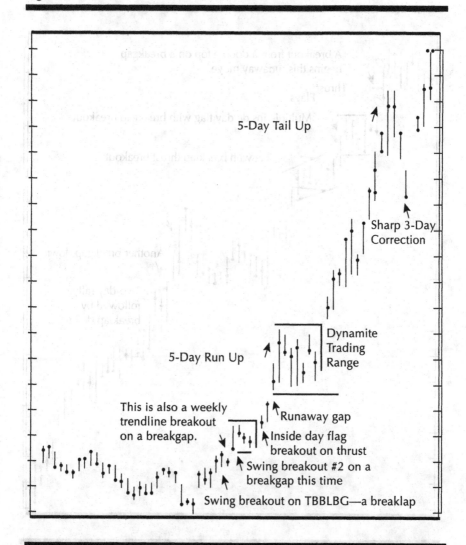

The important point to remember is that once a stock or commodity begins a move that can be characterized as runaway (5/21), then it is assumed to continue to be in a runaway trend until proven otherwise via a correction or trend change. When you get proficient at locating the patterns sketched in the preceding

Figure 7.10 **SAMPLE RUNAWAY DOWN MOVE**

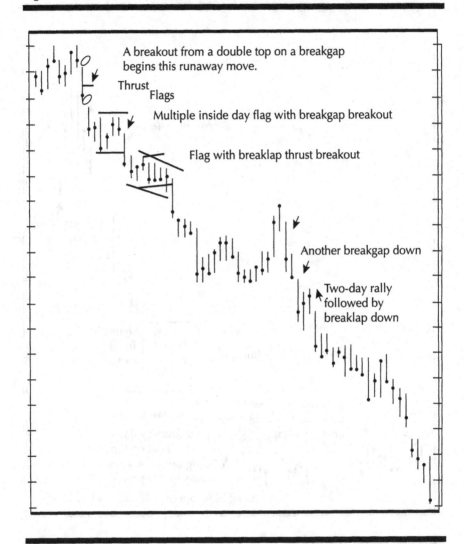

discussion, look for markets with 10 of these runaway characteristics in a 30-bar period or more for the most explosive trends, but the 5/21 laps, gaps, and thrusts is a good proxy.

So, *the first thing the investor should look for to find a runaway trend in any market is runaway technical characteristics.*

EQUITY FUEL

Once we find equities that have exhibited runaway technical characteristics, we next begin to look for a concept we call individual equity *fuel*. The concept of fuel is simple: we are looking for valid reasons to expect the trend we have located to continue into the future. If you have a strong trend that is likely to continue into the foreseeable future, you have a good candidate for further appreciation. Fuel is therefore a summary of some of the most important variables that the top stocks of the past 100 years had in common, which tended to differentiate them from other stocks—and led to huge trends that pushed prices up or down by very large percentages.

Criteria for Runaway up Stocks with Fuel

Technical Strength.   This means that the stock has exhibited runaway characteristics via our 5/21 method at some point since the trend in question began. It also means the stock *has not fallen below its 200-day moving average (MA)* once its trend has begun and it has moved above the 200 MA. Finally the stock must have an O'Neil's *Relative Strength rank of at least 65 if it is undergoing a correction, and at least 80 if it is making new highs.* This ranking is available from *Investor's Business Daily* or *Daily Graphs.*

Consistent Growth or Turnaround Growth.   Consistent growth means (1) the stock has a five-year annual growth rate of 25 percent or higher; and (2) three years of higher annual earnings or two years of higher annual earnings and a next year's estimate of higher earnings than the current year. OR

Turnaround growth means (1) the last two reported quarterly earnings showed earnings up 70 percent or more over year-earlier same quarters, and (2) this quarter's earnings are above last quarter's earnings.

Strong Quarterly Earnings Growth, Earnings Momentum, and Top Earning Per Share (EPS) Ranking.   Strong quarterly earnings growth means that both this quarter and the last quarter show earnings up 25 percent or more over year-earlier similar quarters. AND

Earnings momentum means that either this quarter's earnings are higher than last quarter's earnings or that this quarter's earnings are up over year-earlier similar quarter by a higher percentage than last quarter's earnings were up versus last quarter's year-earlier similar quarter. Put simply, this quarter's earnings growth rate is higher than last quarter's earnings growth rate. AND

Top EPS rank means an *Investor's Business Daily* or *Daily Graphs* EPS ranks over 80.

Reasonable Price.   Criteria are:

1. P/E is 70 percent or less of the lessor of (a) a stock's five-year growth rate (unless the stock is a turnaround growth pick and not a consistent growth pick, in which place the growth rate criterion here does not apply), or (b) the lower of the quarterly earnings growth rate of the last two quarters; *or* the P/E is 50 percent or less of the stock's anticipated growth rate of the next year via analysts consensus estimates. AND

2. P/E is not twice the S&P's P/E or greater. AND

3. Price/Sales is not > 6.

    The bottom line for this criterion is that the stock is not overpriced (items 2 and 3), and that it is selling at a discount to either its current growth or its expected growth rate.

Relatively Undiscovered Stock.   The combined (bank and fund) *institutional sponsorship of the stock should be ideally less than 16 percent of capitalization.* If a stock meets strong themes and trends one can buy it until institutional sponsorship reaches 35 percent, but don't add to it thereafter. In addition, investors should begin taking profits once a stock reaches 40 percent or higher institutional sponsorship. These figures are to be found in O'Neil's *Daily Graphs*, and in the charts of *Investor's Business Daily*.

Low Debt.   The strongest companies use their own internal growth to finance their expansion. This means long-term debt less than 50 percent, actually less than 10 percent in most top stocks. You can relax this qualifying criterion only in specific instances. The two main such situations are when you are trying to exploit a clear secular theme or trend and none of the stocks in that industry meet our criteria but there are one or more that meet all the criteria but low debt. The second instance is when all the companies of the industry in which a stock competes have very high debt levels; in some industries even the best companies need high debt.

Positive Fundamentals and Ratings. Positive fundamentals means that there is a simple, straightforward reason to expect continued earnings growth such as a new product, a technology gap being exploited and not yet fully in use by its expected market, a change in management and anticipated results from restructuring, demographic trends expanding the market, or changes in interest rates or economic environment. You should be able to explain to an uninterested party in plain language why the stock should continue to experience sharp earnings growth for the next few years.

Positive ratings means that if the stock is followed by premier stock rating services such as *Value Line, Zachs,* or *Lowry's* that it has a top or second-to-top rank in most of them and does not have a less than average rank by any of them. You do not need to subscribe to all these services, but you should probably subscribe to one of them or else get our own *Portfolio Strategy Letter,* which screens stocks in this way for you.

Maintenance of Acceptable Risk. Cut risk to original capital and overall risk once any potential problems develop in each market and stock. In our money management rules, you will normally risk up to 2 percent of capital on each position from entry to OPS. If there is any reason for caution, however, you should cut new risk to 1 percent on any new positions or additions. Reasons for caution include (1) the stock itself does not meet new buy criteria because it is no longer reasonably priced or no longer undiscovered; (2) the overall country market that the stock is based in is becoming overvalued or technically questionable, or interest rate trends are no longer clear; (3) top timing models such as the *Chartist* or *International Bank Credit Analyst* are cautious or negative on that overall market; and (4) the stock is a takeover rumor or takeover target where the investor doesn't have inside information.

Ancillary Criteria

Ancillary criteria are not reasons for eliminating stocks from our lists. If an equity meets the preceding criteria, it at least goes on our potential buy list. However, ancillary criteria can help investors to further screen this list to focus on the best opportunities within the stocks meeting our initial criteria. Favorable ancillary criteria usually are exhibited by the top-performing stocks on our lists.

High Alphas and a High Alpha/Beta Ratio.   Alpha essentially measures the ability of a stock to move up independent of market movement. Beta measures a stock's sensitivity to movement in the S&P (or its underlying market). We want stocks that are able to move up regardless of what their underlying market is doing. Ideally, the alpha is over 3 and the alpha/beta ratio is over 3.

Good Daily Graphs Ratings.   This means tools published in O'Neil's *Daily Graphs*, such as Accumulation rating of B or A, Timeliness rating of A or B, Mutual Fund Sponsorship by funds rated A or B.

High Short Interest/Market Cap Ratio but Not Top 5 Percent of Market. Short interest/market cap is the percentage of outstanding stock held in short positions. Although the figure is not nearly as valid as it used to be since it does not differentiate between option and derivative arbitrage and actual shorts, there is still decent evidence that runaway up stocks with high short-interest strongly outperform the market. That is true until short interest/market cap figures get into the top 5 percent of all equities, when stocks begin to underperform markedly.

Beating Analysts' Estimates Recently.   Stocks that are reasonably priced and yet have either (1) beat analysts' earnings estimates for each of the previous two quarters or (2) beat analysts' earnings estimates for four of the previous five quarters tend to outperform the market sharply, though they are rare.

Have High Management/Incentive Ownership.   In general, stocks with over 20 percent of management ownership outperform stocks with less than 20 percent employee/manager ownership. Ownership provides a good incentive for producing strong growth.

Annual or Quarterly Revenue Growth Greater than the P/E.   This is another good gauge that a stock is selling at a very reasonable price.

Group Relative Strength > 70 and a Stock or Industry that Is in Sync with a Theme or Trend.   The best stocks are usually exploiting some trend that is long lasting and will propel earnings for many years to come. Group RS rules help you to locate sectors that might meet these criteria, while stocks exploiting a theme or other group relative strength ranks help you to locate sectors that might meet these criteria, while stocks exploiting a theme whose group rank is also above 70 meet both fundamental and technical guidelines.

MEASURING PRICE AGAINST GROWTH

In the long-run, earnings growth is what fuels stock price gains and has the highest correlation to stock price gains. So earnings gains is the first strong component exerting upward pressure on stock prices. Stocks with high earnings gains also have high potential for stock price appreciation in the market, as long as the price you are paying does not discount too much future growth already.

One way to measure the price you are paying for future growth is the P/E multiple, which is the second component of stock price movement. Investors should realize that the P/E multiple is almost as strong an influence on stock price movement as earnings growth is. When most investors talk about the price of a stock they are really talking about the P/E or the price investors are paying for a given stream of earnings. The P/E is a short-term and more volatile component of a stock's price than its earnings growth. One reason that investors need to avoid negative bear markets is that even in companies whose earnings are rising rapidly, bear markets tend to deflate P/Es across the board. I can show you dozens of stocks that actually doubled earnings during the 1929–1932 bear market or the 1973–1974 bear market or even the 1981–1982 bear market, and still lost over 30 percent of their value (and often 50%–90% of value) because their P/Es dropped so severely. Moreover, high P/E stocks almost always take much bigger hits during a bear market or correction than do relatively low P/E stocks. So stocks priced reasonably in relation to their earnings growth are lower in risk.

On the other hand, almost all the top stocks of the twentieth century that we studied went through a *sustained period of multiple expansion* that helped fuel their stock price gains. This is what allows several hundred percentage or more stock price gains in a brief time frame: it is not just that earnings are skyrocketing, it is also that investors are willing to pay higher and higher P/Es for those skyrocketing earnings that push prices higher. Buying a stock at a reasonable price not only reduces risk, but it also gives an investor leverage on the upside. If a reasonably priced stock is experiencing rapid earnings growth, investors can expect prices to rise with earnings and for the P/E to expand to the expected three-year growth rate of the stock as well.

Suppose that we find two stocks, both expected to grow at a 30 percent rate for the next five years. These are exceptional companies to begin with. One has a P/E of 30, and the other a P/E of 15, both have current earnings of $1 per share. Two years down the road, we can expect the first stock to gain 30 percent each year while maintaining its current multiple of 30. Earnings will move from $1 this year to $1.3 next year and $1.69 the next year. With a 30 P/E that means the stock price will move from $30 now to $50.7, for a gain of 69 percent.

The second stock we can expect to grow 30 percent each year, and for its P/E to rise to 30. Its price should therefore move from $15 (15 P/E × $1 earnings) currently to 50.7 (earnings 1.69 × 30), for a gain of 238 percent. This example shows that P/E expansion vastly increases leverage and returns. Investors do well to remember that almost none of the fixed star performers showed wildly high P/Es (P/E > 1.5 × expected or former growth rates) until they were very near the phase where growth and stock gains slowed down substantially (except when their earnings were very low moving from 0 to 50 cents a share, or within a few quarters from when the stocks moved from a loss to a profit). So when a stock that has been a strong earner and performer becomes wildly overvalued, that is often a signal that something is wrong and the growth rate and appreciation rate of the stock is due for a serious correction. Investors are just expecting too much in current prices.

As Frank Cappiello (of Wall Street Week fame) has highlighted so well in his research, one of the key factors leading to multiple expansion in a stock is increasing institutional ownership. This is why we look for relatively undiscovered stocks that are experiencing rapid growth. Stocks with institutional holdings of less than 16 percent (3%–10% is optimal) are in the phase of just being discovered by institutions. It is often the discovery and accumulation of a stock by institutions that propels its P/E multiple to higher and higher levels most quickly. Thus a stock that is just being discovered by institutions and is still underowned is likely to experience institutional accumulation that will propel its P/E toward its long-run growth rate. So there is potential leverage in owning companies that are just being discovered by funds, banks, and other institutional investors.

There is a downside, however, to high institutional sponsorship of a stock. Once institutions own 35 percent to 40 percent of a stock, they begin to dominate the trading of it. Institutions tend in general to look at similar criteria for dumping stocks. If a heavily institutionally owned stock comes out with surprisingly lower than expected earnings report, or other negatively interpreted news, the stock is much more vulnerable to taking an immediate and sharp drop in price, as huge institutional sell orders all hit the market at the same time. This is why we want to start selling off at least part of a stock in which institutions dominate trading—the risk to holding them is much higher.

We also want companies that have a product or service that is propelling earnings growth, not the leverage employed by the managers. High debt can sometimes increase earnings gains during good times, but it also makes a stock much more vulnerable to rate hikes and slower economic growth. In general, very few of the century's top performers exhibited high debt.

It is one thing for a company to have already experienced rapid earnings gains, and quite another for it to continue to do so in the future. Remember that it is the future earnings potential of a company that you are paying for when you buy it. Don't be a rearview mirror investor. Make sure that the companies you are buying have the potential for earnings growth over the next two or three years that is 40 percent higher than the P/E you are paying. And make sure you understand the business of the companies that you buy and that you have some legitimate reason for expecting future earnings growth, such as a theme or trend or technology gap. Be sure you can explain in simple language the reason one could reasonably expect such high growth from this company in terms of earnings. Finally be sure that rating services that look at such things as balance sheets, analysts' expectations, volume, and other variables look favorably on the companies you are buying (if they rate the stock).

Global Equities

One of the sadder aspects of doing research on global equities is the incredible dearth of information on non-U.S. stocks on a historical basis compared with the wealth of information available for U.S. equities. Sources such as Worldscope, Datastream International, the global Estimate Directory, Bloomberg, and others are striving to fill this void, but the gap is huge, particularly for data prior to the 1960s. More tragic is that even today most non-U.S. equity markets do not have available even a fraction of the information required to compute the pertinent criteria we have outlined earlier in this chapter.

Thus when Tom Johnson and I sought to research foreign equities historically to confirm our U.S. findings, we found similar characteristics as far as the data would take us. We found most of the century's top foreign stocks showed annual profit growth that was among the highest in that market, were among their particular market's top relative strength stocks, displayed runaway technical criteria, were not highly leveraged via debt, were priced reasonably for their growth rates, and very often took advantage of key themes and trends operating within that country or globally. We could not find enough quarterly earnings data, institutional sponsorship data, or analysts' historical estimate data to confirm every element of our U.S. findings. However, the same principles held for what data we could get our hands on.

In addition, the data holes we found historically are often still present in current data. For these reasons, we developed a slightly less rigorous and less aggressive model for picking stocks in foreign markets. It enabled us to outperform country indexes fairly consistently over the long run, and has outperformed most individual country indexes since real-time use in the late 1980s. However, our more lenient criteria for foreign markets makes the degree of our outperformance much less wide than in U.S. markets; therefore when we have the choice of investing in the United States we often prefer it even if its country index is not as strong as other countries because it has substantially more information available and is the most liquid and efficient market on the globe.

Our primary search in non-U.S. equities is for stocks similar to those that we are searching for inside the United States. Therefore we look for these four characteristics:

1. Stocks in top 20 percent of relative strength rankings within a country.
2. Stocks aligned with secular themes and trends that are exploiting a technology gap of some sort.
3. Stocks showing either earnings growth in the last quarter or year in the top 20 percent, or else next quarter or next year projections in the top 20 percent.
4. Among the stocks meeting the preceding three criteria, we then look at those in the bottom third of valuations by P/S ratios or by P/Es in relation to growth rate and that are also in runaway uptrends technically.

As a safety balance against adding too much volatility with these stocks, which are often thinly traded in foreign markets, we also buy stocks with 50 percent of our allocation to non-U.S. countries that are aligned with secular themes and trends we foresee and that meet at least three of our more conservative value and financial strength criteria:

1. Have annual sales in the top third of the market, or market capitalization in the top third of the market.
2. Earnings yield > 14.
3. Price/Book < 1.2 or ½ of market average, or P/E 35 percent less than market average.
4. Dividend yield > 4 percent or twice market average.
5. Historical price stability and financial strength in top 30 percent of market.
6. Shows historical ability to outperform market average in both up and down cycle.

In all situations, there must be a economic or fundamental reason to believe that higher than average earnings growth is likely and the stock should be exploiting some sort of technology gap.

Weeding Down Stock List to Top Global Candidates

We use the criteria described in this chapter to isolate stocks, which are then placed on our "potential buy" list. As mentioned earlier, *this list is the starting point for doing more research.* We want as many factors in our favor as possible. Is the stock exploiting some secular theme or trend that looks compelling? Is it filling a technology gap that has substantial room to grow? Can you provide a sound argument why the company should continue to show 25 percent or more annual earnings growth for at least the next two or three years? Is the company in one of the top countries in the world in terms of overall market situation? How big of a price discount is the stock to its potential growth rate? These are the questions we use to weed out our list until we have 20 to 30 top candidates globally.

MODERN PORTFOLIO THEORY METHODS

Once you have built your top twenty to thirty global equity buy candidates, you have some choices in how you use this information to build a portfolio. This section describes some of the best ways of melding our vehicle selection criteria with our country selection methodologies explored in earlier chapters.

The simplest method is to take 8 to 20 of these top-choice global candidates in relatively different industries and in different countries, and build a portfolio out of them. Using this strategy, you strive to *use our country bond-bill/index relative strength method as a guideline for choosing top equities* that meet our criteria and are involved with those countries; but you are generally using only one or two top stock selections for each country. Additionally if you can't find any stocks you think are truly top global candidates fitting our criteria in a country highlighted as a top candidate, you are giving stock selection a higher priority than country selection and in most instances leaving out exposure to that country. However, even though you can not find an individual equity or two from a chosen country, if your analysis is that the country's overall index is in such an explosive situation that it would be foolhardy to avoid investment there, then simply add an open-ended highly index-correlated mutual fund for that country (or a WEB if it exists), to be one of your top global equity picks in your portfolio. Remember your money management rules of diversifying among countries and asset classes (we will discuss other asset classes in detail in a later chapter). This is actually our favorite of the Modern Portfolio Theory (MPT) choices. However, we usually strive to integrate this method with our stock trading method (to be discussed) in our own trading and fund consulting. Remember to use trailing stops and to exit or lighten up on positions domiciled in countries that turn negative by our timing models.

If you don't have the time and inclination to use the stock trading method we will describe, remember that you can still do very well using our version of the MPT method. The first and most critical element of the MPT method is to be sure you are building a diversified portfolio of at least eight stocks that are in relatively different industries and also in more than one country, preferably three or more of the top countries shown by our 40-week moving average interest-rate/stock market system. You can go up to 20 issues, but going beyond that rarely adds any value to what we call the *MPT core global equity portfolio approach.*

In all our MPT choices, we use the same OPS/trailing stop method. Once you have chosen your 8 to 20 issues, look for the last correction or consolidation pattern prior to a new bull-market high in each issue and put an OPS (open protective stop) below the low price in that correction or consolidation. Be sure you are not violating your total portfolio and individual equity risk money management rules, and be sure you are not risking more than 2 percent between your entry and OPS in any one issue. Whenever a stock in your portfolio consolidates or corrects for 20 days or more and then makes a new high, move your OPS up to below the low of that correction or consolidation as a trailing stop to lock in profits. If a stock is stopped out via a trailing or initial OPS, replace it with a current unrepresented top buy candidate in a different industry. Review the portfolio every six months and build it anew. In other words, every six months make sure that if you were starting a new portfolio you would choose the same issues currently in your portfolio. If you would reject one, exit it. And if there is one you do not have in your portfolio that you would want if building from scratch, add it. Also, if you have held a stock for six months and do not have a profit, in general you should exit it and move to another issue on your six-month review. Under our strategies, it is a rare stock indeed that should be held without a profit for this length of time. Be sure and follow our exit criteria and rules as noted later in this chapter as well.

Whether you use this MPT method or the stock trading method to be described is mostly a question of convenience, how much effort you're willing to put into achieving higher long-term returns, how much trading you are comfortable with, and what you are trying to achieve with stock selection.

There are times when I use MPT, and there are strategies in which MPT is a much better fit with the objectives than our stock trading method. It is important that investors understand how to meld these stock selection techniques with the methods we have built up for global equity country selection in previous chapters. If our 40-week moving average bond-bill/index country selection technique produces a risk/reward mix that you are satisfied with, then the simplest way to follow it is to use open-ended mutual funds (and WEBS) and strive for index-comparable returns in each of your country selections. This is fast and easy.

If you want to boost your returns another 1 percent to 2 percent per year over the long run, use my selection criteria to create your own MPT custom portfolio of 6 to 10 stocks for each country in which you want exposure. You are basically creating your own MPT miniportfolio/fund for each chosen country. This should allow you to beat the index in each country over the long run. You can compute your individual equity risk and make sure that the combined stop-out of all equities in that country does not violate our country money management risk limitation parameters. This takes a little more work than using mutual funds, but is well worth the effort in terms of increased returns, and often decreased risk. This strategy is called an *MPT individual country portfolio.*

Again, if you want to boost your returns further with slightly more risk and volatility, then our MPT core global equity portfolio approach will deliver higher long-run returns. The tradeoff is that sometimes you are stopped out of individual equities even while our other models are still bullish the country. And sometimes, you will be avoiding countries that have been selected (because you can't find top candidate individual equities in those countries) and will be choosing equities from countries that are not in the top tier. These differences may increase volatility somewhat, but in general you are going to get better long-run returns using this strategy. In addition, it is much better for smaller portfolios and requires less monitoring than other strategies.

We have been using these criteria and monitoring these techniques real time since the late 1980s; and we have been publishing our selection for clients since 1992 (in our letter to clients, *Portfolio Strategy Letter*), as well as consulting on hedge fund management since 1989. We generally list our top country choices as well as our top foreign stock picks for investors each month. During this time, the MPT methods have only outperformed our "stock trading methodology" during one calendar year, and our highest return MPT core global equity portfolio approach has produced about two thirds the total return of the stock trading method. Both choices have substantially outperformed both the S&P and each country's relative index during this period. The MPT core global equity portfolio approach (our favorite of the MPT approaches) also has about 1.5 times the risk of the stock trading method. The tradeoff, however, is in time.

STOCK TRADING METHOD

While we certainly respect the validity, simplicity, and effectiveness of the MPT method, we rarely use it in the way we have described. Quite simply, I would never buy a stock unless it generated some sort of technical buy signal—I am just too technically oriented, too much of a trader, and too chicken. Moreover, I would rarely add an entire portfolio at once—I would much rather wait for signals in my top candidate list and build a portfolio slowly with less total risk. So usually I build a wide list of potential top candidates, perhaps 50 in all, and wait for technical pattern-recognition buy signals in them before adding them to a portfolio. We are still building a globally diversified portfolio, this time of 8 to 15 issues, but we are waiting for the technical patterns of each equity to tell us when to invest, and often, how much to invest.

While we use several pattern-recognition tested technical buy patterns to enter stocks, Figures 7.11 and 7.12 show two of my personal favorites. These patterns account for the vast majority of the stocks we buy.

Volume Accumulation Indicators Used in Chart Patterns

- *On-Balance Volume (OBV).* OBV starts at zero and adds total volume to a cumulative total each day that closes higher than the previous day, and subtracts total volume each day

Figure 7.11 **FLAG PATTERN**

A flag pattern looks much like a flag itself. First, there must be a sharp run up in the price followed by a tight consolidation. The consolidation needs to have at least four weeks in the pattern with the highs within 3 ticks of the highest high of the first two weeks of the pattern. The flag cannot correct 37% or more of the previous move from a significant low or high.

1. Has fuel; maximum fuel is better.

2. At least 5 runaway characteristics, usually, 10 or more.

Inside flags like this one where three weeks are within the first make the best flags.

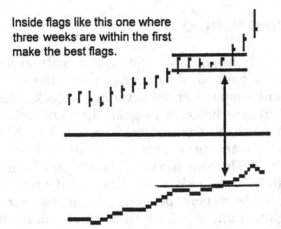

The pattern is triggered when one of four accumulation indicators (OBV, WAD, SWAD, or VOLAC) breaks out to new highs before price breaks above the flag highs.

At that time, enter a buy stop a few ticks above the flag high with an OPS a few ticks below the flag low.

that closes lower than the previous day. Add volume each day that closes higher, subtract volume that closes lower, and keep a cumulative total.

- *Volume Accumulation (VOLAC).* VOLAC is calculated as the percentage each day's close is above or below the midpoint

Figure 7.12 **CORRECTION BUY PATTERN**

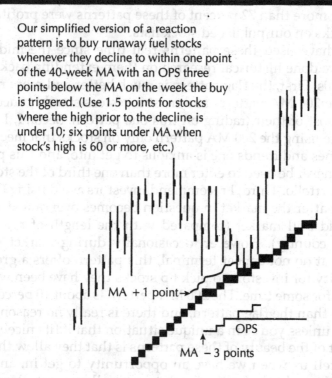

Our simplified version of a reaction
pattern is to buy runaway fuel stocks
whenever they decline to within one point
of the 40-week MA with an OPS three
points below the MA on the week the buy
is triggered. (Use 1.5 points for stocks
where the high prior to the decline is
under 10; six points under MA when
stock's high is 60 or more, etc.)

MA + 1 point→

OPS

↑
MA − 3 points

of that day's range times the day's volume, summed to a
cumulative total.

- *Williams' On-Balance Volume (OBV) or (SWAD).* Williams'
  OBV for stocks, or SWAD, takes each day's ((close − yesterday's close)/(high − low)) − volume, and adds it to a cumulative total (see page 29 of the book *The Secret of Selecting
  Stocks for Immediate and Substantial Gains*).

- *Williams' Advance/Decline of Price (WAD2).* If the close is up,
  then add the (close − true low) to a cumulative total. If the
  close is down, then add the (close-true high) to a cumulative total. The true high is the greater of today's high or
  yesterday's close. The true low is the lesser of today's low
  or yesterday's close.

While the patterns illustrated in Figures 7.11 and 7.12 are not breathtakingly brilliant, they work remarkably well. From 1992 to 1997, more than 72 percent of these patterns were profitable in the stocks on our published stock lists.

We have used these patterns real time since the mid-1980s and have done historical research on them extending back to the late 1800s. First, the flag pattern is much better and more reliable than the 200 MA pattern, and most investors should concentrate all or most of their trading on this one pattern. Second, I would advocate using the 200 MA pattern only on stocks that meet secular themes and trends one is anxious to get into; and this pattern should never be used to enter more than one third of the stocks in one's portfolio. Third, I recommend investors avoid using the MA pattern after the market in question becomes overvalued, or if it is an old bull market (compared with the length of prior ones in that country). However, occasionally during market corrections that do not appear terminal, this pattern offers a great opportunity for investors to pick up stocks they have been wanting to hold for some time. The 200 MA pattern is about 10 percent less reliable than the flag pattern, and there is really no reason to use it at all unless you're in a unique situation that it fits nicely.

Part of the beauty of these patterns is that they allow the market to tell us when we have an opportunity to get in, and they have a formula for limiting risk to a small amount. Remember that the smaller the risk (distance between OPS and entry) while still maintaining highly reliable situations, the higher the reward to our underlying capital we are likely to gain from the opportunity. Therefore, investors not only must weigh the company being bought but also must try to gauge the size of the risk being considered. An extremely tight flag pattern is the optimal situation, because if a stock moves up strongly from your buy point, you will get many times your initial risk in return, and your total portfolio can skyrocket from just one good selection, as Figures 7.13, 7.14, and 7.15 illustrate. These are real-time examples of stocks on our lists that we bought using these patterns.

Take a close look at ECI (Figure 7.13) and Cisco (Figure 7.14) in particular. In the case of ECI, an initial 2 percent risk ended up generating over 41 percent profits to an entire portfolio in just 83 weeks. By the time we exited Cisco in late 1993, it too had the potential to generate portfolio returns of over 40 percent with

Figure 7.13 **FLAGS: THE TIGHTER THE BETTER, PARTICULARLY AFTER A NEW BULL MARKET SIGNAL IS JUST BEGINNING**

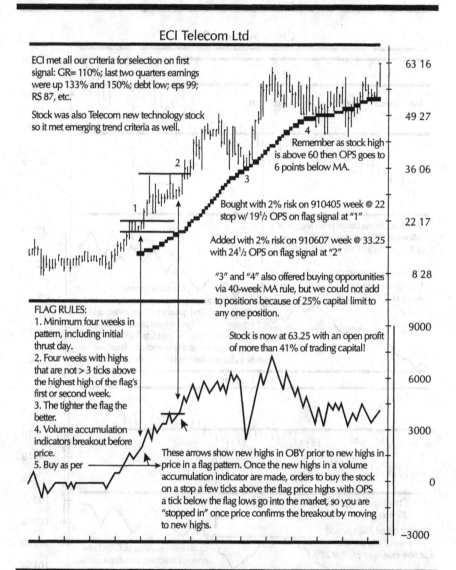

ECI Telecom Ltd

ECI met all our criteria for selection on first signal: GR= 110%; last two quarters earnings were up 133% and 150%; debt low; eps 99; RS 87, etc.

Stock was also Telecom new technology stock so it met emerging trend criteria as well.

Remember as stock high is above 60 then OPS goes to 6 points below MA.

Bought with 2% risk on 910405 week @ 22 stop w/ 19½ OPS on flag signal at "1"

Added with 2% risk on 910607 week @ 33.25 with 24½ OPS on flag signal at "2"

"3" and "4" also offered buying opportunities via 40-week MA rule, but we could not add to positions because of 25% capital limit to any one position.

Stock is now at 63.25 with an open profit of more than 41% of trading capital!

FLAG RULES:
1. Minimum four weeks in pattern, including initial thrust day.
2. Four weeks with highs that are not > 3 ticks above the highest high of the flag's first or second week.
3. The tighter the flag the better.
4. Volume accumulation indicators breakout before price.
5. Buy as per ⟶ These arrows show new highs in OBY prior to new highs in price in a flag pattern. Once the new highs in a volume accumulation indicator are made, orders to buy the stock on a stop a few ticks above the flag price highs with OPS a tick below the flag lows go into the market, so you are "stopped in" once price confirms the breakout by moving to new highs.

Note: Also a good example of how low-risk *trading* can give *superior* results to portfolio allocation investing.

Figure 7.14 **CISCO TOP GROWTH STOCKS OFTEN DO NOT GET OVERPRICED**

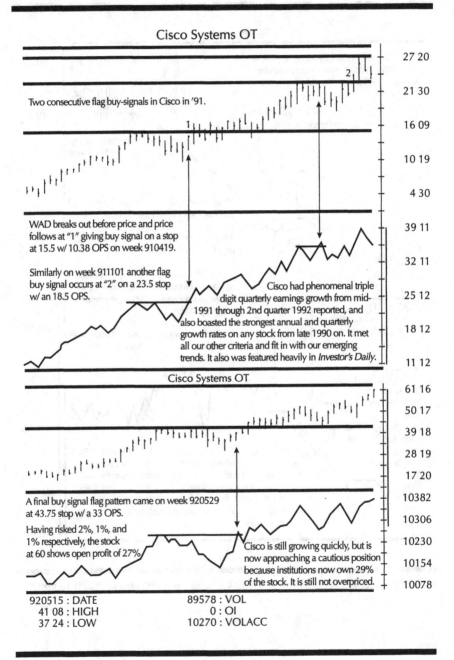

Cisco Systems OT

Two consecutive flag buy-signals in Cisco in '91.

WAD breaks out before price and price follows at "1" giving buy signal on a stop at 15.5 w/ 10.38 OPS on week 910419.

Similarly on week 911101 another flag buy signal occurs at "2" on a 23.5 stop w/ an 18.5 OPS.

Cisco had phenomenal triple digit quarterly earnings growth from mid-1991 through 2nd quarter 1992 reported, and also boasted the strongest annual and quarterly growth rates on any stock from late 1990 on. It met all our other criteria and fit in with our emerging trends. It also was featured heavily in *Investor's Daily*.

Cisco Systems OT

A final buy signal flag pattern came on week 920529 at 43.75 stop w/ a 33 OPS.

Having risked 2%, 1%, and 1% respectively, the stock at 60 shows open profit of 27%.

Cisco is still growing quickly, but is now approaching a cautious position because institutions now own 29% of the stock. It is still not overpriced.

```
920515 : DATE        89578 : VOL
  41 08 : HIGH           0 : OI
  37 24 : LOW        10270 : VOLACC
```

Figure 7.15 VICOR CORPORATION—EXITING WHEN STOCK GETS OVERPRICED

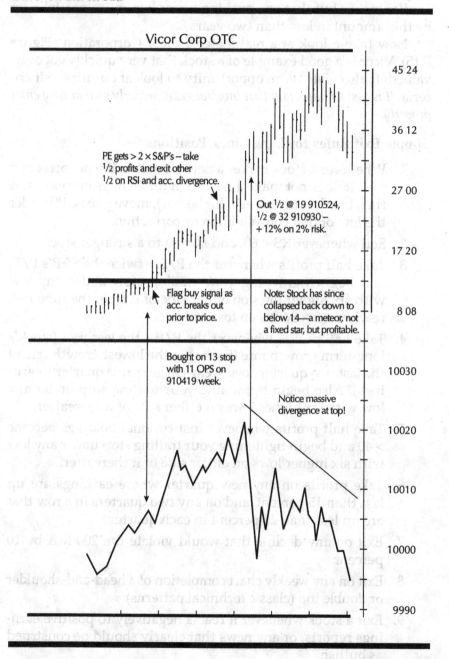

Vicor Corp OTC

PE gets > 2 × S&P's – take
1/2 profits and exit other
1/2 on RSI and acc. divergence.

Out 1/2 @ 19 910524,
1/2 @ 32 910930 –
+12% on 2% risk.

Flag buy signal as
acc. breaks out
prior to price.

Note: Stock has since
collapsed back down to
below 14—a meteor, not
a fixed star, but profitable.

Bought on 13 stop
with 11 OPS on
910419 week.

Notice massive
divergence at top!

2 percent initial risk. We are not talking about the stock going up 40 percent; we are talking about an investor buying six or more similar stocks but that one pushing his or her entire portfolio up by this amount in less than two years.

Now take a look at a real meteor, Vicor Corporation (Figure 7.15). Vicor is a good example of a stock that very quickly got overvalued. It also gives us an opportunity to look at our nine exit criteria. *It is just as important that investors exit properly as that they enter properly.*

Simple Exit Rules for Long Stock Positions

1. Whenever a stock makes a new consolidation or correction (i.e., it does not make a new high for 20 days or more, and then breaks out to a new high later), move your OPS under the low of that consolidation or correction.
2. Sell whenever RS < 60, and switch to a stronger stock.
3. Take half profits whenever the P/E > twice the S&P's P/E, and begin tightening your trailing stop under any low with six higher lows on either side of it from the time P/E reaches > 2 × S&P's on forward.
4. Take half profits whenever the P/E = the lesser of (stock's long-term growth rate (5 year) or the lowest growth rate of the last two quarters over year-earlier same quarter's earnings). Also begin tightening your trailing stop under any low with six higher lows on either side of it thereafter.
5. Take half profits whenever institutional holdings become > 40 and begin tightening your trailing stop under any low with six higher lows on either side of it thereafter.
6. Take profits on any new quarter where earnings are up less than 15 percent, and on any two quarters in a row that are up less than 25 percent in each quarter.
7. Exit on any decline that would violate the 200 MA by 10 percent.
8. Exit on any weekly chart completion of a head-and-shoulder or double top (classic technical patterns).
9. Exit a stock whenever it reacts negatively to positive earnings reports, or any news that clearly should be construed as bullish.

If possible, the preceding exit rules should also apply to stocks in the MPT portfolio as well.

As apparent from Figure 7.16, since we have been publishing stocks meeting these criteria in our monthly letter to clients, they have been beating both the world index and the S&P while being globally diversified and less volatile than either index.

We also have the following criteria for selling stocks short.

Criteria for Finding Short-Sales with Minimum Fuel (Maximum Fuel Criteria are Met by the Best Short-Sale Candidates Only)

1. Earnings: Either (a) or (b) occurs—

   a. A decline in annual earnings and an estimate of either an annual loss or another decline in annual earnings, plus two down quarterly earnings or two negative quarterly earnings.

   b. Two quarterly earnings down 40 percent or more, or two negative quarterly earnings with acceleration in the decline.

Figure 7.16 **STOCK SELECTION TECHNIQUES VERSUS S&P-OWNED INDEX AS PUBLISHED IN PSL SINCE 1992**

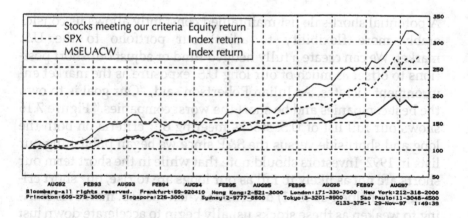

Stocks meeting our criteria	Equity return
SPX	Index return
MSEUACW	Index return

Bloomberg-all rights reserved. Frankfurt:69-920410 Hong Kong:2-521-3000 London:171-330-7500 New York:212-318-2000
Princeton:609-279-3000   Singapore:226-3000   Sydney:2-9777-8600   Tokyo:3-3201-8900   Sao Paulo:11-3048-4500
G133-375-1 29-Nov-97 1:49:39

Source: Bloomberg Financial Markets. Copyright © 1998 Bloomberg LP. All rights reserved.

> If either criterion (a) or (b) is met, the stock remains a short-sale candidate from an earnings criterion standpoint as long as quarterly earnings continue to be lower than year-earlier quarters or continue negative. (For maximum fuel, either the preceding are met or a stock has two quarters in a row of declining earnings and declining sales, and a price/sales ratio (P/S) > 10 and P/E > S&P's P/E.)

2. Runaway technical market characteristics down are displayed on the daily or weekly chart.
3. EPS and RS rank both < 50.
4. Yield 5 percent or < (for maximum fuel must = 0).
5. Debt—must have some, the more the better; over 100 percent ideal (max. fuel > 99).
6. Funds—must have some institutional ownership, > 30 percent is optimum (max. fuel > 20).
7. The worst or second-to-worst rating by Value Line, Zachs, or Lowry's rating services.
8. Max. fuel only—must be a clear bear market in stocks if stock is related to market—according to Chartist, BCA, bond/bill/index rules, or PSL systems.
9. Max. fuel only—forming or formed weekly or monthly pattern of double top, failed rally, or head and shoulders top and P/S > 10.

A potential short-sale list maintained constantly allows us considerably more flexibility to adjust our portfolio to the U.S. market. We can create a fully hedged fund or adjust our short positions to offset as much of our long U.S. exposure as the market environment dictates. As Julian Robertson said, "Our goal is to own the best companies and be short the worst companies." Figure 7.16 shows our full list of U.S. stocks meeting our criteria on both the long and short side versus the S&P since we began publishing our lists in 1992. Investors should note that while in the short term our shorts are not as likely to fall as our longs are to rise, our short criteria have helped us to (1) determine when the U.S. market is starting to weaken as these stocks usually begin to accelerate down just before a broad market decline; and (2) effectively hedge a broad decline as these stocks tend to underperform our longs and the market particularly during corrections. Thus while we do not recommend a fully hedged portfolio at all times, we do recommend covering part or all of your long exposure through shorts during times when the interest rate environment is neutral-negative, when the U.S. technicals are poor, or when overvaluation is extreme enough that systemic market risk is unusually high, but an all-out bearish signal has not yet been given. Only when the U.S. and most global markets have generated universal bearish signals, would we become net short as part of our global allocation strategy. Figure 7.17 shows the performance of our various stock lists (minus commission and slippage estimates) as published in PSL since 1992, including our potential shorting list candidates that have sharply underperformed the market.

Figure 7.17 **U.S. STOCK LIST PERFORMANCE—LONGS AND SHORTS**

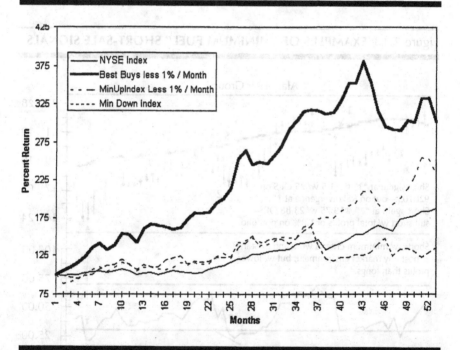

Note: As can be seen, even after allowing for the ridiculously high level of slippage and commissions rate of 1 percent per month, our best buys and minimum up list of potential buys hardily outperformed the NYSE Index since we began publishing it. Similarly, our minimum down list of potential short sales was consistently underperformed by the NYSE Index as well.

Like our longs, investors could use an MPT method or our 200 MA pattern in reverse for short sales of stocks meeting short-sale list criteria, as shown in Figures 7.18 and 7.19. We basically exit short stocks using the following criteria: (1) when they show a positive turnaround in earnings; (2) whenever their P/E gets below their expected growth rate; (3) whenever they violate their 200 MA by 10 percent or more on the upside; (4) take half profits on 40 percent decline from entry and then begin using any high with six lower highs surrounding it as trailing stop; (5) on every new low, use OPS above correction high as trailing stop; (6) exit if relative strength rank or EPS rank ever move above 50 from below it; (7) exit on any weekly chart double bottom or head and shoulder bottom; (8) whenever the stock reacts positively to what should clearly be negative news, or on positive reaction to restructuring or new management.

Figure 7.18 **EXAMPLES OF "MINIMUM FUEL" SHORT-SALE SIGNALS**

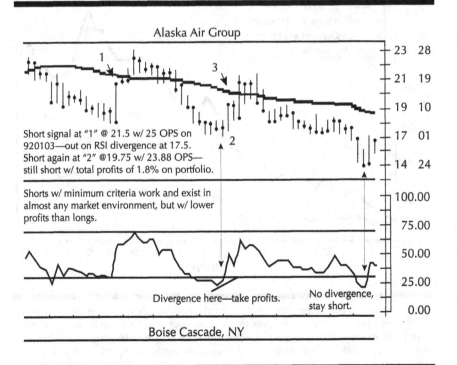

Alaska Air Group

Short signal at "1" @ 21.5 w/ 25 OPS on 920103—out on RSI divergence at 17.5. Short again at "2" @19.75 w/ 23.88 OPS—still short w/ total profits of 1.8% on portfolio.

Shorts w/ minimum criteria work and exist in almost any market environment, but w/ lower profits than longs.

Divergence here—take profits.

No divergence, stay short.

Boise Cascade, NY

Figure 7.19 **EXAMPLE OF 200 MA SHORT SALES**

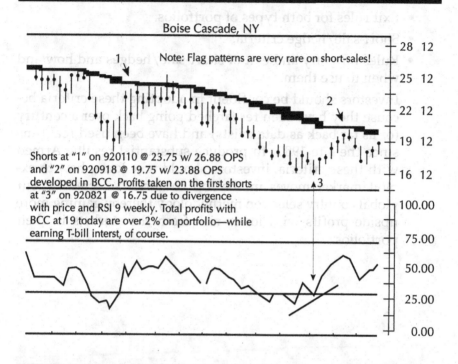

Boise Cascade, NY

Note: Flag patterns are very rare on short-sales!

Shorts at "1" on 920110 @ 23.75 w/ 26.88 OPS
and "2" on 920918 @ 19.75 w/ 23.88 OPS
developed in BCC. Profits taken on the first shorts
at "3" on 920821 @ 16.75 due to divergence
with price and RSI 9 weekly. Total profits with
BCC at 19 today are over 2% on portfolio—while
earning T-bill interst, of course.

SUMMARY

We have covered an enormous amount of ground in this critical
chapter on stock selection. Investors should now understand the
importance of equity selection based on our discussion of the following topics:

- Criteria for selecting top equities in the United States and
  abroad.

- Development of a potential buy list of stocks meeting our
  criteria.

- How to answer critical questions with further research and
  build a list of 20 to 30 top global equities.

- How to take this top list and build a portfolio via either MPT or our own Stock Trading Method.
- Exit rules for both types of portfolios.
- Short-sale/hedge criteria.
- Rules for entry and exit of short-sale/hedges and how and when to use them.

Investors should be confident in adopting these criteria because they have been researched going back over a century (or as far back as data exists) and have been used real time since the late 1980s to produce substantial results. Armed with these criteria, investors should now know how to exploit market moves in the top countries selected by our global country selection methodology thereby gaining more upside profits with lower risk from the markets in their portfolios.

Other Asset Classes and Models to Exploit Them

Up to now, we have treated the global investment world as if equities were the only investment choice available. We have formulated models and techniques for choosing countries to invest in, for avoiding bear market periods, and for choosing specific equities to put into your portfolio. While global equities offer excellent long-run total returns, unparalleled liquidity, and participation in human progress, they are far from being the only investment class available to global investors. And, as our money management rules dictate, global equities should never be the only asset class in your portfolio.

OUTPERFORMANCE AND ASSET ALLOCATION

After I had learned the basic techniques of the European money manager who innovated the concepts we use in our global equity relative strength methodology for choosing countries to invest in, a question I kept asking was "If there were one or two things that you could improve in this model, what would they be?" We discussed this issue at great length. One of the first things we came up with was that it would add great value if we could develop some method of choosing individual equities that would outper-form their selected indexes. In Chapter 7, we have described the outcome of the research effort spawned by this idea.

After long consideration and discussion, we both decided that the low performance of being in cash for prolonged periods was certainly another area for improvement. This brought out the idea of incorporating other asset classes into a portfolio. We then decided that bringing the risk/reward of other asset classes, via similar models to the original model (meaning only when many criteria looked especially positive and with the goal of avoiding negative environments in each selected asset class) would likely add value to the existing system, as well as enhance the return of the portfolio during periods when it had little or no allocation in global equity markets. When I left Europe, in the mid-1980s, I had received the incredible gift of a phenomenal global equity sys-tem, and I also had a good idea of what research I might do to im-prove on it.

After Tom Johnson and I completed our vehicle selection re-search, I began to dig into the asset allocation question. Again, I voraciously read everything I could get my hands on discussing global asset allocation among various asset classes. The first thing I found was a dearth of meaningful research on real global asset classes. There is a ton of information on stock/bond asset alloca-tion choices. Figure 8.1 shows the basic thrust of the data. The bot-tom line is that adding some mix of bonds to a portfolio of stocks tends to cut risk, although it also brings down return, with the generally best risk/reward mix being a somewhat even split be-tween stocks and some duration of bonds.

There were two really slam-dunk clear conclusions I could draw from asset allocation research. The first we covered earlier in this book: Adding global diversification to a stock portfolio adds long-term returns while decreasing long-term risk. The second way that an investor can increase long-term returns while decreasing long-term risk in a statically allocated portfolio is by adding a diversified group of top-rated managed futures or resource-oriented funds, as summarized in Figure 8.2.

While this particular study is far too short-term to be ex-tremely illuminating, other studies done going back much further beyond 1980 generally confirm that *adding managed futures or re-source funds to either a pure equity or equity and bond portfolio tends to*

Figure 8.1 STUFFING FOR BEAR CUSHION

How bonds and cash can soften the fall of your stock portfolio

■ Stocks   □ Bonds   ■ Short-Term Reserves

Your asset allocation	Average annual return	Nmber of years with a loss	Average loss	Two-year loss is '73-'74	Worst annual loss '31
Aggressive growth 100%	10.7%	1 in every 3 (20 out of 71)	-12%	-37%	-43%
Growth 20% 80%	9.9%	1 in every 4 (19 out of 71)	-10%	-30%	-36%
Moderate growth 40% 60%	8.9%	1 in every 4 (16 out of 71)	-8%	-22%	-28%
Conservative growth 20% 40% 40%	7.6%	1 in every 5 (15 out of 71)	-5%	-12%	-19%
Income 20% 20% 60%	6.3%	1 in every 6 (12 out of 71)	-3%	-3%	-12%

Source: Ibbotson Associates, based on model portfolios during 1926–1996. Used with permission. Copyright © 1998 Ibbotson Associates, Inc. All rights reserved. (Certain portions of this work were derived from copyrighted works of Roger G. Ibbotson and Rex Sinquefield.)

dampen drawdown and volatility while slightly enhancing long-term returns. If managed futures can add value during one of the best 15-year runs in stock market and bond market history, they certainly ought to be able to add value when stocks and bonds aren't in a screaming record-breaking bull market. We have done extensive research on this subject, and in general find that an allocation of somewhere between 10 percent and 25 percent in top-rated diversified manager managed futures funds add optimal long-run value to statically allocated portfolios. In fact, this is a substantially clearer additive factor to profitability than is globalizing equity

Figure 8.2 IMPACT OF INCREMENTAL ADDITIONS OF MANAGED FUTURES TO THE TRADITIONAL PORTFOLIO

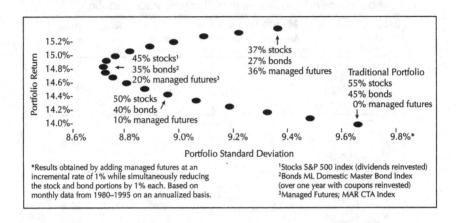

*Results obtained by adding managed futures at an incremental rate of 1% while simultaneously reducing the stock and bond portions by 1% each. Based on monthly data from 1980–1995 on an annualized basis.

[1]Stocks S&P 500 index (dividends reinvested)
[2]Bonds ML Domestic Master Bond Index (over one year with coupons reinvested)
[3]Managed Futures; MAR CTA Index

Source: Used with permission. Copyright © Managed Account Reports Inc. All rights reserved.

investment, or even adding bonds. We will be discussing it in detail in our section on this asset class.

While globalization and the addition of managed futures or resources seemed to be clear conclusions from most asset allocation research, much of the research on asset allocation to date is what I term, "overly academic." First, it is often written by someone with little real-life experience investing in global markets. This has tended to prolong purely unrealistic assumptions such as using standard deviation or volatility as a definition of risk, when in fact these definitions are ridiculous from a true investment standpoint. Upside volatility and sharp moves in a favorable direction are desirable investment traits, and do not accurately reflect any negative potential risk, for example.

Second, authors of academic research on asset allocation tend to believe in some combination of the efficient market hypothesis and/or totally inflexible long-run investment decisions. From this, we get assumptions like the impossibility of adding value via stock selection, country selection, and asset-class selection, as well as static asset allocation models that continue to hold bonds in a wildly inflationary environment despite their potential losses, or stocks during a period of skyrocketing interest rates and weakening economic growth. There are times when it is clearly a poor environment to hold a particular asset-class, yet most research assumes no change in allocation during these periods. Probably because of the assumption of static allocation, there is little research or understanding of the dynamics behind positive and negative return environments in the different asset classes.

One of the most frustrating assumptions in many asset allocation studies is that the definition of asset classes is so tightly constrained that it is not a serious discussion of the truly different investment options an investor faces in the real world. Typically, the world of investing offers, by these authors' assumptions, only stocks and bonds, or perhaps, stocks, international stocks, bonds, and international bonds, if the author is new-world openminded. Only rather recently have managed futures, real assets, and real estate started to be included in the potential mix. This still leaves some terrific investments on the table.

This is not to say that there is no value added from many current studies on asset allocation. Having a good idea what longterm asset allocation tends to provide the optimum risk/reward over the very long term is a valuable starting point from which to begin adjusting to the current and likely investment environment ahead, but it is not the end-all be-all of asset allocation discussions. And, the conclusions drawn are not overly helpful unless a full range of actual investments are chosen among and studied. It is, however, important for investors to understand the one relatively universal axiom that has developed out of asset allocation literature to date: *mixing disparate risky investments lowers portfolio risks while raising returns.*

Perhaps as important as this conclusion is the understanding of why this is so. Two examples of potential investments can illustrate this concept: one is a banking corporation bond that tends to follow interest rates closely; the other is a diversified group of oil wells that are producing but also offer exploration potential. The largest part of the return of our 100 property oil well production/exploration comes from the exploration potential. Thus what makes our bank corporation bond go up or down (interest rates) has little or nothing to do with our oil investment. If both investments have an allowable mix of long-term returns, then they are likely to add synergy to a portfolio because of deriving their profits from almost totally unrelated things. Thus there is little reason to suspect that bond prices will go down at the same time that our oil investment does. Since they are both going up, but due to different factors, mixing them together is likely to smooth long-term performance toward the average of their long-term annual returns.

The best things to mix together in a portfolio thus have an acceptable average annual return together and either derive their long-run returns from totally different and somewhat unrelated activities, or they derive their profit from opposite forces. As seen in past chapters, commodity price rises, such as oil, tend in general to move in opposition to bond prices. This means that to some extent our two proposed investments are likely to be uncorrelated. Bonds are likely to go down in a rapidly rising oil price environment, and conversely, oil prices are likely to come down in a weakening economy, a benefit for bond holders. The more uncorrelated and disparate the investments mixed in a portfolio, the more likely they are to smooth long-term performance, thereby reducing risk.

In a fractional reserve monetary system under a normal inflationary environment, stock prices get hurt by monetary tightening. When the economy begins to overheat and inflation begins to show up on those limited government indicators of inflation (CPI), equities start to expect tightening and they usually decline as interest rates move up to cut off the excessive demand pressures. This is the beginning of a typical negative environment for equities. Now if we could find an asset that typically profits from the same environment that causes queasiness in equities and manages to produce gains on a long-term basis, but especially in the environment described, then we would have an almost perfect smoothing effect on an equity portfolio from creating a mix.

Commodity futures funds are probably the closest thing to this description. The reason is that commodity prices tend to rise from overheating while bonds and equities become nervous. In addition, higher priced commodities mean more price volatility, making profitability more likely for top managers. And an overheating economy means first excessive demand and then a slowing economy that leads to a boom/bust in economically sensitive commodity prices. Since top futures managers are able to profit from both the upturn and downturn, and simply need volatility and trends as the main ingredients in their profitability, this is a promising potential environment for such funds, at exactly the same time that it is a negative environment for stocks and bonds. This is why mixing futures funds with equities is particularly advantageous. It smooths both overall portfolio ups and downs (risk and drawdowns) while enhancing long-term average returns by adding profits in negative years as well as in positive ones. Most top-rated futures funds also produce higher long-run profits than global equities.

So an excellent diversification is an investment that profits long-term but shows enhanced returns at the exact time that something else in your portfolio has trouble. And a worthwhile diversification builds profits in a way that is totally unrelated to the reason something else in your portfolio generates profits. A fair diversification is something often providing different timing of investment gains and losses, but occasionally moving in tandem with most things in your portfolio.

BUILDING A PORTFOLIO

Armed with this simple understanding of diversification and its effect on long-run returns and risk, we can examine some traditional asset allocation choices to dissect their effects on a portfolio.

Would you say global equities are an excellent, good, or fair diversification when matched with U.S. equities? Somewhere around fair-plus is probably accurate. It is true that many markets such as India, China, Japan, Korea, and Colombia have very low historical correlations to U.S. equities. It is also true, however, that in most recessions global equities, even those least correlated with the United States, take a hit just as the United States does. There was virtually no equity market on the globe that did not take some hit from October 1997, for example. World equities, in fact, often take bigger hits than the U.S. blue chips do in such instances. This was true in 1929–1932, 1937, 1973–1974, 1981, 1987, and even the relatively minor 1989–1990. Only Taiwan and Korea escaped 1994, which wasn't even a recession. So while global equities provide some smoothing, in a global recession they are highly correlated with the United States and provide little or no insulation. And, after all, the reason you want diversification is mainly to protect you in negative environments.

What about U.S. bonds? Well that depends on two things—the duration of the bonds and the period in which you get your data to study. For instance if you go back to the post-Civil War era to get your data, you're likely to see bonds in a better light than if you start your study in 1981, or even following World War II. As mentioned earlier, in a gold standard, bonds often move inversely to stocks. Since both produce positive long-run gains, bonds made a much better diversification with stocks prior to the 1920s than they did when the era of inflationary environments was created with the launch of the Federal Reserve Board in the World War I era.

In addition, the lag between bond price movement and stock price movement has become smaller and smaller since the Fed was formed, as the markets slowly caught on to the relationship and as the economy grew more and more addicted to credit. Technical innovations and proliferation of news via new media technology helps speed reactions to events as well. Prior to the 1970s' great inflation, bonds were really a good to good-minus combination with stocks. But after the great inflation period, long bonds in particular have actually become a fair to poor diversification with U.S. stocks. Especially since the 1981 beginning of the disinflation era, bonds and stocks have moved very closely in lockstep.

Adding long bonds to a portfolio since 1981 has done little except cut total returns when combined with U.S. equities. However, if psychology changes again from disinflationary to deflationary, or deflationary fearing, we could again see bonds rally while stocks decline to more realistic earnings expectations. And certainly in Japan, where deflation exists, bonds and stocks are much more inversely correlated. Remember, too, that long bonds are not the only type of bonds. There are junk bonds, zero-coupon bonds, short duration bonds, foreign bonds, distressed bonds, convertible bonds, GNMA's (Government National Mortgage Association), adjustable rate bonds, and so on. We will explore these in more detail in the following section.

EXPLORING ASSET CLASSES

You should now better understand what makes something a good diversification to add to allocation, and what can change that analysis. Now that we understand what makes combinations of investments work together we can examine a broad array of asset classes to determine how we can apply similar techniques to them thus avoiding negative periods and highlighting periods in which they offer a particularly good risk/reward. The following asset classes are discussed: (1) bonds, (2) gold and silver, (3) real Estate, REITs, and trust deeds, (4) arbitrage funds, (5) global hedge funds, and (6) resource and commodity futures funds.

Bonds

First, let's look at different classes of bonds. In a fractional reserve system long-term bonds are simply a speculation on interest rates, pure and simple. If you buy long-term bonds, you are saying you expect rates will go down. Zero-coupons are either a leveraged way of speculating that interest rates will go down, or for short-term zero's, a way of locking in what you expect will be a multiyear high in rates. Buying foreign long bonds is a speculation on that country's interest rates, and on its currency. Buying foreign bond futures is a way of speculating that the country's interest rates will go down without as much currency exposure (because really, only your 1%–5% margin is exposed to the exchange rate change during holding). Buying one-year (short duration) foreign bonds is a way to lock in a currency price and interest-rate combination that you expect both of which will move in a favorable direction. One-year U.S. bonds, short-duration blue-chip preferreds, and adjustable rate bonds are an anchor position—they will give you an extremely reliable positive return, but will also keep you from making double-digit profits if you own too much of them. Junk bonds are a bet that the economy will not weaken significantly. Distressed bonds are a bet that the managers can find turnarounds in bankruptcies and extremely distressed companies and that interest rates won't rise substantially or economic growth decline significantly. GNMAs are a way to lock in rates you expect to slowly decline. If rates decline too fast, most mortgages will refinance and cut the yield on GNMAs. Convertible bonds and convertible preferreds offer a way to build high yields with the potential kicker of capital gains down the road from an underlying security. They are thus a good way of building a long-term position in a depressed equity, market, or industry when a market, industry,

Table 8.1 **THE EFFECT OF DIFFERING ECONOMIC ENVIRONMENTS ON DIFFERENT TYPES OF BOND INVESTMENTS**

Type of Bond	Sample Fund	Environment			
		Economy Weakening	Early Recovery	Recovery	Over Heating
Zero coupon	BTTRX	Aggressive top play	Lighten up	Exit	Short/Avoid
Long-term	VBLTX	Conservative play	Good environment	Lighten up	Exit/Avoid
Short-term	BTSRX	Too cautious	Way to lock in rates	Good cautious choice	Decent play
Foreign Long-Term	RPIBX	N/A	N/A	N/A	N/A
Foreign Short-Term	ICPHX	N/A	N/A	N/A	N/A
Blue Chip Preferreds	VQIIX	Good choice	Steady rates	Exit	Avoid
Adjustible Rate	GSRAX	No advantage	No advantage	Begin buying	Good buy
Adjustible Rate Junk	PPR	Avoid	Best yield buy	Good yield	Best buy
Junk	NTHEX	Worst time to hold	Begin to buy	Best buy	OK
Distressed	Momentum sandalwood	Worst time to hold	Avoid	Buy	OK
GMAs	VFIIX	OK	OK	Lighten up	Exit
Convertible	FCVSX	Avoid	Good	Exit	Avoid
Emerging Market Debt	GMCDX	Avoid	Not yet	Aggressive	Exit

or equity is very undervalued, but not yet on the technical and fundamental path toward marked improvement.

The key points here are (1) there is almost always a bond investment making money in any kind of imaginable environment; and (2) if you can reliably determine which way interest rates and the economy are heading, you can adjust your bond investments to profit from the environment, as shown in Table 8.1.

Synthesizing this table, the aggressive bond investor will move through Stages 1–4 of the Liquidity Cycle by (1) buying long zero-coupon bonds as the economy weakens and goes into recession or soft landing; (2) moving out of zero-coupon bonds and into

Inverted Yield, Rates Declining	Environment				Depressed Industry Improving
	Rates Drop		Rates Rise		
	Slow	Fast	Fast	Slow	
N/A	Aggressive play	Best environment	Worst environment	Negative environment	Negative environment
N/A	Good play	Too conservative	Worst environment	Negative environment	N/A
N/A	Too cautious	Too conservative	OK	OK	N/A
Best environment	N/A	N/A	N/A	N/A	N/A
Cautious play	N/A	N/A	N/A	N/A	N/A
N/A	OK	Too cautious	Bad	Bad	N/A
N/A	OK	Too cautious	OK/Good	Good	N/A
N/A	OK	Too cautious	Good	Good	N/A
N/A	OK	Good	Bad	OK/Fair	Good
N/A	OK	OK	Bad	Fair	Good
N/A	OK	Bad	Bad	Bad	N/A
N/A	N/A	N/A	Avoid	Bad	Best buy
Good	N/A	N/A	Avoid	Avoid	N/A

long bonds or convertibles on the first hints of decent economic growth; (3) moving into junk bonds or emerging market debt as the recovery becomes clearly established; (4) moving into adjustable rate junk, adjustable rate short bonds, and distressed bonds as the economy begins to show signs of overheating.

Investors should note that Stages 1 and 3 in particular often offer investment potential that rivals equity market returns (double-digit teen returns annualized or better). Zero coupons can be especially profitable if you expect rates to drop sharply, whereas junk bonds can be particularly profitable if you expect a significant economic recovery, and emerging market bonds can be very profitable (30% + annual rates) if you expect a strong global recovery.

Here are some examples of different timing systems investors can use to assess the bond market timing environment.

Heine Model. This model was developed by Richard Heine and Nelson Freeburg (*Formula Research*, 901-756-8607). It looks at five variables (all data can be found weekly in *Barron's*) and determines by each one's position versus its moving average (MA) (whether it is bullish or bearish) by adding 1 point if bullish, and 0 if bearish. It then totals all five variables and becomes bullish bonds if the total count is 3 or more and bearish if less than 3. The five variables and respective MA periods in weeks are:

1. Dow Jones 20 bond index and 24-wk MA. If above MA give +1 point, otherwise give 0 points.
2. Long bond Treasury yield and 6-wk MA. If yield is below MA give +1 point, otherwise give 0 points.
3. Thirteen-week T-bill yield and 6-wk MA. If yield is below MA, give +1 point, otherwise give 0 points.
4. Dow Jones Utility Average and 10-wk MA. If Utility Average is above MA, give +1 point, otherwise give 0 points.
5. CRB index and 20-wk MA. If CRB Index is below MA, give +1 point, otherwise give 0 points.

From 1957 to 1995, this model's signals increased the average annual return of the Dow Jones 20 Bond index from buy-and-hold 7.5 percent average annual return with a 21 percent maximum drawdown, to system 12.8 percent average annual return with a 3.4 percent maximum drawdown. (Note that these are average annual returns and not compound annual rates!) On the Benham Target fund 10 years ahead, it produced a 15.2 percent average annual return with a 6 percent drawdown, for more aggressive participation.

An investor using this system as a core timing system, along with ancillary information in previous chapters that help to determine the phase of the Austrian Liquidity Cycle should be able to judge not only when to be bullish bonds, but when to be aggressively bullish and buy zero coupons, versus when to be less bullish and buy junk and emerging market debt. Most of the economic gauges we use for stocks also work well with bonds.

Here's another system investors can use to time bond investments.

Bond-Bill-Utility Model. In this system, you buy bonds when the 30-year government bond yield is below its 10-week moving average and either (a) the 3-month government T-bill yield is below its 38-week moving average, or (b) the Dow Jones Utility Average Index is above its 10-week moving average.

This system model proves bond investing to be as profitable as holding the S&P long-term—but with an unbelievably low 3.2 percent maximum drawdown since 1943 versus the S&P's 52 percent maximum drawdown. The results are shown in System Spreadsheet 8.1. Investors buy the Dow Jones 20 bond index or a long-bond equivalent in buy signals and stand aside in T-bills a money market funds on sell signals.

In this model, we have done for bonds what we did for stocks in Chapters 1 through 5; we have formed a sample model for avoiding negative investment environments. We have slashed risk of drawdown from 21 percent to 3.2 percent, and yet increased compound annual returns from 5.7 percent to 8.7 percent at the same time. Any conservative investor wanting low double-digit consistent income with low risk should seriously consider following this model, while any bond investor should follow this model to better time bond exposure or duration decisions.

Investors should note that one of these two bond systems (the Heine model) is not our own creation, and we owe a debt of gratitude to Nelson Freeburg of *Formula Research* ($195 per year, 901-756-8607) for letting us produce them conceptually. In addition, we have simplified the Heine system in this summary. If you plan on using this system, we suggest you call Nelson Freeburg and buy his back issues on this fantastic bond system (back issues are around $15) so that you have all the details you need.

If you want to have a permanent allocation to bonds, the preceding models, the Austrian Liquidity Cycle (ALC), and Table 8.1 should allow you to invest in the sector of the bond market with the highest profit potential. If you want to use flexible allocation (to be discussed), you will want to use these models and the ALC to tell you the approximate profit potential of investing in the top

System Spreadsheet 8.1 BOND–BILL–UTILITY MODEL

System Description: Buy Bond Total Return Index when 30-year Treasury Bond Yield < 10-week MA and either T-bill Yield < 38-week MA or Dow Jones Utility Index > 10-week MA Exit Bond Total Return Index when the above criteria is not met and hold 3-month T-Bills.

Data Used: Weekly Bond Total Return Index was created by starting with a value of 100 adjusted each week by the percent change of the weekly Dow Jones 20 Bond Index percent change plus $1/52$ of the 30-year Bond Yield. Other data used was the weekly close of T-Bill Yield, weekly close of 30-yearTreasury Bond Yield, and weekly close of Dow Jones Utilities Average.

From: 1/2/43   To: 12/31/97

Entry Date	Entry Price	Exit Date	Exit Price	Profit/ Loss	Days in Trade	Percent Change	Position	Cumulative Return on $100 Investment Bond Total Return and T-Bills	Bond Total Return Only
								100.00	100.00
12/24/43	0.38	12/31/43	0.37	($0.01)	6	0.0%	T-Bill	100.01	
1/7/44	110.69	2/11/44	113.54	2.85	26	2.6	Bonds	102.58	102.57
2/11/44	0.38	3/10/44	0.37	(0.01)	21	0.0	T-Bill	102.62	
3/10/44	113.99	3/17/44	114.11	0.12	6	0.1	Bonds	102.72	103.09
3/17/44	0.38	7/14/44	0.37	(0.01)	86	0.1	T-Bill	102.86	
7/14/44	117.98	7/21/44	117.94	(0.04)	6	0.0	Bonds	102.82	106.55
7/21/44	0.38	8/18/44	0.38	0.00	21	0.0	T-Bill	102.86	
8/18/44	117.97	9/15/44	116.95	(1.02)	21	−0.9	Bonds	101.97	105.66
9/15/44	0.38	9/22/44	0.38	0.00	6	0.0	T-Bill	101.98	
9/22/44	117.34	10/6/44	118.93	1.59	11	1.4	Bonds	103.36	107.44
10/6/44	0.38	1/5/45	0.37	(0.01)	66	0.1	T-Bill	103.46	
1/5/45	123.10	3/23/45	125.47	2.37	56	1.9	Bonds	105.45	113.35
3/23/45	0.38	4/13/45	0.38	0.00	16	0.0	T-Bill	105.48	
4/13/45	125.86	5/4/45	126.5	0.64	16	0.5	Bonds	106.02	114.28
5/4/45	0.38	5/11/45	0.38	0.00	6	0.0	T-Bill	106.02	
5/11/45	126.36	5/25/45	126.73	0.37	11	0.3	Bonds	106.34	114.49
5/25/45	0.38	6/1/45	0.38	0.00	6	0.0	T-Bill	106.34	
6/1/45	126.85	7/27/45	126.91	0.06	41	0.0	Bonds	106.40	114.65
7/27/45	0.38	10/12/45	0.38	0.00	56	0.1	T-Bill	106.49	
10/12/45	126.54	12/21/45	129.2	2.66	51	2.1	Bonds	108.72	116.72
12/21/45	0.38	1/11/46	0.38	0.00	16	0.0	T-Bill	108.75	
1/11/46	130.26	2/22/46	131.68	1.42	31	1.1	Bonds	109.94	118.96
2/22/46	0.38	3/8/46	0.38	0.00	11	0.0	T-Bill	109.95	
3/8/46	131.56	3/15/46	131.85	0.29	6	0.2	Bonds	110.20	119.12
3/15/46	0.38	3/22/46	0.38	0.00	6	0.0	T-Bill	110.21	
3/22/46	131.97	5/10/46	130.47	(1.50)	36	−1.1	Bonds	108.95	117.87
5/10/46	0.38	11/1/46	0.38	0.00	126	0.2	T-Bill	109.16	
11/1/46	125.28	11/22/46	126.25	0.97	16	0.8	Bonds	110.01	114.06
11/22/46	0.38	11/29/46	0.38	0.00	6	0.0	T-Bill	110.02	
12/6/46	125.82	12/13/46	126.85	1.03	6	0.8	Bonds	110.92	114.60
12/13/46	0.38	12/27/46	0.38	0.00	11	0.0	T-Bill	110.94	
12/27/46	127.09	2/28/47	128.75	1.66	46	1.3	Bonds	112.38	116.32
2/28/47	0.38	8/22/47	0.75	0.37	126	0.2	T-Bill	112.60	
8/22/47	128.86	8/29/47	128.44	(0.42)	6	−0.3	Bonds	112.23	116.04
8/29/47	0.77	10/3/47	0.82	0.05	26	0.1	T-Bill	112.32	

System Spreadsheet 8.1 (Continued)

Entry Date	Entry Price	Exit Date	Exit Price	Profit/ Loss	Days in Trade	Percent Change	Position	Cumulative Return on $100 Investment Bond Total Return and T-Bills	Bond Total Return Only
10/3/47	125.85	10/10/47	125.82	(0.03)	6	0.0	Bonds	112.29	113.67
10/10/47	0.83	4/9/48	1.00	0.17	131	0.4	T-Bill	112.78	
4/9/48	125.54	7/2/48	127.59	2.05	61	1.6	Bonds	114.62	115.27
7/2/48	1.00	10/22/48	1.12	0.12	81	0.3	T-Bill	114.99	
10/22/48	126.42	11/5/48	126.26	(0.16)	11	-0.1	Bonds	114.85	114.07
11/5/48	1.13	12/31/48	1.15	0.02	41	0.2	T-Bill	115.06	
12/31/48	127.65	5/6/49	128.48	0.83	91	0.7	Bonds	115.81	116.07
5/6/49	1.15	7/8/49	0.92	(0.23)	46	0.2	T-Bill	116.05	
7/8/49	128.10	2/3/50	135.03	6.93	151	5.4	Bonds	122.33	121.99
2/3/50	1.12	9/8/50	1.31	0.19	156	0.7	T-Bill	123.18	
9/8/50	137.54	9/15/50	137.84	0.30	6	0.2	Bonds	123.45	124.53
9/15/50	1.31	1/5/51	1.38	0.07	81	0.4	T-Bill	123.97	
1/5/51	139.73	1/12/51	139.72	(0.01)	6	0.0	Bonds	123.96	126.23
1/12/51	1.38	2/2/51	1.390	0.01	16	0.1	T-Bill	124.07	
2/2/51	140.83	2/16/51	141.02	0.19	11	0.1	Bonds	124.24	127.40
2/16/51	1.39	7/20/51	1.56	0.17	111	0.6	T-Bill	125.00	
7/20/51	135.26	10/12/51	137.11	1.85	61	1.4	Bonds	126.71	123.87
10/12/51	1.65	2/1/52	1.60	(0.05)	81	0.5	T-Bill	127.39	
2/1/52	137.80	2/22/52	137.88	0.08	16	0.1	Bonds	127.46	124.56
2/22/52	1.64	3/7/52	1.56	(0.08)	11	0.1	T-Bill	127.55	
3/7/52	138.14	4/18/52	138.54	0.40	31	0.3	Bonds	127.92	125.16
4/18/52	1.63	5/23/52	1.73	0.10	26	0.2	T-Bill	128.14	
5/23/52	139.86	6/27/52	140.07	0.21	26	0.2	Bonds	128.33	126.54
6/27/52	1.68	7/25/52	1.85	0.17	21	0.1	T-Bill	128.51	
7/25/52	140.35	8/8/52	140.52	0.17	11	0.1	Bonds	128.67	126.95
8/8/52	1.86	11/7/52	1.80	(0.06)	66	0.5	T-Bill	129.30	
11/7/52	140.71	12/26/52	141.93	1.22	36	0.9	Bonds	130.42	128.22
12/26/52	2.23	7/31/53	2.16	(0.07)	156	1.4	T-Bill	132.22	
7/31/53	138.92	9/4/53	139.04	0.12	26	0.1	Bonds	132.34	125.61
9/4/53	1.96	10/2/53	1.58	(0.38)	21	0.2	T-Bill	132.56	
10/2/53	140.53	9/3/54	151.52	10.99	241	7.8	Bonds	142.92	136.89
9/3/54	1.02	3/25/55	1.37	0.35	146	0.6	T-Bill	143.77	
3/25/55	152.33	4/15/55	152.44	0.11	16	0.1	Bonds	143.87	137.72
4/8/55	1.47	11/4/55	2.18	0.71	151	0.9	T-Bill	145.15	
11/4/55	153.31	12/2/55	153.19	(0.12)	21	-0.1	Bonds	145.03	138.40
11/25/55	2.44	2/3/56	2.40	(0.04)	51	0.5	T-Bill	145.75	
2/3/56	154.50	3/16/56	154.83	0.33	31	0.2	Bonds	146.06	139.88
3/16/56	2.37	3/30/56	2.17	(0.20)	11	0.1	T-Bill	146.22	
3/30/56	154.26	4/6/56	153.47	(0.79)	6	-0.5	Bonds	145.47	138.65
4/6/56	2.40	6/15/56	2.58	0.18	51	0.5	T-Bill	146.18	
6/15/56	151.53	8/17/56	149.84	(1.69)	46	-1.1	Bonds	144.55	135.37
8/17/56	2.60	1/25/57	3.09	0.49	116	1.2	T-Bill	146.28	
1/25/57	144.67	3/29/57	146.38	1.71	46	1.2	Bonds	148.01	132.24
3/29/57	3.03	4/5/57	3.05	0.02	6	0.1	T-Bill	148.12	
4/5/57	146.57	4/12/57	146.75	0.18	6	0.1	Bonds	148.30	132.58
4/12/57	3.15	5/3/57	3.04	(0.11)	16	0.2	T-Bill	148.60	

(Continued)

System Spreadsheet 8.1 (Continued)

Entry Date	Entry Price	Exit Date	Exit Price	Profit/ Loss	Days in Trade	Percent Change	Position	Cumulative Return on $100 Investment	
								Bond Total Return and T-Bills	Bond Total Return Only
5/3/57	145.73	5/24/57	144.83	(0.90)	16	−0.6	Bonds	147.68	130.84
5/24/57	3.12	11/15/57	3.47	0.35	126	1.6	T-Bill	149.99	
11/15/57	138.13	11/22/57	138.92	0.79	6	0.6	Bonds	150.85	125.50
11/22/57	3.15	11/29/57	3.16	0.01	6	0.1	T-Bill	150.96	
11/29/57	139.49	8/15/58	149.99	10.50	186	7.5	Bonds	162.33	135.50
8/15/58	1.52	11/14/58	2.77	1.25	66	0.4	T-Bill	162.98	
11/14/58	147.32	12/19/58	148.31	0.99	26	0.7	Bonds	164.07	133.99
12/19/58	2.90	3/13/59	3.06	0.16	61	0.7	T-Bill	165.23	
3/13/59	148.95	3/20/59	148.73	(0.22)	6	−0.1	Bonds	164.98	134.37
3/20/59	2.76	7/24/59	3.34	0.58	91	1.0	T-Bill	166.64	
7/24/59	145.79	7/31/59	145.97	0.18	6	0.1	Bonds	166.84	131.87
7/31/59	3.05	8/14/59	3.15	0.10	11	0.1	T-Bill	167.06	
8/14/59	146.70	9/4/59	145.78	(0.92)	16	−0.6	Bonds	166.02	131.70
9/4/59	3.89	2/26/60	4.17	0.28	126	2.0	T-Bill	169.26	
2/26/60	147.36	3/11/60	147.95	0.59	11	0.4	Bonds	169.94	133.66
3/11/60	3.64	3/18/60	3.45	(0.19)	6	0.1	T-Bill	170.08	
3/18/60	148.49	5/27/60	149.55	1.06	51	0.7	Bonds	171.30	135.11
5/27/60	3.50	6/3/60	3.18	(0.32)	6	0.1	T-Bill	171.44	
6/3/60	149.69	9/23/60	155.59	5.90	81	3.9	Bonds	178.20	140.56
9/23/60	2.43	11/18/60	2.62	0.19	41	0.4	T-Bill	178.91	
11/18/60	156.05	4/7/61	161.38	5.33	101	3.4	Bonds	185.02	145.79
4/7/61	2.47	4/14/61	2.36	(0.11)	6	0.1	T-Bill	185.13	
4/14/61	161.19	6/9/61	160.61	(0.58)	41	−0.4	Bonds	184.46	145.10
6/2/61	2.44	7/7/61	2.31	(0.13)	26	0.3	T-Bill	184.93	
7/7/61	159.04	8/11/61	157.89	(1.15)	26	−0.7	Bonds	183.59	142.64
8/11/61	2.37	9/1/61	2.32	(0.05)	16	0.2	T-Bill	183.87	
9/1/61	158.50	9/8/61	158.67	0.17	6	0.1	Bonds	184.06	143.35
9/8/61	2.39	9/15/61	2.33	(0.06)	6	0.1	T-Bill	184.17	
9/15/61	158.66	12/8/61	161.97	3.31	61	2.1	Bonds	188.01	146.33
11/24/61	2.54	3/9/62	2.72	0.09	76	0.8	T-Bill	189.46	
3/9/62	164.98	4/13/62	166.98	2.00	26	1.2	Bonds	191.75	150.85
4/13/62	2.72	4/20/62	2.72	0.00	6	0.1	T-Bill	191.88	
4/20/62	167.59	4/27/62	167.91	0.32	6	0.2	Bonds	192.24	151.69
4/27/62	2.74	8/31/62	2.81	0.07	91	1.0	T-Bill	194.15	
8/31/62	169.18	9/28/62	170.65	1.47	21	0.9	Bonds	195.84	154.17
9/28/62	2.75	10/12/62	2.76	0.01	11	0.1	T-Bill	196.08	
10/12/62	171.35	10/19/62	171.88	0.53	6	0.3	Bonds	196.68	155.28
10/19/62	2.75	11/9/62	2.84	0.09	16	0.2	T-Bill	197.03	
11/9/62	172.50	12/14/62	174.75	2.25	26	1.3	Bonds	199.60	157.87
12/14/62	2.81	12/28/62	2.89	0.08	11	0.1	T-Bill	199.84	
1/4/63	175.40	2/1/63	177.10	1.70	21	1.0	Bonds	201.78	160.00
2/1/63	2.92	5/24/63	2.92	0.00	81	0.9	T-Bill	203.68	
5/24/63	181.10	5/31/63	181.43	0.33	6	0.2	Bonds	204.05	163.91
5/31/63	2.97	8/2/63	3.26	0.29	46	0.5	T-Bill	205.16	
8/2/63	182.05	9/13/63	182.75	0.70	31	0.4	Bonds	205.95	165.10
9/13/63	3.34	2/14/64	3.54	0.20	111	1.5	T-Bill	209.00	

System Spreadsheet 8.1 *(Continued)*

Entry Date	Entry Price	Exit Date	Exit Price	Profit/ Loss	Days in Trade	Percent Change	Position	Cumulative Return on $100 Investment Bond Total Return and T-Bills	Bond Total Return Only
2/14/64	186.19	3/6/64	186.58	0.39	16	0.2	Bonds	209.43	168.56
3/6/64	3.59	4/24/64	3.46	(0.13)	36	0.5	T-Bill	210.51	
4/24/64	186.70	8/14/64	191.08	4.38	81	2.3	Bonds	215.45	172.63
8/14/64	3.51	10/9/64	3.58	0.07	41	0.6	T-Bill	216.69	
10/9/64	192.16	10/16/64	192.39	0.23	6	0.1	Bonds	216.95	173.81
10/16/64	3.58	11/6/64	3.56	(0.02)	16	0.2	T-Bill	217.44	
11/6/64	193.38	12/4/64	193.39	0.01	21	0.0	Bonds	217.45	174.71
12/4/64	3.87	12/18/64	3.86	(0.01)	11	0.2	T-Bill	217.82	
12/18/64	193.93	12/25/64	194.09	0.16	6	0.1	Bonds	218.00	175.35
12/25/64	3.87	2/5/65	3.89	0.02	31	0.5	T-Bill	219.04	
2/5/65	195.78	2/12/65	196.25	0.47	6	0.2	Bonds	219.57	177.30
2/12/65	3.90	3/26/65	3.92	0.02	31	0.5	T-Bill	220.63	
3/26/65	196.46	4/30/65	197.48	1.02	26	0.5	Bonds	221.77	178.41
4/30/65	3.92	8/6/65	3.83	(0.09)	71	1.1	T-Bill	224.23	
8/6/65	197.74	8/27/65	197.52	(0.22)	16	−0.1	Bonds	223.98	178.44
8/27/65	3.86	9/16/66	5.45	1.59	276	4.2	T-Bill	233.49	
9/16/66	187.07	9/23/66	186.67	(0.40)	6	−0.2	Bonds	232.99	168.64
9/23/66	5.59	10/14/66	5.47	(0.12)	16	0.4	T-Bill	233.82	
10/14/66	188.49	12/2/66	187.91	(0.58)	36	−0.3	Bonds	233.10	169.76
11/25/66	5.25	12/23/66	4.84	(0.41)	21	0.4	T-Bill	234.12	
12/23/66	189.68	12/30/66	189.85	0.17	6	0.1	Bonds	234.33	171.52
12/30/66	4.75	1/6/67	4.82	0.07	6	0.1	T-Bill	234.60	
1/6/67	191.06	2/17/67	197.60	6.54	31	3.4	Bonds	242.63	178.52
2/17/67	4.58	3/31/67	4.15	(0.43)	31	0.6	T-Bill	244.00	
3/31/67	198.32	5/12/67	196.80	(1.52)	31	−0.8	Bonds	242.13	177.79
5/12/67	3.67	12/29/67	4.99	1.32	166	2.4	T-Bill	248.01	
1/5/68	184.50	2/9/68	189.24	4.74	26	2.6	Bonds	254.38	170.96
2/9/68	4.96	6/14/68	5.71	0.75	91	1.8	T-Bill	258.95	
6/14/68	189.27	8/16/68	196.33	7.06	46	3.7	Bonds	268.61	177.37
8/16/68	5.08	5/9/69	5.98	0.90	191	3.9	T-Bill	279.00	
5/9/69	194.67	5/30/69	193.52	(1.15)	16	−0.6	Bonds	277.35	174.83
5/30/69	6.12	10/24/69	6.98	0.86	106	2.6	T-Bill	284.52	
10/24/69	191.23	11/7/69	193.43	2.20	11	1.2	Bonds	287.79	174.75
11/7/69	7.00	2/20/70	6.78	(0.22)	76	2.1	T-Bill	293.89	
2/20/70	190.97	4/17/70	192.99	2.02	41	1.1	Bonds	297.00	174.35
4/17/70	6.31	7/10/70	6.64	0.33	61	1.5	T-Bill	301.55	
7/10/70	185.11	10/9/70	189.65	4.54	66	2.5	Bonds	308.95	171.33
10/9/70	6.03	11/6/70	5.65	(0.38)	21	0.5	T-Bill	310.51	
11/6/70	189.65	2/26/71	209.48	19.83	81	10.5	Bonds	342.97	189.25
2/26/71	3.50	3/19/71	3.31	(0.19)	16	0.2	T-Bill	343.74	
3/19/71	210.82	3/26/71	211.98	1.16	6	0.6	Bonds	345.63	191.51
3/26/71	3.33	4/9/71	3.70	0.37	11	0.1	T-Bill	346.14	
4/9/71	213.55	4/23/71	212.85	(0.70)	11	−0.3	Bonds	345.00	192.29
4/23/71	3.77	7/16/71	5.38	1.61	61	0.9	T-Bill	348.16	
7/16/71	211.50	7/30/71	212.13	0.63	11	0.3	Bonds	349.20	191.64
7/30/71	5.55	10/8/71	4.53	(1.02)	51	1.1	T-Bill	353.14	

(Continued)

System Spreadsheet 8.1 (Continued)

Entry Date	Entry Price	Exit Date	Exit Price	Profit/ Loss	Days in Trade	Percent Change	Position	Cumulative Return on $100 Investment Bond Total Return and T-Bills	Bond Total Return Only
10/8/71	216.96	10/29/71	220.73	3.77	16	1.7	Bonds	359.27	199.41
10/29/71	4.44	11/5/71	4.23	(0.21)	6	0.1	T-Bill	359.65	
11/5/71	221.32	11/12/71	222.59	1.27	6	0.6	Bonds	361.72	201.09
11/12/71	4.17	12/24/71	4.02	(0.15)	31	0.5	T-Bill	363.58	
12/24/71	225.39	2/4/72	229.99	4.60	31	2.0	Bonds	371.00	207.78
2/4/72	3.37	3/17/72	3.85	0.48	31	0.4	T-Bill	372.55	
3/17/72	232.29	3/24/72	232.22	(0.07)	6	0.0	Bonds	372.43	209.79
3/24/72	3.92	7/7/72	4.14	0.22	76	1.2	T-Bill	376.85	
7/7/72	235.98	7/14/72	236.12	0.14	6	0.1	Bonds	377.08	213.32
7/14/72	4.10	8/4/72	3.79	(0.31)	16	0.3	T-Bill	378.06	
8/4/72	235.78	9/1/72	237.68	1.90	21	0.8	Bonds	381.11	214.73
9/1/72	4.33	11/3/72	4.77	0.44	46	0.8	T-Bill	384.13	
11/3/72	240.49	12/22/72	244.39	3.90	36	1.6	Bonds	390.36	220.79
12/22/72	5.09	9/7/73	8.78	3.69	186	3.8	T-Bill	405.09	
9/7/73	244.59	10/19/73	250.36	5.77	31	2.4	Bonds	414.64	226.18
10/19/73	7.19	10/26/73	6.96	(0.23)	6	0.2	T-Bill	415.36	
10/26/73	250.66	11/2/73	250.70	0.04	6	0.0	Bonds	415.42	226.49
11/2/73	7.20	1/4/74	7.41	0.21	46	1.3	T-Bill	420.90	
1/4/74	252.32	1/11/74	254.51	2.19	6	0.9	Bonds	424.56	229.93
1/11/74	7.62	2/8/74	6.95	(0.67)	21	0.6	T-Bill	427.26	
2/8/74	255.50	3/15/74	255.66	0.16	26	0.1	Bonds	427.53	230.97
3/15/74	7.92	10/11/74	6.70	(1.22)	151	4.8	T-Bill	447.90	
10/11/74	234.42	11/22/74	247.20	12.78	31	5.5	Bonds	472.32	223.33
11/22/74	7.53	11/29/74	7.33	(0.20)	6	0.2	T-Bill	473.17	
11/29/74	247.56	12/6/74	246.79	(0.77)	6	-0.3	Bonds	471.70	222.96
12/6/74	7.52	1/3/75	7.11	(0.41)	21	0.6	T-Bill	474.67	
1/3/75	245.73	3/14/75	261.63	15.90	51	6.5	Bonds	505.38	236.36
3/14/75	5.62	5/9/75	5.36	(0.26)	41	0.9	T-Bill	510.02	
5/9/75	256.82	7/25/75	265.40	8.58	56	3.3	Bonds	527.06	239.77
7/25/75	6.25	10/31/75	5.69	(0.56)	71	1.8	T-Bill	536.38	
10/31/75	269.40	12/5/75	270.59	1.19	26	0.4	Bonds	538.75	244.46
12/5/75	5.55	12/26/75	5.34	(0.21)	16	0.4	T-Bill	540.65	
12/26/75	271.93	2/27/76	289.42	17.49	46	6.4	Bonds	575.43	261.47
2/27/76	4.87	4/23/76	4.76	(0.11)	41	0.8	T-Bill	580.00	
4/23/76	298.25	5/14/76	295.52	(2.73)	16	-0.9	Bonds	574.69	266.98
5/14/76	5.07	7/2/76	5.37	0.30	36	0.7	T-Bill	578.87	
7/2/76	298.43	2/11/77	331.10	32.67	161	10.9	Bonds	642.24	299.12
2/11/77	4.63	4/8/77	4.59	(0.04)	41	0.8	T-Bill	647.10	
4/8/77	333.13	5/13/77	336.60	3.47	26	1.0	Bonds	653.84	304.09
5/13/77	4.82	6/3/77	4.99	0.17	16	0.3	T-Bill	655.85	
6/3/77	340.15	8/5/77	346.37	6.22	46	1.8	Bonds	667.84	312.92
8/5/77	5.42	9/30/77	5.98	0.56	41	0.9	T-Bill	673.76	
9/30/77	353.70	10/14/77	352.22	(1.48)	11	-0.4	Bonds	670.94	318.20
10/14/77	6.16	8/11/78	6.81	0.65	216	5.3	T-Bill	706.50	
8/11/78	358.95	9/15/78	364.07	5.12	26	1.4	Bonds	716.58	328.91
9/15/78	7.70	2/9/79	9.19	1.49	106	3.3	T-Bill	739.88	

System Spreadsheet 8.1 *(Continued)*

Entry Date	Entry Price	Exit Date	Exit Price	Profit/ Loss	Days in Trade	Percent Change	Position	Cumulative Return on $100 Investment Bond Total Return and T-Bills	Bond Total Return Only
2/9/79	358.03	2/23/79	357.04	(0.99)	11	−0.3	Bonds	737.84	322.56
2/23/79	9.29	6/8/79	9.55	0.26	76	2.8	T-Bill	758.59	
6/8/79	362.70	7/27/79	372.91	10.21	36	2.8	Bonds	779.95	336.90
7/27/79	9.48	8/3/79	9.15	(0.33)	6	0.2	T-Bill	781.71	
8/3/79	374.21	8/10/79	375.34	1.13	6	0.3	Bonds	784.07	339.09
8/10/79	9.32	12/7/79	11.93	2.61	86	3.2	T-Bill	809.11	
12/7/79	344.90	1/11/80	333.87	(11.03)	26	−3.2	Bonds	783.24	301.63
1/11/80	11.94	4/18/80	13.82	1.88	71	3.4	T-Bill	809.69	
4/18/80	320.23	7/25/80	348.89	28.66	71	8.9	Bonds	882.16	315.20
7/25/80	7.88	9/5/80	10.12	2.24	31	1.0	T-Bill	890.74	
9/12/80	336.35	9/26/80	331.74	(4.61)	11	−1.4	Bonds	878.53	299.70
9/26/80	10.46	1/2/81	13.91	3.45	71	3.0	T-Bill	904.53	
1/2/81	321.69	1/9/81	326.12	4.43	6	1.4	Bonds	916.98	294.62
1/9/81	13.60	4/3/81	12.50	(1.10)	61	3.3	T-Bill	947.29	
4/3/81	320.04	4/10/81	317.48	(2.56)	6	−0.8	Bonds	939.71	286.82
4/10/81	14.15	6/12/81	14.98	0.83	46	2.6	T-Bill	964.08	
6/12/81	322.02	7/3/81	320.59	(1.43)	16	−0.4	Bonds	959.80	289.63
7/3/81	13.91	10/30/81	13.35	(0.56)	86	4.8	T-Bill	1005.55	
10/30/81	312.57	1/1/82	324.27	11.70	46	3.7	Bonds	1043.18	292.95
1/1/82	11.69	2/26/82	12.43	0.74	41	1.9	T-Bill	1063.10	
2/26/82	333.23	3/12/82	341.53	8.30	11	2.5	Bonds	1089.58	308.55
3/12/82	12.06	3/19/82	12.91	0.85	6	0.3	T-Bill	1092.72	
3/19/82	341.56	5/28/82	360.57	19.01	51	5.6	Bonds	1153.54	325.75
5/28/82	11.48	8/20/82	8.62	(2.86)	61	2.8	T-Bill	1185.73	
8/20/82	378.66	11/26/82	451.87	73.21	71	19.3	Bonds	1414.97	408.23
11/26/82	7.94	12/31/82	7.98	0.04	26	0.8	T-Bill	1426.61	
12/31/82	452.85	4/1/83	487.94	35.09	66	7.7	Bonds	1537.15	440.82
4/1/83	8.68	4/15/83	8.17	(0.51)	11	0.4	T-Bill	1543.00	
4/15/83	494.83	5/27/83	501.58	6.75	31	1.4	Bonds	1564.05	453.14
5/27/83	8.46	9/23/83	8.99	0.53	86	2.9	T-Bill	1609.39	
9/23/83	494.84	11/11/83	498.86	4.02	36	0.8	Bonds	1622.46	450.68
11/11/83	8.83	7/27/84	10.30	1.47	186	6.5	T-Bill	1728.62	
7/27/84	499.13	3/8/85	593.55	94.42	161	18.9	Bonds	2055.63	536.23
3/8/85	8.73	3/22/85	8.64	(0.09)	11	0.4	T-Bill	2063.49	
3/22/85	593.30	7/26/85	675.42	82.12	91	13.8	Bonds	2349.10	610.19
7/26/85	7.23	10/25/85	7.18	(0.05)	66	1.9	T-Bill	2393.76	
10/25/85	694.12	4/25/86	838.73	144.61	131	20.8	Bonds	2892.47	757.73
4/25/86	5.86	5/30/86	6.15	0.29	26	0.6	T-Bill	2910.03	
5/30/86	833.17	9/12/86	857.55	24.38	76	2.9	Bonds	2995.18	774.73
9/12/86	5.24	10/31/86	5.18	(0.06)	36	0.8	T-Bill	3017.69	
10/31/86	870.83	12/26/86	895.92	25.09	41	2.9	Bonds	3104.63	809.40
12/26/86	5.49	1/9/87	5.53	0.04	11	0.2	T-Bill	3112.10	
1/9/87	907.96	2/6/87	920.06	12.10	21	1.3	Bonds	3153.58	831.20
2/6/87	5.58	6/26/87	5.64	0.06	101	2.2	T-Bill	3224.39	
6/26/87	887.00	7/24/87	886.88	(0.12)	21	0.0	Bonds	3223.95	801.23
7/24/87	5.55	1/8/88	5.90	0.35	121	2.7	T-Bill	3310.21	

(Continued)

System Spreadsheet 8.1 *(Continued)*

								Cumulative Return on $100 Investment	
								Bond Total Return and	
Entry Date	Entry Price	Exit Date	Exit Price	Profit/ Loss	Days in Trade	Percent Change	Position	T-Bills	Bond Total Return Only
1/8/88	907.00	3/4/88	960.38	53.38	41	5.9	Bonds	3505.02	867.63
3/4/88	5.62	6/17/88	6.44	0.82	76	1.7	T-Bill	3564.67	
6/17/88	961.06	7/22/88	964.82	3.76	26	0.4	Bonds	3578.61	871.64
7/22/88	6.76	9/16/88	7.21	0.45	41	1.1	T-Bill	3618.13	
9/16/88	985.57	11/11/88	1016.30	30.73	41	3.1	Bonds	3730.94	918.15
11/11/88	7.54	12/30/88	8.22	0.68	36	1.1	T-Bill	3771.29	
12/30/88	1009.63	1/6/89	1006.48	(3.15)	6	-0.3	Bonds	3759.52	909.28
1/6/89	8.24	1/20/89	8.30	0.06	11	0.4	T-Bill	3773.10	
1/20/89	1020.14	2/10/89	1029.06	8.92	16	0.9	Bonds	3806.09	929.68
2/10/89	8.57	4/14/89	8.71	0.14	46	1.6	T-Bill	3865.87	
4/14/89	1024.96	9/8/89	1121.12	96.16	106	9.4	Bonds	4228.56	1012.85
9/8/89	7.88	10/6/89	7.83	(0.05)	21	0.7	T-Bill	4256.44	
10/6/89	1122.34	10/13/89	1129.34	7.00	6	0.6	Bonds	4282.98	1020.27
10/13/89	7.63	11/3/89	7.78	0.15	16	0.5	T-Bill	4303.82	
11/3/89	1136.78	1/12/90	1148.59	11.81	51	1.0	Bonds	4348.53	1037.66
1/12/90	7.57	5/18/90	7.67	0.10	91	2.7	T-Bill	4467.87	
5/18/90	1146.72	5/25/90	1151.85	5.13	6	0.4	Bonds	4487.86	1040.61
5/25/90	7.74	6/1/90	7.80	0.06	6	0.2	T-Bill	4496.16	
6/1/90	1158.87	6/22/90	1168.39	9.52	16	0.8	Bonds	4533.10	1055.55
6/22/90	7.74	8/3/90	7.50	(0.24)	31	1.0	T-Bill	4576.43	
8/3/90	1187.8	8/10/90	1184.95	(2.85)	6	-0.2	Bonds	4565.45	1070.51
8/10/90	7.23	9/21/90	7.39	0.16	31	0.9	T-Bill	4606.22	
9/21/90	1168.44	9/28/90	1165.34	(3.10)	6	-0.3	Bonds	4594.00	1052.80
9/28/90	7.32	10/5/90	7.18	(0.14)	6	0.2	T-Bill	4602.04	
10/5/90	1172.49	12/14/90	1219.21	46.72	51	4.0	Bonds	4785.41	1101.46
12/14/90	6.86	12/21/90	6.78	(0.08)	6	0.2	T-Bill	4793.26	
12/21/90	1227.86	12/28/90	1228.70	0.84	6	0.1	Bonds	4796.54	1110.04
12/28/90	6.52	2/8/91	5.97	(0.55)	31	0.8	T-Bill	4835.16	
2/8/91	1271.18	4/19/91	1295.44	24.26	51	1.9	Bonds	4927.44	1170.33
4/19/91	5.57	8/2/91	5.58	0.01	76	1.7	T-Bill	5010.54	
8/2/91	1333.18	11/22/91	1405.69	72.51	81	5.4	Bonds	5283.06	1269.93
11/22/91	4.58	11/29/91	4.44	(0.14)	6	0.1	T-Bill	5288.85	
12/6/91	1407.98	1/10/92	1446.88	38.90	26	2.8	Bonds	5434.97	1307.15
1/10/92	3.85	4/17/92	3.60	(0.25)	71	1.1	T-Bill	5494.16	
4/17/92	1466.53	6/26/92	1497.29	30.76	51	2.1	Bonds	5609.40	1352.69
6/26/92	3.67	7/3/92	3.59	(0.08)	6	0.1	T-Bill	5614.32	
7/3/92	1503.61	9/18/92	1569.24	65.63	56	4.4	Bonds	5859.37	1417.69
9/18/92	2.89	10/30/92	2.97	0.08	31	0.4	T-Bill	5880.29	
10/30/92	1570.45	11/6/92	1567.96	(2.49)	6	-0.2	Bonds	5870.96	1416.53
11/6/92	3.05	11/20/92	3.13	0.08	11	0.1	T-Bill	5878.81	
11/20/92	1572.42	12/4/92	1582.93	10.51	11	0.7	Bonds	5918.10	1430.06
12/4/92	3.31	12/11/92	3.29	(0.02)	6	0.1	T-Bill	5922.79	
12/11/92	1590.06	1/8/93	1604.42	14.36	21	0.9	Bonds	5976.28	1449.47
1/8/93	3.15	1/15/93	3.07	(0.08)	6	0.1	T-Bill	5980.78	
1/15/93	1602.62	4/23/93	1673.65	71.03	71	4.4	Bonds	6245.85	1512.02
4/23/93	2.82	5/7/93	2.88	0.06	11	0.1	T-Bill	6253.57	

System Spreadsheet 8.1 *(Continued)*

Entry Date	Entry Price	Exit Date	Exit Price	Profit/ Loss	Days in Trade	Percent Change	Position	Cumulative Return on $100 Investment	
								Bond Total Return and T-Bills	Bond Total Return Only
5/7/93	1686.01	5/14/93	1689.21	3.20	6	0.2	Bonds	6265.44	1526.07
5/14/93	2.89	6/11/93	3.14	0.25	21	0.2	T-Bill	6280.59	
6/11/93	1700.63	6/18/93	1699.66	(0.97)	6	−0.1	Bonds	6277.01	1535.51
6/18/93	3.05	6/25/93	3.10	0.05	6	0.1	T-Bill	6281.58	
6/25/93	1701.09	9/24/93	1740.34	39.25	66	2.3	Bonds	6426.52	1572.26
9/24/93	2.93	1/28/94	2.96	0.03	91	1.1	T-Bill	6494.79	
1/28/94	1769.49	2/4/94	1769.45	(0.04)	6	0.0	Bonds	6494.64	1598.56
2/4/94	2.99	8/12/94	4.43	1.44	136	1.6	T-Bill	6599.86	
8/12/94	1705.99	8/19/94	1707.21	1.22	6	0.1	Bonds	6604.58	1542.33
8/19/94	4.59	8/26/94	4.62	0.03	6	0.1	T-Bill	6611.82	
8/26/94	1706.37	9/2/94	1716.85	10.48	6	0.6	Bonds	6652.43	1551.04
9/2/94	4.61	12/16/94	5.76	1.15	76	1.4	T-Bill	6745.29	
12/16/94	1688.62	3/10/95	1760.36	71.74	61	4.2	Bonds	7031.86	1590.35
3/10/95	5.77	4/7/95	5.76	(0.01)	21	0.5	T-Bill	7065.81	
4/7/95	1803.54	7/21/95	1927.49	123.95	76	6.9	Bonds	7551.41	1741.34
7/21/95	5.46	7/28/95	5.47	0.01	6	0.1	T-Bill	7561.27	
7/28/95	1911.66	8/11/95	1911.84	0.18	11	0.0	Bonds	7561.98	1727.20
8/11/95	5.41	8/18/95	5.40	(0.01)	6	0.1	T-Bill	7571.76	
8/18/95	1910.44	11/24/95	1992.00	81.56	71	4.3	Bonds	7895.01	1799.62
11/24/95	5.34	12/1/95	5.32	(0.02)	6	0.1	T-Bill	7905.09	
12/1/95	1995.17	3/1/96	2032.66	37.49	66	1.9	Bonds	8053.63	1836.35
2/23/96	4.78	5/10/96	5.02	0.24	56	1.1	T-Bill	8139.52	
5/10/96	1989.48	5/31/96	1998.94	9.46	16	0.5	Bonds	8178.22	1805.89
5/31/96	5.03	6/21/96	5.08	0.05	16	0.3	T-Bill	8204.44	
6/21/96	2001.28	7/5/96	2019.93	18.65	11	0.9	Bonds	8280.90	1824.85
7/5/96	5.12	8/16/96	5.04	(0.08)	31	0.6	T-Bill	8333.26	
8/16/96	2050.91	8/23/96	2046.79	(4.12)	6	−0.2	Bonds	8316.52	1849.12
8/23/96	5.06	9/27/96	5.18	0.12	26	0.5	T-Bill	8360.11	
9/27/96	2066.41	12/13/96	2110.15	43.74	56	2.1	Bonds	8537.07	1906.36
12/13/96	4.83	12/20/96	4.76	(0.07)	6	0.1	T-Bill	8546.93	
12/20/96	2116.29	1/3/97	2124.70	8.41	11	0.4	Bonds	8580.89	1919.50
1/3/97	5.08	1/10/97	5.02	(0.06)	6	0.1	T-Bill	8591.31	
1/10/97	2115.38	1/31/97	2124.37	8.99	16	0.4	Bonds	8627.83	1919.21
1/31/97	5.06	5/2/97	5.22	0.16	66	1.3	T-Bill	8742.62	
5/2/97	2133.53	8/8/97	2221.26	87.73	71	4.1	Bonds	9102.11	2006.74
8/8/97	5.15	9/5/97	5.01	(0.14)	21	0.4	T-Bill	9141.33	
			Percentage of Years Profitable					100%	76%
			Maximum Drawdown					3.20%	21.10%
			Compound Annual Return					8.72%	5.71%

sector of the bond market for the current environment. Particularly during periods when zero coupons, junk, EM-debt, and foreign long-bonds look promising—if the profit potential looks good via models and economic gauges and understanding—then one should compare the potential profit and risk with other asset classes such as global equities. Make either a small or a major allocation to these bond sectors depending on how their returns and risk posture looks in comparison to other asset classes (discussed in detail later on). Bank Credit Analyst also has some excellent bond models for U.S. and global bonds, and investors could subscribe to their various excellent services as well as subscribing to our own *Portfolio Strategy Letter (PSL)*, which reviews our bond model recommendations in the high yield section. All system followers should subscribe to Nelson Freeburg's wonderful publication *Formula Research* ($195 per year, 901-756-8607). It is like having your own expert system analyst for such an incredibly low price, it is almost unbelievable.

There are several main points for investors here. First, it is possible to significantly improve the risk/reward of investing in bonds by using simple economic gauges and timing systems, and by rotating into the best sector for that particular market environment. By doing both, we can actually bring bond investment returns up to total returns of buy and hold equities over the long run. Second, there are times when even if the equity market is bullish, asset classes like junk bonds, emerging market bonds, and zero-coupon bonds can actually show better profitability than stocks, while having somewhat disparate performance. Finally, the correct bond sector is often a better place for investment capital than T-bills/cash, during periods when global equity models are not positive.

Gold and Silver Equities

From mid-1993 to mid-1994, we became mildly excited about gold stock opportunities and put as much as 12 percent of portfolio capital (in *PSL* and funds we consult for) into gold plays that ended up producing profits of around 25 percent while gold itself rose from the 350 level to a peak of 417 before declining back to just under 400 when we exited positions (we kept a 1% position). This is the last time we have been bullish gold stocks in our

Portfolio Strategy Letter models or in our hedge fund consulting. It was also the last time gold staged any sort of decent rally. How were we able to exploit the small move in gold in 1993–1994 while still exiting and avoiding painful investment from 1985 to 1994 and then from mid-1994 through 1997? Very simple. We used timing models (to be described).

Gold and precious metal stocks are not a hedge against uncertainty, not a hedge against a stock market decline, not a hedge against a bond market decline. Gold stocks tend to rise with inflationary expectations, or pronounced shortages, period. Gold has been in a bear market basically since its heyday of the late 1978 through January 1980, when it soared from around $120 to over $800. During this Great Inflation, gold and gold stocks were the assets to hold, while stocks and bonds were trash. Because history often repeats itself, investors still need to watch gold stocks as a legitimate asset class. If reflation ever takes off, it might be a critical component in your investment arsenal.

Our timing models for gold stocks follow. Investors can use funds (like INPMX) or buy top relative strength gold stocks when models turn bullish in unison and the environment seems ripe for higher inflation. Aggressive investors foreseeing far higher gold prices can also load up on marginal mining companies—those companies whose cost of mining gold is above current prices for maximum gains.

Kaeppel/Davis/Freeburg K-Ratio System.   Jay Kaeppel, research director at Essex Trading Company, first popularized the K-ratio, or ratio of gold stocks to gold bullion. Here again is Nelson Freeburg's reworking of the concept into an excellent system:

K-ratio = *Barron's* Gold Mining Index (GMI) divided by Handy Harmon's gold bullion price, on a weekly basis.

Figure 8.3 shows how gold stocks and bullion have performed under different K-ratios since late 1975.

Whenever the K-ratio falls below 1.2, gold shares move up an average of 39.8 percent over the next 3 months, 73.7 percent over the next 6 months, and 134.4 percent over the next 12 months. Conversely, when the K-ratio moves above 2.15, gold shares fall by an average of 8.7 percent over the next 3 months, decline by an

Figure 8.3 **K-RATIO AND GOLD STOCKS**

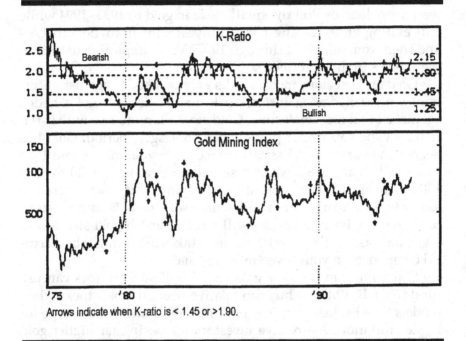

Note: Arrows indicate when K-ratio is < 1.45 or >1.90.

Note: Arrows indicate when K-ratio is < 1.45 or > 1.90.

Source: Formula Research.

average of 15.7 percent over the next 6 months, and fall by 20.4 percent over the following 12 months. Thus the K-ratio has some usefulness as a gold timing indicator.

Adding Ned Davis' Standard Deviation Bands. Next take a 46-week moving average of the K-ratio, and then calculate the standard deviation over the same 46-week period. Plot the 46-week MA and put lines 2.3 standard deviations above and below the MA. Buy when the 46-week MA falls below the lower *SD* line and then rises above it again. Sell when the 46-week MA rises above the upper *SD* line and then falls below it again. This is the long-term model signal.

Now for the intermediate-term signal, use a 4-week MA of the K-ratio and calculate the *SD* over that period. Plot *SD* bands 1.3 standard deviations above and below the 4-week MA. Use the opposite logic for buy and sell signals with the intermediate system: Buy when the 4-week MA moves above the upper *SD* band and then falls below it; and sell when the 4-week MA moves below the lower *SD* band and then moves above it. This is our intermediate-term signal.

Now combine the intermediate-term and long-term signals so that any buy signal is taken and any exit signal is taken. Here are the results of this system. The system produces a 28.8 percent gain per annum versus 2.6 percent BH since late 1975 (as illustrated in Figure 8.4). The maximum drawdown was 21 percent. The system is profitable two thirds of the time and is invested long 44 percent of the time. The average trade lasted 13 weeks. The sell signals also work well. If you combine short and long signals you would have achieved a 33 percent GPA, but with a 38 percent maximum drawdown; 21 of 33 short trades were profitable.

Figure 8.4 **COMBINED K-RATIO LONG-TERM AND INTERMEDIATE-TERM SYSTEM SIGNALS AND PERFORMANCE**

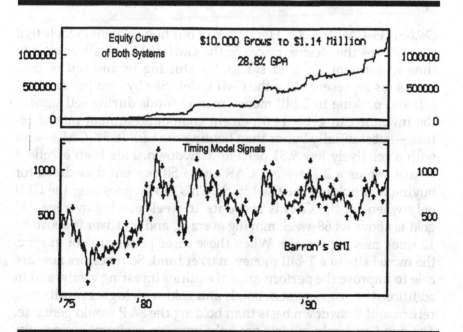

GMI-Bullion-Swiss Franc Momentum Model. This model is simply based on concurrent positive or negative momentum in gold stocks, gold bullion, and the Swiss franc versus the dollar.

Buy when the weekly GMI close is 8 percent above a weekly GMI low close; *and* the Swiss Franc (versus dollar) is above its 9 wk MA; *and* gold bullion is higher than it was 26 weeks ago.

Once long exit when the GMI weekly falls 8 percent or more from a prior weekly GMI close.

Since 1975, this model has produced a 21.3 percent GPA, with 59 percent of all trades profitable and a 19 percent maximum drawdown. It was invested only 29 percent of the time. When this model is bullish, gold shares move up at a 93 percent annual rate.

If you like these two systems, again I have left out some details, please purchase them from their originator *Formula Research* (for only $15).

Combination of Two above Models. The K-ratio system and the momentum system are both bullish only 18 percent of the time; when they are both bullish, however, gold shares move up at an astounding 118 percent annual rate. Not a bad time to consider options, futures, or aggressive marginal mining shares.

Gold-Silver-GMI Model. Here's one of our homegrown models that simply uses the closing prices of the GMI, gold and silver cash to time investments in gold stocks. By shifting in and out of gold stocks (as represented by the GMI Index; See System Spreadsheet 8.2) and parking in T-bill money market funds during sell signals, the investor can get a 14.6 percent compound annual rate of return—substantially better than holding the S&P (8.5% CAR)—and with a relatively low 9.51 percent drawdown. This is an excellent return versus a 2.3 percent CAR and a 50 percent drawdown for buying and holding the GMI itself. This model goes long the GMI only when (a) the GMI is above its 16-week moving average, (b) gold is above its 68-week moving average, and (c) silver is above its 12-week moving average. When these three prices are not in sync, the model sits in a T-bill money market fund. So investors now are able to improve the performance of equities investing vastly; and in addition, they can invest in bonds and gold with higher profits on a return and drawdown basis than holding the S&P would generate. The bond and gold models not only improve performance greatly,

System Spreadsheet 8.2 **GOLD SYSTEM**

System Description: Buy GMI Index when GMI Index > GMI Index 16-week MA and gold prices > gold price 68-week MA and silver prices > 12-week MA. Exit GMI and buy 3-month T-bills when these conditions are no long true.

Data Used: Weekly close of GMI Index, weekly close of Handy Harmon Gold Index, weekly close of Handy Harmon Silver Index and weekly close of 3-month T-bill Yield.

From: 3/1/75   To: 12/31/9

Entry Date	Entry Price	Exit Date	Exit Price	Profit/ Loss	Days in Trade	Percent Change	Position	GMI Total Return with T-Bills	GMI Buy and Hold
								100.0000000	100.0000000
3/21/75	5.38	5/23/75	5.12	($0.26)	46	1.0%	T-Bills	100.9859761	
5/23/75	478.96	6/6/75	483.35	4.39	11	0.9	GMI	101.9115825	102.8951570
6/6/75	5.26	8/1/75	6.32	1.06	41	0.9	T-Bills	102.7872100	
8/1/75	510.90	8/8/75	515.24	4.34	6	0.8	GMI	103.6603682	109.6838744
8/8/75	6.46	11/12/76	4.89	(1.57)	331	8.5	T-Bills	112.4911578	
11/12/76	283.03	11/19/76	267.68	(15.35)	6	−5.4	GMI	106.3902523	56.9835019
11/19/76	4.89	11/26/76	4.60	(0.29)	6	0.1	T-Bills	106.5146145	
11/26/76	280.88	12/17/76	283.80	2.92	16	1.0	GMI	107.6219296	60.4151144
12/17/76	4.36	12/24/76	4.27	(0.09)	6	0.1	T-Bills	107.7340965	
12/24/76	272.36	1/14/77	276.79	4.43	16	1.6	GMI	109.4864172	58.9228313
1/14/77	4.61	1/21/77	4.67	0.06	6	0.1	T-Bills	109.6070703	
1/21/77	273.98	1/28/77	264.41	(9.57)	6	−3.5	GMI	105.7785439	56.2873869
1/28/77	4.70	2/18/77	4.63	(0.07)	16	0.3	T-Bills	106.0954581	
2/18/77	274.68	4/8/77	275.28	0.60	36	0.2	GMI	106.3272088	58.6013837
4/8/77	4.59	7/22/77	5.21	0.62	76	1.4	T-Bills	107.8049452	
7/22/77	275.19	7/29/77	268.50	(6.69)	6	−2.4	GMI	105.1841556	57.1580628
7/29/77	5.16	8/5/77	5.42	0.26	6	0.1	T-Bills	105.3138967	
8/5/77	273.70	8/12/77	278.43	4.73	6	1.7	GMI	107.1338994	59.2719532
8/12/77	5.35	9/9/77	5.55	0.20	21	0.4	T-Bills	107.6134410	
9/9/77	280.56	11/18/77	281.84	1.28	51	0.5	GMI	108.1044062	59.9978712
11/18/77	6.09	1/6/78	6.14	0.05	36	0.9	T-Bills	109.0486616	
1/6/78	309.60	2/10/78	290.33	(19.27)	26	−6.2	GMI	102.2612982	61.8052155
2/10/78	6.48	2/17/78	6.45	(0.03)	6	0.2	T-Bills	102.4197013	
2/17/78	294.70	2/24/78	292.82	(1.88)	6	−0.6	GMI	101.7663283	62.3352847
2/24/78	6.46	3/3/78	6.43	(0.03)	6	0.2	T-Bills	101.9234782	
3/3/78	295.24	3/31/78	296.34	1.10	21	0.4	GMI	102.3032229	63.0846195
3/31/78	6.31	5/26/78	6.48	0.17	41	1.0	T-Bills	103.3576797	
5/26/78	294.65	6/9/78	290.83	(3.82)	11	−1.3	GMI	102.0176956	61.9116551
6/9/78	6.63	6/16/78	6.62	(0.01)	6	0.2	T-Bills	102.1793794	
6/16/78	300.26	11/3/78	348.69	48.43	101	16.1	GMI	118.6602538	74.2288451
11/3/78	8.45	1/19/79	9.41	0.96	56	1.9	T-Bills	120.8973068	
1/19/79	344.44	4/13/79	335.24	(9.20)	61	−2.7	GMI	117.6681371	71.3656200
4/13/79	9.65	4/27/79	9.12	(0.53)	11	0.4	T-Bills	118.1657655	
4/27/79	352.88	8/3/79	360.94	8.06	71	2.3	GMI	120.8647455	76.8366152
8/3/79	9.15	8/24/79	9.60	0.45	16	0.6	T-Bills	121.5697096	
8/24/79	412.25	10/26/79	404.59	(7.66)	46	−1.9	GMI	119.3108279	86.1287919
10/26/79	12.93	11/9/79	12.10	(0.83)	11	0.6	T-Bills	119.9869068	
11/9/79	413.03	11/16/79	401.77	(11.26)	6	−2.7	GMI	116.7158307	85.5284726
11/16/79	12.03	11/30/79	11.02	(1.01)	11	0.5	T-Bills	117.3311695	
11/30/79	433.99	2/22/80	702.12	268.13	61	61.8	GMI	189.8213340	149.4667376
2/22/80	13.16	2/29/80	13.70	0.54	6	0.3	T-Bills	190.4184772	
2/29/80	730.37	3/7/80	720.60	(9.77)	6	−1.3	GMI	187.8712908	153.4007451
3/7/80	15.14	6/6/80	8.04	(7.10)	66	4.0	T-Bills	195.3505142	
6/6/80	679.97	8/15/80	827.83	147.86	51	21.7	GMI	237.8296339	176.2277807
8/15/80	8.72	8/22/80	9.41	0.69	6	0.2	T-Bills	238.3253808	
8/22/80	864.83	10/31/80	1200.83	336.00	51	38.9	GMI	330.9185239	255.6317190
10/31/80	12.33	8/27/82	7.75	(4.58)	476	23.4	T-Bills	408.2965036	

(Continued)

System Spreadsheet 8.2 *(Continued)*

								Cumulative Return on $100	
Entry Date	Entry Price	Exit Date	Exit Price	Profit/ Loss	Days in Trade	Percent Change	Position	GMI Total Return with T-Bills	GMI Buy and Hold
8/27/82	542.58	11/26/82	659.61	117.03	66	21.6	GMI	496.362669	140.4172432
11/26/82	7.94	12/3/82	8.28	0.34	6	0.2	T-Bills	497.304769	
12/3/82	767.68	3/4/83	862.96	95.28	66	12.4	GMI	559.027360	183.7062267
3/4/83	7.94	4/22/83	8.03	0.09	36	1.1	T-Bills	565.393590	
4/22/83	944.99	4/29/83	925.55	(19.44)	6	-2.1	GMI	553.762513	197.0303353
4/29/83	8.15	5/6/83	8.04	(0.11)	6	0.2	T-Bills	554.841357	
5/6/83	961.16	6/10/83	995.88	34.72	26	3.6	GMI	574.883901	212.0021288
6/10/83	8.64	6/24/83	8.98	0.34	11	0.4	T-Bills	577.060673	
6/24/83	978.25	7/1/83	926.92	(51.33)	6	-5.2	GMI	546.781578	197.3219798
7/1/83	9.09	1/10/86	7.05	(2.04)	661	23.9	T-Bills	677.671285	
1/10/86	560.45	2/7/86	547.88	(12.57)	21	-2.2	GMI	662.472199	116.6322512
2/7/86	6.99	8/15/86	5.60	(1.39)	136	3.8	T-Bills	687.562739	
8/15/86	472.50	11/21/86	501.21	28.71	71	6.1	GMI	729.340361	106.6971794
11/21/86	5.39	1/16/87	5.38	(0.01)	41	0.9	T-Bills	735.761753	
1/16/87	564.54	6/12/87	855.22	290.68	106	51.5	GMI	1114.603334	182.0585418
6/12/87	5.59	7/31/87	6.14	0.55	36	0.8	T-Bills	1123.539699	
7/31/87	951.91	8/14/87	952.78	0.87	11	0.1	GMI	1124.566561	202.8270357
8/14/87	5.93	9/4/87	6.19	0.26	16	0.4	T-Bills	1128.817512	
9/4/87	1006.41	9/18/87	967.19	(39.22)	11	-3.9	GMI	1084.827266	205.8946248
9/18/87	6.32	10/9/87	6.49	0.17	16	0.4	T-Bills	1089.197694	
10/9/87	954.20	10/16/87	930.21	(23.99)	6	-2.5	GMI	1061.813652	198.0223523
10/16/87	6.96	5/27/88	6.34	(0.62)	161	4.5	T-Bills	1109.217075	
5/27/88	665.75	6/17/88	678.34	12.59	16	1.9	GMI	1130.193482	144.4044705
6/17/88	6.44	11/17/89	7.68	1.24	371	9.5	T-Bills	1237.775294	
11/17/89	801.78	12/29/89	827.15	25.37	31	3.2	GMI	1276.941099	176.0830229
12/29/89	7.77	8/10/90	7.23	(0.54)	161	5.0	T-Bills	1340.583131	
8/10/90	787.54	8/31/90	777.90	(9.64)	16	-1.2	GMI	1324.173524	165.5987227
8/31/90	7.49	1/4/91	6.52	(0.97)	91	2.7	T-Bills	1360.131430	
1/4/91	713.89	1/18/91	663.21	(50.68)	11	-7.1	GMI	1263.573892	141.1836083
1/18/91	6.12	4/23/93	2.82	(3.30)	591	14.4	T-Bills	1445.655393	
4/23/93	639.21	8/6/93	730.07	90.86	76	14.2	GMI	1651.146936	155.4167110
8/6/93	3.10	10/22/93	3.06	(0.04)	56	0.7	T-Bills	1662.566821	
10/22/93	789.63	2/11/94	828.04	38.41	81	4.9	GMI	1743.439117	176.2724854
2/11/94	3.24	6/24/94	4.18	0.94	96	1.2	T-Bills	1765.043870	
6/24/94	779.49	7/1/94	757.47	(22.02)	6	-2.8	GMI	1715.182723	161.2496009
7/1/94	4.20	9/2/94	4.61	0.41	46	0.8	T-Bills	1728.384846	
9/2/94	826.24	10/14/94	849.83	23.59	31	2.9	GMI	1777.732008	180.9111229
10/14/94	4.92	3/31/95	5.64	0.72	121	2.4	T-Bills	1819.896128	
3/31/95	759.61	5/12/95	699.90	(59.71)	31	-7.9	GMI	1676.841142	148.9941458
5/12/95	5.63	5/26/95	5.72	0.09	11	0.2	T-Bills	1680.978464	
5/26/95	734.00	6/2/95	741.16	7.16	6	1.0	GMI	1697.376019	157.7775412
6/2/95	5.64	6/9/95	5.48	(0.16)	6	0.1	T-Bills	1699.664434	
6/9/95	745.06	6/16/95	771.42	26.36	6	3.5	GMI	1759.798053	164.2192656
6/16/95	5.57	9/15/95	5.34	(0.23)	66	1.5	T-Bills	1785.572434	
9/15/95	769.68	9/22/95	763.97	(5.71)	6	-0.7	GMI	1772.325866	162.6333156
9/22/95	5.25	1/5/96	5.04	(0.21)	76	1.6	T-Bills	1800.499492	
1/5/96	744.37	3/8/96	836.26	91.89	46	12.3	GMI	2022.765164	178.0223523
3/8/96	4.89	3/15/96	4.95	0.06	6	0.1	T-Bills	2025.129624	
3/15/96	832.51	3/29/96	836.72	4.21	11	0.5	GMI	2035.370697	178.1202767
3/29/96	4.99	12/31/97	5.18	0.19	459	9.1	T-Bills	2221.101111	

Percentage of Years Profitable	87%	40%
Maximum Drawdown	-9.5%	50%
Compound Annual Return	14.6%	2.3%

but also allow investors to get better-than-equity returns with lower-than-equity drawdowns from assets relatively uncorrelated with stocks—providing substantial diversification benefits.

Real Estate, REITs, and Trust Deeds

While real estate historically tends to have a positive correlation to equities, that correlation is often pretty low. In the fractional reserve paper money Federal Reserve System, rising inflation is often good for real estate but bad for stocks (at least until the bond market catches on and forces real interest rates to sky-high levels thereby choking off real estate speculation). Going back to the 1800s, there has also been a distinct valuation cycle in real estate versus stock prices, where the average price of a home per stock index unit has moved up and down to clearly defined zones several times in each direction. Today, stocks are trading at the level where real estate normally gains on equities over the long run. This long-run valuation cycle theory has been popularized by Gray Cardiff (Sound Investing), and it certainly bears watching.

It is fair to say that there are indeed some circumstances in which real estate will gain while equities will not, particularly in a rising inflation period (P/Es tend to contract when inflation is rising). This is why historically at least the correlation between the two assets is relatively low, though not inverse. In addition, real estate investment trusts (REITs), the liquid stock equivalent of real estate, have very high yields of 5 percent to 10 percent (from rents), which make them somewhat less prone to serious declines than equities in general.

On the other hand, since REITs have expanded as an asset class in the 1990s, their correlation with equities has been extremely high. In 1990, 1994, and in both corrections of 1997, REITs have declined in lockstep with equities. And since both equities and REITs are now highly sensitive to interest rates (and/or deflationary drops in growth), they will continue to be more heavily correlated than a study of history would reveal. This pulls REITs down to only a fair diversification in my book, similar to international equities. Certainly if you can find a REIT that meets our selection criteria, it would have good profit potential, high yields, and diversification benefits, but investors should not regard REITs as a truly sound disparate asset to equities in the near future. Nonetheless given a choice of asset classes over the next decade, I would choose real estate over equities because of valuation problems with equities.

International real estate is probably a better diversification in certain circumstances. If you can find a country that has artificially low interest rates or is sterilizing currency appreciation, as Asia was until 1995 and 1996, then you have a system where a real estate bubble is being rigged. Participate until valuations get overdone and then exit early. In all cases, you want a combination of favorable liquidity environment, hot-spot reasons for your particular real estate to appreciate, and preferably some technology gap or demographic reason for your real estate to be in higher and higher demand. The ultimate value check on real estate is rent/yield. If the yield is not higher than T-bills (or short rates in your particular country), you are getting overvalued. And keep in mind the three most important things in real estate—location, location, and location.

One- or two-year trust deeds, or short-term mortgages can be another good anchor for your portfolio particularly if they are in your local area and you can personally check out the property underlying them. In Fall 1997, in the booming Silicon Valley-San Francisco Bay Area of California, one could still get one-year trust deeds with 60 percent or lower loan to equity, yielding from 10 percent to 12 percent. The key is to find borrowers who should be able to pay, but do not meet the normal requirements of banks or mortgage lenders for high-quality credit. Examples I find often are people who are about to inherit money or who don't have a "normal" job, but would like a home-equity loan to expand or start their own business. What you are looking for is someone who should not have trouble paying back the loan, but who does not meet requirements on a typical loan application. Consultants often fit this category. So do many retirees, who are placed in awkward situations by stupid tax laws. It is not uncommon to find retirees who realize that they are much better off after taxes borrowing money on their house than they are pulling beyond the mandatory amount out of their IRA. The reasons are twofold. First, the loan is tax-free cash, while the IRA or Keogh withdrawal is taxed heavily. Second, the higher mortgage payments are tax-deductible, which basically allows retirees to pull more money out of their IRA or Keogh later with lower overall taxes than without the higher mortgage. I don't recommend that you go above 65 percent loan to equity (and only go above 60% on one-year trust deeds), because in the rare and sorry event of nonpayment you want to be able to have no problem getting back your principal plus interest. Check out the history of the mortgage company you are using for your trust deed investment, and try to stick with companies that have better than 95 percent rates of repayment history. The bottom line is that an 11 percent to 12 percent reliable yield is one of the better anchors available to an investor. Particularly if you are a conservative investor, some part of one's portfolio should almost always be allocated to such anchors—and these make up a far better alternative to cash when our models are defensive toward some or most global equity markets, although they are less liquid than arbitrage funds, which offer similar returns.

There are some types of real estate oriented loans I advise strongly against. Remember our wealth equation. You want to use the force of your unspent productivity (your capital) to do good things for humankind and change the world in a positive way. I strongly advocate avoiding what I term "negative-karma" investments. Here are two examples, though I am sure there are many more. In real estate, one can often reap short-term financial gains by taking advantage of other people's misfortune. You might buy trust deeds with extremely low loan-to-equity terms (40% or lower usually) from borrowers who are unlikely to be able to pay the loan so that you can purposely foreclose on a desired property. There are actually mortgage companies that specialize in such things.

One famous example is that of a partnership founder who actually sought out alcoholics in Oakland and offered loans on their property, realizing that few of them would ever be able to repay. The partnership returned 30 percent to 40 percent a year for the first few years until someone put a bullet through the general partner's head. Do not try to take advantage of people to make money—try to add real value in a positive way. Another example is the use of tax liens. Many states now allow for excessive interest rates or even foreclosure of delinquent tax liens on property, which investors can finance for the tax authorities. Helping the government to steal property out from under people and enforce excessively high tax rates is not my idea of making the world a better place. We have already seen the effects of high taxes in Chapter 6—voting for and advocating the advantages of lower taxes is a better approach than becoming a tax collector with your capital. It is not what I personally would want to be remembered for. Nor does making money require you to be a cruel jerk or to side with evil. Life is too short to have people hating you for what you do with your capital—particularly when you can use it for so many purposes that are positive forces in the world.

The bottom line is that REITs and specific properties with special characteristics make up fair diversifications and should particularly be included in portfolios when they meet our selection criteria. Trust deeds are an excellent anchor that can help dampen market volatility effects on your portfolio and are especially good investments for conservative investors who find low double-digit returns are acceptable in the long term.

Arbitrage Funds

Although selected trust deeds can act as an effective anchor to your portfolio, providing minimally acceptable returns through thick and thin, they have the drawback of being illiquid. What if you could find an investment that offered pretty consistent low-risk, low double-digit returns that was fairly liquid? In fact, that is what top-rated arbitrage funds offer. That is why our two favorite anchor investments are triple-i's arbitrage funds first, and Monroe Trout's futures funds second. They are some of the best uncorrelated investments we know of with minimally acceptable yet consistent thick-and-thin returns.

If you want to check out how truly uncorrelated an arbitrage fund is, verify how its net asset value behaved during the late October 1997 global stock market panic. There are several types of arbitrage funds, some of them more uncorrelated than others. Many arbitrage funds like the U.S.-based Merger Fund and GAM-arbitrage mainly deal with takeover situations in which they are often buying the consumed and selling short the buyer when a disparity in value exists. Funds like this are relatively uncorrelated with stocks, but in a panic situation they will decline in value because the stocks they own are subject to the same panic liquidation as other stocks, and because they have usually recently been bid up to levels where most investors can take a quick profit.

While these arbitrage funds are likely to be considerably less volatile than stocks, they are not totally uncorrelated. We prefer funds such as APAM, Fenchurch, Kingate Global, Farallon Fixed Income Offshore, and triple-i global, which exploit a number of derivative-valuation disparities, particularly in expiring futures versus the cheapest-to-deliver instrument. These situations have nothing to do with stock market panics and are therefore almost completely uncorrelated with stock market events. Triple-i has had only seven losing months since 1982, the largest being 1.01 percent and drawdowns under 3 percent during this entire period, while producing average annual gains of over 12 percent.

The main drawback to these types of funds is that you either need high minimum investments (Fenchurch, Farallon, and APAM) or you need an offshore account of some sort to participate in them. It is well worth the trouble, however, to open a Swiss bank account (which you can even do in retirement accounts), just to have some of triple-i's fund (Nauticus A is available through Euro-Dutch in the Bahamas as a feeder to triple-i) in your portfolio. Particularly for conservative accounts, this should be a consistent and heavy allocation. Even for aggressive accounts, some portfolio allocation is always warranted, and when equity investment is deemed risky by models, this should be one of your highest rated alternatives. An almost risk-free 12 percent a year with monthly liquidation is pretty darned hard to beat.

Global Hedge Funds

Here is another asset class that is not very highly correlated with global equities and yet produces higher average annual returns, with lower risk levels. Any large portfolio should constantly have at least 10 percent to 20 percent in either a broadly diversified grouping of top-rated hedge funds, or in a fund of funds. It is imperative that you invest in a broadly diversified grouping of different top managers for this portion of your allocation, and I would not advise ever having over 50 percent of allocation to this group (unless it is via Trout or Midas).

It is important to diversify into hedge funds because Mutual funds are mostly very constrained in terms of what they can invest in. Most mutual funds are 90 percent to 100 percent invested in their chosen asset class no matter what the environment. This is why most U.S. equity mutual funds lost over 60 percent of value during the 1973–1974 bear market. In essence, mutual funds say you are already making the decision that you want exposure to this asset class when you buy this fund, so you are responsible for this assets group's total and relative returns, to its investors. Mutual funds rarely build the flexibility into their prospectus to sell short, or invest in other asset classes in a meaningful way. Thus a good mutual fund will slightly outperform its relative asset class during bull markets and in bear markets—but it will be extremely highly correlated with its relative benchmark index, whether that be the S&P, a small cap index, a bond index, small-cap growth, large-cap value, or whatever. The bottom-line is that if the environment is poor for the underlying index of a mutual fund, a mutual fund investor is in deep trouble.

By contrast, most hedge funds are "total return" funds, meaning that their managers are striving to produce positive investment gains in any market environment. Most hedge funds are either limited partnerships with a maximum number of U.S. investors allowed (which is finally being changed) or offshore funds, where the costs and regulatory environment give the manager much more flexibility in terms of assets that can be utilized to produce profits. Most of the top managers in the world are offshore hedge-fund managers so that they have enough flexibility to use futures, short sales, currency markets, arbitrage and other vehicles to produce profits for their investors no matter what the stock and bond market environments. There are traditional hedge funds, like the Ermitage Selz Fund or Maverick Fund, that keep a relatively stable balance between longs and shorts in a particular market (United States, in this case). Traditional hedge funds are not betting on the direction the stock market moves but on the stock-picking ability both on the long and short-side of its manager. Many hedge funds utilize long and short stock positions, but also allow their managers to utilize futures, forex, Reg S, private placements, and other vehicles to produce profits. This very fact often allows hedge funds to profit from the same factors leading global equities into trouble, making them a diversification that produces higher than stock market average annual returns with risk lower than that of the stock market (for a basket of top managers). In this category, Julian Robertson's Jaguar and Momentum Stockmaster are our favorite funds.

Because of their total flexibility, some hedge funds are particularly risky. Since hedge funds often employ leverage, occasionally a sharp market move will force some manager into closing down a fund with a large or full loss to investors. The recent Asian market crisis of October 1997 and Niederhoffer's reaction to it, forced his fund out of business. A similar situation developed with a mortgage hedge fund in the 1994 bond market crash. While both of these managers had displayed large enough drawdowns in the past to not be the highest quality rated by most rating services, Niederhoffer had an impressive total return history up until 1997, albeit with occasional large drawdowns. This is why it is important to diversify among a broad array of funds. A sample fund of hedge funds that had investments in Niederhoffer's fund, for example, took a manageable 5 percent hit from his debacle, much better than the 100 percent hit investors in his fund alone took.

In addition, because there is often higher potential risk to these investments than a manager's track record will show historically, investors should be cautious about putting too much allocation into even a fund made up of a diversified group of hedge funds. A 10 percent to 20 percent allocation to a fund of funds or diversified group of highly rated funds is prudent for most portfolios; during dangerous market environments, higher return seekers could increase that to as high as 50 percent (in extreme cases) while still maintaining a historically acceptable level of risk and reward.

It is also important for investors to understand what type of hedge fund they are investing in. Opportunistic funds tend to have among the best performance history, although some macromanagers like Soros, have incredibly good performance on the whole as well. The term "hedge fund" has developed a broad set of meanings. Some funds people could describe as hedge funds are of a much lower risk posture than we have described. We would not at all be uncomfortable putting significantly higher allocations than we have described into these lower risk funds such as Trout's (which we would call a futures fund), Triple-i's (which we would call an arbitrage fund), or the funds I consult for, the Midas Fund (which follow the strategies described in this book to try and achieve very low-risk above-average returns) and Midas High Yield Fund (which follows a much more conservative strategy aimed at capital preservation first, and focuses mainly on bonds and high yield strategies).

Hedge funds are more likely to produce a long-run consistent profit performance than are stock funds. Stock funds can produce high teen average annual returns for a decade or more during a secular bull market, and then all of a sudden produce negative annual returns for the next decade, as we have seen. Hedge funds may have periods of very sharp gains and then periods of small gains and an occasional loss, but losses for many years in a row are much less likely because they are not dependant on bull markets for their gains. Hedge funds get their gains from the superior vehicle selection and trend identification of their managers. If the global secular bull market in equities stalls, an investor is much more likely to achieve profits by investing in someone like Julian Robertson or George Soros, who has produced profits in many types of environments being both long and short, than investing with Fidelity Magellan, for example. If you're investing for the long term, it is much better to allow a top manager to have the flexibility to adapt to changing environments. Think how much the environment has changed in the past 30 years; it may change even more in the next 30 years. Knowing that, would you prefer a manager to be flexible, or one who is tied down to investing in just one asset class?

For my own money, I also prefer the incentive structure of a hedge fund. Most hedge funds pay managers very sparingly unless they produce profits, which they get a piece of. While mutual fund managers will get paid a similar salary if they are up or if they lose 50 percent (while the market is down 60%), hedge fund managers are only paid when they produce profits for you. The bottom line is that I think hedge funds belong in most investors' portfolios. The next questions then become—which hedge funds, and how does one invest?

While there are some private partnerships for large accredited investors in the United States, the only true hedge fund available inside the United States for smaller investors is Caldwell & Orkin Market Opportunity Fund (COAGX), which can be bought through most brokers such as Schwab. While this excellent hedge fund is always long and short the U.S. market and has the flexibility to adjust its net long or net short position, it is limited to this arena. It is thus much more likely to be able to profit from a bear market than most other mutual funds, but does not have the ideal flexibility we prefer when investing in only one fund. But if you are going to stick to the United States, this is probably your best bet, and it is run by two excellent managers. There is also a new limited liability partnership called Plutus

(650-233-9091) that provides investors a way to legally access many top hedge funds for a low minimum.

However, if investors take the simple step of just opening a Swiss or offshore bank account, a world of new opportunities opens up. (Plutus will give investors legal access to this world within the United States.) While offshore funds aren't allowed to have U.S. investors directly, since Swiss and most offshore banks buy their funds via an omnibus account, U.S. investors can have access to offshore funds through offshore bank accounts. With offshore status, there are some excellent funds of funds that allow a small investor to get a diversified holding of many of the world's top hedge funds. Our suggested starting points would be either *Haussmann Holdings NV* ($100,000 minimum, Netherlands Antilles 514-393-1690), one of the oldest multimanager funds of funds available, or *Momentum Rainbow Fund* ($25,000 minimum, Bermuda 441-71-581-5841).

Other funds of funds include *Fraternity Fund* (John Anthony, $25,000 minimum, 599-9-671-922), which is a way for investors to own a broad array of the funds under management by Soros Fund Management. Momentum Performance Strategies Limited in Bermuda (441-71-581-5841) also offers a broad list of funds of funds in the hedge fund arena, including *Momentum All-weather*, which combines Monroe Trout's fund with the Sandalwood Fund, which is itself a fund of funds in distressed debt securities; *Momentum Universal Hedge*, a fund of hedge funds; and Momentum Emerald. *Altin, Ltd.* (Switzerland, 4141-760-6257) is another relatively new entrant to the fund of funds universe, which offers an excellent selection of top-rated low- and high-risk hedge funds. And investors with offshore accounts can also always buy the *Midas Fund*, Cayman Islands (contact Mark Boucher 1-650-233-9091, fax 233-9092), which mimics the investment strategy described in this book, as well as its more conservative brother *Midas High Yield Fund*, Cayman Islands. The new U.S. LLP, Plutus will give U.S. investors legal access to these funds as well (650-233-9091).

Even relatively cautious investors will benefit from the true diversification offered by funds of hedge funds, and should allocate at least 10 percent to this asset class. More aggressive investors could put 15 percent to 25 percent into these funds as a long-term holding. Be sure to stick mainly with funds of funds, and only those that are investing in some of the world's top managers.

Resource and Commodity Futures Funds

Probably one of the best diversifications for global stock funds are resource or futures funds. While some commodity funds have been given a bad name, many of the top managers in the world on both a risk and reward basis are either futures fund managers or else rely heavily on futures for their profitability. We have already discussed how the secular inflation that hurts stocks often plays right into the hands of managers of futures funds. With top managers who can produce gains in nearly any environment, this area is likely to improve long-run portfolio profitability in addition to dampening any negative stock market periods. Just as in global hedge funds, however, it is critical that you stick with only the very top of the proven managers—or funds of funds based on them.

I advocate a two-tiered approach to investing in commodity funds. The *first* is to *build a core position of 10 percent to 15 percent in top funds* of funds based on the best managers in the world. *Our overall favorite futures fund is one managed by Monroe Trout,* via either *Momentum Assetmaster* (Bermuda, 441-71-581-5841) or *Oceanus Fund* (Bahamas, contact Jay Tausche, 1-316-267-9227). Trout has managed to produce mid-double-digit annual gains with drawdowns under 10 percent and profits in 8 out of every 10 months. Trout's funds, along with triple-i's arbitrage funds are my favorite safe haven. Trout has the extra advantage of being able to produce higher profit potential as well.

Once you have some Trout in your portfolio, I like either funds of funds or else a self-made grouping of at least three other managers. Here are some of my favorites. *Commodities Corp Switzerland* (41-22-346-1400) is our favorite fund of funds in the commodity region. This fund has produced better than S&P average annual returns with lower drawdowns and higher reliability by investing in many of the world's top commodity fund managers. The only setback to this fund is high minimums, in the $1,000,000 and up range. *GAM US$ Trading Fund* (Isle of Man, 441-624-632-700) is our next favorite. Caxton Global Investments Ltd. (Bermuda, 44-295-8617) is also an excellent high-return bond for $1,000,000 and up. Finally, for the very small investor and U.S.-based as well, is *Shearson Diversified Futures* (1-800-825-7171, $5,000 minimum, pensions and IRAs okay).

Next we like some of the premier independent manager funds such as *Nauticus C*-Tudor (Jay Tausche, 1-316-267-9227), managed by the legendary Paul Tudor Jones, and *Chesapeake Fund* ($25,000 minimum, pensions and IRAs okay, contact Richard Bornhoft 303-572-1000), managed by one of the top turtles in the world, Jerry Parker, Jr. Both *Hasenbicler AG.* (Eschenbachgasse 11, A-1010 Vienna, Austria, 43-1-587-3344) and *Medallion-B* (Jay Tausche, 1-316-267-9227) are also favorite funds, but these only make sense if the premium over net asset value they charge is less than 5 percent. Investors should use these funds to form their core holdings in futures funds.

After investors have a core holding of 10 percent to 15 percent in the top-rated all environment futures funds, I suggest potentially adding to a group of more commodity price sensitive futures funds and instruments when our commodity timing models dictate good potential uptrends in resources and industrial commodities.

To review the basics of the industrial commodity price cycle, which is linked to the ALC, historically commodity prices tend to bottom and get support whenever they sell below the average cost of production long enough to cause cutbacks in production. Producers cut back or shutdown when they cannot make a profit due to lower prices, and eventually supply falls to a depressed level of demand. Inventories and stock of commodities fall off when they are undervalued. Goods do not move as quickly when demand is weak, so why hold them in storage? As the Austrian Liquidity Cycle moves toward increased growth rates, demand suddenly begins to heat up a little because the economy needs more raw commodities to produce the higher supply of finished goods being demanded by consumers. Low inventories are quickly drained. Very quickly, shortages develop in raw industrial commodities. Now production is at a relatively low level that cannot pick up immediately because commodities are grown or mined with at least a one-year lag (in general). So rising demand exists with very little flexibility in production. Prices begin to move up and another upwave in the commodity cycle has begun.

Intermediate producers see prices moving higher and they respond by beginning to accumulate inventory to avoid having to pay higher prices down the road. Demand picks up in response to inventory buildup by intermediate producers, and prices rise further. Excess demand leads to shortages, and shortages lead to panic by some producers who must have the raw commodities to produce the goods they produce—prices are bid up higher and at a faster rate. Economic growth in the whole economy begins to overheat and demand for raw commodities is at a peak level. Producers of raw commodities expand their growing or mining in response to higher prices, but it will not take effect until it is already too late. Eventually, demand falls back down at about the same time that the onslaught of new supply for increased production hits the market. Prices retreat into a sharp downtrend as demand falls and supply increases. So goes the classic commodity cycle.

What this analysis suggests is that we can apply timing principles to raw industrial commodity trends in much the same way that we apply them to bond and stock trends. It also suggests that one of the main engines fueling higher industrial commodity prices is increasing global growth.

Our model has three parts:

1. Look for evidence of increasing global growth via either an increase in the Organization for Economic Cooperation and Development (OECD) industrial production figures; or a rising OECD Leading Economic Indicator Diffusion Index that is above the current OECD industrial production rate.

2. Look for technical momentum in the Commodity Research Bureau (CRB) metals index to lead technical momentum in the CRB raw industrials index via (a) a weekly close by the CRB metals index that is 5 percent or more above the lowest weekly close since the uptrend began; and (b) a weekly close by the CRB raw industrial index that is 4 percent or more above the lowest weekly close since the uptrend began.

3. Exit on any move down by the weekly CRB metals index close by 5 percent or more from its highest weekly close since the uptrend began, and a move down by the CRB raw industrial index weekly close of 4 percent from its highest weekly close since the uptrend began.

Basically, we need evidence of stronger economic growth developing and confirmation of a move up by both CRB metals and CRB raw industrial commodities. During these periods, commodity indexes and funds generally move up at a 23 percent annual rate, allowing tremendous opportunities to resource investors. Take advantage of these trends by loading up on commodity index and index sensitive commodity funds.

Investors can buy Goldman Sachs index futures (for aggressive investors) or buy the U.S. mutual fund based on the Goldman Sachs commodity index, Oppenheimer Real Asset Fund (QRAAX, for conservative investors), along with index-sensitive commodity funds such as Di Tomasso's AGF 20/20 Managed Futures Fund (Canada, 416-367-3981) and ED&F Man's AHL Commodity Fund (Dublin, $30,000 minimum, 1-305-539-9047). The nice thing about these trends is that they usually coincide with an economic over-heating that eventually produces a more negative stock environment at the same time that these funds are gaining most rapidly. Therefore, commodity futures funds should become yet another arrow in the quiver of global investors. Use top all-around managers for consistent diversification as well as adding to commodity funds that are economically sensitive during clear increasing global growth trends.

SUMMARY

In studying alternative asset classes and ways for investors to utilize them, we learned first that *mixing disparate risky investments lowers portfolio risks while raising returns.* It is important to understand how and why this operates and under what conditions it is true. Next, we looked at bonds and discovered that there are many types of bonds we can rotate among to fit the economic environment for maximum profit. In addition, a core bond timing model and several other models help us key in on when bonds offer superior risk/reward potential compared with other asset classes.

We discussed our Gold-Silver GMI timing system, and how it has kept us out of a negative asset class during negative periods. We looked at Real Estate, and REITS, and how to use them in a portfolio. We also discussed how trust deeds (or short-term mortgages) can become part of the core anchor of a portfolio by producing consistent double-digit gains annually.

We then looked at a new asset class to most readers, arbitrage funds and analyzed why the top funds in this class offer superior double-digit consistent performance and should be included in every portfolio as an anchor of performance.

After that, we delved into the world of global hedge funds and explained why most portfolios should have some exposure to a fund comprised of the top hedge funds in the world as a core position. It became clear that hedge funds and futures funds offer superior diversification with stock funds because they are often able to profit especially strongly from the exact variables that cause stock funds trouble in producing gains. And finally we reviewed how to use futures funds—first with Trout and funds of top-rated futures funds as core holdings, and next by using our commodity timing model to tell you when resources offer superior opportunities for profits.

In Chapter 9, we discuss ways for putting together all that we have learned so far into a fully integrated portfolio allocation and management system to help build high profits with low risk on a consistent basis far beyond what is possible solely with global equities.

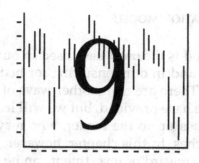

Asset Allocation Models and Global Relative Strength Analysis— Constructing a Portfolio

In Chapter 8, we examined asset classes that make up truly disparate investments, which are much better matched with traditional assets in a diversified portfolio. We also developed flexible timing models for many asset classes that were similar to the timing model we developed for global equities utilizing technicals, valuation, and liquidity.

USING ASSET ALLOCATION MODELS

The reader can use all these tools in many ways. We are going to suggest two possible alternatives. The first is to create an improved static asset allocation model for three relative risk postured investors. The second is to use all of the models and information developed thus far along with a new tool called "global asset-class relative strength analysis" to develop a flexible asset allocation system that strives to be diversified yet is limited to the top risk/reward areas on the globe for every environment.

329

The second method is the one I have used in our *Portfolio Strategy Letter* since 1992, and in our consulting for hedge fund management since 1989. There are many other ways of using the wealth of information we have provided, but we will leave alternative innovative techniques up to the reader, who may focus on one or two such approaches. In this chapter, however, we illustrate that the long-run risk/reward of investment can be improved so dramatically with the two main asset allocation techniques we advocate, that most investors will want to use one of these methods for at least a core part of their overall portfolio.

Table 9.1 shows comparative risks for investments. We have already learned that conventional buy-and-hold investing can involve very large risks. The long-run drawdown of holding U.S. and international stocks since World War II, for example, has been around 50 percent, while the long-run drawdown of holding U.S. bonds has been around 21 percent. And we have learned techniques for improving both the return and risk posture of these investments via timing models. Our stock timing model utilizes the 40-week moving average of T-bonds, T-bills, and a stock index for each country, along with a relative strength gauge to help us focus in on the top global equity environments and to avoid potentially negative periods. We learned about the bond-bill-utility bond model, which can also help drastically cut the drawdown of investing in bonds while improving their return. And we learned similar timing models for precious metals stocks and for resource price-sensitive funds.

When we allocate in a static portfolio, it makes sense to look for a superior risk/reward ratio in any allocation we give to global equities. Certainly, if we gain reward and reduce risk when we use our timing models for investments in global equities, bonds, gold, and commodities, we can gain even more advantage by combining these models and using each one for each asset class in our portfolio. This then represents the asset-class category "flexible" shown on Table 9.1. Thus "global stock flexible" means we are using our global stock timing model for this portion of our allocation (the return is computed as the lowest of either the relative country index return or the return of all stocks meeting our criteria combined, if such information is available) to reduce risk and increase long-term profitability. Bonds "flexible" means we are using our Heine Model on a

Table 9.1 **THE MAGIC OF REAL DIVERSIFICATION AMONG TRULY DISPARATE ASSETS**

Asset Class	Conventional Conservative (%)	Our Systematic Static Conservative (%)	Conventional Moderate Risk (%)	Our Suggested Moderate Risk Static (%)	Conventional Aggressive (%)	Our Suggested Aggressive Static (%)	Our Suggested Aggressive Static (%)
U.S. stocks	33.0		50.0		33.0		
U.S. small caps					33.0		
U.S. stocks flexible							
International stocks					33.0		
Global flexible		20.0		30.0		40.0	60.0
Bonds	33.0		50.0				
One-year bonds							
Bonds flexible		20.0		20.0		15.0	20.0
Junk bonds		5.0		5.0			
Gold and silver equities flexible		5.0					
REITs							
Trust deeds (1 year)		10.0		5.0		5.0	
Arb funds (III)		10.0		10.0		5.0	10.0
Hedge fund of funds (Haussmann)		5.0		10.0		10.0	15.0
Trout		10.0		10.0		5.0	15.0
Futures fund of funds (Com Corp)		10.0		10.0		20.0	30.0
Real assets							
Real assets flexible		5.0					
Cash—T-bills	33.0						
1970–1997 average annual return	10.3	est. 13.8	11.8	est. 15.5	14.9	est. 17.0	20.0
1970–1997 reliability	79.0	90.0	68.0	89.0	65.0	86.0	79.0
1970–1997 maximum drawdown	23.5	11.0	33.0	14.2	54.0	15.3	18.6
Long-run returns (est.)	8.0	12.0	9.0	14.0	12.0	15.0	18.0
Long-run reliability (est.)	70.0	85.0	62.0	82.0	60.0	80.0	70.0
Long-run maximum drawdown (est.)	25.0	15.0	36.0	17.0	60.0	20.0	30.0

long-term bond fund for that portion of our allocation. "Real assets flexible" uses the change in the cash Goldman Sachs commodity index for buy periods of our resource model. "Gold and silver equities flexible" uses the return of the GMI for periods when both gold models were positive, and so on. By combining the lower drawdowns and higher returns of our global equity model with the lower drawdown and higher returns of our bond and other asset-class models, we can generate a portfolio that is much more reliable in producing gains in every year, and with much higher long-run returns than we could get without such a combination. If we can then further add to such a portfolio more diversification among other asset classes that are truly disparate investments, we can enhance gains, reliability, drawdown, and volatility even more.

The result of all this can be dramatic for investors, as is evident by comparing a conventional conservative portfolio found in most asset allocation research, with a portfolio that combines assets that are more disparate and asset classes utilizing timing models. The conventional conservative asset allocation is one-third U.S. stocks (we used the S&P total return), one-third bonds (we used 20-year T-bond total return), and one-third cash (we used 3-month T-bill total return). This is for an investor near retirement who is less concerned with annual return than with principal preservation. Since 1970, this mix of assets has produced around a 10.3 percent average annual return (not compound annual return, but average annual return), produced a positive gain 79 percent of the time, and had a maximum drawdown of a whopping 23.5 percent. And remember that more than half of this period was during one of the largest secular bull markets in stock and bond markets this century. If we do our best to estimate the average annual returns of similar such assets this century, we come up with a more realistic estimate of true probable gains in the long run, which come out to about an 8 percent average annual return, making money in 70 percent of years, and having a maximum drawdown near 25 percent. Somehow, this does not sound very appetizing to most conservative investors.

Can we improve this classic static asset allocation choice for the conservative investor? In a statically allocated portfolio designed for a cautious investor, we diversify extremely broadly without more than 20 percent in any one asset class and make sure that we have lots of disparate investments. Like the high-cash position of the conventional portfolio, we put 30 percent in anchor investments such as arbitrage, Trout, and one-year trust deeds. We then diversify broadly among all the asset classes we have covered, with our highest concentration (20%) in flexible global bonds and flexible global stocks. Trout and Triple-i do not have historical track records going all the way back to 1970. To account for any such fund without a long-enough history, we assume the investors substituted the one-year bond for these investments in years prior to their being tradable, and in addition we use the worst year of each fund's return and add it at the worst possible time for the rest of the portfolio twice as often as each respective fund had a single-digit return year or lower during its actual trading history. In this way, *we are being very conservative in our estimate* of likely returns for years before these funds began trading.

The result is something conservative investors can be much more excited about. We have cut the maximum drawdown for this period from 23.5 percent to 11 percent, and investors using such an allocation can realistically expect a maximum drawdown of around 15 percent over the long run. Not only have we slashed drawdown by 53 percent, but we have also given our investor a portfolio that will make money 90 percent of years instead of 79 percent, and returns an average of 13.8 percent instead of an average of 10.3 percent since 1970. Over the long run, an investor can realistically expect a 12 percent return with 85 percent reliability instead of an 8 percent average annual return with 70 percent reliability. This 34 percent increase in average annual return with a 14 percent increase in reliability and a 53 percent cut in maximum drawdown shows the magic of combining truly disparate asset classes and using timing models on risky asset classes.

The moderate investor has even more to gain. The conventional moderate-risk portfolio is half bonds and half stocks. Since 1970, this combination has produced an 11.8 percent average annual gain, profits in 68 percent of years, and a hefty 33 percent maximum drawdown. We put 50 percent in flexible global stocks and flexible bonds, 25 percent in anchors like Trout, arbitrage funds, and trust deeds, 5 percent in junk bonds, and 10 percent each in futures and hedge funds of funds. The portfolio is still very diversified, but more concentrated in higher return investments. The average annual return jumps from 11.8 percent to 15.5 percent, the portfolio is profitable in 89 percent of years instead of 68 percent, and the maximum drawdown plummets from a heart-stopping 33 percent to just 14.2 percent. Long-run investors should expect something on the order of 14 percent average annual returns on a 17 percent maximum drawdown with this portfolio, instead of 9 percent on a 36 percent drawdown.

Our aggressive suggested static portfolio produces similar across-the-board gains. The conventional aggressive portfolio invests one-third each in U.S. stocks, in international stocks (world index in $ terms total return), and in small cap (Dimensional Advisors 9/10 Small Company Fund is proxy)—all three of which are highly correlated. Instead, we diversify among seven high-return categories that are also disparate investments and relatively uncorrelated. Our highest concentration is in flexible global stocks followed by futures funds of funds, flexible bonds, and hedge funds of funds. The result is a 17 percent average annual gain versus a 14.9 percent return, profits in 86 percent of years versus 65 percent of years, and most significantly, a drop in maximum drawdown from a whopping 54 percent to an acceptable 15.3 percent. Realistically, investors can expect 15 percent plus annual gains, 80 percent reliability, and a maximum drawdown around 15 percent with this mix.

We also put in an even more aggressive posturing for your information, which uses some leverage (50%) but still manages to keep drawdowns to below the conventional "conservative" level. Here we increase our allocations to global flexible and futures funds, as well as maintaining an anchor in Trout and arbitrage, which can pay for our leverage. Under this portfolio, we achieve a 20 percent annual rate of return since 1970, while still keeping our maximum drawdown under 19 percent for that 28-year period.

It is significant that our most aggressive posture actually produces almost double the return of the conventional conservative portfolio (20% versus 10.3%) while cutting the drawdown from 23.5 percent to just under 19 percent and keeping reliability the same at 79 percent. This may allow investors to rethink their definitions of what conservative and aggressive really are. A conservative investor who could stomach a 23.5 percent drawdown before surely can accept the performance of an aggressive investor using our suggested allocations. Realize too that we have made very conservative estimates in coming up with these calculations. For example, we assumed no real benefit from stock selection.

Investors should also note that even if you take out our timing models and use the S&P and world index returns for stocks and the U.S. 20-year bond total return for bonds, adding truly disparate investments in the allocations we have shown still manages to produce significantly lower drawdowns and higher returns than conventional allocation shows in every portfolio demonstrated in Table 9.1.

Our most conservative allocation actually produces more average annual profit for the 1970–1997 period than do either U.S. or global stocks, with a drawdown that is 77 percent less than either single asset class.

Thus our combination of timing models and of mixing truly disparate investments can show long-term investors dramatic gains in returns while cutting risk to the bone—we have largely achieved our goal of significantly improving risk/rewards to investing.

Most investors should pick a category of risk and suggested allocation and stick closely to the allocation we have given. This means setting up an offshore bank account of some type for most U.S. investors, or using Plutus LLP to access other funds, but doing so is clearly worth the trouble. For those hell-bent on staying purely U.S., COAGX is the available hedge fund, Shearson Diversified Futures and Chesapeake are the available futures funds, and Merger Fund (MERFX) is the available arb fund. While none of these is my first or even second pick, you should derive significant long-run benefits from using these in the appropriate portfolio mix.

Investors should realize however that *the world is fast-changing, and there are limitations to static asset allocations.* The more experienced an investor you are, and the more proficient you become at using the models and tools we have described, the more profit you will gain from a flexible asset allocation methodology in the long run. After all, the ideal asset allocation method concentrates most of one's risk and capital in the best risk/reward investments on the planet at any one time. In our next section we describe tools for determining when to stray from our proposed static allocations to concentrate more heavily in a particularly advantageous asset class.

GLOBAL RELATIVE STRENGTH: RADAR SCREEN
FOR FLEXIBLE ASSET ALLOCATION

Our philosophy and approach toward flexible asset allocation can be summarized as follows: *invest selectively and carry a big net.*

Investing selectively means that we try to go only with the real cream in terms of trends. First, we want our potential investment to show up on our radar screen of top relative strength compared with all other investments and asset classes on the globe. Next we want the right technical configuration. We want evidence of a strong runaway trend, for the trend to be clearly in the direction we are looking at, and for some sort of low-risk, highly reliable pattern to be developing so that we can enter with reliability and low risk. We also want as many variables as possible in our favor. We want the Austrian Liquidity Cycle (ALC) to be favorable, valuation to be fair or good, and for there to be some reason for expecting the trend to be able to continue for at least two years into the future. The country of the potential investment should be among the top ideas from the perspectives of our models and our understanding of the dynamics of growth. We would like a technology gap, demographic factor, or some trend or theme to be part of the wind behind the sails of our potential investment. And we would want our best understanding of the situation to be in favor of our investment. When asked, we would like to be able to explain what makes this investment one of the top 10 to 20 trends available today. What we are really looking for in a potential investment is an alignment of as many of the things we have discussed in this book as possible.

Carrying a big net means looking at and analyzing every possible investment we can find. William O'Neil in his great services does a tremendous job of looking at his definition of relative strength across most of the stocks available in the U.S. market. That is fine when the U.S. market is king. But why stop there? The investment world is our oyster as global investors. Why not compare global stocks, global bonds, hedge funds, futures funds, arbitrage funds, small cap U.S., small cap Japan, large cap value, small cap value, Portuguese banks, trust deeds, and on and on. What we strive to do is look at everything out there that is possible to categorize and invest in. Every asset class and every group that we can find. Then we do an asset-class relative strength (RS) analysis, and countrywide relative strength analysis of total returns. And finally we do a global relative strength analysis across all the asset classes and groups that we have looked at. We do this analysis for each asset class, for each country we are interested in, and globally using a relative strength of 1 week, 1 month, 2 months, 3 months, 6 months, 9 months, 12 months and a (2×1 week, 2×1 month, 2×2 months, 2×3 months, and 1×6, 9, and 12 months) weighted average. We then look at each of these relative strength durations and see what hits our top 10 or 20 categories in each one (or our bottom 10 or 20 if looking for short categories). This look at relative strength (all based on U.S. dollar total returns) of varying durations and among different asset classes, countries, and globally becomes our radar screen for scouting for potential top trends to place in our investment portfolio.

So not only do we want to be selective, but we want our potential investment's category to come up on one of our relative strength radar screens. Investors can gain an incredible feedback loop of information from studying these radar screens. Note that the radar screens do not include individual equities, but do include various sectors. We have learned a great deal about sector movement from studying our radar screens over the years. Remember that we do not just want to see a group come up on our screens, we want to see it and understand why it is likely to continue to move further up the duration of our radar screens for a prolonged period of time.

For example, a large number of recurring observations can be made in many countries fairly consistently across times during similar liquidity cycles. Figure 9.1 helps illustrate one of the observations that seems to work across countries.

A large body of data in the United States in particular seems to support the thesis that small caps deliver substantially higher total returns than mid caps or large caps over the long run, albeit with substantially higher risk. And in fact, much of the better individual selection screens we found to work consistently were more or less designed to catch smaller cap or lower mid-cap issues on the verge of shooting into higher cap categories.

The long-run analysis often stops just as it is starting to bear fruit. Amazingly, much research shows the outperformance of small caps long-term, stops there, suggests some long-term allocation to small caps, and simply moves on. This is similar to finding a potentially huge vein of gold on a piece of land and then

Figure 9.1 SMALL CAPS NEED TOP-LINE GROWTH

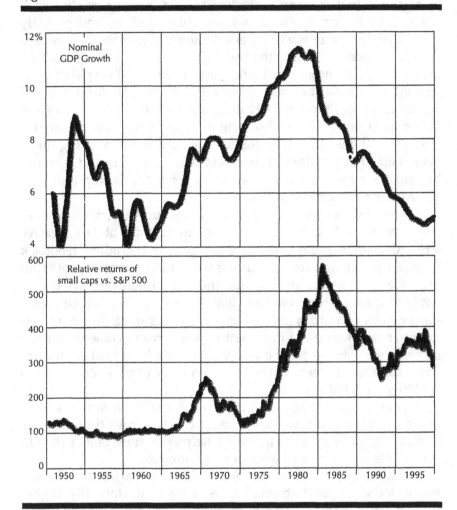

Note: Small-cap stocks outperformed big stocks during times when nominal GDP was booming, but have lagged when it was slowing. Could nominal GDP be bottoming?

Source: Ibbotson Associates, based on model portfolios during 1926–1996. Used with permission. Copyright © 1998 Ibbotson Associates, Inc. All rights reserved. (Certain portions of this work were derived from copyrighted works of Roger G. Ibbotson and Rex Sinquefield.)

immediately selling the property without doing any further research to see how much gold is there, and how best to mine it. If you look closer and try to understand the how and why of a potentially lucrative piece of information uncovered by research you will often learn not only where the fruit of profits lie, but also when they are most ripe for the picking.

Although small caps show marked outperformance over the long run, they generally outperform in lightning streaks of time and spend long periods underperforming significantly, especially during weak market periods. Do these streak periods of small caps have anything in common? As Figure 9.1 shows, the outperformance of small caps correlates almost perfectly with rising periods of nominal GDP growth. This is why many observers often conclude that the market top is not in until small caps have their day. As most bull markets since World War II have ended with economic overheating, this has indeed been the right environment for small caps. Recent history confirms this analysis. If you look at the largest nominal GDP increasing quarters of 1991–1993, you will find small cap outperformance. 1994's soft landing hit small caps very hard. The recovery since 1995 failed to generate much nominal growth acceleration, hence large-cap outperformance. Finally in mid-1997 nominal growth began to accelerate, even reaching what Fed Greenspan described as unsustainable growth. During this period, small caps had their best rally in years. However as soon as the Asian crisis begin to imply slower growth in the United States potentially, smaller caps took a much bigger hit than large caps in the October decline and have been much more slow to recover as evidenced by the performance of the Russell 2000. Do not expect a seriously long-lived outperformance until stronger growth and accelerating nominal GDP growth are evident.

The same analysis applies to other countries such as Japan. Japanese OTC companies exploded into a historic degree of outperformance starting in the summer of 1989 when overheating in the Japanese economy was beginning and nominal growth was accelerating. While the Nikkei peaked at the end of December 1989, the Japanese OTC market continued on a tear, gaining another 40 percent before peaking at the end of June 1990. In this way, the Japanese secular peak was very similar to the 1972 period in the United States when an overheating economy sent the U.S. OTC into new high ground while the rest of the market had trouble.

Since the mid-1990 peak, however, the Japanese OTC market has faced decelerating growth, and it has declined by over 80 percent, while the Nikkei is off just 48 percent in the same period.

Knowing this, an investor can watch for small caps to begin hitting radar screens whenever the prospect for improving growth is present in a country and begin positioning in the top companies meeting our criteria. Conversely, if several small-cap indexes for a particular country begin to hit our radar screens in succession, check out whether improved growth prospects are developing. If there is evidence supporting higher growth rates, you can position on a new trend that is likely to produce especially large profits. Conversely if little evidence of improved growth is available, you can wait for RS charts further out to show small caps along with secure evidence of quickening growth before emphasizing small caps in your allocation. It may just be a blip on the radar screen caused by a short-term sharp correction. What you are looking for is lots of confirming evidence.

In most countries, investors are better off shifting from small-cap growth to small cap value once serious overheating begins—and be sure to jump ship when rates start to send short rates and bonds on the wrong side of their 40-week moving averages. The more experience you get looking at the radar screens in conjunction with the ALC, understanding, and other tools we have developed, the more quickly you can find a group or asset class that is likely to outperform and is better emphasized in a portfolio.

In 1995, for example, we matched the S&P's hefty returns without much equity exposure at all. Early in the year, we were 70 percent allocated to selected bonds, mostly in New Zealand and South Africa. Another key point is illustrated by New Zealand bonds that repeats itself again and again. In 1993–1994 New Zealand's economy began to overheat with its inflation rate rising to levels under which their central bank would not receive a salary. Naturally, New Zealand's central bank responded by tightening credit and proceeded to engineer a steeply inverted yield curve. New Zealand's currency was among the strongest across the entire set of durations in our global currency RS analysis. Thus when New Zealand's bonds begin to hit our radar screen for RS and clear signs of economic slowdown had developed along with positive technical signs near the end of 1994, we knew we had the potential for currency gains and strong capital gains from holding Kiwi bonds.

By the time we took profits in mid-1995, we had over 20 percent in total returns from these bonds, which was much higher than most global equity markets experienced in early 1995. And it was in a trend that had everything going for it so that it seemed reliable: valuation was very positive, following an inversion is the best time to buy bonds, technical factors were newly positive, and the ALC showed strong potential for the stringent central bank to make bondholders happy, while real interest rates were over 8 percent. By almost all forms of analysis, it looked like a slam dunk, so we allocated the maximum allowed by our money management rules to this situation. This is exactly what flexible asset allocation is all about—being able to position your capital in the trends that appear to be among the best on the planet by all the forms of analysis developed in this book.

We suggest experienced investors start off with our static allocation model that fits the profile they are looking for. Then begin watching our RS radar screens carefully. Strive to find trends that are developing that have many factors in their favor and that look to be among the best developing trends you can think of. Only enter on technical buy or sell patterns and with limited risk. Start out with 1 percent risk per trade. Begin allocating slightly more to these situations as you gain confidence both watching the radar screens and identifying better than average trends and the right instruments to exploit them. Soon you will be able to flexibly adjust your optimum static allocation toward the best trends and instruments on the globe. You can always look to our services or other top services such as Daily Graphs, Bank Credit Analyst, Portfolio Strategy Letter, Zachs, Value Line, Formula Research, and the others that we list in the appendix for help in melding your individual strategy.

Finally, it is important for investors to look carefully at applying these techniques in history to get a true picture of what it is like to follow such a strategy. Our strategies, like most, are fairly simple when understood fully, but they are not easy. It is one thing to see long-term performance numbers, it is quite another to live through the hardships necessary to achieve those numbers. It is easy to remember your strategy is sound when it is performing well. It is much more difficult when your strategy is underperforming.

Our European money manager benefactor often lamented getting heat from clients during the final phase of a bull market in any U.S. or European market. His models would often exit prematurely and would place him in low-yielding cash during a period when euphoria was high and optimism made it seem like not being invested was foolhardy. And although we have strived to diversify and to select higher returning safe investments than cash, our own real-life experience is somewhat similar. A true weakness of our methodology is that one is often left prematurely in lower-risk vehicles while the later stages of a bull market, which are often the most explosive, roll on. Thus as the performance of the monthly recommendations made to our clients in our *Portfolio Strategy Letter* shows (see Figure 9.2), while we have managed to substantially outperform both the S&P and the World index since 1992, we substantially outperformed during the earlier stage of the liquidity cycle, and have been overly cautious during 1996 and 1997. This is the cost of avoiding risky markets—you may often miss some good ones. This may seem not so tough—

Figure 9.2 **COMPARISON OF TOTAL PSL PORTFOLIO VERSUS S&P 500 AND WORLD INDEX**

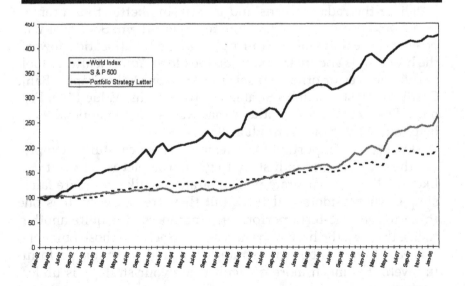

but during these periods it is not easy to be in conservative investments while every idiot is making a fortune in a particular local market. The track record we have achieved on a published monthly basis is reviewed in Figure 9.2 to show that a real-time effort at using these methodologies has largely accomplished our goal of decent performance with low risk. The funds we consult for have done even better real time during this same period. This is not just a theoretical dissertation. However, investors should understand a characteristic of this strategy—outperformance usually comes during the early phases of the Liquidity Cycle and during economic downturns. Underperformance commonly occurs during the later periods of the Liquidity Cycle. Such underperformance when everyone else is doing better is often difficult to stomach, but it is critical in avoiding the downturn from the excesses built up in the later stages of a cycle. I hope to have given you enough courage, understanding, and information that you will be able to stick to the strategy not just when it outperforms, but when it inevitably does not do as well.

SUMMARY

This book provides as much information as practicable for accomplishing our goal of producing dependable gains better than those of equities long-term with significantly lower risk. We have covered timing via ALC, valuation, and technicals to help slash the risk of global equity investing. We have covered individual equity selection criteria that took us years to research and have helped us generate huge gains for the funds we consult for. These are the criteria you should apply to outperform the country indexes in the countries you are investing in. We have covered critically important money management strategies for slashing individual vehicle, country, sector, and asset-class risk. I have tried to help you master the investment process and understand the how and why of our strategies, not just look at their performance; and to see that understanding what generates profits and how markets operate is as important to your success as any system we can give you because it will teach you to find good fish holes forever and not just point you toward good fish holes today. Next, we covered other asset classes—not just conventional ones, but asset classes that we have found are much more truly disparate than stocks and bonds so that combining them in a portfolio will give higher returns and lower risk. We covered timing systems for bonds, gold stocks, and resource-sensitive funds so that you will know when good opportunities are developing in these areas and be able to invest in them long-term with lower risk and higher returns. We covered some anchors and core holdings for your portfolio such as arbitrage funds, Trout's funds, trust deeds, and adjustable-rate junk funds. Core holdings are funds of funds in top-ranked futures managers and funds of funds dedicated to top-ranked hedge fund managers. We then went on to asset-allocation where I compared traditional allocations with ones empowered by the principles we had learned throughout the book to show you how you can now achieve better than average returns with much lower risk than you ever imagined possible. And I ended by showing you how to use our radar screens of RS rankings to help key in on the very best trends and improve on the performance of your relevant static allocation category.

I hope that throughout this process you have become a more astute and better investor, and that you will now be much better able to position your capital for the embetterment of humankind and yourself.

APPENDIX A

Strategies for Short-Term Traders

This discussion of short-term trading appears as an appendix for a very good reason: I firmly believe that most of the people trading on a short-term basis should not be doing so. Short-term trading should (1) be reserved for only a very small portion of your overall portfolio; (2) only be used by experienced investors who are already on top of global market trends in the ways advocated in this book; (3) only be used by people who have traded as a full-time business successfully for a number of years; (4) never be used by novice or beginning traders; and (5) be utilized by traders who understand that it may not consistently improve your risk/reward performance.

I have nothing against short-term trading in and of itself. In fact, I made a living trading short-term patterns for several years. And I certainly do not think that short-term trading is bad for the markets. The more short-term traders there are, the more liquid each market is, and the easier it will be for the average investor to get a quick, orderly, and minimally marked up fill on his occasional order to sell 1000 Microsoft.

On the other hand, for many if not most traders and investors, short-term trading can become almost like a drug that eats up one's time, resources, and investment capital. Anyone who has even the remotest inkling of trouble with gambling should stay as far away as possible from short-term trading.

Furthermore, traders should realize that short-term trading is a grind most of the time. Most strategies require the investor to stay glued to the screen. If you are on a bathroom break and your method signals a trade and you miss it—boom, that could be the best trade of the year. In addition, most short-term strategies have a severe weakness when compared with the trading strategies described earlier in this book—their reward/risk ratios are very poor compared with longer term strategies. The reason is simple. Short-term periods have less fluctuation to capture, so the rewards are rarely 10 or 20 times the initial risk, as can often be the case on a good intermediate-term trade lasting many months or even years.

For this reason, in the approaches suggested here to investors who are hell-bent on utilizing short-term methods, I strive to get investors to *look for short-term patterns with the potential to expand the time horizon of the trade.* For example, you want to get in on a trade with half-hourly bar chart sized risk, but you also want to look for situations where you will be holding the position for many days, if the trade turns out and can capture a decent sized move on a daily or even weekly bar chart. Similarly, if you are looking at 5-minute bars, you will want to try to find trades that have the potential of turning into decent half-hourly bar chart sized moves, maybe even a daily bar chart sized move. We are looking at shorter-term charts to try to enter what have the potential to be much longer-duration moves. This is the best way to utilize short-term approaches, because instead of facing a relatively poor reward/risk ratio (which is a time-consuming grind with little upside), investors are hunting for a home-run trade with phenomenal reward/risk occurring in a relatively short period (many days or weeks instead of many months to years).

These approaches are only for experienced professionals who can devote full time to the markets. Be sure you have mastered the other approaches in this book before looking at these methodologies. Any short-term traders who have skipped much of the book and turned directly to this section for quick gratification are missing out on much of what will help them profit most. Short-term trading involves using high leverage. And if there is anyone who needs full understanding of the global economic, liquidity, valuation, technical, and Austrian alchemy perspective, it is the person who is employing high leverage. The short-term trader will get more benefit from understanding the rest of the material in this book, than will any long or intermediate time-framed investor or trader. A thorough understanding of fuel and its impact can allow a short-term trader to avoid huge hits from unforseen shocks, as well as allow a short-term trader to focus efforts on areas with unusually high potential for longer-lasting larger profits than otherwise.

That being said, one of my companies has some short-term trading oriented courses from the late 1980s that I still sell. And Larry Connors and I are thinking of putting together an update of more current and new short-term patterns for experienced traders. Please call or write Larry if you are interested (Oceanview Financial Research, 23805 Stuart Ranch Road, Suite 245, Malibu, CA 90265; 310-317-0361).

Larry Connors is a friend, associate, and fellow hedge fund manager, who wrote *Investment Secrets of a Hedge Fund Manager*, with Blake

Hayward, and *Street Smarts,* with Linda Raschke of Market Wizard's fame, and publishes the fine monthly letter *Professional Traders Journal* (310-317-0361). The following short-term pattern for trading runaway moves was written by me for Larry's letter, and he has graciously allowed me to reprint it here (with permission) for your benefit. It is one of my favorite short-term trading methods, and illustrates how to expand the time frame of your trades.

TRADING RUNAWAY MOVES

One of the most reliable and profitable situations a stock or futures contract can develop, is after a strong breakout of a flag-type trading range. A flag trading range is a pattern where a vehicle runs up strongly and then consolidates for a prolonged period of time before breaking out to the upside again. Particularly in stocks, but also in futures, strong breakouts from flag trading ranges often lead to prolonged moves higher. In fact, simply trading flag trading ranges in their own time frame can be a very profitable endeavor.

However, for the purposes of short-term trading patterns, we will be discussing how to take advantage of these situations in order to position short-term by mixing time frames. In mixing time frames, one will often find that he/she is able to position with low, short-term bar risk distance between an open protective stop and entry, and yet participate in a move that is many, many times initial risk and develops into a longer than short-term move. This is how capital can be multiplied many-fold without significant risk—by finding low-risk trades that return many times that risk, and by finding short-term risk opportunities that have the potential to develop into longer-term moves than the original time frame one is looking at.

For our examples, and in our own use of this pattern, we first look at daily bars and then go to half-hourly bars for the pattern. In other words, we screen a half-hourly pattern with a longer-term bar chart. Even shorter-term traders could do the same thing on a shorter time frame. One could look at a half-hourly bar chart to screen 5 or 10 minute bar patterns for instance. The key point is that you are entering with entry points set on a shorter time frame—and may be able to capture a move that develops into a longer time-frame run-up in order to profit many multiples of your initial risk.

The pattern we are going to show you is called the "flag within a flag pattern."

As a brief side note, investors using these patterns should understand that they can achieve better results, both in terms of reliability and profitability, by concentrating on commodities that meet our run-away criteria and stocks that meet our runaway-up-with-fuel criteria as explained in [book Chapter 7] our Science of Trading course and published monthly in our letter to clients, *Portfolio Strategy Letter*. Adding these filters is certainly not necessary to very profitably trade these patterns, but it does also enhance results rather dramatically.

Investors lacking a list of runaway-up-with-fuel stocks, as well as all those traders seeking as many investment opportunities as possible, should go through a daily process of reviewing all the stocks on the new high list. We're looking for stocks making new highs after having just broken out of at least a 17-day flag trading range pattern. Again, the flag pattern is a sharp runup in price followed by a consolidation for 17+ days that does not retrace 38 percent of the initial runup. We are looking for prices to break out on a gap from the prior close or on a large-range day [thrust, really a TBBLBG, see Chapter 7].

Let's look at an example to clarify (Figures A.1 and A.2). Tuboscope, Inc. (symbol TUBO) began to make the 52 week new high list in mid June when it broke out of a six-month trading range. (It also met our runaway-up-with-fuel criteria). It moved up from a low of 11½ on 2/11 to 20⅜ on 7/3, an 8⅞ point move. From 20⅜ it developed a consolidation pattern that declined to 18⅝, a drop of 1¾ points, or 19.7 percent of the

Figure A.1 **TUBOSCOPE DAILY**

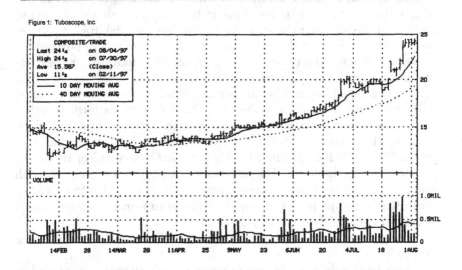

Source: Bloomberg Financial Markets. Copyright © 1998 Bloomberg LP. All rights reserved.

Figure A.2 **TUBOSCOPE HALF-HOURLY**

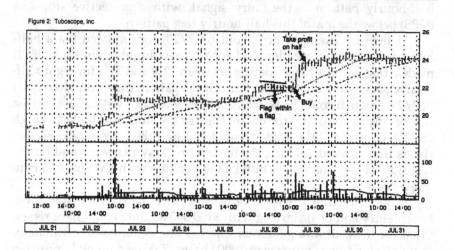

Figure 2: Tuboscope, Inc

Source: Bloomberg Financial Markets. Copyright © 1998 Bloomberg LP. All rights reserved.

prior upmove (< 38 percent). The consolidation lasted 17 days or longer before a breakout developed on a gap on 7/23. Our criteria for a flag breakout on a daily chart were met. Note that we need to first find daily flag patterns making new 52-week highs before looking for what will ultimately be our two shorter-term patterns. In this way we are adding a short-term element to an already profitable situation.

Now an investor could certainly buy the breakout and use an OPS (open protective stop) just below 18⅝ with pretty low risk for a decent trade, meeting the criteria established in our course's flag pattern. But we're going to show you how you can get far more bang for your buck by adding a short-term pattern to this already lucrative setup. We suggest investors monitoring the new high list daily put alarms above the high levels of all those stocks that have made new highs and have consolidated in a flag pattern for 17 days or more without retracing 38 percent of the prior upmove, so as not to miss an opportunity. One could use CQG, Bloomberg, TradeStation, Investigator, or even several sources on the internet (like Quote.com) to set these alarms.

The short-term flag within the longer-term breakout works as follows. Once you get alerted of a breakout or a new high following a breakout go to the half-hourly chart. Often, following an initial upthrust half hour, a stock will consolidate, making a short-term flag pattern of four bars or more than does not retrace 38 percent or more of the last half-hourly upswing. A breakout above the high bar of this half-hourly pattern is the entry signal, with a protective stop-loss (OPS) below the low of this half-hourly flag pattern.

TUBOS for example, broke out on 7/23, consolidated via a half-hourly stochastic correction and rose to new highs again on 7/28. It made a flag pattern consolidating between $22\frac{1}{4}$ and $21\frac{3}{4}$ for eight half-hourly bars before breaking to new highs again in the second half hour of 7/29, where it could be purchased at $22\frac{3}{8}$ to $22\frac{5}{16}$ with a $21\frac{5}{8}$ ops—a risk of only $\frac{3}{4}$ points. By the end of the day the stock had traded as high as $24\frac{1}{4}$, closing at $23\frac{5}{8}$. Traders could exit half the trade when original risk is first covered, making the trade a breakeven at worst and let the rest ride. This is one way to build a big position with low risk in a runaway stock.

A trader risking 1 percent of capital per trade (risk = distance between entry and ops) starting with $100,000 account could have risked $1,000 or if we allow a generous slippage and commission estimate of $\frac{1}{4}$ point, could have purchased 1000 shares. Taking a quick $\frac{1}{2}$ position profit at $23\frac{3}{8}$ to clear risk would have yielded $475 after commissions and open profits at the close were $625 on the remaining $\frac{1}{2}$ positions profit of 1.1 percent in a day with the strong possibility of being able to hang on to 500 shares of a stock that has just broken out of a trading range and is likely to move much higher with no more risk to original capital (at least theoretically) because the profit taken on the first $\frac{1}{2}$ position more than covers the risk on the second $\frac{1}{2}$. We have just locked in a large potential profit with very little risk—and a portfolio filled with several of these trades can return large amounts of profit with very little risk of capital, which is what we're trying to accomplish as traders.

Remember that once a stock or future emerges from its flag base it will go on our list to watch for this pattern each time it moves into new 52-week high territory until it gets overvalued (stock: $P/E \geq$ its five-year growth rate or its current quarterly earnings growth rate), overowned institutionally (stock: 40 percent or higher institutional + bank ownership of capitalization), overbought (weekly, daily, and monthly RSI above 85), until the trend turns (below 50 day ma is good rule of thumb but prefer GTI trend method as explained in course and coded in Investigator software), or until the Relative Strength drops below 65 on a reaction or below 80 on a new high. In other words, once a stock breaks out of a flag if it continues to not violate any of the above criteria we still watch for internal half-hourly flags on each new 52-week high because the stock still shows strong potential for a big move. The prime time to buy is just after a breakout, but one can continue to watch for this short-term pattern even if the stock has broken out recently and continues to be one of the strongest in the market as shown in the following example (Figures A.3 and A.4).

CTS first broke out of a trading range flag in early April and traded sharply higher making the new high list almost daily into early June, where it formed another flag and broke out in early July. On July 23 it made a strong close to new highs on a wide half-hourly bar. It was still undervalued via its quarterly and five-year growth rate compared to P/E, still owned less than 40 percent by institutions, not yet wildly overbought on a weekly, daily, and monthly basis all at once, was definitely in a strong uptrend with RS above 90. And making new highs yet again. It clearly qualified for a potential short-term internal flag pattern. The next morning it consolidated for five half-hourly bars below the highs of the last bar of July 23 ($75\frac{1}{2}$) with a low of $75\frac{1}{8}$. When it broke above $75\frac{1}{2}$ if you bought the high of that half hour you got in at $75\frac{5}{8}$ and could have used a 75 OPS—a risk of only $\frac{5}{8}$ of a point. 1100 shares could be purchased with 1 percent risk. July 24 closed at $79\frac{13}{16}$ a profit of 4.19 points or almost five times your initial risk! If you took quick profits on $\frac{1}{2}$ position at $76\frac{5}{8}$ you still ended up over $2,600 on the day (2.6 percent) and have no original capital at risk in a very explosive stock that has continued to move higher.

Figure A.3 **CTS DAILY**

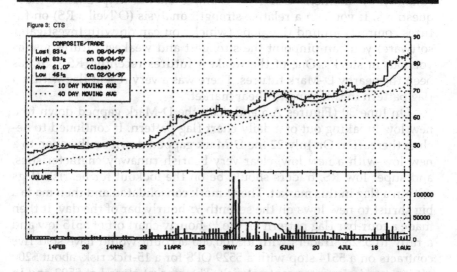

Source: Bloomberg Financial Markets. Copyright © 1998 Bloomberg LP. All rights reserved.

Figure A.4 CTS HALF-HOURLY

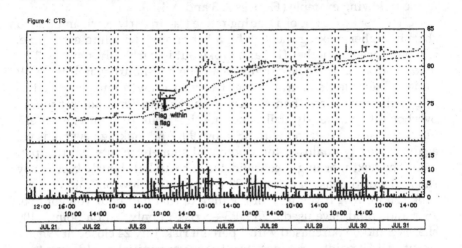

Figure 4: CTS

Source: Bloomberg Financial Markets. Copyright © 1998 Bloomberg LP. All rights reserved.

What about bear markets and what about futures. Surely if the pattern is robust it should hold up in runaway down vehicles as well as runaway up markets. Our next example should help answer those questions. If you run a relative strength analysis (O'Neil's RS) on futures contracts around the globe (which you can do with Investigator software) you can pinpoint the strongest and weakest futures just as you can in stocks. One of the weakest futures recently (RS < 5) has been the nearby D-Mark futures. There was a very recent flag within a flag pattern in this runaway bear market.

On June 30 (Figures A.5 and A.6), the D-Mark gapped down to a new low breaking out of a daily chart flag pattern. It continued to decline thereafter. On July 22 the D-Mark gapped down on the open to a new low-with a new low, clear very bearish runaway characteristics, and super low RS, traders should be on the lookout for bearish flags within a flag in this market. The D-mark consolidated and then made a big thrust to new lows on the seventh ½-hourly bar of the day. It then made a four-bar flag pattern on the ½-hourly chart off of 5515 low and a rally to 5528. Traders with a $100,000 account would have sold five contracts on a 5514 stop with a 5529 OPS for a 15-tick risk, about $200 after commissions per contract risk. The market closed at 5502 and in order to cover risk traders would have taken a quick $400 profit after

Figure A.5 D-MARK DAILY

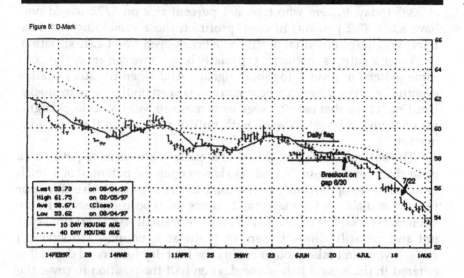

Source: Bloomberg Financial Markets. Copyright © 1998 Bloomberg LP. All rights reserved.

Figure A.6 D-MARK HALF-HOURLY

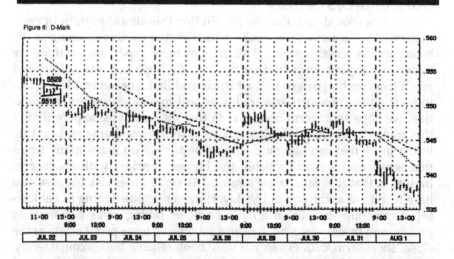

Source: Bloomberg Financial Markets. Copyright © 1998 Bloomberg LP. All rights reserved.

commissions on three contracts, keeping two open with risk more than covered by profits taken. With the D-Mark continuing to collapse and at 5385 today, traders who took a 1 percent risk on 7/22 would now have $3200 (3.2 percent) in open profit on those remaining two contracts with large potential profits on a break-even worst-case situation.

When a futures contract is especially bearish we can apply the exact same pattern in reverse for short signals. And when the stock market eventually turns lower in a bear market, we can do the same in stocks. Until such time that new 52-week lows move above new 52-week highs, we recommend investors stick with bullish patterns in the U.S. stock market.

The bottom-line is that this simple pattern allows us to get in on a good short-term day-trade, and also leaves open the potential of a much more lucrative opportunity in the some of the most explosive stocks or futures available in the markets. It allows us to position heavily in the strongest stocks, but in a way that takes very small risk to original capital and yet still allows traders to profit at sometimes astronomical rates. If you can't take enough profits the first day (or second day if it is entered in the second half of the day) on half the position to cover the risk on the remaining half then get out and wait for another opportunity. Cautious traders may only want to take trades in the first half of the day so that they don't have to take overnight risk unless they have large open profits and have booked profits on a day trade in the first half position. More cautious traders may also want to book the whole profit at the close unless the close is at least as far above your entry as your original OPS was below it.

Traders should note that we are finding this simple pattern in new-high stocks at least twice a week—which should continue as long as the broad market remains strong. This is many more opportunities than any trader can exploit with limited capital. We hope you can watch and profit from such a pattern in the future, and that it becomes a key arrow in your quiver of short-term trades toward maximum profits. In addition, we hope short-term traders note that the huge upside potential of this trade comes from taking a risk on a short-time frame and getting into a move that can last much longer and move up many many times that small initial risk. Probably the biggest problem with short-term trading is that it is rare to get a reward 10 or 20 times risk because you have to get out at the end of the day. However by positioning in vehicles set to move up sharply on a daily basis, by taking quick day-trade ½ profits, and by only staying in overnight when a large profit exists at the close, short-term traders can not only book reliable trades consistently, but can often find a ten-bagger without taking very large risks—and without having to wait years to realize it by using this pattern.

APPENDIX B

Recommended Books, Services, Data Sources, and Letters

LETTERS AND SERVICES

1. Everything by the **Bank Credit Analyst Research Group** (1002 Sherbrooke Street West, Suite 1600, Montreal, Quebec, Canada H3A 3L6; 516-499-9706). Our two favorite publications are *International Bank Credit Analyst* and *Emerging Market Analyst*, which do the best job of any service we have found of covering the liquidity cycle for most tradable countries around the world. They can provide an incredible amount of data and models to readers. Also excellent are their *Bank Credit Analyst* and *BCA Foretrends*. While these services are a bit more expensive than most newsletters, they are much more comprehensive and a bargain for what you get. You may have a bit of learning curve to get through if you are not familiar with economic jargon and concepts.

2. Back and future issues of Nelson Freeburg's **Formula Research, Inc.** ($195 per year, 4745 Poplar Avenue, Suite 307, Memphis, TN 38117; 901-756-8607). The Heine Model as well as many of our gold models and other timing models come from the excellent market timing research done by Nelson Freeburg. For the technically or system oriented trader, this service is an absolute must. Freeburg scans the globe for new ideas to put into models that beat buy and hold in each asset class applied to with lower risk on a monthly publication basis. Freeburg is not afraid to use other people's ideas

355

if they work. His service is like hiring a full-time research staff for an unbelievably low price. Highly recommended.

3. Larry Connors' **Professional Traders Journal** (Oceanview Financial Research, 23805 Stuart Ranch Road, Suite 245, Malibu, CA 90265; 310-317-0361). Particularly for technically and short-term oriented traders, this too is an unbelievably rich source of research and (computer and real-time) tested ideas to apply to improve your trading, published monthly. Connors has innovated some excellent ideas such as his classic volatility indicator comparing short-term and long-term volatility and looking for a return to the long-term mean. A real gem and bargain at $295 per year.

4. Dan Sullivan's **The Chartist** and **The Chartist Mutual Fund Timer** (P.O. Box 758, Seal Beach, CA 90740; 562-596-2385). Dan Sullivan is another long-time innovator whose work on relative strength and timing systems has put his services at the very top of all long-term systems and services in terms of performance both on a risk and reward basis. Sullivan has managed to beat indexes while sidestepping the bulk of most major bear markets for over 20 years. His timing model is excellent, utilizing technical and monetary components—and his discipline is unmatched. He also has managed accounts available ($100,000 minimum, contact Bill Mais) which, although highly correlated with U.S. equities, offer a much lower risk and better way to participate in U.S. stocks than a typical mutual fund. The service is also a great bargain at $150 per year.

5. Jay Schabacker's **Mutual Fund Investing** (Phillips Publishing, 7811 Montrose Road, Potomac, MD 20854-3394; 1-800-211-8558). Schabacker's "Business Cycle" which underlies his movement among different mutual fund groups, is essentially the Liquidity Cycle. This conservative and somewhat traditional manager has done an excellent job of steering investors into low-risk yet very profitable funds in a diversified approach. Schabacker always gives investors his favorite sectors, favorite bond sector, favorite foreign funds, and favorite U.S. areas of investment with each issue. For the person who has very little time to donate to monitoring the markets and who is U.S. oriented, this is one of the best services around. Jay's book, *Winning in Mutual Funds* is also highly recommended.

6. Top-quality rating services such as **Value Line, Zacks,** and **Lowry's**. Investors should subscribe to at least one of these services (probably Value Line first, Zacks second, and Lowry's third) to help screen out the best potential stocks. Investors who can afford it, should subscribe to all three. Some services, such as *Portfolio Strategy Letter*, provide an initial screen of stocks by these services.

7. Our own **Portfolio Strategy Letter** (Investment Research Associates, 334 State Street #106-267, Los Altos, CA 94022; 650-233-9091), which follows the flexible asset allocation strategy and other strategies described in this book on a monthly basis. The letter also lists U.S. and foreign stocks on our watch list that meet our criteria, gives our global asset-class relative strength rankings, and allows investors to follow our diversified high yield ideas, which are more conservative yet have beat the S&P since 1992 with less than half the risk. Information on Midas Hedge funds is also available to accredited and non-U.S. domiciled investors. The *Portfolio Strategy Letter* model portfolio has achieved an over 400 percent (vs. 250% for S&P and 190% for world index) gain since March 1992 when publishing began, without sustaining a drawdown over 8 percent.

8. William O'Neil's services: **Investor's Business Daily,** and **Daily Graphs,** as well as O'Neil's classic book, *How to Make Money in Stocks*. O'Neil is not only one of the great innovators in the field, he has done more to popularize the concepts of relative strength, strong earnings growth, and technical patterns than almost anyone on the globe. His paper *Investors Business Daily* is simply the best paper out there for investors in U.S. equities. Investors will note that we have borrowed many ideas from O'Neil's CANSLIM selection criteria in our own selection criteria. That is simply because O'Neil's concepts work under rigorous historical testing. While we also try to buy decent value and place more emphasis on just discovered institutional accumulation than O'Neil, investors would be foolish not to utilize the research that O'Neil makes available to investors for a bargain price. Almost every serious investor should not only read *IBD*, but also subscribe to *Daily Graphs*, O'Neil's bottom level service that looks weekly to monthly at 6,000 or so stocks and lists more factors in one graphics section than any other chart I have ever seen anywhere. Every investor should consider these services as the highest priorities for better investments. I simply cannot recommend them highly enough.

9. Other suggested services or publications include: Mark Skousens **Strategies and Forecasts** (see Phillips Publishing, 7811 Montrose Road, Potomac, MD 20854-3394; 1-800-211-8558), **Barron's** (which gets my award for the best information at the cheapest price of any letter or service), **The Wall Street Journal; Forbes; Technical Analysis of Stocks and Commodities Magazine; Anthony Robbins' Power Talk tapes** and **Date with Destiny Seminar;** and the **Investment Psychology Seminars** of Van Tharp.

DATA SERVICES AND SOFTWARE

For many small investors and traders, just finding the data necessary to keep track of indexes and interest rates for many non-U.S. countries is a new and difficult process. Where can investors find such data? And where can investors find macroeconomic data on the United States and other countries?

1. **Global Exposure** (8800 Venice Boulevard, Suite 217, Los Angeles, CA 90034) is probably one of the cheapest (around $200 a year) services that provides an unbelievably complete set of macroeconomic, interest-rate, and index data on the United States. Almost all the macro models in the book can be monitored via this service's SCB database.

2. The cheapest source of information on international interest rates and stock index prices is in the weekend **Financial Times,** which can be purchased at most newsstands. The *Times* is also an excellent source of information on offshore fund prices.

3. A bit more expensive, but certainly worth it, are **International Bank Credit Analyst** and **Emerging Market Analyst** (1002 Sherbrooke Street West, Suite 1600, Montreal, Quebec, Canada H3A 3L6; 516-499-9706), which are monthly reports that produce more charts and information on the macroeconomic/stock/interest rate picture of over 40 countries around the globe, than any other pure data service we have seen. Considering the breadth of information contained in these reports, the services are a phenomenal bargain.

4. **Portfolio Strategy Letter** (Investment Research Associates, 334 State Street #106-267, Los Altos, CA 94022; 650-233-9091), although not a data service, produces a monthly following of the status of our models and allows readers to follow along via the dictates of our strategies for around $300 a year (with book-buyer discount).

5. For more sophisticated investors and managers, we have used the services **Bloomberg, Datastream International,** and **Worldscope,** and believe that although these are expensive ($2,000 a month and up), they offer the most complete international coverage that is available worldwide. Investors wanting more information on hedge funds might also look into **Nelson's** Rating Service, and **Managed Account Reports** Guides.

6. We use a wide-range of software services, but some of our favorites include Meta-stock, TradeStation, CQG, AIG, Ganntrader, GET, and a relative newcomer that has programmed some of my own work

and has O'Neil's relative strength pattern formulated into it is **Investigator** (Pinpoint Strategies, 650-969-MONY).

BOOKS

Trading

1. Bogle, John. *Bogle on Mutual Funds.* New York: HarperCollins, 1996.
2. Cappiello, Frank. *Finding the Next Super Stock.* Cockeysville, MD: Liberty Publishing, 1982.
3. Connors, Larry, and Blake Hayward. *Investment Secrets of a Hedge Fund Manager.* Chicago: Probus Publishing, 1995.
4. Connors, Larry, and Linda Raschke. *Street Smarts.* Malibu: M. Gordon Publishing Group, 1995.
5. O'Neil, William J. *How to Make Money in Stocks.* San Francisco: McGraw-Hill, 1995.
6. O'Neil, William J. *The Investor's Business Daily Almanac of 1992.* Chicago: Probus Publishing, 1992.
7. O'Shaughnessy, James. *What Works on Wall Street.* San Francisco: McGraw-Hill, 1996.
8. Schabacker, Jay. *Winning in Mutual Funds.* San Francisco: American Management Association, 1996.
9. Schwager, Jack D. *Market Wizards.* New York: New York Institute of Finance, 1989.
10. Soros, George. *Alchemy of Finance.* New York: John Wiley & Sons, 1994.
11. Sperandeo, Victor. *Trader Vic—Methods of a Wallstreet Master.* New York: John Wiley & Sons, 1991.
12. Train, John. *The New Money Masters.* New York: Harper Perennial, 1989.
13. Zweig, Marty. *Winning on Wall Street.* New York: Warner Books, 1986.

Economics

1. Figgie, Harry. *Bankruptcy 1985.* Harry Figgie is a Grace Commission member.
2. Gilder, George. *Wealth and Poverty.* New York: Basic Books, 1981.

3. Pilser, Paul. *Unlimited Wealth*. New York: Crown Publishers, 1990.
4. Rand, Ayn. *Capitalism: The Unknown Ideal*. New York: Signet, 1967.
5. von Mises, Ludwig. *Human Action*. Chicago: Henry Regnery Company & Contemporary Books, 1966, rev.
6. Wilson, *Bureaucracy*. New York: Basic Books, 1991.

Future Trends

1. Drucker, Peter F. *Innovation and Entrepreneurship*. Harper Business, 1993.
2. Peters, Tom. *Thriving on Chaos*.
3. Popcorn, Faith. *Clicking*. New York: HarperCollins, 1996.
4. Popcorn, Faith. *The Popcorn Report*. New York: Doubleday Bantam Dell, 1991.

Personal Development

1. Carnegie, Dale. *How to Win Friends and Influence People*. New York: Pocket Books, 1964.
2. Covey, Stephen. *The Seven Habits of Highly Effective People*. New York: Fireside Books, 1990.
3. Hill, Napolean. *Think and Grow Rich*. New York: Fawcett Crest, 1960.
4. Robbins, Anthony. *Awaken the Giant Within*. New York: Simon & Schuster, 1991.
5. Tharp, Van K. *The Investment Psychology Guides*. Institute of Trading Mastery, 1986.

Other Sources

1. *Investor's Business Daily*. P.O. Box 6637, Los Angeles, California 90066-0370.
2. *Lowry's*.
3. *Value Line*. 220 East 42 Street, New York, New York 10017-5891.
4. *Zucks Research*. 155 North Wacker Drive, Chicago, Illinois 60606.

FREE REPORT

For investors wanting more information on how to use sentiment tools and incorporate its important signal into your trading, please send us (Investment Research Associates, 334 State Street #106-267, Los Altos, CA 94022) the following information:

Your Name, Address, Phone Number, along with any comments you may have on this book and the information in the book.

On request, we will also be delighted to send you a free copy of our monthly letter to clients, *Portfolio Strategy Letter*, which follows the dictates of the models included in this book.

Master Spreadsheet of Systems Performance

Throughout the chapters in this book, I have included spreadsheets displaying the profit/loss or annual rate and trades of many different types of strategies. In this appendix, I include a master spreadsheet showing all the other spreadsheets in the book, along with category and summary of data types and rules. Armed with this master spreadsheet, a reader can easily look in one source and see at what point various monetary tools become bullish or bearish. The systems shown in Chapter 2 are referred to as "monetary" systems and "economic gauges." The spreadsheets in Chapter 4 are referred to as "technical breadth" and "sentiment."

System Spreadsheet **MASTER**

Category	Indicator	Signals	Annual Rate of Return	Data Used
Monetary	3-Month T-Bill Yield	3-Month T-Bill Yield 12-Month ROC ≤ 6.0% 3-Month T-Bill Yield 12-Month ROC > 6.0%	18.8% 2.2%	Monthly 1/29/43–12/31/97
Monetary	Dow Jones 20 Bond Average	Dow Jones 20 Bond Average 12-Month ROC > -1.5% Dow Jones 20 Bond Average 12-Month ROC ≤ -1.5%	17.4% -0.3%	Monthly 1/29/43–12/31/97
Monetary	30-Year Government Bond Rate	30-Year Treasury Bond Rate 12-Month ROC ≤ 9% 30-Year Treasury Bond Rate 12-Month ROC > 9%	14.8% 0.9%	Monthly 1/29/43–12/31/97
Monetary	Yield Curve	30-Year T-Bond Yield/3-Month T-Bill Yield < 1.0 30-Year T-Bond Yield/3-Month T-Bill Yield > 1.15	-7.5% 19.1%	Monthly 1/29/43–12/31/97
Monetary	Monetary Composite	3-Month T-Bill Yield 12-Month ROC ≤ 6.0%, Dow Jones 20 Bond Average 12-Month ROC > -1.5%, and 30-Year Treasury Bond Rate 12-Month ROC ≤ 9%	20.1%	Monthly 1/43–12/97
Market Trend and Interest Rate	S&P 500 and T-Bill or T-Bond 40-Week Moving Averages	S&P > S&P 40-Week MA and either T-Bill Yield < 40-Week MA or T-Bond Yield < 40-Week MA		Weekly 1/2/43–12/31/97
Economic Gauges	Capacity Utilization	Capacity Utilization Index ≤ 81.5% Capacity Utilization Index > 88.5%	20.4% -6.3%	Monthly 1/29/43–12/31/97
Economic Gauges	Industrial Production	Industrial Production Index 12-Month ROC ≤ 5.6% Industrial Production Index 12-Month ROC > 7.0%	13.2% 1.1%	Monthly 1/31/45–12/29/97
Economic Gauges	CPI Inflation and GDP Quarterly Growth	CPI Inflation ≤ 3.2% and GDP Quarterly Growth ≤ 4% CPI Inflation > 3.2% and GDP Quarterly Growth > 4%	19.2% 2.9%	Monthly 4/30/59–12/29/97
Economic Gauges	CPI ROC fast and slow	Fast CPI ROC < Slow CPI ROC Fast CPI ROC ≥ Slow CPI ROC	13.2% 1.0%	Monthly 1/29/43–12/31/97
Economic Gauges	CRB Index	CRB Index 12-Month ROC ≤ -1% -1% ≤ CRB Index 12-Month ROC ≤ 5 CRB Index 12-Month ROC > 5%	21.5% 21.2% -4.8%	Monthly 1/31/77–12/31/97
Economic Gauges	Unemployment Change	Civilian Unemployment Rate > 29 months ago Civilian Unemployment Rate ≤ 29 months ago	16.1% 4.4%	Monthly 1/31/47–12/31/97
Technical Breadth	OTC Momentum Model	Buy on 7.9% rise from trough. Sell on 7.9% decline from peak.		Daily 2/1/63–12/31/97
Technical Breadth	11-Day Advance/Decline Ratio	Advance/Decline Ratio 11-Day MA > 1.9. (Exit after 3 months.)	29.2%	Daily 1/4/43–12/31/97
Technical Breadth	NYSE Up Volume	Up volume percent of total volume 5-day MA > 77%. (Exit after 3 months.)	25.3%	Daily 1/29/43–12/31/97
Commodity Sensitive	Sensitive Materials Index	Sensitive Material Index 18-Month ROC ≤ 18% Sensitive Material Index 18-Month ROC > 18%	18.4% -10.4%	Monthly 1/31/57–12/31/97
Sentiment	Consumer Sentiment	Consumer Sentiment Index ≤ 99.5 Consumer Sentiment Index > 99.5	14.2% -2.5%	Monthly 1/31/57–12/31/97
Sentiment	Help Wanted	Help Wanted Index 17-Month ROC ≤ -21 Help Wanted Index 16-Month ROC > 24	27.8% -2.1%	Monthly 1/31/51–12/31/97
Monetary	3-Month T-Bill Yield	3-Month T-Bill Yield 12-Month ROC ≤ 6.0% 3-Month T-Bill Yield 12-Month ROC > 6.0%	18.8% 2.2%	Monthly 1/29/43–12/31/97
Monetary	Dow Jones 20 Bond Average	Dow Jones 20 Bond Average 12-Month ROC > -1.5% Dow Jones 20 Bond Average 12-Month ROC ≤ -1.5%	17.4% -0.3%	Monthly 1/29/43–12/31/97
Monetary	30-Year Government Bond Rate	30-Year Treasury Bond Rate 12-Month ROC ≤ 9% 30-Year Treasury Bond Rate 12-Month ROC > 9%	14.8% -0.9%	Monthly 1/29/43–12/31/97
Monetary	Yield Curve	30-Year T-Bond Yield/3-Month T-Bill Yield < 1.0 30-Year T-Bond Yield/3-Month T-Bill Yield > 1.15	-7.5% 19.1%	Monthly 1/29/43–12/31/97

(Continued)

System Spreadsheet MASTER (Continued)

Category	Indicator	Signals	Annual Rate of Return	Data Used
Monetary	Monetary Composite	3-Month T-Bill Yield 12-Month ROC ≤ 6.0%, Dow Jones 20 Bond Average 12-Month ROC > -1.5%, and 30-Year Treasury Bond Rate 12-Month ROC ≤ 9%	20.1%	Monthly 1/43–12/97
Economic Gauges	Capacity Utilization	Capacity Utilization Index ≤ 81.5% Capacity Utilization Index > 88.5%	20.4% -6.3%	Monthly 1/29/43–12/31/97
Economic Gauges	Industrial Production	Industrial Production Index 12-Month ROC ≤ 5.6% Industrial Production Index 12-Month ROC > 7.0%	13.2% 1.1%	Monthly 1/31/45–12/29/97
Economic Gauges	CPI Inflation and GDP Quarterly Growth	CPI Inflation ≤ 3.2% and GDP Quarterly Growth ≤ 4% CPI Inflation > 3.2% and GDP Quarterly Growth > 4%	19.2% 2.9%	Monthly 4/30/59–12/29/97
Economic Gauges	CPI ROC fast and slow	Fast CPI ROC < Slow CPI ROC Fast CPI ROC ≥ Slow CPI ROC	13.2% 1.0%	Monthly 1/29/43–12/31/97
Economic Gauges	CRB Index	CRB Index 12-Month ROC ≤ -1% -1% ≤ CRB Index 12-Month ROC ≤ 5 CRB Index 12-Month ROC > 5%	21.5% 21.2% -4.8%	Monthly 1/31/77–12/31/97
Economic Gauges	Unemployment Change	Civilian Unemployment Rate > 29 months ago Civilian Unemployment Rate ≤ 29 months ago	16.1% 4.4%	Monthly 1/31/47–12/31/97
Technical Breadth	11-Day Advance/Decline Ratio	Advance/Decline Ratio 11-Day MA > 1.9. (Exit after 3 months.)	29.2%	Daily 1/4/43–12/31/97
Technical Breadth	NYSE Up Volume	Up volume percent of total volume 5-Day MA > 77%. (Exit after 3 months.)	25.3%	Daily 1/29/43–12/31/97
Commodity Sensitive	Sensitive Materials Index	Sensitive Material Index 18-Month ROC ≤ 18% Sensitive Material Index 18-Month ROC > 18%	18.4% -10.4%	Monthly 1/31/57–12/31/97
Sentiment	Consumer Sentiment	Consumer Sentiment Index ≤ 99.5 Consumer Sentiment Index > 99.5	14.2% -2.5%	Monthly 1/31/57–12/31/97
Sentiment	Help Wanted	Help Wanted Index 17-Month ROC ≤ -21 Help Wanted Index 16-Month ROC > 24	27.8% -2.1%	Monthly 1/31/51–12/31/97
System	Bond System	30-Year Treasury Bond Yield < 10-Week MA and either T-Bill Yield < 38-Week MA or Dow Jones Utility Index > 10-Week MA	14.6%*	Weekly 1/2/43–12/31/97
System	S&P 500 and T-Bill or T-Bond 40-Week Moving Averages	S&P > S&P 40-Week MA and either T-Bill Yield < 40-Week MA or T-Bond Yield < 40-Week MA	10.2%*	Weekly 1/2/43–12/31/97
System	OTC Momentum Model	Buy on 7.9% rise from trough. Sell on 7.9% decline from peak.	18.2%*	Daily 2/1/63–12/31/97
System	Gold System	GMI Index > GMI Index 16-Week MA and gold prices > gold price 68-Week MA and silver prices > 12-Week MA	8.7%*	Weekly 3/1/75–12/31/97

* Compound interest

Index

|||||| |||| | || ||||||||||
9 780471 185383

9 780471 185383